‖‖‖ ‖ ‖‖‖‖‖‖‖‖‖‖‖‖ ‖‖‖ ‖‖‖
I0131228

CULTURAL IDEALS OF HOME

Spanning the nineteenth to twenty-first centuries, this book investigates how home is imagined, staged and experienced in western culture.

Questions about meanings of 'home' and domestic culture are triggered by dramatic changes in values and ideals about the dwellings we live in and the dwellings we desire or dread. Deborah Chambers explores how home is idealised as a middle-class haven, managed as an investment, and signified as a status symbol and expression of personal identity. She addresses a range of public, state, commercial, popular and expert discourses about 'home': the heritage industry, design, exhibitions, television, social media, home mobilities and migration, smart technologies and ecological sustainability. Drawing on cross-disciplinary research including cultural history and cultural geography, the book offers a distinctive media and cultural studies approach supported by original, historically informed case studies on interior and domestic design; exhibitions of model homes; TV home interiors; 'media home' imaginaries; multiscreen homes; corporate visions of 'homes of tomorrow' and digital smart homes.

A comprehensive and engaging study, this book is ideal for students and researchers of cultural studies, cultural history, media and communication studies, as well as sociology, gender studies, cultural geography and design studies.

Deborah Chambers is Professor of Media and Cultural Studies at Newcastle University, UK. Her most recent publications include *Changing Media, Homes and Households* (2016), *Social Media and Personal Relationships* (2013) and *A Sociology of Family Life* (2012).

DIRECTIONS IN CULTURAL HISTORY

Series Editors: Gillian Swanson and Ben Highmore

The *Directions in Cultural History* series directs history towards the study of feelings, experiences and everyday habits. By attending to the world of sensation, imagination, and desire at moments of change, and by coupling this to the materials and technologies of culture, it promotes cultural history as a lively and vivid arena for research. The series will present innovative cultural history in an accessible form to both scholars and upper level students.

The Making of English Popular Culture
edited by John Storey

Light Touches
Cultural Practices of Illumination, 1800–1900
Alice Barnaby

Photography
The Unfettered Image
Michelle Henning

Cultural Ideals of Home
The Social Dynamics of Domestic Space
Deborah Chambers

For more information about this series, please visit: https://www.routledge.com/Directions-in-Cultural-History/book-series/DICH

CULTURAL IDEALS OF HOME

The Social Dynamics of Domestic Space

Deborah Chambers

Routledge
Taylor & Francis Group

LONDON AND NEW YORK

First published 2020
by Routledge
2 Park Square, Milton Park, Abingdon, Oxon OX14 4RN

and by Routledge
52 Vanderbilt Avenue, New York, NY 10017

Routledge is an imprint of the Taylor & Francis Group, an informa business

© 2020 Deborah Chambers

The right of Deborah Chambers to be identified as author of this work has been asserted by them in accordance with sections 77 and 78 of the Copyright, Designs and Patents Act 1988.

All rights reserved. No part of this book may be reprinted or reproduced or utilised in any form or by any electronic, mechanical, or other means, now known or hereafter invented, including photocopying and recording, or in any information storage or retrieval system, without permission in writing from the publishers.

Trademark notice: Product or corporate names may be trademarks or registered trademarks, and are used only for identification and explanation without intent to infringe.

British Library Cataloguing-in-Publication Data
A catalogue record for this book is available from the British Library

Library of Congress Cataloging-in-Publication Data
Names: Chambers, Deborah, 1954- author.
Title: Cultural ideals of home : the social dynamics of domestic space / Deborah Chambers.
Description: Abingdon, Oxon ; New York, NY : Routledge, 2020. | Series: Directions in cultural history | Includes bibliographical references and index.
Identifiers: LCCN 2019052771 (print) | LCCN 2019052772 (ebook) | ISBN 9781138637924 (hardback) | ISBN 9781138637931 (paperback) | ISBN 9781315205311 (ebook)
Subjects: LCSH: Home--Social aspects. | Dwellings--Social aspects. | Households--Social aspects. | Domestic space--Social aspects.
Classification: LCC GT2420 .C53 2020 (print) | LCC GT2420 (ebook) | DDC 392.3/6--dc23
LC record available at https://lccn.loc.gov/2019052771
LC ebook record available at https://lccn.loc.gov/2019052772

ISBN: 978-1-138-63792-4 (hbk)
ISBN: 978-1-138-63793-1 (pbk)
ISBN: 978-1-315-20531-1 (ebk)

Typeset in Bembo
by Taylor & Francis Books

CONTENTS

ACKNOWLEDGEMENTS

The idea for this book emerged while I was working on an earlier book, *Changing Media, Homes and Households* (2016). This sparked an interest in addressing the bizarre nature, uncanny history and veiled power relations that frame the ways in which the 'ideal home' is imagined and enacted – particularly in homeowning nations such as the UK and USA. Leading to a focus on the discursive complexities involved in the idealisation of 'home' in Western culture, the project prompted me to investigate 'home' itself as a mutable entity and contested concept in social and cultural life. I have therefore progressed a couple of themes addressed in the earlier book by drawing not only on cultural history, sociological and media studies perspectives but also on leading scholarship in cultural geography and other social science disciplines. Needless to say, the subject matter is so vast and complex that the following chapters can only cover a selected but pertinent range of themes. That said, I hope the themes and issues raised in the book will make a contribution to debates in what is a vital field of study – a field rendered all the more critical in a period framed by the post-2008 global recession, the datafication of homes, intensified migration and home mobilities, and the ecological crisis.

I wish to extend my thanks and gratitude to the people and range of events that I have been invited to, which provided me with the opportunity to give talks on topics that contributed to ideas in the book, and enabled me to gain valuable feedback. These include Helen Ikla, for the Architecture Programme event on 'Domestic Desires' at the Royal Academy of Arts, London; Iris Kleinecke-Bates for the Material Cultures of Television conference at Hull University; Sabina Mihelj and Emily Keightley for the Media and Time symposium at Loughborough University; Annette Hill, Magnus Andersson and Magnus Johansson for the International Research Workshop on Mobile Socialities and International Symposium on Media Mixing, at Lund University; Katarzyna Kopecka-Piech for the Workshop of the Academia Europaea Knowledge Hub on Mediatization, at the University of Wroclaw; and for the opportunity to participate at the European Communication Research and Education Association conference, Faculty of Communication Sciences, University della Svizzera Italiana, Lugano and International Association for Media and Communication conference, School of Communication, Complutense University of Madrid.

I gratefully acknowledge and thank the editors and anonymous reviewers of *Media, Culture and Society* and James Leggott, Principal Editor and the anonymous reviewers of *Journal of Popular Television* for publication of articles that relate to and support the subject matter of some of the chapters; and Maren Hartmann, Elizabeth Prommer, Karin Deckner, and Stephan Görland for the opportunity to develop my ideas on corporate-made speculative films and videos of the 'future home' in their book, *Mediated Time* (Palgrave Macmillan, 2020) which relates to some of the case study material in Chapter 9 on homes of the future.

I am very appreciative of the excellent advice and support given by Natalie Foster, Editor at Routledge, during the planning stage of this book and also by Gillian Swanson (Series Editor of Directions in Cultural History with Ben Highmore) who generously devoted time to review the manuscript and offer valuable suggestions during its final stage. I am also grateful to the copy editor, Peter Stafford, for his excellent work.

I wish to thank the School of Arts and Cultures at Newcastle University for the research leave I received for a semester which enabled me to complete the book. I am also grateful to my colleagues at Newcastle University for their intellectual inspiration, valuable discussions and also for creating a stimulating and supportive intellectual environment. In particular, I thank James Ash, David Baines, Gonul Bozoglu, Soudeh Ghaffari, Joss Hands, Peter Hopkins, Sarah Hill, Peter Golding, Darren Kelsey, Chris Haywood, Majid Khosravinik, Rhiannon Mason, Andrew Newman, Karen Ross, Tina Sikka and Chris Whitehead. Finally, I thank Lis Joyce for her wonderful support and forbearance throughout all the stages of completing this book.

INTRODUCTION

Themes and issues

Questions about the meanings of 'home' and domestic culture in late modernity are triggered by dramatic changes in values and attitudes towards the dwellings we live in and the dwellings we desire or dread. This book explores the shifting imaginings and meanings of 'home' in a Western context. With an emphasis on how 'home' is idealised as a haven, managed as an investment, and signified as status and personal identity, it traces the dynamics of 'home' as an as an icon and a moral imperative. The cultural, social and political forces that shape 'home' as a private, intimate and bounded space are explored to consider the public and outside influences and the social pressures brought to bear on beliefs about this space. To reveal the multiple ways in which home is conceived and imagined, the book deals with the complex interplay between home, heritage, materiality, consumer culture, media technologies and identities between the late nineteenth and twenty-first century. This time span encompasses dramatic social upheavals and environmental challenges that have deeply impacted home imaginaries including two world wars, severe economic depressions, the global financial crisis of 2008 and climate change.

Correspondingly, a mounting sense of crisis surrounds 'home' invoked by related disruptions of traditional home encounters and identities which involve both persistent and fluctuating power dynamics of gender, sexuality, class, race and ethnicity. Events and social trends relating to consumerism, suburbanisation, globalisation, economic austerity, climate change, migration and digital technologies coincide with social anxieties about mobile populations, changing gender roles and family values, new intimacies and household types, renavigations of 'public' and 'private' boundaries, and the urgent need for environmentally sustainable homes. At the same time, an intimate, cosy and idealised version of home prevails in popular culture from TV programmes on stately homes, house-hunting, home makeovers and social media home curation.

Traditional discourses, lifestyle advice, digital communication technologies and smart home rhetoric re-navigate home ideals in relation to changing attitudes about 'normal' households and family life. But who is steering these ideals, for what purposes, to what ends and with what effects on popular visions and personal encounters with 'home'? How are these cultural discourses and technologies received, acted upon, questioned and challenged? The book deals with these questions to consider expressions of home as privatised, porous, vulnerable, secure, heteronormative, queer, mobile, smart or environmentally sustainable. A range of public, state, institutional, commercial, popular and expert discourses are explored encompassing the heritage industry, interior and industrial design, national and international exhibitions, television and social media, smart technologies and ecological sustainability. Continuities and ruptures in traditional meanings and values associated with home over time and across these discursive sites are examined to consider the implications of idealised and abject notions about this dwelling. Taken together, and with a focus mainly on the US and UK contexts, the aim is to assess how government, commercial and popular rhetoric about ideal homes and 'proper' home life are constructed, reproduced and permeate our everyday lives. It scrutinises the ideological roles played by these institutions and agents in shaping *dominant* discourses which convey the normal 'home' as an essentially middle-class and nuclear family project framed by ambitions of home ownership. How alternative modes of imagining and experiencing home systematically or inadvertently exclude and marginalise certain social groups are considered as part of this aim by addressing alternative domesticities, home mobilities, migration and household sustainability.

Approach and perspectives

A growing interest in the home as a site of social and cultural inquiry confirms a strong fascination with home and domesticity in the media, popular culture and everyday life. This book explores this fascination from a cultural and sociological perspective to contribute to the multi-disciplinary nature of studies of home. The mounting interest in home gave rise to the journal *Home Cultures* in 2004, committed to 'the critical understanding of the domestic sphere, its artefacts, spaces and relations, across timeframes and cultures' and to several special issues on geographies of home and domestic spaces in journals such as *Cultural Geographies* (see, for example, Blunt 2005). These are among a range of journals that have established the architectural, design and geographical roots of key debates about home cultures and domestic space. However, they also draw on work from other social sciences and humanities, confirming the importance of an interdisciplinary approach for studies of home set out in this book.

This book extends beyond an emphasis on home as a dwelling to examine the intersecting influences of official, popular cultural and commercial initiatives and moral priorities on home imaginings and encounters. The themes and approaches within the following chapters are situated mainly within the disciplines of cultural history, contemporary cultural studies, media studies and sociology combined with geographical perspectives. As such, the book is not positioned within a housing studies perspective. Rather, it draws on and engages with pioneering research arising from studies of home and domestic space within design history, cultural geography, social anthropology, feminist studies and queer theory, as well as cultural history and media and communication studies to highlight power relations of nation, race, gender and class. Extending the practice of history beyond traditional disciplinary boundaries, cultural history provides a vital lens through which to consider both popular and high cultural traditions and diverging interpretations of historical events associated with 'home'. The study of records and academic accounts of the social, popular, intellectual and artistic representations of past societies including traditional culture and early media offers glimpses of the historical struggles over meanings of home that underpin or contradict today's home imaginaries. Bridging past and present meanings of home, the book is also characterised by a particular emphasis on the historical and contemporary impacts of media content and technologies on home cultures. It addresses the domestic adoption of analogue and digital media technologies, media representations of domestic culture and makeover and property TV, smart home futures and the mediatisation of home. Exploring how home is constituted, imagined, mediated and materially encountered in the past and present, the chapters critically set out and engage with a series of empirical and theoretically informed case studies.

With a focus on meanings of home in nations that have a homeowning tradition, the book's accent is on the Western socio-cultural contexts of the UK and USA, where home ownership is a central feature of the economy. It enquires into the reasons why these Western cultures are captivated by home ownership as a key dimension of nationhood, citizenship and identity. Innovative research from other homeowning countries, particularly from Australia, are also drawn on. Many facets of home culture in these home owning countries have been circulated globally, thereby broadening the book's relevance. Correspondingly, global trends are examined, particularly in relation to debates about migration and home mobilities that foreground the precarious nature of 'home', identity and belonging. A series of original case studies contributes to the book's enquiry into the parallels and discrepancies between discourses and enactments of 'home'. These include the roles of interior and domestic design and exhibitions in the creation of model homes; the home adoption of television and computers in the shaping of 'media homes'; multiscreen homes and the making of new kinds of screen-based 'home time'; corporate media visions of 'homes of tomorrow' and smart home futures. The intention, then, is to offer a critically engaging set of linked enquiries across the chapters to reveal shifting home ideals and the contested, fluctuating and ambiguous nature of 'home'.

These home imaginaries tend to promote middle-class lifestyles and sets of values. Yet, importantly, such home ideals affect us all. The aim is to uncover the cultural processes that symbolise ideal homes and influence our encounters with home as an internal and mutable space. 'Home' is often described as a stage set (Chapman 1999), one on which desire, nostalgia and aspirations are staged and mediated via representations continually beamed into our home via television and Internet. 'At the same time, these qualities of home are tangled up with judgement, one-upmanship, vanity and financial burdens – all involved in creating a complex, but widely accepted discourse of materiality' as Gene Bawden (2011 online) states. Certain home ideals draw on imaginaries of past 'stately homes' involving complex heritage discourses as a 'staged authenticity' (West 2016; see Chapter 1). This staging of home as an authentic space relies on potent but fluctuating imaginaries of national heritage and personal agency. This book focuses on idealisations of home across a range of sites including home decoration manuals, exhibitions, media representations of home and discourses of smart home futures.

Invoked and endorsed by popular TV dramas such as *Downton Abbey*, heritage ideals 'monumentalise' home through powerful discourses that veil the legacy of slavery in heritage home imaginaries (described in Chapter 1). This mode of home idealisation is entangled in images of grand 'stately homes', past architectural styles and the promotion of antiques to style contemporary homes that conform to 'good taste', as elaborated in the following chapters. Twentieth century exhibitions comprised a major promotional strategy and cultural force in conveying and consolidating 'good design' and decent middle-class family values through government policy and state and commercial spectacles of home interiors. These examples of the 'staging' of home have targeted women as consumer citizens, to confirm and consolidate their roles as homemaker. As such, the role of design and exhibitions, particularly between the late nineteenth and mid-twentieth centuries, forms a key focus of the first group of chapters to understand the role of state and market-led initiatives in designing and staging the model home (see Chapters 1 to 4). These strategies were reconfigured through the medium of TV programmes in the mid-twentieth century and, more recently in the form of lifestyle and property TV which rose to prominence from the late twentieth and early twenty-first centuries (discussed in Chapter 4 and 5).

The adoption and role of media technologies and media content in the home provide a related focus to trace the cultural processes involved in the mediatisation of the home. Chapter 4 describes the entrance of television and computers into the home in the twentieth century to consider the national and household strategies involved in the formation of the 'media home'. Both the growing influence of TV programmes and social media in the production and circulation of ideal home discourses are considered. The book charts the promotion, household adoption and domestication of these technologies and of TV programmes and schedules that have mobilised distinctive middle-class version of the 'media home'. Media representations of home delivered by highly popular property and lifestyle TV programmes about house-buying and home makeovers are addressed in Chapter 5 to consider how these home ideals are performed and re-enacted via social media, with a focus on the social media network, Pinterest. Chapter 6 offers a case study of the multiscreen home and the rise of a new kind of 'media time'. Households actively stretch time using mobile second screens, streaming devices and the development of habits such as binge-watching and the 'blue light' activity of night-time mobile device use (also see Chambers 2019). And Chapter 8 assesses the implications of digital media use in the context of home mobilities by considering the use of mobile communication technologies among transnational migrants. The rise of what we might call the 'virtual home' and the hybridisation of space as a key feature of the mediatisation of home are examined.

The multi-scalar home

'Home' not just a staged space but also an enacted place. The idealisation of this apparently private domain is formed, informed and performed via imaginings of home on multiple scales involving a series of material and discursive strategies invoked by official, commercial and moral agents and navigated or subverted by homemakers. Within the field of geography, home is approached as a material and imaginative site conceived through multiple scales – as household, community, nation, state and empire. But home is not simply a location, it is also a cultural form and an emotional desire. A house becomes a home when shaped by and instilled with social and cultural meanings. In their seminal book, *Home*, cultural geographers Alison Blunt and Robyn Dowling (2006) conceive of home as a *spatial imaginary* involving relations between feelings, attachment, and dwelling: 'a set of intersecting and variable ideas and feelings, which are related to context, and which construct places, extend across spaces and scales, and connects places' (Blunt and Dowling 2006: 2). While house and home are habitually associated with a physical residence, home is also invoked by intimate relationships or affiliations that extend beyond the dwelling. Blunt and Dowling emphasise the relationship between the imaginative and the affective by drawing attention to the emotions involved in our encounters with this residence as a physical space, in terms of the need for belonging and emotional support as well as shelter and security. This conceptualisation of home enables us to distinguish between 'home' and 'dwelling'. It also foregrounds the multi-scalar spatial imaginaries that underscore the various conceptions of home – as a house, a neighbourhood, town, nation and as a transnationally negotiated imaginary.

The multi-scalar notion of home enables us to approach the dwelling as a dynamic space involving transnational attachments among international migrants, refugees, transnational families and diaspora communities (Blunt, 2005). The geographical emphasis on scale highlights the *relationality* of space and the significance of connectivity (Amin 2002; Massey 2004). It enables us to recognise that both movement and stasis are implicated in meanings of home and to question conventional oppositions between 'nomadic' and fixed exemplars of home. This approach prompts a reconsideration of local-global relations within the context of mobility, flow and systems (Bauman, 2000; Castells, 2000). Accordingly, *multi-scalar* and *relational* considerations of the local invite a rethinking of globalisation as 'the nesting of local scales of organization and action within national, international, and transnational ones, and the politics of inter-scalar contestation' (Amin, 2002: 386, Lewis, 2015).

An acknowledgement of the spatial imaginary involved in multi-scalar ideas that define 'home' also enables us to approach homemaking as sets of activities performed across multiple scales, sometimes concurrently. For migrants, home-making means finding ways to create a sense of home in a new region or country. This can be expressed by material objects selected and assembled together in the making of home to generate a sense of familiarity and homeliness. Objects symbolise attachment to a 'place' which is remote, but which nevertheless summons a sense of 'home' (Ralph and Staeheli 2011). Material objects and cuisine not only remind migrants of their homes of origin but may form the core of 'home' by invoking and sustaining relationships far from the country of settlement. Familiar material objects can cushion individuals from the tensions of outside forces and foster feelings of identity and of belonging to a place, whether it be the home they occupy or a specific place they retain connections with (Tolia-Kelly 2004: 317). The meaning of home in such circumstances is not inevitably grounded in a fixed location but cultivated through recurring affirmations of a relationship between householders and material objects (Jacobs and Smith 2008; Miller 2001). The role of material objects in sustaining links with the home country are discussed in Chapter 8 in the context of home mobilities.

These instances demonstrate that while home can be approached as a house, neighbourhood, city, region, nation and homeland, the multiple scales involved are not separate from one another. Conceived as relational and changing, home is recognised as a plural and fluctuating concept that refers to places, practices and power. A focus on metaphors of the family and homeland in relation to the multi-scalarity of home also draws attention to the role of multi-scalar ideas of home that associate home with 'country' and 'nation' by leaders of nations. The affective deployment of 'home' in political backlashes against multiculturalism via government, news and social media confirms that 'home' is a highly contested political category, one regularly and *increasingly* used as a tool of exclusion as well as belonging. For example, in many countries, full citizenship is refused for those who find themselves uprooted. Citizenship relies on claims of attachment to place (Morley 2000: 26).

At the other end of the scale, homelessness involves marginalisation and urban dispossession. The homeless are controlled through restraint and those who have escaped repression in their countries are held in asylum centres (see Blunt and Dowling 2006 126–131; Morley 2017). Those in detention centres and refugee camps are denied rights to a homeland and a home. As Blunt and Dowling emphasise: '...home is a site/imaginary of alienation as well as belonging; home-liness and unhomeliness co-exist and define each other' (Blunt and Dowling 2008: 569). Multi-scalar spatial imaginaries are pivotal, then, to accounts of modernity, imperialism and nationalism and thus to householders' encounters with home and domesticity as expressions of personal and communal identities. Taken as a whole, a multi-scalar approach uncovers the significance of home for relations that function across multiple dimensions: social, political, economic, cultural interconnecting political forces at domestic, national and transnational scales.

Home imaginaries

Normative conceptions of an idealised home influence the material form and cultural expression of dwellings. The emphasis on 'material and imaginative geographies of home' – as imagined physical spaces and lived experiences – relates to home as an *ideal* domestic space with particular qualities and characteristics that shape social identities. Thus, if home is 'lived as well as imagined', it also involves imaginings of an 'ideal' home. Notions of the 'ideal' are abstractions from 'real' homes. But they continuously influence our encounters with home. As Blunt and Dowling put it, 'A central focus of imaginaries of home is their idealisation: certain dwelling structures and social relations are imagined to be 'better', more socially appropriate and an ideal to be aspired to' (Blunt and Dowling 2006: 88). Idealised homes promoted in media discourses, public policy and commercial ventures stage middle-class versions of home as 'ideal' by routinely depicting intimacy and belonging in the form of a heterosexual nuclear family, usually in a detached, suburban owner-occupied house. Perpetuated in expert and popular discourses, these imaginaries of home offer us visions of what home and home comforts *should* be.

In the following chapters, I use the term 'home imaginaries' to analysis idealised visions of home as part of dominant imaginaries that shape our aspirations. This term enables a consideration of the struggles over meanings of home and subversions of traditional and modern ideals of home as a site conceived of traditional family harmony; a late modern site of mobility, agency and digital change, and of environmental risk. To highlight the contested and conditional nature of home imaginaries, alternative domesticities and the 'queering' of domesticity are discussed in Chapter 7. Debates about how to achieve environmentally sustainable homes are discussed in Chapter 10. Supporting Blunt and Dowlings' use of the term 'spatial imaginaries' in relation to multi-scalarity, I also draw on philosopher Charles Taylor whose work on 'modern social imaginaries' questions the distinction made between "ideas" and "material" factors as rival causal agencies'.

Rather than treating 'imaginary' as just a figment of the imagination, Taylor (2003, 2007) uses a *socialised* idea of imaginary framed by social practice theory. To paraphrase Taylor, human practices are, at one and the same time, 'material' and 'modes of understanding' which are often inseparable from one another (Taylor 2007: 212). While Blunt and Dowling emphasise the important spatial dimensions of imaginaries, for Taylor a socialised conception of imaginary explains how 'people imagine their social existence [...] how things go on between them and their fellows, the expectations that are normally met, and the deeper normative notions and images that underlie these expectations' (Taylor 2003: 106). This consideration of imaginary emphasises the *collective* as well as *individual* practices involved in conducting our social lives. Since Taylor's social imaginary foregrounds the expectations entailed in managing everyday life, this allows us to consider the *expectations* involved in 'home imaginaries'. These imaginaries comprise the beliefs, aspirations towards and expectancies associated with the perfect or 'ideal home'.

Such imaginaries are navigated in relation to visions of dream dwellings generated on a national scale by public agencies and on an individual and household scale among homemakers. Thus, by approaching imaginaries as more than just an image in the mind, we can focus on the social practices involved in the production and lived practices linked to home imaginaries. Informed by Taylor's notion of social imaginary and Blunt and Dowling's idea of 'spatial imaginaries', the following chapters use practice theory to extend beyond a representational approach. This opens up considerations of 'home imaginaries' as a set of powerful discourses that endorse and promote visions and enactments of the idealised home.

Home ideals and performed practices

Pierre Bourdieu's concept of 'field' as a system of social positions and practices contributes to an understanding of how home imaginaries are shaped by interactions between institutions, rules and everyday practices. For Bourdieu (1993), fields of practice such as art, education, religion, and law are organised around their own distinctive but often overlapping set of rules, knowledges, and forms of social and cultural capital. Government, commercial and moral agents attempt to shape home imaginaries, led by experts in intersecting fields of art, architecture and design, heritage, television, social media, science, technology and so on. Each field has its distinct set of professional positions and practices which implicate the production and consumption of home culture by forming trajectories of 'taste' guided by government policy, commercial strategies and moral imperatives.

Home imaginaries of idealised homes are guided, then, by specific social actors. 'Home professionals' or 'home experts' such as architects, engineers, designers, advertisers, exhibitions, technological gadgets, lifestyle gurus and property experts perform in relation to government, commercial and moral programmes. These social actors take on the role of authorities and connoisseurs to create visions of the ideal home. Their professional practices are diverse but the home imaginaries they contribute to are *material* as well as *imagined*: real as well as residing in the mind (Tutton 2017: 480). Combining a textual and materialist analysis, Richard Tutton offers a material-discursive approach by drawing on Taylor to overcome the division between the 'real' and the 'imaginary' within social imaginaries. As a site performed through material-discursive practices, we can say that discursive constructions of 'home' are not merely imaginative but are entirely *social practices*. A material-discursive analysis highlights, then, the notion of performativity involved in the dynamic enactment and mediation of idealised homes via home professionals and self-made experts who guide us in our homemaking practices, from advice manuals to homemaker TV shows and social media influencers.

Performing on behalf of state and commercial mediators, 'home' experts are social actors who attempt to shape our everyday values and attitudes towards home as a sought-after ideal. Their expert practices are provisional yet recognisable processes comprising familiar competences and conventions that evolve around 'tastes'. Bourdieu's theorisation of 'taste' is developed in his seminal text *Distinction: A*

Social Critique of the Judgement of Taste, where he refers to these social actors as cultural intermediaries and 'taste-makers' (Bourdieu 1984). For Bourdieu, cultural tastes distinguish people's social class positions. They work to create the ideal home as a desired object and desired mode of living, not just in homeowning cultures. Performing as social constructs, tastes are experienced by individuals as personal preferences and dispositions. While these tastes are attained by social conditioning they are continually negotiated by dominant and marginalised groups, each seeking to preserve or improve their position within society (Maguire and Matthews, 2012: 16). As social classes distinguish themselves through taste, cultural capital plays a key role in societal power relations by providing the means for a cultural form of domination and hierarchy (Gaventa 2003: 6).

Bourdieu frames 'taste' as part of consumption practices. These practices not only reflect class position but reproduce those class positions by disseminating 'good taste' *through* the consumption of goods. As such, individual taste operates as a social construct which is continuously and often subtly manipulated by cultural industries – involving intermediaries from designers to lifestyle gurus. In the context of homemaking, these expert taste makers or 'needs merchants' mediate between the spheres of production and consumption as part of 'an economy that requires the production of consuming tastes and dispositions' (Maguire and Matthews, 2014:15). The term 'cultural intermediary' is therefore used in the following chapters to consider to how tastes are formed, legitimated, circulated and challenged in ways that distinguish between social classes. 'In sum, taste is a mechanism of social reproduction: it enables the continuation – and veils the arbitrariness – of hierarchies between and within class groups' (Maguire and Matthews, 2014: 16). This approach to home imaginaries – as a set of practices mediated by home experts as 'taste makers' – offers conceptual tools to explore the dynamics of the idealised home, as a tastefully styled dwelling aspired to, sought after and contested. The emphasis on the performative quality of home imaginaries, as enacted by both professional practices and homemaking practices, confirms the *relational* and entwined imaginings and practices involving experts and homemakers in relation to one another.

Home imaginaries are produced and disseminated in ways that beckon and mobilise action by householders as homemakers. Experts serve to inspire, persuade, motivate and steer our expectations of home and our commitments to home ownership. They offer advice, practical guidance, lifestyle coaching and moral counselling to support homemaking practices through a host of decoration manuals, exhibitions, brochures, retail stores, advertising, magazines, lifestyle and property TV shows, and via websites and apps. While the 'ideal' home is largely unattainable, the extensive homemaking work that goes into improving and perfecting our homes involves multiple sensations and sensory practices that summon, augment and coordinate gendered, raced and class identities. Some of these homemaking practices are highly pleasurable, some are disagreeable or taxing, and some are downright frustrating, disheartening or oppressive. This range of responses affects our emotional states, identities and sense of well-being since home experts approach us as *neoliberal subjects* in charge of our own destinies.

Neoliberalism and the entrepreneurial self

Neoliberalism describes a distinctive cultural process charactering late modernity which encourages people 'to be active, entrepreneurial, self-optimising subjects' (Elias et al. 2017: 5). In late capitalist consumer culture, individuals are not treated as passive consuming subjects but as agents who actively engage with consumer culture in a project of self-improvement. In this respect, home is regarded as an extension of the enterprising or entrepreneurial self – as a project in constant need of updating and improvement – forming a key dimension of the project of the self (Rose 1992). As such, homemaking activities are part of a wider preoccupation with and regulation of *the self* and *home* in late modern society. The perception that our homes require constant attention, involving continuous modification and upgrading, generates personal feelings of a perpetually unstable and *precarious home*, one in need of ongoing surveillance and reassessment. Homemaking puts pressures of time, money and effort on us, particularly on women, as 'aesthetic entrepreneurs' (Elias et al. 2017: 37). Via homemaking practices, the homemaker becomes the ideal neoliberal subject. Through multiple actions, she is under relentless pressure to redecorate, refurbish, refurnish and upgrade the home interior in an effort to create the perfect home. The aesthetic entrepreneur is a subject judged by her capacity to consume, thereby reinforcing the link between femininity and consumption as a necessary component of the management of home (Bronwyn Davies 2005; and see Chapter 2, 3 and 5).

Despite the neoliberal emphasis on personal agency, choice and the pleasures of homemaking as forms of self-expression and personal authenticity, home makeovers promoted by advice manuals, TV programmes, magazines and lifestyle gurus involve ambivalent subjective experiences. They entail emotions, moods and affect, producing pleasure but also dissatisfaction and frustration with largely inaccessible ideals. Yet they form an essential part of the 'gendered management of affect' (Saraswati 2013:12). By hailing women as entrepreneurial homemaking subjects, home imaginaries work to conceive of 'home' as a sensual space, a site of sentiment, affect, memory and imagination. This active work of homemaking involves practices such as home curation via social media platforms like Pinterest and Instagram. These websites signal the rise of an active curatorial self (discussed in Chapter 5). Homemaking is therefore a feminist issue as well as an issue of class and race, since the emotional and aesthetic labour involved is systematically feminised yet often invisible and unacknowledged. The making of home is an active agency and site of emotion with no ending: 'always in progress, always being made' (Pink 2012: 191).

Home precarities and the crisis of home

Idealised homes tend to obscure the destabilising aspects of home life. As part of the book's critical assessment of ideal home discourses, the term 'home precarities' is employed to highlight some of the major ways in which these ideals are undermined or even reinforced. Home is conceived as a threatened and threatening space. While the home is conventionally viewed as a space of sanctuary linked with cosy feelings of homeliness, it is also depicted as a space under threat from the outside, a threat from which we must protect ourselves and our families. A mounting sense of crisis associated with 'home' is conveyed in popular cultural, academic and policy discourses prompted by a series of global, national, local and micro-social trends and uncertainties. This sense of crisis is generated by the fluctuating social and cultural events and conditions that impact on ideas, perceptions and experiences of 'home'. Notable among these are the global financial crisis of 2008 and ensuing collapse of the housing market; intensified migration and home mobilities; the growth in smart home technologies; the digital surveillance of home activities; and the impact of global warming on homes and households.

'Home precarity' refers a set of palpable and contrived social conditions and dispositions that perform a key role in shaping our encounters with home. Home precarities underscore challenging and difficult conditions such as domestic violence, homelessness, migrant resettlement and the challenges of household sustainability required to respond to climate change. Whether these adversities are normalised or dramatised, they form part of home imaginaries. They invoke notions of a fragile, vulnerable, threatened, insecure and unstable home. The term 'home precarities' is therefore employed in this book to consider these domestic uncertainties and vulnerabilities. The term 'precarity' has been advanced as a key concept in social and political sciences, emerging from the work of Lauren Berlant (2011). Precariousness is referred to by Berlant as the intrinsic condition of vulnerability and dependence arising from societal structures. For Berlant, precarity is a social condition arising from unequal relations of power and the intensified precariousness experienced by some subjects who are, or are perceived to be, more vulnerable than others. In geography, precarity is employed to address the social and economic deterioration of security labour markets. For example, in the Global North, the term points to the insecurities and uncertainties generated by the 2008 financial crash and resulting culture of austerity. The word precarity is increasingly used to describe the marginal working conditions that now characterise late capitalism (see, for example, Standing, 2011; Waite 2009; Gill and Pratt 2008; Peck 2012; Ferreri et al. 2017; Harris 2015).

However, more recent work in cultural geography explores the ways in which precarity functions at a *cultural* level 'through imaginaries of and assumptions about how day-to-day life is, and should be, lived' (Harris and Nowicki 2018: 388). Cultural precarity is conveyed via a series of affects and social imaginaries that pinpoint, mobilise and normalise ideas of uncertain, insecure or vulnerable life in late modern society. I use the term 'home precarities' as a feature of home imaginaries to draw attention to both the destabilisation *and* validation of ideal homes within a range of domestic conditions and predicaments. Home precarities highlight the fundamental instabilities and uncertainties that accompany and prompt a reassessment of home imaginaries involving the 'ideal home'. Idealisations of home cannot function without some notion of home precarities as the antithesis to home ideals.

Not only are the precarious, vulnerable circumstances of certain kinds of home set in opposition to home ideals. Home precarities are also regularly exploited to support dominant values that perpetuate idealised homes. As such, home precarities are both *palpable* and *contrived* and deeply entangled with inequalities of gender, class and race. In specific and diverging circumstances, they are invoked, internalised and acted upon as discursive social practices.

An example of contrived home precarities is exemplified in Chapter 1 which details how a sense of decline and loss is associated with English country houses. This sense of home precarity has functioned from the twentieth century as a national crisis to idealise and monumentalise apparently vulnerable dwellings as stately homes that come to represent the nation. However, it conceals the palpable precarities associated with African slave labour that supported the construction, restoration and residence of many of Britain's country houses. As discussed in Chapter 1, commemorations of the bicentenary of the abolition of the British slave trade in 2007 provoked several national institutions to reassess the legacy of slavery in relation to landed wealth and British estates. This reassessment raises questions about how these interconnections and how country houses, as part of our national heritage, are to be understood and engaged with today by Britain's diverse communities and by citizens in Africa and the Caribbean.

The idealisation of home also involves palpable home precarities for women within gendered domestic circumstances which are normalised as part of home imaginaries. While home can be a 'homely' place of comfort and security for women, the home can also be a site of isolation, frustration and social pressures as part of *prescribed* gender roles. The gendered constituents of palpable home precariousness concern women as homemakers, caregivers and as domestic workers whose unpaid labour takes place in often highly precarious domestic circumstances. It is now recognised that most violence against women occurs in the home or in other private spaces as part of a pattern of coercive and manipulative behaviour. While often viewed as a private matter, global assessments reveal that one in three women experience physical or sexual violence from an intimate partner or from a person other than her partner in their lifetime (García-Moreno et al. 2015; see Black et al. 2011). Moreover, violence in the home is a key cause of homelessness and destitution among women with domestic abuse accounting for around one in ten homelessness applications in the UK (Campaigns report 2018). Evidence in the UK also reveals that many migrant women do not report incidents of domestic abuse to the police for fear of having their right to stay in the UK removed (Step Up Migrant Women UK 2017). The emphasis on privacy and intimacy in dominant discourses of home have therefore been critiqued within feminist perspectives by pointing to the ways in which these palpable home precarities are normalised, contrived to conceal the gendered power relations that shape home life (see Duncan and Lambert 2003; Martin and Mohanty 1986).

Underscored by the global financial crash of 2008, palpable home precarities form part of home imaginaries within experiences of home dispossession and the dramatic decline in access to mortgages in homeowning countries such as the US and UK. Home is no longer a secure investment. Yet, surprisingly, property TV programmes multiplied in number after the global financial crash of 2008 by exploiting palpable home precarities as part of the financialisaton of homes within neoliberal economic discourses. Chapter 5 explores the relevance of the global economic crisis for home imaginaries by considering how the financial crisis has been navigated within contrived home precarities to popularise post-crisis property TV programmes thereby intensifying the idealisation of home. These examples indicate that palpable and contrived home precarities go hand in hand with idealisations of home.

The rhetoric of war and technological prowess over other nations employed within imaginings of home as a political and 'military weapon' (Colomina 2001) are addressed in Chapter 4. The chapter indicates that the appeal to this mode of home precarity not only fuels and justifies anxieties around security and risk. It also promotes and venerates a privatised and defensive home as a contrived precariousness that justifies the promotion of market-led, technologised smart home futures. Chapter 9 shows that smart home discourses draw on these *contrived* home precarities to play on our fears of an invasion of home from outside. The promotion of visions and anxieties about a vulnerable and insecure home open to security breaches generates a contrived need for electronic alarms systems and digitally controlled surveillance of the home's perimeters. Paradoxically, it is the very same smart home discourses that have fuelled fears about the invasion of home privacy by security companies and tech giants. These companies can monitor household activities and collect data for marketing purposes through devices such as voice-activated assistants including Amazon's Alexa and Google Home. And smart homes are now vulnerable to cyberattacks on hardware, software and data used around the home. Anxieties about this surveillance and datafication of home form part of today's palpable home precarities alongside the growing recognition that homes and household routines need to be radically changed to become part of the solution to climate change. Yet, fundamentally, the appeal to home precarities associated with war and outside threats closes down alternative discourses that could generate constructive policies and practices to address climate change.

Contrived home precarities impede policies and practices needed to create environmentally sustainable homes as shared national and community projects. In the dramatically titled *Housing Bomb: Why Our Addiction to Houses Is Destroying the Environment and Threatening our Society*, environmentalists Nils Peterson, Tarla Rai Peterson and Jianguo Liu argue that our desires for ideal homes, bigger homes and second homes have 'built our way to ruin' by adding to the environmental crisis. Arguing that 'affluence and technology will not rescue society from a housing bomb' they warn us that the growing addiction to houses has 'taken the humble American dream and twisted it into an environmental and societal nightmare' (Peterson et al. 2013:1–3). Fears of an uncertain future can generate a sense of anxiety and restlessness since this future becomes impossible to foretell. Yet effective and sustainable responses to the palpable precarity of global warming, to reduce our carbon footprint at the level of the household, are complex and challenging. This is addressed through a series of issues and examples that inform Chapter 10. In this final chapter, palpable home precarities associated with the need to make homes environmentally sustainable are examined to uncover potential solutions.

By way of a conclusion to the book, we can confirm, then, that 'home' is a provisional and deeply contested concept. Home imaginaries entail sanctioned and contested idealisations and yet also precarities that challenge or even shape and support certain political and cultural agendas – about how we should conduct our everyday lives and according to what values. Traditional discourses that promote idealised homes are being contested in an era characterised by multiple trends and tendencies, some of which are positive and some of which have been and continue to be deeply damaging, both socially and environmentally. The following chapters emphasise that, on the one hand, home represents an urgent yet imprecise public predicament which continuously demands the attention of private citizens. On the other hand, home is vigorously defended as the exclusive domain of the state or financial and cultural experts. As a central material-discursive form, 'home' therefore comprises a generalised political as well as cultural category. It emerges as a set of distinctive social practices and routines, and a key site of struggle over contemporary identities, values and ways of living. Consequently, imaginaries of home are inspiring and performative but also intimidating, inconsistent and contradictory. 'Home' is all-pervasive yet also elevated from mundane, everyday life.

Structure of the book

Guided by the broad set of approaches and concepts set out above, the book provides a focus on the ways in which home is defined and circumscribed by outside, public agents and the ways in which dominant home imaginaries are performed, questioned or subverted at the level of households and daily life. The following chapters emphasise the multiple meanings of home and domesticity, confirming the vital importance of critiquing dominant discourses of home, conventional domesticities and heteronormative living arrangements.

Chapter 1 explores heritage homes. It considers the ways in which certain homes are reconfigured as sites of public commemoration and memory by the heritage industry. The chapter's themes are introduced by examining the influence of period dramas, such as *Downton Abbey* on discourses of heritage. The chapter then returns to the historical events and public debates that led to the elevation of the country house as a symbol of national 'heritage'. The roles played by major heritage institutions and cultural practices in generating collective memories are traced to explain how the country house came to stand for the nation, involving a sentimentalising of class inequalities and idealisations of the homes of the landed gentry. The following section examines research on the relationship between slavery and the British country house which prompts a reassessment of the legacy of slavery within the material-discursive practices of heritage home imaginaries, raising questions about social inequalities and racial oppression that underpin and politicise home ideals.

Chapter 2 traces the changing meanings of domestic space in the late nineteenth and early twentieth century to reflect on how the ideal home was conceived, promoted and idealised by forces beyond the home. Tracing the gendered constructions of home underpinning the feminisation of domestic space, it addresses moral alignments of domesticity in the nineteenth century that led to the idea of refined homemaking among the upper and upper-middle classes corresponding with ideas about the civilising effects of tasteful home décor. A series of key examples focus on advice manuals and exhibitions, to consider the leading aesthetic principles and cultural policies that shaped both visual and moral discourses of 'home' and household arrangements as *gendered* and *classed* spaces. Examples such as the annual Ideal Home Exhibition and New York World's Fair 1939–1940 reveal how exhibitions displayed model homes to convey dramatic changes in the meaning and purpose of home: from a place of decorativeness to one of efficiency and Modernist designs. The chapter explains that by the early twentieth century, women were summoned and reassigned as 'consumer citizens'.

Chapter 3 chronicles the rise in home ownership, domestic design awareness and consumerism in mid-twentieth century Britain and the United States. Post-World War II reconstructions of home life gave rise to the social desire for a modern suburban home as a consuming unit. The fluctuating imaginaries of the ideal family home and suburban living in the UK and US perpetuated inequalities of class, gender and race within the organisation of home life as an expression of national pride. Promoted by state and commercial initiatives, the ideal home conveyed by post-war exhibitions in the UK such as the Festival of Britain (1951) involved the promotion of 'good design' as a moral imperative. The chapter provides a case study of how dream houses displayed at the New York World's Fair of 1964–1965 were intimately tied to the grand theme of national identity and the Cold War. The intersection of military and domestic concerns in the US highlights the exploitation of the Cold War theme involving domestic consumer goods as a measure of national progress and superiority over other nations. The Kitchen Debate epitomises the overtly political nature of home, domestic modernity and middle-class affluence.

In mid-twentieth century Britain and America, 'home' was reconfigured as a mediatised space, reflecting the cultural dynamics of each country. Foregrounding the intersecting processes of domestic modernity and suburbanisation, **Chapter 4** examines the introduction of television and computers into the home. It provides an account of the display of television sets in model living rooms at national exhibitions in the UK and USA to show how television was designed and promoted for the ideal home. The chapter explores how the entrance of television and then computers into domestic space reshaped household dynamics and the spatial and temporal flows of home life. It reveals the extensive efforts that went into normalising television through programming and scheduling and how households negotiated domestic routines to adapt household dynamics to the media home. Traditional ideas about home in relation to 'public' space were destabilised by the adoption of media into the home. Domestication theory is introduced to offer a lens through which to consider the allied early introduction of computers into the home. The chapter traces the ways in which the computer drew paid work into the home and the gendered distinctions involved in computer-aided home working. This teleworking was used predominantly by women to combine their domestic and work duties, confirming that new technologies often function to reinforce as well as contest gendered roles and hierarchies.

Chapter 5 focuses on popular cultural re-imaginings of home in lifestyle and property TV programmes and via social media curation with a study of Pinterest. Together, these mediums idealise 'home' and cast light on home precarities associated with property ownership after the global economic crisis of 2008. Divided into two sections, the chapter first assesses how homes are conveyed in lifestyle and property TV programmes and then charts how homemaking is performed and re-enacted via social media. The chapter considers why and how television became such an influential medium after the global economic crisis. Two significant issues are tackled in this chapter. The first is the culpability of property and lifestyle TV in relation to the financial crisis of 2008. The second is how dreams of home ownership and exploitations of home dispossessions have been projected in gender-bound ways as post-crisis forms of entertainment. The digital mediation of home is signified by social media sites that facilitate users to transform their homes into personalised sites of self-display.

Extending the theme of home mediatisation, **Chapter 6** explores the changing dynamics of today's multiscreen home by examining the ways that digitalisation and mobilisation of personal and familial relationships shape home life. The chapter identifies new routines and temporal arrangements that lead to new kinds of mediated 'home time'. The chapter shows how domestic screens alter and re-order our concentration, our rhythms and our attentiveness to schedules through enhanced media affordances such as speed, immediacy of access, liveness and binge-watching. The chapter argues that rather than just constraining our time, digital screens enable us to subvert and actively reshape temporal routines and the associated needs of work, sleep and timekeeping that characterise late modernity.

Chapter 7 moves beyond the heteronormative ideology of home and domesticity to address modes of homemaking that subvert and transform them. Alternative domesticities are explored to consider struggles and contestations over traditional and new meanings of home in late modernity, from traditional family values to postmodern notions of mobility, agency and change. The chapter first examines how these changes have been mediated by popular media accounts of home. By chronicling the ways domestic life has been reconfigured by changes in intimate affiliations, for example among lesbian and gay couples, it then addresses a range of ethnographic case studies to explain the implications of new domestic living arrangements. The chapter highlights new ways of thinking about home in relation to the queering of domesticities.

Ideas of home relate not only to our possessions, material environment, household structure and type of home but also to our sense of place as 'identity'. Focusing on the theme of home place and identity, **Chapter 8** explores the diverse ways in which home is imagined in relation to transnational mobilities to highlight the multi-scalar nature of home. It examines mobile meanings of home relating to affinities with homeland, belonging and attachment to places and memories of place. The first section examines both positive and precarious experiences of transnational migrant movement in relation to ideas of home and belonging by examining materialities of home. How migrant's visions of home are shaped by gender, life experience, religion and related socio-cultural circumstances are considered as key elements of these processes. The second section considers mediated home mobilities by addressing the ways in which media and communication technologies support migrant families' connections with their home country as a manifestation of the transnational features of today's mediatised home. The chapter shows how home encounters are shaped by flows and movements that involve digital communication technologies which support the creation of a *virtual home*.

Chapter 9 explores the motives and discourses underlying 'homes of the future' and smart home futures. The first section considers visions of smart home futures in the early, mid and late twentieth century by examining 'homes of tomorrow' that symbolised progress and national prowess. A case study of corporate films and videos of the 'future home' from the 1950s to the present is presented to assess dominant corporate motives and narratives that sustain 'future home' prophecies. In addition to exhibitions, trade shows and media accounts, these corporate-made speculative films and videos of the 'future home' have played a major part in anticipating and popularising what I call 'home futurism'. The following sections deal with contemporary transformations in smart home technologies including the impact of the Internet of Things on domestic life. It addresses home surveillance and the datafied home by identifying the role of corporate 'future-makers' in the creation of future home imaginaries. Gendered power relations are reproduced through an implied encoding of a masculine discourse of smart expertise configured around the digital maintenance involved in sustaining a smart home. In terms of adopting and maintaining smart home systems, the 'digital housekeeping' involved in setting up and maintaining the technology is largely undertaken by men. By prioritising masculine discourses of technologised homes, smart homes have failed to address housework needs while celebrating the home as an efficient workspace. In the context of global warming, the market-led enthusiasm for smart solutions generates questions about the role of this technology to support energy-efficient 'eco-friendly' sustainable homes to lower their carbon footprint.

Chapter 10 addresses key debates, rhetoric, policy initiatives and proposed solutions for environmentally sustainable and energy saving homes. This final chapter highlights the palpable home precarities associated with climate change and how the need for sustainable homes challenges deep-seated values and routines associated with 'normal' home life. First, it chronicles household energy use and sustainability by taking Europe as a cross-national regional example. The second section examines state and free market strategies towards green policies followed by an exploration of examples of 'green' or 'eco-homes' homes. The final section considers popular culture and news discourses. While social network sites offer vital media sources for sharing knowledge and advice on environmental sustainability, a strong sense of denial remains in many mainstream news and popular media accounts of climate change. The theme of lifestyle TV is revisited in a new light in this final section, by referring to the role of 'eco-lifestyle' television as a major site of imaginative experimentation in alternative, transformative lifestyles to support green living exemplified by the work of Tania Lewis (2012; 2015). Overall, the book's chapters seek to emphasise that competing ideas about the purpose of home correspond with competing notions of social and cultural life.

References

Amin, A. (2002) 'Spatialities of globalisation', *Environment and Planning A*, 34(3), 385–399.

Bauman, Z. (2000) *Liquid Modernity*. Cambridge: Polity Press.

Bawden, G. (2011) 'Home theatre: Staging the domestic interior', *Double Dialogues*, 14. www.doubledialogues.com/article/home-theatre-staging-the-domestic-interior/ (accessed 31 August 2019).

Berlant, L. (2011) *Cruel Optimism*. Durham, NC and London: Duke University Press.

Black, M.C., Basile, K.C., Breiding, M.J., Smith, S.G., Walters, M.L., Merrick, M.T., Chen, J., and Stevens, M.R. (2011) *The National Intimate Partner and Sexual Violence Survey (NISVS): 2010 Summary Report*. Atlanta, GA: National Center for Injury Prevention and Control, Centers for Disease Control and Prevention, Atlanta, Georgia. www.cdc.gov/violenceprevention/pdf/nisvs_report2010-a.pdf (accessed 2 July 2019).

Blunt, A. (2005) 'Cultural geography: Cultural geographies of home', *Progress in Human Geography*, 29, 505–515.

Blunt, A. and Dowling, R. (2006) *Home*. London: Routledge.

Blunt, A. and Dowling, R. (2008) '"*Home: A response and future directions*" in Jennifer Hyndman Authors meet critics: reviews and response', *Social and Cultural Geography*, 9(5), 557–572.

Bourdieu, P. (1984) *Distinction*. London: Routledge & Kegan Paul.

Bourdieu, P. (1993) *The Field of Cultural Production*. Cambridge: Polity.

Campaigns report. (2018) 'A safe home'. APPG for Ending Homelessness, All-Party Parliamentary Group for Ending Homelessness: Homelessness prevention for care leavers, prison leavers and survivors of domestic violence. www.crisis.org.uk/media/240459/cri0198_domesticabusebill_appg_report_2019_aw_web.pdf (accessed 10 August 2019).

Castells, M. (2000) 'Materials for an exploratory theory of the network society', *British Journal of Sociology*, 51, 5–24.

Chambers, D. (2019) 'Emerging temporalities in the multiscreen home', *Media, Culture and Society OnlineFirst*, 1–19. doi:10.1177/0163443719867851.

Chapman, T. (1999) 'Stage sets for ideal lives: Images of home in contemporary show homes', in T. Chapman and J. Hockey, *Ideal Homes? Social Change and Domestic Life*. London: Routledge, pp. 44–58.

Colomina, B. (2001) *Domesticity at War*. Barcelona: ActarD Inc.

Davies, B. (2005) 'The (im)possibility of intellectual work in neoliberal regimes', *Discourse: Studies in the Cultural Politics of Education*, 26(1), 1–14.

Duncan, J.S. and Lambert, D. (2003) 'Landscapes of home', in J.S. Duncan, N.C. Johnson and R.H. Schein (eds), *Companion to Cultural Geography*. Oxford: Blackwell, pp. 382–403.

Elias, A., Gill, R. and Scharff, C. (2017) 'Aesthetic labour: Beauty politics in neoliberalism', in A. Elias, R. Gill and C. Scharff (eds), *Aesthetic Labour: Rethinking Beauty Politics in Neoliberalism*. Basingstoke: Palgrave Macmillan, pp. 3–50.

Ferreri, M., Dawson, M., and Vasudevan, A. (2017) 'Living precariously: Property guardianship and the flexible city', *Transactions of the Institute of British Geographers*, 42(2), 246–259.

García-Moreno, C., Zimmerman, Z., Morris-Gehring, A., Heise, L., Amin, L.A., Abrahams, N., Montoya, O., Bhate-Deosthali, P., Kilonzo, N. and Watts, C. (2015) 'Addressing violence against women: A call to action', *The Lancet*, 385 (9978), 1685–1696.

Gaventa, J. (2003) *Power after Lukes: A Review of the Literature*. Brighton: Institute of Development Studies.

Gill, R. and Pratt, A. (2008) 'In the social factory? Immaterial labour, precariousness and cultural work', *Theory, Culture & Society*, 25(7–8), 1–30.

Harris, E. (2015) 'Navigating pop-up geographies: Urban space-times of flexibility, interstitiality and immersion', *Geography Compass*, 9(11), 592–603.

Harris, E. and Nowicki, M. (2018) 'Cultural geographies of precarity', *Cultural Geographies*, 25(3), 387–391.

Jacobs, J.M. and Smith, S.J. (2008) 'Living room: Rematerializing home', *Environment and Planning A*, 40, 515–519.

Lewis, T. (2012) '"There grows the neighbourhood": Green citizenship, creativity and life politics on eco-TV, *International Journal of Cultural Studies*, 15(3), 315–326.

Lewis, T. (2015) '"One city block at a time": Researching and cultivating green transformations', *International Journal of Cultural Studies*, 18(3), 347–363.

Maguire, J.S. and Matthews, J. (2012) 'Are we all cultural intermediaries now? An introduction to cultural intermediaries in context', *European Journal of Cultural Studies*, 15 (5), 551–562.

Maguire, J.S. and Matthews, J. (2014) 'Introduction: Thinking with cultural intermediaries', in J.S. Maguire, and J. Matthews, *The Cultural Intermediaries Reader*. London: Sage Publications, pp. 1–12.

Martin, B. and Mohanty, C.T. (1986) '"Feminist politics": What's home got to do with it?', in T. De Lauretis (ed.), *Feminist Studies/Critical Studies*. Bloomington: Indiana University Press, pp. 191–211.

Massey, D. (2004) 'Geographies of responsibility', *Geographical Annals*, 86(1), 5–18.

Miller, D. (2001) 'Possessions', in D. Miller (ed.), *Home Possessions: Material Culture behind Closed Doors*. Oxford: Berg, pp. 107–122.

Morley, D. (2000) *Home Territories: Media, Mobility and Identity*. London: Routledge.

Morley, D. (2017) *Communications and Mobility: The Migrant, the Mobile Phone, and the Container Box*. Oxford: Wiley-Blackwell.

Peck, J. (2012) 'Austerity urbanism: American cities under extreme economy', *City*, 16(6), 626–655.

Peterson, M.N., Peterson, T. and Liu, J. (2013) *The Housing Bomb: Why Our Addiction to Houses Is Destroying the Environment and Threatening our Society*. Baltimore: Johns Hopkins University Press.

Pink, S. (2012) 'Domestic time in the sensory home: The textures and rhythms of knowing, practice, memory, and imagination', in E. Keightley (ed.), *Time, Media and Modernity*. Basingstoke: Palgrave Macmillan, 201–224.

Ralph, D. and Staeheli, L. (2011) 'Home and migration: Mobilities, belongings and identities', *Geography Compass*, 5(7), 517–530.

Rose, N. (1992) 'Governing the enterprising self', in P. Heelas and P. Morris (eds), *The Values of the Enterprise Culture: The Moral Debate*. London: Routledge, pp. 141–164.

Saraswati, L.A. (2013) *Seeing Beauty: Sensing Race in Transnational Indonesia*. Honolulu: University of Hawai'i Press.

Standing, G. (2011) *The Precariat: The New Dangerous Class*. London: Bloomsbury Academic.

Step Up Migrant Women UK. (2017) 'Latin American Women's Rights Service. Safe reporting of crime for migrants with insecure immigration status'. Press release, May 2017.www.amnesty.org.uk/press-releases/uk-domestic-abuse-bill-risks-failing-migrant-women (accessed 10 August 2019).

Taylor, C. (2003) *Modern Social Imaginaries*. Durham, NC: Duke University Press.

Taylor, C. (2007) *A Secular Age*. Cambridge, MA: Harvard University Press.

Tolia-Kelly, D. (2004) 'Materializing post-colonial geographies: Examining the textural landscapes of migration in the South Asian homes', *Geoforum*, 35, 675–688.

Tutton, R. (2017) 'Wicked futures: Meaning, matter and the sociology of the future', *The Sociological Review*, 65(3), 478–492.

Waite, L. (2009) 'A place and space for a critical geography of precarity?' *Geography Compass*, 3(1), 412–433.

West, H. (2016) 'Artisanal food and the cultural economy: Perspectives on craft, heritage, authenticity and reconnection', in J.A. Klein and J.L. Watson (eds), *The Handbook of Food and Anthropology*. London: Bloomsbury, pp. 406–434.

1

HERITAGE HOMES

Introduction

Across the world, the past homes of aristocratic, famous and wealthy people have been transformed into museum sites that influence and also raise questions about the idealisation of present-day homes. The explosion of interest in 'stately homes' has been inspired by films and British TV period dramas such as *Downton Abbey*. This chapter examines home as a site of history. The grand country houses built in Britain's countryside between the seventeenth and nineteenth centuries have become potent cultural symbols. They play a central role within discourses of 'heritage' as part of national and regional attempts to forge a sense of common identity. As a timely intervention, the English country house offers a lens through which to explore the formation of elite homes as icons of public commemoration.

The public appeal of the English country house accelerated following the decline of the great estates before and after World War I. From the late nineteenth and early twentieth century, photographs and news about the country house season figured in lifestyle magazines and newspapers' society pages. These pages offered the middle classes filtered access to home interiors that displayed the luxury homes and lifestyles of the upper classes (Davidoff 1986). The growth in British heritage films in the 1980s, adaptations of Jane Austen novels in the 1990s, followed by films such as Ian McEwan's *Atonement* (2001) and murder mystery films such as *Gosford Park* (2002) have provided a cinematic focal point for the country house, elevating these grand homes to the status of a national icon. Likewise, historical popular television dramas such as *Brideshead Revisited* (1981), *Downton Abbey* (2010–2015) and documentary TV programmes such as BBC1's *The Edwardian Country House* (2002), Channel 4's *Country House Rescue* (2008) and Julian Fellowes's *Great Houses* on ITV (2013) fuel our fascination with homes of the past.

These popular narratives function as a vital source of inspiration on tastes and styles of contemporary home furnishing. But their impact also extends much further than this. They perform as phantasmagorias of 'home'. Historic homes work to generate and sustain powerful ideas about how ideal homes are to be imagined, presented and experienced today. As a key setting for popular dramas, the contemporary cultural appeal of the grand country house is carefully nurtured by leading cultural agents including heritage institutions such as the National Trust and English Heritage. The aim of these cultural intermediaries is to ensure that the grand houses, their art works and landscapes are celebrated as 'heritage homes' to unite and define the nation. They do so by venerating refinement, connoisseurship and civility associated with the domestic living of past and present titled and wealthy families in ways that feed into popular beliefs about 'ideal' homes today.

Critical explorations of today's country houses are rare. However, a global popular fascination with the 'period' country house situates 'home' at the centre of debates about heritage, nation and empire. An analytical reflection on the country house as 'heritage' provides pointers about how certain collective memories of 'home' are constituted, based on contrived home precarities. By re-evaluating traditional interpretations of country houses and how they circumscribe social attitudes to 'home', this chapter uncovers cogent values about home as time and place, conveyed through heritage, memory, nation, class and race by re-evaluating traditional interpretations of country houses and how they circumscribe social attitudes to 'home'. It traces the roles played by major heritage institutions and cultural practices in generating collective memories which shape and come to underpin idealisations of the contemporary *middle-class* home as a 'staging of authenticity' (West 2016). To understand how heritage homes have become sites of desire, the chapter explains that historical institutions and popular dramas are mediators engaged in *monumentalising home*. It draws on a body of research on slavery and the British country house conducted as part of the commemorations of the 2007 bicentenary of the abolition of the British slave trade which prompts a reassessment of the legacy of slavery within the material-discursive practices of heritage home imaginaries. Marked by questions of power and representation as a furtive part of this process of home 'monumentalisation', these elite homes veil social hierarchy and enslavement, involving social inequalities and racial oppression, that underpin and politicise home ideals.

The 'Downton effect'

The popular period drama, *Downton Abbey* was first aired in Britain on ITV in September 2010, and then four months later in the United States on PBS. The series conveys the growing popularity of heritage television for contemporary audiences. Winning a string of prestigious awards, this big-budget costume drama attracted millions of faithful viewers globally. An upsurge in visitors to English country houses, with a year-by-year rise in numbers, was so noticeable that this renewed interest was named the 'Downton Effect' in press releases by Visit England.[1] Nearly a third of tourists to the UK visit a historic house or castle,[2] with eight of the top ten National Trust paid-for locations being country houses and parklands (National Trust 2013: 72), and 13 million people visit the Historical Houses Association's privately-owned houses, involving around five hundred properties (Historic Houses Association, 2014). As Oliver Cox points out, 'The "Downton Effect" has also been linked to a surging demand for Savile Row suits, bowler hats, butlers, afternoon tea, riding side-saddle, tiaras, vintage lingerie, luxury wallpaper and interior design, and country houses themselves' (Cox 2015: 114). This trend has, of course, been welcomed with open arms by the heritage industry. The transatlantic appeal of the English country house of past centuries is further indicated by a series of exhibitions launched in 2014 in the United States, in Wilmington, Delaware and Houston, Texas.

Historians and media commentators describe *Downton Abbey* as a reassuring symbol of an ideal past evoked at a time of economic and social upheaval in Britain and other Anglophone nations. As Katherine Byrne puts it, 'Downton provides a sanitised, yet seemingly "authentic", portrait of a period of instability and rapid change, which its writers have identified as having much in common with our own present' (Byrne 2013). The series embodies the 'cult of the country house' within a plot that evolves around an aristocratic family, the Crawleys, whose grand Yorkshire estate is financially threatened. This threat of losing Downton, as an expression of the precarity of home, is symbolised as a threat to both personal identity and English national heritage (Baena and Byker 2015). Since the property has been in the family for several generations, Lord Crawley's entire identity is rooted in the estate: the place and the desire for the property to be passed on to his heir. This forewarning establishes the country house as a nostalgic symbol. As such, the story is connected to a set of English narratives that represent the country house in a state of decline, involving a sense of loss and nostalgia for an idealised past. Its plot and stylised format are reminiscent of literary adaptations such as the popular series *Jewel in the Crown* (Granada, 1984) and *Brideshead Revisited* (Granada, 1981). It shares qualities with the British heritage films of the 1980s, such as *Another Country* (1984), *A Passage to India* (1985) and *A Room with a View* (1986), constituting a cycle of films that are essentially conservative and nostalgic in their mode of address (Higson 1993: 110). These narratives come together to form a genre that associates the country house with the English character and sense of identity, ranging from novels such as Evelyn Waugh's *Brideshead Revisited*, E.M. Forster's *Howard's End* and Darlington Hall in Kazuo Ishiguro's *The Remains of the Day* (Baena and Byker 2015).

Downton Abbey draws on the appeal of the country house as 'collective remembrance' and 'country house fetishism' (Baucom, 1999: 5) by offering audiences a vision of such an estate within a ritual of re-conceiving and preserving a bygone sense of Englishness. *Downton Abbey* therefore represents a powerful emotional emblem of nationality and heritage 'worth sacrificing for and preserving' (Baena and Byker 2015: 263). The aesthetic splendour of the series is aimed at triggering sentimental longings through a range of visual codes such as clothing, furniture, modes of social etiquette and long shots that describe the landscape's magnificence.

Focusing on the relationships within the Downton household, the plots of each instalment follow life 'below stairs' as well as in the grand reception rooms. Two distinct social classes of aristocracy and domestic servants cohabit this grand space to generate ongoing ruptures and social polemics. However, these evolving tensions are set within a wider environment of harmonious co-existence. The lives of the three Crawley daughters are entangled in these two social classes set within two different ways of life: one receding, where women have little power and one ascending where power is anticipated for women. The servants' roles in the household are scripted as expressing respectful, dignified tasks that uphold the family's aristocratic bearing, as a quintessential part of the English national heritage. Accepting the unequal relations of the household as part of the natural order, the butler and housekeeper view their work as deeply honourable. As Baena and Byker state, 'The overall mood of the series is thus one of celebration where at least regular characters seem to know their place and accept it, reinforcing a rather nostalgic view of an English past heritage' (Baena and Byker 2015: 267).

This traditional representation of a consistent domestic realm where the house-holders 'know their place' creates an idealised vision of the past designed to stir reminiscence for a bygone English identity. The narrative reinstates and justifies aristocratic and elitist behaviour and beliefs, restored by the depiction of benevolent employers in charge of a large household of servants. Television dramas and film settings like *Downton Abbey* and *Brideshead* cross from imagined to mediated visions of grandeur (Bawden 2011). These stage sets reflect and amplify class aspirations, class divisions and fantasies of status within stratified societies that function as 'an idealisation of the higher strata' (Goffman 1969). The narrative strategy of evoking a 'lost and longed for earlier period' serves to endorse a sentimental disavowal of class tension. Indeed, the evocation of nostalgia explains the series' success and its cultural worth (Hodge 2011). The discourse of reminiscence in *Downton Abbey* corresponds with wider social concerns associated with national and cultural iden-tities in terms of lineage, belonging and traditional values. The emotional dimen-sions of the drama uncover and mediate cultural values of nation and nationhood that haunt contemporary society, as values that seem to be precariously dissolving. As Hodge (2011) states, 'All of this points to the fact that in our flexible modern environment, with all its attending fragmentation, we see an increasing reliance on popular media narratives for negotiating our social and cultural identities.'

Substantial tourism revenue has been generated by opening English country houses to the public (Cox 2015: 210). However, the challenge for historians and the heritage industry has been to find ways to tap into the popularity of dramas such as *Downton Abbey* to draw in visitors to the complex cultural backdrops of these 'stately home' narratives (Cox 2015). Importantly, this genre of television drama continues to present the country house as a lived-in space. Creator of *Downton Abbey*, Julian Fellowes, suggests that his work has made a significant impact on curatorial trends by recounting the daily lives not only of the former upper classes but also the servant community who contributed to the running of the country house (Waterfield and Julian Fellowes 2012: 65). The claim, then, is that *Downton Abbey* has triggered a desire to promote grand homes by addressing the competing individual experiences of servants and landed families and how the country house contained and shaped these narratives.

Yet certain curators and scholars argue that *Downton Abbey* has not generated a new curatorial direction as such. Rather, the series has simply consolidated a prevailing approach in the staging and narrativisation of country houses. After all, exhibiting servants' quarters is not new. Cox (2015) points to Erdigg Hall, obtained by the National Trust in 1973 for its detailed information about the servants who worked there in the past, rather than the grandeur of its architecture or contents (see Waterson 1990). Similarly, the National Trust has invested in the restoration of Victorian kitchens at Dyrham Park near Bath and the domestic service areas at Ickworth in Suffolk. Nevertheless, the presentation of English country houses as a living force to appeal to visitors runs counter to conservation agendas. Cox states that:

> Servants' quarters, which require the least amount of prior knowledge for meaningful interpretation and engagement by the public, tend to enjoy the longest visitor dwelling times. For academic historians, this retreat to the servants' quarters is symptomatic of the discrepancy between history's popularity and the inadequate historical literacy of much of the population. (Cox 2015: 116)

This notion of a 'retreat' to the servant's quarters implies visitor ignorance and a disregard of the finer aesthetic features of country houses such as architecture, art and porcelain collections. Conversely, a more recent approach is to regard museum visitors as agents of their own encounters with English country houses, inspired by their own socio-cultural backgrounds, experiences and trajectories. This requires house curators to abandon orthodoxies in order to engage with house museums and open up other possibilities and experiences (Young 2007). Yet while the servants' quarters of country houses can inspire a sense of involvement among visitors-as-tourists, most custodians and academics are more interested in the décor and artefacts of reception rooms occupied by the rich or noble family.

The strategy tensions facing the heritage industry in the display of country house, between authenticity and popularised visitor immersion, were revealed in 2014. A public uproar was caused by a remark made by Sir Simon Jenkins, then chairman of the National Trust. Addressing techniques of presenting the country house in an interview, Jenkins remarked that 'There are things we can learn from Disney' (Cox 2015: 117). This came close to inferring that the English country home might be a 'simulacrum'. For Baudrillard, a simulacrum is an imitation or simulation of reality (Baudrillard 1983: 1994). In this sense, today's Disneyland culture can be characterised as a simulational culture. This culture of hyperreality involves a loss of distinction between 'reality' and 'image'. The country house appears to represent, to *stand for* something imagined and not real. But instead, the country house *hides* a reality. It prevents us from seeing the real workings of dominant groups in power.

Country houses are not only conserved as 'heritage homes' but also preserved as a set of powerful middle-class values about 'home', involving the conservation of a class-bound set of cultural values encompassing social ranking, middle-class reverence and an idealisation of elites. Promoted within the dominant discourses of British country houses, these class-bound values are underpinned by the socio-economic power structures of colonialism, slavery and empire on which the country house thrived. The 'connoisseurship' and 'family lineage' perspectives within academic studies of the collections and genealogies of mainland Britain's landed elite tend to be masked by the structures of power corresponding with these legacies (Bressey 2013). The 'Downton effect' and revelations of the roles played by colonialism, slavery and empire in the histories of country houses prompts the need for a closer look at how homes of the wealthy were preserved and transformed into sites of heritage that stood for the whole nation, and represented the pinnacle of respectable home living. Drawing on Baudrillard, we might say that the symbol of the country house as a prestige home involves a rewriting of social class inequality (conveyed as a noble service, by workers to the elite) and a denial of the role of slavery in sustaining and preserving the economic fortunes of country estates. Bearing this in mind, the legacy of slavery in the history of the country house is discussed below.

Monumentalising home

The Victoria & Albert Museum, London (V&A) staged an exhibition in 1974 called 'The Destruction of the Country House' during a moment of crisis in heritage politics and the history of country house preservation (Adams 2013). Supported by archival research, Ruth Adams' analysis of the event and its response in the media provides a record of public debate about heritage during a pivotal period of the 1970s. The exhibition appealed to home precarities by presenting the view that England's grand country houses were under threat and that if these iconic estates were neglected, then key features of English national history, culture and identity would also be under threat. By associating these homes with English heritage, the V&A endorsed the protection of the country house by recasting the architectural legacy of the aristocracy from a sectional interest to a national cause. The exhibition thereby succeeded in galvanising popular appeal and support for a privileged minority interest. A number of critics contested the growing accent on heritage in British culture, within heritage politics, including Patrick Wright's *On Living in an Old Country* (1985) and Robert Hewison's *The Heritage Industry: Britain in a Climate of Decline* (1987). Their main grievance was that Britain's history was being sanitised and commercialised by a conservative, retrograde ideology which was turning the country into a theme park – again, a Disneyfication and simulacrum of events that refutes the social class inequalities and racial oppression on which country houses were founded.

Although upheld as part of public policy discourse, 'heritage' has never been clearly defined. Rather than an objective classification, 'heritage' is a relational, subjective concept with a distinctive political, ideological and aesthetic purpose.

Heritage functions to reclassify pasts 'so as to infuse them with present purposes' (Lowenthal 1998: xv). It reformulates or reconceptualises artefacts, sites and land-scapes as national asset or 'treasures' worthy of rescue within what Laurajane Smith calls an 'authorised heritage discourse' (Smith 2006: 29–30). This discourse promotes the idea that these houses, lands and artefacts must be protected and venerated for future generations not only for educational purposes but also to create a sense of cohesive identity founded on the past. Heritage homes are, then, a highly politicised process 'subject to contestation and bound up in the construction, reconstruction and deconstruction of memory and identity' as maintained by Sara McDowell (2008: 43). She goes on to say that 'Memory always represents a struggle over power and is thus implicated in the "who decides?" questions about the future.' While oppositional discourses can occur, they tend to be eclipsed by dominant explanations that reaffirm the encounters of white, European upper middle and ruling class men who populate the professions involved in preserving historical sites and homes of the landed gentry (Smith 2008: 162).

The staging of a continuously under-threat *national* heritage was a key strategy, as a contrived precarity, used to validate heritage in the first annual report of the National Heritage Memorial Fund for 1980–81 (Hewison 1987: 136–7). Ruth Adams (2013: 3) suggests that: '"Threat" is not only a ubiquitous trope of heritage discourse, but a defining characteristic.' Country houses have been enhanced as powerful symbols of this heritage by the assertion that they and heritage itself, are 'in danger' (Hewison 1987: 193; Wright 1985: 73). The Gowers Committee was appointed by the Labour government in 1948 to find ways to preserve and maintain houses of historical or architectural interest after World War II. And the National Trust was tasked to administer those country houses, supported by the state. Despite the enormous expense, the Gowers Committee stipulated that the 'way of life' of country house inhabitants must be preserved – alongside the buildings and land – via tax exemptions and grants. These houses were still inhabited by their families who were reclassified as 'tenants'. In exchange, the public would gain value from a preserved heritage that included the whole package: houses and occupants. The public would receive certain access rights for educational and tourism objectives.

The alternative term, 'stately home' was gradually introduced to describe country houses with the aim of representing these *private* homes as *public* assets to signal their value to the whole nation (Cannadine 1992). Thus, the idea of a country house as something confiscated, requisitioned and remote was erased by the presentation of an English country house as a monumentalised family space, open to the public. From the 1950s and 1960s, some landed families established their country houses as businesses with profit-making initiatives supported by *Country Life* magazine. Established in 1897, *Country Life* provided property coverage of manorial estates and other upmarket residential properties and a focus on the pleasures of rural life including hunting, farming and equestrian news. However, inflation and higher taxes in the late 1960s led to the demolishing of several houses considered to be a burden or even monstrosities if they conformed to architectural tastes no longer fashionable.

The V&A launched a touring exhibition in 1964 called 'Vanishing History', under the directive of the Standing Conference for Local History, to foreground a need to document old buildings due for demolition (Adams 2013). This acted as a trigger for country house owners to crystallise around their own interests, as a *cause*. With a growing number of their homes being opened to the public, owners were now familiar with the idea of performing a civic role as curators of heritage. With this aim in mind, the Historic Houses Association was established in 1973 as an independent body that evolved from the British Travel Association to foster public appreciation of the country house as a vital feature of English history and culture. At the time, private country houses were accepted as venues of leisure and entertainment and, to some degree, as repositories of nationally valuable cultural artefacts. But they were not yet associated with loftier abstract ideas of heritage as symbols in need of special protection (Mandler 1997; Adams 2013). The Historic Houses Association appointed John Cornforth, the architectural editor of *Country Life* magazine, to conduct a wide-ranging survey of country houses in 1972 to provide concrete evidence in which to anchor these emotional claims. Called 'The Country Houses in Britain: Can they Survive?', the survey was labelled 'independent' even though it was subsidised by a sizeable number of country house owners as well as the printing costs paid by the British Tourist Authority.

The country house lobby gained momentum during a severe recession in 1974, when a Labour government proposed a wealth tax and withdrawal of tax relief on agricultural land and art works not on public display. This raised alarm among members of the heritage alliance who feared that country houses and their contents would be broken up and either sold or demolished in response to the new charges. A campaign against the wealth tax called 'Heritage in Danger' was launched by Conservative Member of Parliament, Patrick Cormack and art dealer Hugh Leggatt. Other organisations joined in making submissions to the Parliamentary Committee including Country Landowners' Association, the Historic Houses Association, the Museums Association, the Tate Gallery, the British Museum, the Historic Buildings Council, the Standing Commission on Museums and Galleries, the British Tourist Authority, the Reviewing Committee on the Export of Works of Art, the National Art Collections Fund and the Antique Dealers' Association (Adams 2013).

In the same year, a V&A exhibition called 'Destruction of the Country House' was mounted to support the preservation of the stately home. It functioned, simultaneously, to promote opposition to the wealth tax (Mandler 1997: 404). The show publicised the positive role played by homes of the landed gentry in local communities as well as the cultural value of these estates. As Adams comments:

> The explanatory panels in the exhibition portrayed country estates as the 'best' of English society in microcosm and as models of a self-sufficient Communitarianism ... However, such solidarity could only be assured within a hierarchical society in which everyone 'knew their place'. (2013: 7)

The exhibition also drew attention to the social composition of the heritage lobby as a privileged elite that encompassed the landed aristocracy, landowners, officer class and 'hangers-on' (Strong 1999: 202).

The explicit aim of the exhibition was to elicit an emotive response from visitors, as explained by Adams (2013). This was exemplified by a theatrical set at the exhibition, titled the 'Hall of Lost Houses' that looked like a neo-Classical portico being smashed by a wrecking ball with photos of some among the thousands of country houses destroyed in the twentieth century. Although effective in provoking emotional reactions, this dramatic approach revealed the event's political implications: of sanctioning a return to a way of life that was questionable and now obsolete. The wall panels interpellated visitors using a direct, brusque tone such as:

> In modern times no other country has been party to such artistic destruction in a period of peace. To have destroyed so much of beauty over such a length of time is a stain on our national history. We are all to blame in some way. If you leave this hall of destruction feeling grieved and shameful, then we who have prepared this exhibition will be confident that people and government will not allow it to happen again. (Text taken from preparatory document, dated 12 September 1974, held in V&A Archive, quoted in Adams 2013: 8)

The empathy between the V&A and country houses was fostered by the role of curators who were from similar cultural and intellectual backgrounds as the country house owners. This group of professionals acted as cultural intermediaries who not only united the owners with the museum and heritage lobby but also connected this cohesive group with 'the masses' by interpreting and conveying ideas about 'heritage' to the public (see Bourdieu 1984; Adams 2013: 8–9). The restyling, rebuilding or desertion of English country houses within the history of country houses and their estates undermines the notion of inheritance as continuity. But the 'Destruction' exhibition countered this notion of decline by uniting country houses and their occupants as a heritage package and by correlating tradition with the public good. Few people outside aristocratic circles were concerned for the landed gentry experiences of living in damp, draughty and dilapidated country bastions. As such, exhibitions such as 'Destruction' served the purpose of appealing to inheritance as continuity. Ancestry was associated with entitled stewardship to signify social continuity (Lowenthal 1998: 92): 'Country-house owners are the hereditary custodians of what was one of the most vital forces of cultural creation in our history' (quoted in Hewison 1987: 193).

With the wealth tax proposal dropped in 1975, the V&A's Country House exhibition had achieved its aim. Through public policy, country houses were now recognised as national heritage with their established owners continuing to live in the properties as custodians or trustees (Mandler 1997). These events show how the English country house formed the centrepiece of a political debate about Britain's tax system. By appealing to myths of aristocratic decline and hardship, country house owners were able to access charitable support. Reinventing themselves in this way, they moved from moneyed landowners to unpaid curators of national heritage. Non-aligned observers were dismayed at the extreme choices proposed, of 'philistine confiscation or a dream of squirearchy, brute socialism or brute feudalism' (Mandler 1997: 404). Although some estates were dissolved in the ensuing years, most of country house owners, such as Chatsworth, managed to increase their wealth through new business ventures (Adams 2013: 12).

After 1975, heritage lobbying in the UK expanded with an increasing emphasis on conservation in public and government opinion. This emphasis was galvanised by a new pressure group called SAVE Britain's Heritage created in 1975, European Architectural Heritage Year, by a group of journalists, historians, architects, and planners who campaign publicly for endangered historic buildings and are active on the broader issues of preservation policy. In 1983, the Historic Buildings and Monuments Commission for England (later renamed English Heritage), was set up to run the national system of heritage protection and manage a range of historic properties. A more business-oriented approach to national heritage was now adopted to develop the commercial potential of historic buildings and monuments. This brave new 'heritage industry' was run not only by the old-style cultured generalists but also by entrepreneurs. The incorporation of the big house into the heritage landscape allowed its meaning to be extended beyond the social and spatial signifier of elite culture (Hodge 2011).

The conflation of the country house and 'heritage' underpinned a set of strategies to invoke a powerful set of values about home and social class. The country house lobby promoted a discourse that articulated the idea of the decline of the landed gentry family and a vanishing 'way of life' as a loss of heritage. This monumentalising of homes of the elite, by appeals to a sense of loss, sought to unify the nation around a naturalised social hierarchy, as part of the presentation of collective memory. A key feature of this process of monumentalising is the arousal of public feeling that supports a rhetoric of national recovery (Wright 1985: xiii) which functioned to promote powerful ideas of true British identity. By invoking the idea of the 'imagined community' (Anderson 1991), the stately home is reclassified as a heritage site that stands for the whole nation. The country houses of the aristocracy are no longer simply homes of the past but a collective cause of benefit to the whole nation through the principles of national heritage (Strong 1999). As such, the country house becomes a powerful symbol of tradition, a marketing tool for the preservation of a lost utopia (Deckha 2004; Adam 2013). The homes of the landed gentry now symbolise Britain as a nation.

This marketing tool has been effective, as verified by Laurajane Smith (2006: 137). In interviews with visitors to stately homes, she found that they seldom refer to these 'families' as 'aristocracy', 'ruling class' or in terms of social hierarchy. The discourse of the country house visit tends to be linked affectionally with the notion of 'the family'. This use of the term 'family' invokes a sense of respectable 'homeliness' which works to naturalise social inequalities. A masking of the mechanisms of power that support the stately home allows this history to be a *shared*, national story. However, a critique of the apparent whiteness of English country houses involves a major reconstruction of British history by broadening and challenging dominant discourse to include histories about slavery, colonial expansion and empire (Bressey 2013), providing a very different account of home precarity.

Slavery and the Country House

English Heritage commissioned research to reassess relations between transatlantic slavery and those country house properties now in their charge as part of the 2007 commemoration of the bicentenary of the abolition of the British slave trade. Until then, revisionist estimates of the profits generated from slaving and the slave trade suggested that, whilst not insignificant, they accounted for a small share of British domestic income between the mid-1700s and the mid-1800s. However, commemorations of the bicentenary of the abolition of the British slave trade in 2007 prompted several national institutions to reassess the legacy of slavery. Of the 33 country houses surveyed as part of the bicentenary research, 26 were found to have links to slavery or abolition with four further sites then commissioned in 2008. The findings of these and other related studies were presented at the 'Slavery and the British Country House' conference in 2009.[3] Published as a conference volume in 2013 edited by Marge Dresser and Andrew Hann, the research revealed the tangled connections between landed wealth, British estates and the labour of African slaves. Understandably, such relations were disregarded or concealed for centuries. The book represents a radical change of approach by English Heritage, shifting from disavowal and cover-up to gradual, *ongoing* disclosure. The findings ruptured pre-existing nostalgic narratives, provoking a reassessment of heritage homes and how these homes convey social relations in the past and the present (Hodge 2011).

In the *Slavery and the British Country House* research, four themes emerge from the mapping of the legacies of slavery on to the British country house (Dresser and Hann 2013). The first is confirmation that between the 1660s and the 1820s, the wealth derived from the Atlantic slave economy and slave labour supported the construction, restoration and residence of many of Britain's country houses. Also, a wider network of indirect links between these properties and slavery existed. Second, both merchants and the landed elite involved in the rise of country homes from the late 1600s, drew on ideas of refinement, propriety and decorum to dissociate themselves from their links with the Atlantic slave trade. Whilst the landed elite consolidated their status, merchants actively sought to enter this social class and align their families with the landed estates. Recording the history of the now demolished Rutland country house, Normanton Hall, Nuala Zahedieh (2013: 71) confirms a correspondence between Britain's involvement in the Caribbean and an intensive period of country house building. A significant number of those who generated their wealth from the late seventeenth century and early eighteenth centuries' slave-based plantation system were eager to purchase and build country houses (Zahedieh 2013: 76).

A third theme arising from the research is that although slavery and country house aesthetics seem to be diametrically opposed, the aesthetics and wider cultural tastes displayed in the country houses were linked with dealings of slavery. This includes classical designs, ornate interiors, ornamentations, collections of art and furniture and scenic landscaping. Researchers are now investigating the role of slavery origins or derivations in the collections of slave-owners. Laurence Brown confirms that classical slavery motifs adorn the Palladian style eighteenth-century Marble Hill House in Twickenham and the nineteenth-century Baring-family-owned Northington Grange in Hampshire. He confirms that 'it was Atlantic slavery that had directly financed the construction of these arcadian worlds' (Brown 2013: 97). Similarly, Victoria Perry explains how slavery profits supported the aesthetics of romantic landscaping and eighteen-century 'scenic tourism' in Britain through the example of Piercefield estate on the River Wye near Chepstow (Perry 2013).

A fourth theme resulting from the work on slavery and the country house concerns issues of *belonging*. Questions are generated about how these connections should be approached and understood by Britain's diverse citizenry and by those in Africa and the Caribbean. The curators of individual stately homes are now impelled to make decisions about *whose* historical accounts to present. Whilst it is right to acknowledge that a property has been funded by a slave plantation, this testimony may mean different things to different people. As Madge Dresser and Andre Hann state:

> The identification of particular individuals of colour associated with that property might well have a particular resonance for those members of the public for whom a visit to an historic property might afford not merely a day out but an encounter with heartfelt questions of family history, identity and belonging. And that personalised connection has an impact beyond those who count themselves among the descendants of the enslaved and the colonised to reach into our very notions of who 'belongs' to Britain. (Dresser and Hann 2013: 14)

Using the new database from the Legacies of British Slave Ownership project, Nicholas Draper (2013) provides a national summary of the number of slave owners who owned country houses on the British mainland in 1834. He traces the use of profits from slavery in several properties. The Slavery Abolition Act of 1933 activated the emancipation of enslaved people in most British colonies. The British state agreed to pay out compensation amounting to £20 million to slave owners and additional beneficiaries of slavery. The agreed payment included mortgagees and annuitants who had monetary claims secured on the enslaved. This involved identifying every person in Britain who held 'slave property' in the colonies at the point when the slave system ended. Owners or occupiers of country houses can now be identified by matching them with known slave owners at the time of emancipation through the Slave Compensation Records. The records not only document people in Britain who received large sums for compensation in the

1830s. They also hold the addresses in Britain of the absentee slave owners, including country house owners. This data offers scholars the opportunity to identify cases where this inflow of cash financed the building of country houses, the rebuilding of old ones and the luxury expenditure on art collections and furniture (Draper 2013).

The slave compensation archives indicate that between 5% and 10% of British country houses were owned by slave owners. In some areas and wider regions, the percentage was higher (Draper 2013: 20). However, the compensation records only record slave owners and beneficiaries at the *end* of slavery, making it difficult to assess the changing connections with slave ownership over time. Nevertheless, the records provide substantial detail, relevant to the wider collective effort of tracing the links between slavery and the British country house. Nicholas Draper states: 'In the case of Antigua, some three dozen country houses are readily identifiable with slave owners or other beneficiaries of slave compensation' (as set out in the Appendix to the *Slavery and the British Country House* volume). Draper goes on to say:

> The list includes well-known sites of slave ownership such as Dodington Park in Gloucestershire, the family home of the Codringtons ... as well as major houses such as the National Trust's property at Greys' Court in Oxfordshire belonging to the family of the Stapleton baronets of the Leeward Islands, and Brentry House in Gloucestershire, built by Humphrey Repton in 1802 and owned by John Cave in the 1830s. (Draper 2013: 20)

Likewise, Madge Dresser (2013) traces the multifaceted links between local merchants and gentry families and the profits and management of the colonial slave trade in England's West Country. Her work reveals not only that Bristol's merchants occupied grand, rural residences in the mid-eighteenth century, but also that more established gentry families may have profited from slavery as colonial office holders or plantation owners by renovating or buying properties. As Dresser states, 'The profits made from slave plantations, the slave trade and the trade with slave colonies enabled to varying extents these West Country proprietors of stately homes to play increasingly genteel roles as magistrates, MPs and patrons of the arts' (Dresser 2013: 41).

Over 20 rural retreats outside Liverpool built in the eighteenth and early nineteenth centuries by slave traders, plantation managers or merchants trading in slave-produced goods have been identified by Jane Longmore (2013). With the spread of the suburbs many of these country houses have been demolished. As Longmore emphasises, this highlights how easily slavery's influence on a region's archaeological heritage can be overlooked. Longmore investigates how far the social ambitions of the leading Liverpool slave traders were achieved. They were attained by entering a higher social class through marriage, and via the advancement of their children's education, marriages and careers and purchase of landed property to ensure the reproduction of social capital (Bourdieu 1984). As Longmore states:

One by one, the mansions disappeared as the expanding city engulfed them and made them less desirable ... in a guide to the country houses of the North West, published in the 1990s: 'more fine old houses have been demolished in south Lancashire than in any other part of England in the twentieth century'. (Robinson 1991: 145 in Longmore 2013: 51)

The City of Liverpool's Information Officer described these vast mansions still in existence in 1957 as properties 'built only for the specific purpose of displaying Victorian families to the best advantage' and also as 'a burden on the community' (Millington 1957: 6–7 quoted in Longmore 2013: 44). The challenge of looking after the former homes of the wealthy seemed entirely inappropriate in a city urgently anticipating the enormous 1960s slum clearance programme (Longmore 2013).

Sheryllynne Haggerty and Susanne Seymour (2013) studied the distinctive ways in which the Bolsover Castle and Brodsworth Hall related to slavery in the eighteenth century. They demonstrate the explicit connections with slavery of a British prestige property, Brodsworth Hall by focusing on Peter Thellusson, owner of the former Brodsworth Hall between 1791 and 1797. Whilst not a slave trader, he invested in a wide range of slavery-related merchandises and land. One of the two subsequent heirs to his fortune built the existing Hall in the 1860s. Yet Bolsover Castle in Derbyshire which was owned by the third Duke of Portland from 1762 to 1819, appears at first sight to be unconnected to slavery. However, Haggerty and Seymour found that the Duke played a string of well-established roles as Prime Minister, Secretary of Home Affairs and as a member of the landed elite which involved the preservation of Caribbean slave regimes.

The 1807/2007 commemorations reveal, then, the presence of black men and women working as free and enslaved servants on the country house estates. However, this dimension of British history is regularly supressed in the central narratives conveyed at heritage sites. Bressey (2013:114) argues that:

> The relationship between whiteness, British greatness and great estates remains largely unchallenged by major heritage institutions. This contributes to an idealisation of a certain understanding of our past; assumptions still prevail that black people do not belong in the history of country houses and did not contribute to their creation, maintenance or preservation.

As Bressey points out, political parties such as the British National Party exploit these notions of 'old England'.

Present-day inclusive narratives and engagement

Following on from the findings of the bicentenary, the heritage sector has been slow to address past connections between the slave trade and the British country house. The challenge facing the heritage industry is to find ways to present historical narratives about the links between the country house and the slave trade in a manner that would enable *all* visitors to gain an awareness of the slave history. Mindful of the sensitive dynamic involved, this would also involve offering minority ethnic groups whose heritage is directly related to the Atlantic slave trade, ways to interpret that history. Two examples of how this can be done are presented in the *Slavery and the British Country House* research. Cliff Pereira (2013) provides a case study of the London Borough of Bexley. He explains the effects of community activism on the Borough's presentation of its historic properties. As late as 2007, Bexley conceded the potential of publicising the West Indian and East Indian connections of its heritage properties. A number of sites are regarded as part of the borough's heritage such as the Jacobean manor of Hall Place and its gardens (Bexley Village), the Georgian mansion of Danson House and its encompassing parkland, Red House designed by William Morris with architect Philip Webb in 1859 (Bexleyheath), and Lamorbey House (Sidcup) (Pereira 2013: 123).

The East Indian and West Indian trades were interlinked in their influences: the Atlantic slave trade impacted on the British landscape of the country house, on the manor house and estate and, most significantly in terms of the populating of Britain. Bexley's grand houses and estates that were linked to the East and West India trades involved capital from the trades supporting the construction of local alms-houses, schools and the maintenance of churches. The East and West Indian trades were also connected on personal and business levels and by commodities and the trade routes themselves. Throughout the twentieth century, the borough's historic properties were not mentioned and seldom visited by the various ethnic minority groups living in Bexley. They were inaccessible to the public, being either in ruins or in private hands (Pereira 2013: 129). As Pereria states, 'The challenge has been in making this factual narrative and attached cultural sensitivities accessible to all communities in the borough' (Pereira 2013: 129).

Recognition of black and Asian history at heritage sites in Bexley has been galvanised by public and collective pressure among minority ethnic groups themselves in reaction to hostile political movements. Black and Asian groups have used local history fairs, national festivals and Black History Month to call attention to their roles in the hidden histories of the country at local and national level. This initiative has been combined with the support of museum directors, heads of local studies and the Mayor of Bexley. These projects have involved community specialists during all the stages of the process (Pereira 2013). An exhibition of the findings was followed by a book published on *The Great Estates*, focusing on the owners of six estates in the borough. Coinciding with the book's publication in 2000, Bexley Heritage Trust (BHT) was founded as a non-profit organisation to manage Hall Place and provide a hub for heritage in Bexley. BHT then took responsibility for the management of Danson House.

Against a backdrop of racially motivated attacks on African Caribbean and Asian people in the South London area, leading to two deaths including that of teenager, Stephen Lawrence in 1993, BHT joined forces with Bexley Archives and Local Studies and the Bexley Commission for Racial Equality. They worked together to launch the Connections 2001 exhibition and then Connections 2002, to address the sensitive issues of Bexley's heritage in an inclusive manner. Placing community cohesion at the heart of education as part of the borough's cultural sector involved narration and community engagement. Led by BHT, the heritage sector used mobile exhibitions to 'take the British country house and its inclusive narrative to the communities in order to attract new visitors to its properties, encourage communal harmony and preserve its heritage' (Pereira 2013: 128). A significant outcome of research in Bexley has been the identification of African and Asian residents in the Bexley area before 1900. Recognition of the attendance of black and Asian people to the 'grand' estates is not motivated by a desire to raise visitor numbers. As Pereira says:

> Rather this is a historical reality that needs to be documented and brought into the public realm, alongside 'working class' and domestic servant narratives. After reading *The View from Shooters Hill*, one African-Caribbean resident of Bexley commented: 'when I walk through the park now, I think of my ancestors who made it for me; when I walk past a building I recall the black person who lived there centuries ago, I feel I belong here'. (Pereira 2013: 130)

In these ways, Bexley's heritage sector has strived to publicly acknowledge the role of migrant peoples within the historical underpinning of modern Bexley with an emphasis on the hybrid quality of heritage. This has allowed the possibility for a recuperation of a sense of connection and belonging.

A second example with similar aims comprises a series of events launched in Bristol in 2007 as part of a multimedia consultation exercise to commemorate its links with the transatlantic slave trade, at the behest of the National Trust. Rob Mitchell and Shawn Sobers (2013) deal with the links between history and memory in Bristol in their documentation of the project which included film screenings, city tours, poetry readings, museum exhibitions, theatre productions and television documentaries. The pioneering consultation involved asking Afro-Caribbean and other marginalised groups for their views of Dyrham Park (Gloucestershire), Clevedon Court and Tyntesfield (both North Somerset). The project also explored how those responsible for the properties have approached and can approach, in the future, the topic of slavery. Mitchell and Sobers worked with four groups to explore the properties and their histories, and to produce creative responses to their findings. One of the elders from the Bath Ethnic Minority Senior Citizens Association, called Daisy, who has been trying to trace her family history, had to give up when she realised that the enslaved Africans who were sent to the Caribbean were not documented as effectively as those who arrived in the Americas. In Daisy's words: 'we don't know who we belong to [back in Africa]. It's like we are non-entities, we are nothing, we don't count for anything'. The project demonstrated that 'silence among figures in authority can breed replacement myths among the people, especially the young' (Mitchell and Sobers 2013: 135).

Conclusion

As a symbol of the most coveted kind of 'home', the English country house evokes a complex discourse of nostalgia designed to generate a desire 'to develop a sense of national identity from elicit emotions associated with the nation's past' (Baena and Byker 2015: 262). Heritage discourses and popular dramas naturalise power relations that shape this ideal home. The monumentalising of the houses of the landed gentry involves discourses of re-collection that present a past which functions for the present. These discourses are actively reproduced through cinematic and television popular narratives, sustaining dominant values that shape the aestheticisation of middle-class homes today as part of a 'staged authenticity' (West 2016) to evoke ancestral status and convey wider ideas about elegance, connoisseurship and civility. Referring to the decline and destruction of English estates that mobilise popular narratives such as *Downton Abbey*, Baena and Byker (2015) point out that 'If an Englishman's home is his castle, then the possibility of losing Downton implies more than merely the loss of property: it becomes a threat to personal identity'(Baena and Byker 2015: 263). As such the country house involves a fetishisation of forms (Baucom 1999). The loss of property and inability to recover the home of the past is a contrived home precarity that has great emotional appeal, one that many can relate to, in some way or another.

Attachment and belonging are senses powerfully staged not only in popular discourses of home but also in historical, archaeological and heritage discourses surrounding the home (Paynter 2002, Smith 2006, Hodge 2009). The particular nostalgia associated with country houses essentially involves a continuous 'search for authentic origins and stable meanings' (Tannock 1995: 453). The memory and desire invoked in period dramas such as *Downton Abbey* frame an idealised home which is echoed by the heritage industry's framing of an idealised past. As such, heritage homes are powerful simulacra that operate as memory-sites. Promoting a feeling of community, the collective nostalgia associated with the country house forms a contrived precarity that functions to obscure social differences and forms of exploitation associated with race, gender and class.

This chapter has shown how recent scholarship that highlights the legacy of slavery questions earlier heritage discourses of the country house. The 1807/2007 commemorations verify the links established between the wealth derived from slavery and the British country house. This research confirms that black men and women worked as free and enslaved servants for the country house estates, as a feature of British history obscured in the main heritage accounts. Yet the grand homes of the landed gentry have been largely promoted, unopposed, by major heritage institutions which stage the idealisation of the country house. However, the revelation that country houses are expressions of wealth, power and privilege enables a critique of the socio-economic dynamics and the cultural values sustained by the monumentalising of these 'great country homes'.

The work of scholars and heritage practitioners, and the commitment by English Heritage to commemorate the bicentenary of the abolition of the British transatlantic slave trade indicate that the memorialising of 'home', culture and place are in a continuous state of flux. The apparent fixity of the 'stately home' is, then, exposed as a phantasmagoria. This academic reassessment of the country house now uncovers possibilities for multiple interpretations of these houses. If the working classes and 'domestic servants' are part of the history of country houses so too are people of African Caribbean heritage. Nostalgic discourses can enable 'recuperation of previously overlooked historical material and practices' (Tannock 1995: 457), and as Christina Hodges states, this can enable the development of 'new perspectives on what has been remembered and forgotten within processes of memory' (Hodge 2011: 131). As such, the nostalgia associated with these properties can function, in both public and private realms, in ways that allow them to be encountered both as part of a wider cultural dynamic and as personally subjective experiences that open up new understanding of how 'homes' are produced, lived and idealised.

Notes

1 VisitEngland, available at www.visitengland.org/media/pressreleases/2012_trends.aspx./ (accessed 24 July 2014).
2 'Downton Abbey and Harry Potter Locations a Major Drawcard for Tourists', Visit-Britain, available at http://media.visitbritain.com/News-Releases/DOWNTONABBEY-AND-HARRY-POTTER-LOCATIONS-A-MAJOR-DRAWCARD-FOR-TOURIS TSe651.aspx./ (accessed 21 July 2014) (cited in Cox 2015).
3 The 'Slavery and the British Country House' conference held at the London School of Economics in 2009 was co-organised by English Heritage with the University of the West of England and the National Trust.

References

Adams, R. (2013) 'The V&A, the destruction of the country house and the creation of 'English Heritage', *Museum and Society*, 11(1), 1–18.

Anderson, B. (1991) *Imagined Communities: Reflections on the Origin and Spread of Nationalism*. London: Verso.

Baena, B. andByker, C. (2015) 'Dialects of nostalgia: Downton Abbey and English identity', *National Identities*, 17(3), 259–269.

Baucom, I. (1999) *Out of Place: Englishness, Empire, and the Locations of Identity*. Princeton: Princeton University Press.

Baudrillard, J. (1983) *Simulations*. New York: Semiotexte.

Baudrillard, P. (1994) *Simulacra and Simulation*. Michigan: University of Michigan Press.

Bawden, G. (2011) 'Home theatre: Staging the domestic interior', *Double Dialogues*, 14. www.doubledialogues.com/article/home-theatre-staging-the-domestic-interior/ (accessed 20 July 2019).

Bourdieu, P. (1984) *Distinction: A Social Critique of the Judgment of Taste*. Cambridge, MA: Harvard University Press.

Bressey, C. (2013) 'Contesting the political legacy of slavery in England's country houses: A case study of Kenwood House and Osborne House', in M. Dresser and A. Hann (eds), *Slavery and the British Country House*. London: English Heritage.

Brown, L. (2013) 'Atlantic slavery and classical culture at Marble Hill and Northington Grange', in M. Dresser and A. Hann (eds), *Slavery and the British Country House*. London: English Heritage, pp. 89–97.

Byrne, K. (2013) 'Adapting heritage: Class and conservatism in Downton Abbey', *Rethinking History: The Journal of Theory and Practice*, 18(3), 311–327.

Cannadine, D. (1992) *The Decline & Fall of the British Aristocracy*. London: Penguin.

Cox, O. (2015) 'The "Downton boom": Country houses, popular culture, and curatorial culture', *The Public Historian*, 37(2), 112–119.

Davidoff, L. (1986) *The Best Circles: Society, Etiquette and the Season*. London: The Cresset Library.

Deckha, N. (2004) 'Beyond the country house: Historic conservation as aesthetic politics', *European Journal of Cultural Studies*, 7(4), 403–423.

Draper, N. (2013) 'Slave ownership and the British country house: The records of the Slave Compensation Commission as evidence', in M. Dresser and A. Hann (eds), *Slavery and the British Country House*. Swindon: English Heritage, pp. 17–28.

Dresser, M. (2013) 'Slavery and West Country houses', in M. Dresser and A. Hann (eds), *Slavery and the British Country House*. Swindon: English Heritage, pp. 29–42.

Dresser, M. and Hann, A. (eds) (2013) *Slavery and the British Country House*. Swindon: English Heritage.

Goffman, E. (1969) *The Presentation of Self in Everyday Life*. London: Penguin Press.

Haggerty, S. and Seymour, S. (2013) 'Property, power and authority: The implicit and explicit slavery connections of Bolsover Castle and Brodsworth Hall in the eighteenth century', in M. Dresser and A. Hann (eds), *Slavery and the British Country House*. Swindon: English Heritage, pp. 78–88.

Hewison, R. (1987) *The Heritage Industry: Britain in a Climate of Decline*. London: Methuen.

Higson, A. (1993) 'Representing the national past: Nostalgia and pastiche in the heritage film', in L. Friedman (ed.), *British Cinema and Thatcherism*. London: UCL Press, pp. 109–129.

Historic Houses Association. (2014) *Heritage Means Business: Enabling Britain's Inspirational Places to Meet New Challenges*. London: HHA.

Hodge, C.J. (2009) 'Materialities of nostalgia at the old homestead', *Archaeologies: Journal of the World Archaeological Congress*, 5(3), 488–510.

Hodge, C.J. (2011) 'A new model for memory work: nostalgic discourse at a historic home', *International Journal of Heritage Studies*, 17(2), 116–135.

Longmore, J. (2013) 'Rural retreats: Liverpool slave traders and their country houses', in M. Dresser and A. Hann (eds), *Slavery and the British Country House*. Swindon: English Heritage, pp. 43–53.

Lowenthal, D. (1998) *The Heritage Crusade and the Spoils of History*. Cambridge: Cambridge University Press.

McDowell, S. (2008) 'Heritage, memory and identity', in B. Graham and P. Howard (eds.), *The Ashgate Research Companion to Heritage and Identity*. Farnham: Ashgate, pp. 37–53.

Mandler, P. (1997) *The Fall and Rise of the Stately Home*. London: Yale University Press.

Millington, R. (1957) *The House in the Park*. Liverpool: Town Clerk's Dept. for the Corporation of the City of Liverpool.

Mitchell, R. and Sobers, S. (2013) 'Re:Interpretation: The representation of perspectives on slave trade history using creative media', in M. Dresser and A. Hann (eds), *Slavery and the British Country House*. Swindon: English Heritage, 132–139.

National Trust. (2013) *Annual Report 2012/13*. https://nt.global.ssl.fastly.net/documents/annual-report-2012-13.pdf (accessed 20 July 2019).

Paynter, R. (2002) 'Time in the valley: Narratives about rural New England', *Curr Anthropol*, 43 (supplement), S85–S101.

Pereira, C. (2013) 'Representing the East and West India links to the British country house: The London Borough of Bexley and the wider heritage picture', in M. Dresser and A. Hann (eds), *Slavery and the British Country House*. Swindon: English Heritage, pp. 123–131.

Perry, V. (2013) 'Slavery and the sublime: The Atlantic trade, landscape aesthetics and tourism' in M. Dresser and A. Hann (eds), *Slavery and the British Country House*. Swindon: English Heritage, pp. 98–105.

Robinson, J.M. (1991) *A Guide to the Country Houses of the North-West*. London: Constable.

Smith, L. (2006) *Uses of Heritage*. London: Routledge.

Smith, L. (2008) 'Heritage, gender and identity', in B. Graham and P. Howard (eds), *The Ashgate Research Companion to Heritage and Identity*. Farnham: Ashgate, 159–178.

Sobers, S. and Mitchell, R. (2013) 'Re:Interpretation: The representation of perspectives on slave trade history using creative media', in M. Dresser and A. Hann (eds), *Slavery and the British Country House*. Swindon: English Heritage, pp. 132–139.

Strong, R. (1999) *Country Life 1897–1997: The English Arcadia*. Basingstoke and Oxford: Boxtree.

Tannock, S. (1995) 'Nostalgia critique', *Cultural Studies*, 9(3), 453–464.

Waterfield, G. and Fellowes, J. (2012) 'Perspectives on the historic house: Giles Waterfield interviews Julian Fellowes', in G. Waterfield and R. Parker (eds), *Looking Ahead: The Future of the Country House*. London: Royal Geographical Society, pp. 64–71.

Waterson, M. (1990) *The Servants' Hall: The Domestic History of a Country House*. London: National Trust.

West, H. (2016) 'Artisanal food and the cultural economy: Perspectives on craft, heritage, authenticity and reconnection', in J.A. Klein and J.L. Watson (eds), *The Handbook of Food and Anthropology*. London: Bloomsbury, pp. 406–434.

Wright, P. (1985) *On Living in an Old Country: The National Past in Contemporary Britain*. Oxford: Oxford University Press.

Young, L. (2007) 'Is there a museum in the house? Historic houses as a species of museum', *Museum Management and Curatorship*, 22(1), 59–77.

Zahedieh, N. (2013) 'An open elite? Colonial commerce, the country house and the case of Sir Gilbert Heathcote and Normanton Hall', in M. Dresser and A. Hann (eds), *Slavery and the British Country House*. Swindon: English Heritage, pp. 71–77.

2

IDEALISING HOMES AND HOMEMAKING

Introduction

In Britain, North America and Northern Europe, widespread urbanisation over the course of the nineteenth century coincided with marked changes in ideas about 'home' and its relationship to the public world of politics, employment and the economy. Corresponding with public anxieties about shifting class and gender relations, these changes gave rise to idealisations of domestic space that remain familiar today. They were expressed by growing public concerns about morality, new domestic standards and new forms of self-improvement. Through a series of key examples, mainly from the US and UK, the chapter considers the leading aesthetic principles and cultural policies that shaped both visual and moral discourses of 'home' and household arrangements as *gendered* and *classed* spaces. These discourses marked 'home' as an institution and setting shaped by feminine virtues of privacy, morality and aesthetic discernment. Despite their apparently private nature, such moral principles were conscientiously promoted and regulated by state and commercial public institutions. They were advanced by cultural intermediaries which included architects, designers, artists, educators and social reformers. If these cultural agents monitored the aesthetic 'tastes', consumer choices and domestic routines associated with home, they also involved a strict social class ranking, within articulations of public discernment and personal expression of domestic space.

The chapter shows how this notion of 'taste' – relating to principles of home décor, decorum and domestic routines – served to project and delineate ideas of virtuous homemaking. Designated, initially, for upper and middle-class women, 'taste' comprised a moral worth whose influence ultimately extended to women of *all* social classes. Advice about home decoration, etiquette and domestic routines systematically universalised and naturalised homemaking as a quintessentially 'feminine' predisposition. This guidance coincided with and consolidated the ideological separation of spheres: the masculine sphere of work and politics, and the feminised sphere of domesticity (Davidoff and Hall 2002; Vickery 1993). A range of advice publications imparted guidance on feminine decorum and taste including manuals, books and magazines. These forms of advice then extended to department stores, exhibitions and World Fairs as staged events which, by the early twentieth century, summoned and reassigned women as 'consumer citizens'. Consumerism, a scientisation of home management and home modernisation were promoted by these mediators.

Refined homemaking in the nineteenth century

To avoid the city slums, the middle classes moved to smart new terraces built on the outskirts of towns, from the mid-nineteenth century. The construction of houses on the edges of cities marked a spatial division between work and home. By renting semi-detached or detached villas, middle-class occupants were able to separate themselves from city slums and protect their privacy. Stylish nineteenth-century suburban developments conveyed a sense of detachment from urban centres. Culminating in nineteenth-century housing, the rise of the merchant classes coincided with the privatisation of everyday family life and domestic customs. Among these upper- and middle-class inhabitants, the process of privatisation was marked by separate spaces within the home, conveyed in the layout of Victorian middle-lass houses. The work of the kitchen, maintained by paid servants, was divided from the public interactions of the parlour. The addition of private bedroom space away from these communal rooms stabilised the idea of home as a retreat and setting for leisure. The late nineteenth-century notion of home as a place of non-work was also idealised in the designs of this urban space.

Although the homes of the landed gentry represented spectacles of grandeur and discernment displayed at public receptions such as society balls and parties, the Victorian upper middle-class drawing room symbolised the home as a retreat (Davidoff 1986). At the same time, the Victorian drawing room constituted a focal 'public-private' space. Conceived as a private space that was open to callers, day-to-day domestic activities of the family were shaped by the social conventions of welcoming invited guests into this reception room. The room was organised as a display space with furnishings, ornaments, carpets and wall hangings selected to exhibit the family's status and identity to wider society. As such, this permanently on-display yet 'private space' was constantly scrutinised by outsiders – not only by guests but also by cultural agents. Architects, artists and designers delivered practical advice on interior decoration and home management to confirm the domestic fabric and moral worth of that space. The domestic space of the late nineteenth-century upper-middle classes was, then, a *staged* space, one involving the performance of respectability and reputation (Anderson 2013). The aspiration to impress guests gradually extended beyond the upper and wealthy middle classes to the working-class homemaker seeking respectability through stylishness (Massey 1990: 8).

House decoration advice manuals emerged in Britain and America as part of a range of aesthetic strategies to steer women in cultivating special standards of domestic taste and design in the middle-class Victorian house. In particular, the surge in nineteenth-century domestic advice literature offered guidance to women among the new middle classes on their role as homemakers and consumers. As a significant cultural and historical genre, these guidebooks on home decoration formed a repository of codes and values about domestic culture illuminating the roles of women as homemaker during an era of rapid social change. Spreading first to the middle classes, advice books and journals on home decoration and lifestyle grew in popularity on both sides of the Atlantic in the nineteenth century. They conveyed the home as a setting for ideal domestic life through interior design styles, furniture and ornaments. If advice discourses circulated inventive design ideas, they also enabled middle-class women to negotiate their way through the ordeal of modern living 'thus aiding their integration into modern society' (Lara-Betancourt and Hardy 2014: 132). The publications became cheaper and more accessible to the working classes by the end of the century. They were framed by the liberal philosophy of self-help and self-improvement and underpinned by the spread of literacy, a growth in leisure and rising incomes among a broadening group of the population.

Advice literature assigned strict gender roles influenced by Christian values. Books, articles and pamphlets addressed women directly as the homemaker responsible for the home's décor. Emphasising that the family and the home were vital for a moral Christian life, it was considered the woman's duty to ensure the drawing room was a civilising setting, suitably bedecked and enhanced by tasteful and decorative carpets, furniture, wall stencils and ornaments. The respectability of the house, gauged by guests and other outsiders, was not just conveyed by the dwelling's architecture and interior décor. It was also implied by the feminine decorum of the hostess in terms of her moral virtue, refinement and attentiveness to the comfort of visiting family and guests (Tange 2008: 167). Distinctive standards and ideals of domestic femininity shaped women's clothing, physical movement, habits and beliefs (Anderson 2013, Hamlett 2010). These ideals were then reflected in the drawing room's interior, fashioned by elaborate connections between consumption, display and exchange. Defined as a feminised space, the drawing room was directed by the 'lady of the house' in her distinct roles as wife, household manager and hostess (Tange 2008). However, formality took precedence over comfort in the drawing room of the mid-Victorian middle classes. Highlighting the Christian stance of the drawing room, this drawing room was referred to as a 'solemn shrine', not a place to relax but a place that offered a minimum of repose and a 'strict artificiality' (Grant Allan 1880: 312, quoted in Anderson 2013).

Decoration manuals foregrounded the gendered nature of society, emphasising divisions between the 'masculine' dining room and 'feminine' drawing room. The prescriptive nature of nineteenth century décor was conveyed by values and ideals that circumscribed choices in interior design, colour schemes and furniture styles to contrast home from the world of work (Forty 1986: 102). Antique and handcrafted furniture was favoured over new mass-produced furniture since the latter was judged as distasteful and unrefined. As such, these manuals revealed significant tensions between domestic conventions and personal taste. Tracing the move towards a constrained individualisation in drawing room adornment, Anne Anderson explains that antique and handcrafted furniture presented an ideal opportunity for women to express discernment. She states, 'Although a woman might be yet another 'thing' in the drawing room, she could challenge female passivity by fashioning a distinctive environment that expressed her personality' (Anderson 2013: 40). This gradual individualisation of the archetypal drawing room acted as a precursor to the idea of the *personalised* design of the modern 'living room'. The feminised act of decorating gradually came to represent a form of self-expression and self-fulfilment for women. Embodying aspirational identities, the *act* of decorating signified modernity by conveying a modern, creative and feminine performance (Sparke 2008). The expectation was that the homemaker would stamp her 'individuality' on the house, despite this expression of uniqueness and refinement being an unattainable ideal (see Chapter 5 which highlights the role of social media in similar contemporary goals).

Furnishing rooms with antiques was a relatively new custom among the wealthy middle classes of America and Britain in this period. Favoured among aesthetes as expressive of connoisseurship, antiques and objects of art became signs of drawing room elegance and gracious living. Handcrafted antiques conveyed their owners' personality and invoked ancestral heritage, personal sentiments and an 'authentic' lifestyle untainted by industrial mass production. Refinement expressed a type of protest with old collectable objects serving to elevate their owners above vulgar middle-class consumerist attitudes. In fact, the whole drawing room was often approached as a work of art. This room formed a public spectacle that designated the feminine homemaker as 'decorateur', as a scene setter or inventor of the interior to convey her flair, originality and creativity through décor. Ironically though, this custom inspired a new fashion and consumerist conformity. As well flaunting seventeenth- or eighteenth-century antiques, the Victorian drawing room displayed Persian carpets, renaissance bronzes, as well as curios and ceramics from China, Japan and the Near East. Confirming complex trade links across the world, these objects were combined with family heirlooms, souvenirs and other collectables with the aim of forming an agreeable ambience as part of the art of the 'personal touch' (Anderson 2013: 51).

This expression of discriminating taste involved an eclecticism described as the 'cosmopolitan interior' that served to promote a metropolitan view of middle-class femininity that criss-crossed the empire (Neiswander 2008). The feminine custom of collecting heirlooms, mementoes and souvenirs was guided by sentimental value as well as the need to display good taste. Importantly, these commodities were sold by appeals to their emotional value through their association with purchasers' feminine identity as a material expression of the self (Sparke 2008). The tensions involved in this expression of femininity were clear. On the one hand, this domestic space represented the materialisation of a woman's authentic self through expressions of individual taste, untainted by fads or fashion. On the other hand, good taste was founded on well-informed selection and display, comprising a discernment guided by distinct aesthetic codes.

By the end of the nineteenth century, the drawing room had become a battleground over good taste, governed by class distinctions (see Bourdieu 1984). Groups of painters, architects, designers, and writers appointed themselves as vanguards of taste by pioneering an admiration for old artefacts as an expression of refinement. Appeals to respectability by the new wealthy middle classes were undermined by criticisms of bad taste in drawing room décor. The choices in décor made by women as homemakers were denigrated as unrefined and gaudy. New furniture was frowned upon for lacking lineage and morality. With their unrestrained desires, women of the new upper-middle classes were targeted as a problem group, condemned for gaining prosperity too hastily and following fashion impetuously. They were scorned for their 'dangerous appetites' and lack of restraint in purchasing 'superfluous and flimsy knick-knacks that overwhelmed the drawing room' (Vallance 1904: 110 in Anderson 2013: 45). Women of households aspiring towards upward mobililty were placed in a precarious position: a home precarity contrived by experts and experienced palpably by women themselves. This gendered predicament comprises a seam that runs through home imaginaries to the present day.

Complaints were made by these vanguard taste makers that homes were crammed with extravagant, hideous sentimental objects (Stewart 1984). With its corniced ceilings, heavy curtains and dark furniture, this domestic space was gradually condemned by connoisseurs as ostentatious and cluttered. Contempt for new, machine-made mass-produced carpets and furniture by architects, artists and designers functioned to elevate the upper classes. Women were offered a narrow set of options for expressing their identities in this system of 'taste' in the expression of their roles as homemaker. Yet, judged by what they bought, they were soon typecast by architects, artists and designers as reckless consumers, as hoarders of bric-a-brac. Feminine creativity was regularly derided by male connoisseurs such as Aymer Vallance, a colleague of William Morris, who blamed women for turning 'drainpipes, set up on ends, into vases for bulrushes and dried grasses; milking stools into flower-stands; cauldrons into coal scuttles; whereby square pianos, disembowelled of their works, become "silver tables", and sedan chairs, fitted with shelves, become china cabinets' (1904: 111–12, in Anderson 2013: 49). In the *Art of the House*, Rosamund Marriott Watson shunned mediocre amateur embellishment by women, chastising the unrestrained female decorator who could not hold back from ruining furniture and china. And if the drawing room was referred to as the 'lady's temple', husbands were depicted as long-suffering bystanders forced to escape to the gentlemen's club. The notion of bad taste functioned, then, as a discerning form of aesthetic classification and ranking to signify the vulgarity, excess and inferiority of the upwardly mobile middle classes (Bourdieu 1984).

Throughout this period, English country house stereotypes influenced ideological constructs that connoted an essential Englishness which validated status and ranking. In turn, these ideals fuelled cultural movements such as 'Merry England'. By around 1900, newly built residential estates were designed in styles ranging from Tudor, Elizabethan, Jacobean, Stuart and Georgian to express a sense of nationalism through imaginings of 'Olde England' (Long 1993). As described in Chapter 1, the period country house forms a stage on which reminiscences such as Merrie Old England are projected to this day (see Judge 1991). Utopian visions of an idyllic domestic past were propelled by a sentimental nostalgia for a utopian, pastoral way of life. The drawing room formed the heart of this dream, complete with glowing logs in the inglenook fireplace, warm carpets and soft seating, and antique furniture, paintings and curios to invoke a haven of geniality and comfort. The sentiments associated with this spectacle home articulate a longing for certain attributes of an earlier society thought to be missing in modern times. They corresponded with a re-evaluation of a nation described as 'a world that has never actually existed, a visionary, mythical landscape, where it is difficult to take normal historical bearings' (Judge 1991: 131). In the United States, the English country house style was promoted in the early twentieth century by taste makers such as Nancy Lancaster. Through selected fabrics and the arrangement of furniture, the techniques of these American taste makers were to nurture an individualism and a distinctive feminine modernity as the embodiment of elegance and sophistication (Wood 2005: 110 in Anderson 2013: 55).

Through the use of interior decorating manuals, women among the upwardly mobile middle classes grappled with the tension between expressing personal flair and observing defined aesthetic codes. One of the first eminent books that delivered artistic instructions on home decoration in the UK appeared in 1867. Written by Charles Eastlake, it was titled *Hints on Household Taste* and assembled from a series of articles he wrote for *Cornhill Magazine* (Long 1993). This was followed by a series published by Macmillan between 1876 and 1879 on The Art at Home which included W.J. Loftie's *A Plea for Art in the Home* (1878). H.J. Cooper's the *Art of Furnishing on Rational and Aesthetic Principles* (1876) was followed by *The Art of Beauty*, published in 1878 by Chatto and Windus. *The Art of Decoration* appeared in 1881, written by celebrated author of the time, Mrs Haweis. Among the most influential authors was Mrs J.E. Panton who wrote 33 books on home decoration and management including *From Kitchen to Garrett* in 1887 which went into more than ten editions. A leader in home decoration and management publications, Mrs Panton was among the first of many women in England to set up a business of engaging women of suitable 'social status' and 'taste' to administer the decoration of a whole house including curtains, chair covers and wallpaper (Long 1993). Decoration and home crafts advice became a respectable job for women of taste, though one often scoffed by men as a trivial vocation (Beckett and Cherry 1987). Many of the earlier titles were written for the upper-middle classes.

These trends reveal that the fashioning of the nineteenth century home as an 'old home' filled with antiques and curios was not simply a specific construction of feminine and family identity. Influenced by country house imaginaries, the metaphors of 'old' and 'antique' enabled a staging of authenticity within middle-class homes through appeals to heritage and lineage. Importantly, then, the interior design of the private home was a public issue directly linked to a chain of civic and commercial influences, moral premises and power relations. This chain reproduced the dynamics of class, gender, and race by encompassing Christian beliefs, art movements, government-sponsored design training, manufactured goods, nation and British empire. Supported economically by colonialism and the slave trade, these ambiguous yet uncompromising taste codes served to classify domestic space into distinctive classed and gendered rankings. They conferred the natural superiority of upper-class breeding and heredity as aesthetic discernment (Bourdieu 1984). In terms of gender relations, the masculine derision of women's roles and habits as custodians of domestic ornamentation functioned to confirm male superiority over feminised domestic space.

The rise of the domestic manual

During the same period, domestic advice manuals on cooking, housekeeping and childrearing were published, containing more practical advice on economy, repairing and 'making do' (Long 1993: 21). Attempts to formalise and teach principles of domesticity is exemplified by the rise of literature on homemaking in the United States. One of the most widespread nineteenth-century domestic manual by Catharine Beecher and Harriet Beecher Stowe was their 1869 treatise, *The American Woman's Home; or, Principles of Domestic Science*. Catharine Beecher was an educator and social reformer and half-sister to abolitionist Harriet Beecher Stowe. Beecher applied scientific principles to cooking, housework and parenting. Her work inspired the principles of scientific management in the home and the rise of 'home economics', discussed below. Beecher emphasised the importance of providing young women with a liberal education even though she disagreed with female suffrage, arguing that the public domain should be left to men.

Like decoration manuals, nineteenth-century books on domestic economy confirm the extent to which the home of the middle classes was shaped by values delivered from beyond the home in the public sphere. *The American Woman's Home* was not only a treatise on the domestic arts. The book upheld the moral and religious ideals of American domesticity. The introduction to the 1991 reprint by Joseph S. Van Why describes *The American Woman's Home* as 'a bible of domestic topics' underpinned by Protestant principles. Intriguingly, Kristin Jacobson (2008) compares *The American Woman's Home* with the twenty-first-century television programme *Extreme Makeover* to reveal the continuities across the centuries: 'Both texts function as "technologies" of the American Dream, or as material, moral, and political guides' (see Chapter 5). Beecher and Stowe's *The American Woman's Home* offered guidance to readers on all possible aspects of homemaking. Advice ranged from the phase of building the home, strategies of selecting stoves and chimneys, to the upkeep of earth-closets. Yet the kind of home portrayed in their book was out of reach for many of its readers, in terms of household income. The manual came to be used more as a wish-list. Containing specific ideas and assumptions about race, class and gender, these texts played a vital role in defining a domestic culture as a *national* project that privileged middle-class, white family values (Jacobson 2008). The mission of these domestic advice manuals was to make routine domestic duties as appealing as possible to their female readers.

Importantly, *The American Woman's Home* arose from a need to deal with a domestic and gender crisis triggered by the American economy's cycle of economic expansion and contraction after the Civil War (1861–1865). The main purpose of this manual was to enhance the housekeeper's standing in American culture by championing the homemaker and traditional family values set against the temptations of hedonism and the scourge of poverty and homelessness (Jacobson 2008). Framed as a *moral* issue, the domestic prowess of white, middle-class women was asserted by Beecher and Stowe during a time when their assigned status and duties appear to be challenged by Woman's Rights' conventions. This anxiety pointed to a crisis in the education of 'modern girls' who were thought to be brought up lacking the practical skills required to perform the domestic duties needed to support their families and direct servants. The purpose, then, of *The American Woman's Home* was to depict domesticity as something appealing for 'modern girls' by enhancing domestic labour as something analogous to performing Christs' work (Jacobson 2008: 109).

Inspired by American advice manuals, domestic guidebooks in the UK contained handy, everyday recipes for medicines, cooking cleaning and other household tasks. The earliest book intended for the middle classes with servants in the UK was Mrs Beeton's *Book of Household Management* 1861. This influential text underlined how difficult it was not only to manage the home as a complex arrangement of financial, social and material excess but also to manage social class relationships with servants. The *Book of Household Management* supports the argument that women were assigned their own distinct and 'complementary' gender roles, asserting the importance of shaping the character of the next generation of men (see Davidoff and Hall 2002). A cheaper volume costing half the price targeted a wider market from 1865, titled the *Everyday Cookery and Housekeeping Book*. A succession of books on cookery and gardening by Mrs Beeton then became available by the 1890s, for around a shilling. The triumph of these manuals is demonstrated by the expanding market for books on the domestic economy in the late nineteenth century, particularly among those of the 'respectable servantless class' or lower middle classes, exemplified by *How to Keep House* in 1902, by Mrs D.C. Peel.

A feminist reassessment of the history of feminised domesticity by Dolores Hayden publicises the work of American 'material feminists' from the 1870s such as Melusina Fay Pierce Mary Livermore, and Charlotte Perkins Gilman (Hayden 1981). Highlighting palpable home precarities encountered by women, materialist feminists campaigned against women's confinement to domestic life as the source of their subservient position in society. The ambitions of these feminists were to design homes that supported *socialised* domestic tasks and childcare. In their quest for equality and economic autonomy, the ambitions of this group of women was to reconfigure childcare and domestic tasks as communal activities that required a revolutionising of American homes (Hayden 1981).

This quest prompted an interrogation of the underlying power relationships between women, men and children in modern society. Hayden describes the pioneering plans and inventive schemes of these determined campaigners. They constructed kitchen-less houses in conjunction with a public kitchen and community dining club. Charlotte Perkins Gilman, a material feminist known for her work as a novelist and social reformer, argued for changes in housekeeping and child-raising practices in her book *Women and Economics* (1898). To relieve the pressures on women to contribute to a strengthening of the public sphere, she developed proposals for house design conducive to working women and their families in the early twentieth century (Hayden 2002: 11). Notwithstanding the important work of these campaigners, domestic advice manuals – with their stress on the moral virtues of a traditional domestic femininity – predominated.

Magazines provided another source of conventional homemaking guidance in the period 1880 to 1914. On both sides of the Atlantic, the market for magazines expanded during the late nineteenth century alongside the rise in women's literacy. Most of the late-eighteenth and early-nineteenth-century general magazines in Britain reflected the tastes of the leisured classes since they were the only people who could afford to pay for them (Long 1993: 23). The tone of moral sobriety in these mid-nineteenth-century magazines is exemplified by the *Ladies' Treasury* (1857–95) which expressed a conservatism through topics such as needlework, paper-flower making and hobbies to fill the prolonged period of leisure endured by women in the home. These magazines were initially targeted at an upper-class readership. However, a demand for cheaper magazines corresponded with the rising incomes and aspirations of the middle classes to accommodate a wider female audience (Long, 1993: 23). The *Englishwoman's Domestic Magazine* by Samuel Beeton from 1852 dealt with the management of the home by offering practical advice on cookery and fashion, for tuppence. The habitual association of domesticity with femininity naturalised the idea of house management as *women*'s work.

Women homemakers as consumer citizens

The increasing domestication of early twentieth-century society as a central ideology is underpinned by a series of state and commercially led initiatives in Britain and the US. These initiatives addressed women homemakers as consumer citizens. In the commercial context, the growing interest in and demand for home furnishings among Britain and America's late nineteenth-century middle classes prompted the rise of the department store. These retail outlets not only sold items of furniture but also ready-made room schemes (Long 1993: 24). In the UK, department stores that supplied the expanding middle classes included Liberty's, Selfridges, Harrods and Debenhams. Famous stores in the US such as Macy's and

Bloomingdales, and David Jones in Australia now supplied furniture displayed in showrooms. In London, dedicated furnishing shops such as Hampton's, Heals, Maples, and Waring and Gillow's offered professionally coordinated furnishings and interior detailing as well as showroom-displayed individual items of furniture.

The retail links with high art are also exemplified by a close relationship with department stores in the 1920s and 1930s in New York, developed by the Metropolitan Museum of Art (Wasson 2015: 613). As well as publishing pieces in specialised home decorating and design magazines such as *Magazine of Art* and *Arts and Decoration*, the museum produced articles about the value of art education in women's magazines such as *Country Life, Ladies' Home Journal, Ladies Home Companion* and *House Beautiful*. The museum even offered classes in art history to department store clerks, emphasising the museum's connections with retail and consumerism. As Wasson states, 'the Met addressed the American home as if it were a de facto museum satellite' (Wasson 2006: 174). In 1927, an exposition of modern design sponsored by the museum was held at Macy's department store. The Met supplied certain objects and museum-like designs to be exhibited alongside talks given by the Met on the history of art and design (Friedman 2003, 18–19). Importantly, this alliance not only suited the museum's objective of popularising its mission. It also lent credibility to Macy's claims as a connoisseur, as a taste maker. The show's objective to connect 'art with everyday household life' was fully achieved. Fifty thousand visitors showed up over the one-week exposition, an audience size that dwarfed visitor numbers at the museum's main site nearby (Wasson 2015). This collaboration between commercial institutions and art museums reveals the breadth and depth of the public agenda of promoting good taste in the home.

Exhibitions

Alongside advice manuals, magazines, journals and department store displays, national exhibitions played a key role in promoting a consumer-led, home-centred society. As staged events, exhibitions represented official, commercial and expert attempts to influence styles in interior décor and the values associated with home culture. Resonating with the technique used in department stores, model interiors formed an important exhibition strategy to engage with manufacturers, retailers and the buying public in shaping a feminised domestic space, framed by consumerism. In the UK, commercial initiatives were exemplified by the Ideal Home Exhibition, worthy of focus, here. Founded in 1908 and sponsored by the *Daily Mail* newspaper, this spectacular annual event illustrates several emerging trends. The exhibition acted as the newspaper's publicity tool to generate advertising revenue and attract women readers. Demonstrating the influence of news media, the event showcased the latest housing, interior designs and consumer durables.

The remarkable significance of the Ideal Home Exhibition was underscored by its monumental scale. Home interiors were presented as spectacles to attract the gaze of the middle-class 'housewife'. With its carnivalesque atmosphere and theatrical displays of consumer goods, this event performed a vital role in promoting new technological developments as *domestic* artefacts as well as innovations in interior design (Ryan 1997). The organisers of the Ideal Home Exhibition employed relentlessly inventive tactics to connect the exhibition to the grand themes of national identity, modernity and progress with 'Britishness' expressed as an Imperial national identity, particularly before World War II. Here, the *domestic* culture of the nation was set against and elevated above that of other nations, involving the search for an 'ideal' perception of home through an articulation of the role of the Empire in the formation of domestic culture. Patronised by visiting royalty and celebrities of the day, this influential exhibition presented home interiors as a stage on which to attract female visitors with disposable income.

The 1908 launch of the exhibition was underpinned by the changing nature of a consumer culture, a culture which itself contributed to the rise of a more complex collective sense of 'consumer citizenship' among women. Nevertheless, the fusion of the words 'ideal' and 'home' veiled yet hinted at the tensions and contradictions between the 'homely' and the 'aspirational' (Curtis 1998). Attentive to the way 'home' symbolises both individual and familial identity by linking ideas of 'past' and 'future', the Ideal Home Exhibition drew on contradictory tropes of nostalgia and modernity to conjure up a domestic ideal. On the one hand, these tropes were framed by art, modernity, science and technology. On the other hand, they drew on ideas that appealed to the traditional, the familiar, the glamorous and the exotic. The exhibition's organisers embraced the challenge of fusing visions of an ideal past *and* an ideal future, one that would seem innovative, aspirational and at the same time, would appear familiar, cosy and traditional. These complex ideas were expressed through spectacles of scale and enclosure: not just furnished room displays but whole houses built and displayed with each room carefully fitted out, decorated and equipped with the latest technologies.

Whilst the Great Exhibition of 1851 had promoted British manufacturing and technology to the world, the emphasis at the Ideal Home Exhibition was on publicising – to the nation – consumer goods, interior design and new technologies associated with home. Here, the impulse was to introduce modern domestic technology into the household and to define the homemaker as a 'modern', 'efficient' housewife (Reiger 1985:2). The celebration of modernity and progress was expressed by displaying labour-saving devices, and the quest to turn 'home' into a space of leisure and aesthetic appeal (Curtis 1998: 266). To emphasise the new status of women as consumer citizens, the exhibition enlisted women through women's organisations such as the Women's Institute. Members of these women's organisations offered advice and even training to help housewives embrace or cope with a new era of homemaking and domestic consumption that involved new domestic technologies. Demonstrations were regularly given of new inventions for the modern home, from electric lighting to washing machines and vacuum cleaners. In these ways, the event played a key role in 'modernising' discourses of the ideal home.

The aim of giving women as consumers a sense of power was managed not only by demonstrations but also by generating a sense of choice and cultivating a direct relationship with women as homemakers. As well as stimulating newspaper profits by serving a new female audience and readership, the Ideal Home Exhibition expressed the possibilities of *curating* domestic space (see Chapter 5). That said, the exhibition also involved condescending interventions by male architects and designers (Long 1993). At the same time, by referring to the lifestyles of the rich and famous, the event managed to sensationalise everyday, domestic culture. As Long states: 'Photographs of the rich and famous and of the country house Season were also an important means whereby information about the homes and lifestyles of the upper classes was made accessible to the middle classes' (Long 1993: 26).

These examples indicate the key role played by the Ideal Home Exhibition in promoting homemaking as a glamorous pastime and a national issue as strategies for influencing public taste and generating consumption. David English states, 'Indeed, the Exhibition established itself as a 3-dimentional advice manual, its founders recognising that few possessed the gift to create an "ideal home" unaided' (English 1992: 7). And as English goes on to observe, the promotional literature accompanying the 1910 Exhibition underscored (heteronormative) nuclear family values by claiming resolutely that 'No home can really be ideal unless it contains at least one man, one woman, and if possible, one baby, or else a good substitute'. In these ways, the exhibition formed an imaginative stage on which the contradictions of a consumer society were played out (Ryan 1997).

The exhibition formed part of a growing trend of spectacularising the domestic interior by displaying model rooms as representations of the inner life of idealised homes (see Chapter 3). At the 1910 exhibition, a competition held to furnish and decorate an 'ideal home' costing £600 comprised a model home with a drawing room, dining room study, four bedrooms and a nursery: a home beyond the reach of most of the British population at the time. The event also displayed a real eight-bedroomed home and a similar full-scale ideal house was built at the 1912 exhibition with eleven rooms (*Ideal Home Catalogue* 1912, pp. 9–10, in Long 1993). Home manuals of the time complemented the Ideal Home Exhibition, such as Mrs Humphry's *Book of the Home* 1909, which offered advice on furnishing houses with either 10 or 7 rooms on a budget. As Long states, 'it seems that when contemporaries use the term "ideal home", they were referring to a house at the mid to top end of the middle-class scale, within financial reach for some and to be aspired to by others, but not way beyond the reach for the middle classes as a whole' (Long 1993: 32). Yet the standard middle-class house at the time in the 1870s to 1880s, was the small terraced home. The yawning gap between the affluent ideal and the hard-up reality of the homes of most exhibition visitors was unmistakable. However, the Ideal Home Exhibition did acknowledge social disadvantage by creating a spectacle of the primitive and the alien. In 1922, a miner's cottage was re-assembled to show how such a dwelling digresses from the modern ideal while at the same time invoking a sense of the noble labouring classes.

The scientific management of homes

Attempts to *rationalise* the domestic sphere were made in the Unites States by employing the principles of scientific management which were popularised by the beginning of the twentieth century. Advanced by Frederick Taylor in the late 1880s, scientific management aimed to streamline the production and distribution of goods on a mass scale by speeding up repetitive factory and clerical work. What is little known is that these scientific methods of industrial production, determined by time and motion studies, were applied earlier to the 'domestic economy' of the home through the 'science of household management'. Although the term 'home economics' was not commonly used until the early twentieth century, efforts to formalise housework efficiency date back to the mid-1800s (see Gregg 2018). These principles of science-based efficiency in the home were progressed in the early twentieth century by American home economist Christine Frederick. The aim of efficiency science in the home was to reduce the amount of time women spent in housework and minimise the drudgery it involved. The principles of scientific management are, then, rooted in the discourses of the domestic advice manuals mentioned above, initiated in the mid-1800s by Catharine Beecher in her *Treatise on Domestic Economy for the Use of Young Ladies at Home* (1841). These principles shaped the design of kitchens from the early twentieth century. With an emphasis on designing and describing devices as labour-saving, attempts to ratio-nalise the domestic sphere led to the idea of homemaking as 'scientific' and the housewife role as 'modern'. Frederick then endorsed planned obsolescence as an essential element of an industrialised economy. The argument was that 'creative waste' allowed the smooth-running of the industrial economy because lasting, durable, well-made objects clog the market, thereby compromising the effective-ness of mass production.

Drawing on the principles of science, this kind of management of house-wives, families and homes included advice on hygiene, food nutrition, eti-quette and childcare (Blunt and Dowling 2006: 53–54; Forty 1986). Whilst home economics and scientific management principles were prescriptive, they gave women an avenue through which to navigate the world in the 1940s and 1950s. (Blunt and Dowling 2006: 53–54). Attempts to rationalise the domestic sphere materialised in the form of the Frankfurt kitchen in 1926 designed by Austrian architect Margarete Schütte-Lihotzky for a social housing project in Frankfurt, Germany. Regarded as the predecessor of the modern fitted kitchen, the Frankfurt kitchen was a landmark in domestic design. This was the first time that a kitchen had been conceived and approached as a unified whole, designed specifically as a low-cost unit to facilitate efficiency. After World War I, when German cities were suffering severe housing shortages, a range of social housing projects were built to supply affordable apartments to working-class families. With limited funds, apartments were designed to standardised specifications to be small but comfortable in order to keep costs down (Hebler 2009).

The Frankfurt kitchen design was influenced by Christine Frederick's aim of rationalising work in the kitchen. Forming part of ergonomics, Schütte-Lihotzky saw her planned kitchen as essential to all social classes, from middle-class women lacking servants to working-class women forced to juggle multiple jobs that might risk public health (Hebler 2009; Schütte-Lihotzky and K. Zogmayer 2004). These principles of scientific management were intended to 'rationalise' the household not only by shortening the time spent on 'unproductive' house-work to lengthen women's factory work time. They also supported emancipatory goals of elevating women's status in the home by lightening women's housework load and allowing them to engage in other pursuits. The commercial success of this modern, fitted kitchen was demonstrated by its instalment in over 10,000 units in Frankfurt.

Yet women found these kitchens difficult and inflexible. Designed for one person, the space was too small for more than one person to work in the kitchen. And the design failed to account for the fact that children would be able to reach the low-reach storage cupboards. Later, this 'work kitchen' design was heavily criticised for isolating the housewife from the household since only one person could squeeze into the space. Rather than 'professionalising' the role of the housewife, it physically confined these tasks to women, thereby undermining the emancipatory principles involved. Nevertheless, between the 1930s and 1960s, the Frankfurt kitchen was adopted and adapted in other countries such as Swit-zerland and Sweden with easy-to-clean surfaces (Hebler 2009). And by the early twentieth century, progressive social workers were publicising the 'science of right living' to the working class and immigrants in Europe. It was held that improve-ments in people's habits and behaviour could enhance the quality of life for these social groups and thereby stabilise society as a whole.

The state promotion of 'good design' in the home

In addition to the commercial initiatives exemplified by the Ideal Home Exhibi-tion, interior design and homemaking formed a central plank of state agendas in the early twentieth century to boost trade and elevate the quality of home life as *national* concerns. In Britain, the techniques of exhibiting show homes, room set-tings and domestic items were adopted in design exhibitions during the interwar years to shape domestic tastes and homemaking practices. The government regar-ded these strategies as vital for aspirational couples and those families with little flair or know-how in questions of taste. In 1932, a Board of Trade Committee report on Art and Education emphasised the need to display the best examples of the new industrial art to raise national design standards and promote design consciousness among the public (Board of Trade 1932). At its request, a series of national Mod-ernist exhibitions were mounted. For example, in 1935, the Royal Society of Arts launched the exhibition 'British Art in Industry' to boost export trade and educate British and overseas publics on the importance of 'good design' in British manu-facturing goods.

At a time when British industrial art was moving away from the Arts and Craft movement, the Modernist style was embraced in Britain through the work of a group of prominent designers. These designers rejected the cramped, dark, depressing architecture and furniture of the nineteenth century. Instead, the Modernist aesthetic aspired to transform raw materials into an art form by advocating a minimalist style using clean lines and utilitarian design. Modernism had a far-reaching effect on the design of domestic interiors. The Bauhaus dictum, 'form follows function', was adopted by Modernist architecture and design in reaction to excessive ornamentation of earlier Victorian machine-made products. This allowed Modernists to reduce designs to geometric shapes with clean lines regarded as synonymous with clean lives. It was in this period that architects and designers sought to convince governments of the virtues of Modernism as an answer to contemporary social problems (Darling 2007). A belief in the role of functionalism, industrial design, technology and machinery to create a better world, galvanised Modernist designers who were committed to the idea that modern interior spaces play a central role in enhancing modern domestic experiences.

Exhibitions included the Industrial Art in Relation to the Home Exhibition held at Dorland Hall in London in 1933, the Royal Academy in 1935 and the Council for Art & Industry (CAI) Working Class Home Exhibition in London in 1937. These events were organised by crusading organisations such as the Design and Industries Association (DIA), founded in 1915 by an alliance of designers, businessmen and industrialists whose goals chimed with the government Board of Trade's objectives of improving design in households across the nation. The DIA exhibited furnished show houses within a mission to improve manufactured products both functionally and visually. From the late 1920s, the organisation embraced the progressive trends of Modernism which began to influence British design. With its slogan 'Nothing Need be Ugly', the DIA set about changing the way products were designed and perceived by the public within a morally charged discourse (Woodham 2004).

The DIA influenced the founding of the Council of Industrial Design in 1944 (now called the Design Council). As the brainchild of the Board of Trade, the British wartime government launched the Council of Industrial Design (COID) to promote 'good design' and 'economic efficiency' as intersecting principles by associating 'good design' with 'good living' and model homes (Maguire 1997). Its main objective was to support Britain's post-war economic recovery by advancing British manufacturing, stimulate export trade and cultivate national pride through 'good' design. Design exhibitions were not only part of the government policy of influencing the expansion of British exports. They also performed as instruments of internal political education and ideology. A major objective of the COID was to raise national design standards and promote design consciousness among the public as well as manufacturers by constructing new regimes of good taste in the home (Woodham 2004: 465).

In its attempt to purge the nation of bad taste in styling and the worst excesses of mass-market taste, the COID advocated aesthetic and moral absolutes for the

British nation through its design values: 'In general, the pattern was to tell the public what it should like' (Jeremiah 2000: 167). The COID's post-war magazine provided copious examples of bad taste in design within its strategy of promoting good taste. By now taking an interest in the British Modern Movement and the new breed of industrial designers, the BBC launched several radio programmes in 1933 about design including *Design in Modern Life*; Gordon Russell on *The Living room and Furniture*; Wells Coates on *Dwellings*; Elisabeth Tenby on *The Kitchen* (McCarthy 1979). Through these state-led initiatives, the status and prospects of 'home' and domestic life were aligned to British manufacturing and trade to elevate commercial needs and project a forward-looking aesthetic suited to domestic interiors.

An English designer, craftsman and educationalist, Gordon Russell was a key figure in British design, he became Director of the COID in 1947 (Russell 1968). As chairman of the Utility Design Panel, Russell led the development of utility furniture during World War II. The Utility Furniture Scheme is an example of the functional demands of military operations carried over into civilian life. Driven by a shortage of timber and labour for decorative designs during and after the war, this extraordinary state initiative extended into a period of post-war austerity lasting until 1952. During this time new furniture was rationed, made available only to newly married couples and members of the working class who were bombed-out and needed to be rehoused. The aim was to produce well-designed affordable furniture that made the most efficient use of scarce timber through a range of approved designs produced in the *Utility Furniture Catalogue* of 1943. Providing an unparalleled opportunity for government-backed design reformers to implement their ideas on home furnishings and décor, the scheme advocated a 'stripped down' aesthetic. Lacking in ornamentation, utility furniture designs formed state-led initiatives that demonstrate the remarkable influence of government on ideals and values which shaped the material fabric of home life in peacetime as well as wartime.

Such initiatives were pursued in other countries such as Sweden where state intervention in home design was epitomised by design principles that supported the ideals of a Swedish welfare society shaped by strong egalitarian values (Kristoffersson 2014). In the 1930s and 1940s, architects and interior decorators came together with planners and teachers of home economics as part of a campaign against 'the unnecessary ugliness' of past customs and bad taste. During this period, Sweden had been suffering from some of the most inferior housing standards in Europe. The government prioritised modern housing and modern living to address the problem. Despite well-intentioned advice and like British initiatives, this state promotion of 'good design' involved condescending messages that summoned housewives to adopt practical, discreet and restrained domestic styles. The emphasis on an aesthetics of everyday life in Sweden was framed by ideas about morality involving the promotion of a peaceful, light and subtle functional home to create a site for open, balanced and rational households.

The well-known home furniture company IKEA was launched in 1943 as part of this government drive to improve housing and home design (also see Chapter 5).

New housing estates and apartment blocks were built in Sweden in the 1950s and 1960s within this unparalleled state campaign. The need for inexpensive furniture by the occupants of all these new homes contributed to IKEA's early success. The provision of state housing involved circumscribed design principles (Garvey 2017: 104). Studies of domestic activities generated detailed measurements that became guidelines for the 'correct' height of kitchen countertops and the appropriate distance between the sink and the oven. This led to a succession of compulsory architectural rules recommended by the government and stipulated for the building industry to ensure municipal funding of projects. Echoing British attempts to use design to improve the moral fabric of home life, the Swedish government exploited design as a medium for direct political intercession during the twentieth century (Lindqvist 2009; Sandberg 2011; Garvey 2017).

'Liberalising' housewives in the world of tomorrow

Contrasting with the circumstances in the UK and Sweden, early twentieth-century developments in designs for the home in the US were largely commercially led. However, the values promoted at the New York World's Fair 1939–1940 resonate with those of Britain's Ideal Home Exhibition and merit consideration here, given its enormous impact on home imaginaries. Conceived by a group of New York businessmen at the height of the Great Depression, the aim of this international exhibition was to attract much-needed business to New York City. The New York World's Fair was an ambitious and spectacular event. It was the first large trade exposition to showcase industrial and artistic progress with a focus on visions of the future (Edgerton, 2007). It was devised to raise the mood of the nation by introducing Americans to the 'world of tomorrow'. The World's Fair staged a vision of a near future of technologies supplied by industry yet guided by societal ideals to generate a nobler nation and more virtuous world led by consumerism and democracy. These predictions of a bright future for the world were proclaimed even as the war was amassing in Europe (see Samuel 2007).

The Fair presented a captivating range of science, technology, architecture, theatricality and politics. The exhibits aimed to prove that technological advancements would enhance the average Americans' standards of living by securing peace, prosperity and increased leisure time in the near future. On this optimistic stage, domestic technologies played a central role in embracing the electric home and the newly emerging technology of television for the home (addressed in Chapter 4). Among companies that built vast pavilions to showcase their new products were the electric and manufacturing company Westinghouse, and the major television manufacturer RCA Corporation which owned the National Broadcast Company (NBC) (see Chapter 4). They 'wrapped their exhibits in public relations rhetoric which worked to convince visitors that corporations were not simply profit-hungry businesses that sold consumer goods, but rather vital components of a democratic society that provided the tools needed to build a better tomorrow' (Becker 2001: 361).

During this period, electrification was novel with regions of the US not yet connected. In 1939, the Westinghouse pavilion exhibited domestic appliances under the banner of 'freedom', by projecting an emancipated life juxtaposed with the life of an intransigent 'Mrs. Drudge'. This vision formed the foundations of the famous 'kitchen debate' that was to erupt 20 years later between then US Vice-President Richard Nixon and Soviet premier Nikita Khrushchev (discussed in Chapter 3). The inferred freedom for women went far beyond promises of liberating the housewife. These visions implied the political freedom associated with the market autonomy of capitalism (Beck and Dorrian 2018: 22). The Fair was promoted in a film depicting a fictional middle-class family called the 'Middleton Family - Babs, Bud, and their parents' – who were shown viewing the sights of the Fair including the lavish displays of new products designed to make life easier and affordable including the electric dishwasher, modern fitted kitchens and a raft of electric appliances. As Beck and Dorrian (2018) state, 'Right from the beginning of the film it is clear that what is at stake is the future – and indeed the future of the family as it is entwined with the future and productivity of the nation as a whole' (Beck and Dorrian 2018: 22–23).

The theme of 'The World of Tomorrow', returned to in Chapter 9 on 'home futures', embodied efforts to recover a national story of progress. A dream of future progress was venerated, one that had previously been destabilised by World War I, the Great Depression, the uncertain future of another war in Europe, and the rise of totalitarian regimes (Duranti 2006: 664). The World of Tomorrow theme also promoted the ideals of the emerging new middle class, as exemplified by the 'Middleton Family', to express the promise of a suburban America organised around consumerism and dreams of a cohesive, peaceful society. Yet this vision of a future democracy harboured deep racist and sexist undertones. One of the most visited exhibits was called the 'Typical American Family', a promotional scheme involving an essay contest that non-white families were unequivocally barred from. The scheme was collaboratively sponsored by the Ford Motor Company, the Johns Manville Company, the U.S. New Federal Housing Administration and World's Fair authorities. The all-white winners of the Typical American Family were rewarded with a free trip to the World's Fair in a Ford automobile. The winners were also accommodated on the Fair's site as an actual display in a nuclear family house constructed by the Federal Housing Administration and clad with asbestos siding – a recent miracle invention by the Johns Manville Company (McIntosh 1996: 9).

Incongruously, by the summer of 1939 visitors to the New York World's Fair were spurning the futuristic themes by showing a preference for the nostalgic mock-up villages in the Amusement Area with names such as 'Merrie England' and 'Old New York' (Maloney and Kinkead 1940). Such was the power of dreams of a utopian past. The World of Tomorrow theme was therefore dropped by 1940 in favour of promoting the 'carnival' mood of the Amusement Area and in response to mounting tensions in Europe. It was now organised around a new theme, For Peace and Freedom, with the projection of a giant country fair. Accordingly, 'this season it would be nostalgic narratives rather than narratives of progress that would provide fairgoers with an illusion of harmony and coherence' (Duranti 2006: 674). Nevertheless, memories of the 1939–40 New York World's Fair reaffirmed a nostalgia for the very idea of progress, as Duranti points out. With varying degrees of success, such exhibitions sustained a distinctive narrative of domesticity that attempted to fix ideas and values that shaped gender, class and race distinctions in the early twentieth century. These ways of promoting home imaginaries wrapped in dominant middle-class values represented the shift from the 'long nineteenth century' to modernity.

Conclusion

This chapter has traced the changing meanings of domestic space between the late nineteenth and early twentieth century through a series of key examples to explain how the ideal home was conceived, promoted and venerated by forces beyond households. As an expression of gendered and classed status, the moral construction of domesticity in the nineteenth century corresponded with ideas about the civilising effects of tasteful home décor. 'Home' was systematically structured by a range of public techniques and social hierarchies transposed as the purpose of the home itself. These regimes of taste and decorum were employed as part of a range of powerful cultural and economic strategies to impart moral values that prescribed the modern home of the time. This home was publicly coded as a *feminine* domain through representations of an expressive, sentimentalised and sensitive space that functioned to create a boundary between private and public worlds. Importantly, this set of cultural trends formed part of a broader and enduring impulse which underscores the recommendation culture of the digital age, explored in later chapters.

Home design came under the jurisdiction of the male expert from the late nineteenth century to manage the moral codes associated with the spiralling range of goods available to women as individual consumers. As homemakers, women and their homes became the object of potential surveillance and judgement not only by visitors to the home but also by this raft of cultural intermediaries ranging from architects, designers, artists, writers, social reformers, retailers and exhibition organisers. These taste makers served class, state and commercial interests while acting as mentors to women as homemakers. Aesthetic authority and moral superiority were expressed as interchangeable values through expert advice on the appropriate gender roles, protocols and aesthetic values required to create a home of refinement and decorum.

By the early twentieth century, a distinctive discourse of domestic modernity began to fix meanings of gender and class, deeply framed within consumer culture (see Chapter 3). Some women managed to navigate professional roles as social reformers and writers of advice and domestic manuals, a practice that now saturates and defines today's popular culture. However, throughout this history of upper- and middle-class home idealisation, taste formed a profound site of struggle over domestic meanings and practices. On the one hand, and corresponding with a bourgeois sensibility, this 'good taste' offered women choice and consumption as a form of pleasure in the act of buying for, decorating and managing their homes. Homemaking was designated as an expression of individual flair and self-expression. On the other hand, the homes and homemaking choices of women among aspirational and upwardly mobile classes were regularly vilified and inhibited by these practices, revealing the palpable home precarities experienced by women in their navigation of domestic space. Indeed, across all social classes, women were habitually undermined and scorned by professionalised groups of mainly male taste makers, within a set of narratives that expressed gendered relations of power and framed homemaking as a moral issue.

If exhibitions and retail stores celebrated scientific and technological advancement, they also endorsed the desirability of the homes of the aristocracy, the rich and the famous to create projections of an ideal home that was nostalgic and glamorous yet out of reach to most visitors and shoppers. As a site for consumption, 'home' crystallised women's emerging status as aspirational subjects and consumer citizens. As the following chapter shows, from the early to mid-twentieth century, national exhibitions were much more than cultural forces that endorsed women and their homes as conduits of consumption. The idealisation of home space was galvanised both by celebrations of a sentimental past and visions of a progressive future that served to promote national agendas. By the early twentieth century, the spectacularised ideal home – in all its guises and with all its ambiguities – came to play a fundamental role in promoting the white, nuclear family as a symbol of the nation.

References

Allan, G. (1880) 'The philosophy of drawing rooms', *Cornhill Magazine*, 41, 312–326.

Anderson, A. (2013) 'Drawing rooms: A backward glance – Fashioning an individual drawing room', in G. Downey (ed.), *Domestic Interiors: Representing Homes from the Victorians to the Moderns*. London: Bloomsbury, pp. 38–60.

Attfield, J. (ed.) (1999) *Utility Reassessed: The Role of Ethics in the Practice of Design*. Manchester: Manchester University Press.

Beck, J. and Dorrian, M. (2018) 'The time capsule and the cut up: Negotiating temporality, anticipating catastrophe', *Theory, Culture & Society*. https://westminsterresearch.westminster.ac.uk/download/00d680ad8ffc734587b6297ec7dc7f26f2969b557aaef3d01f256ff93800290d/141142/BECK_%26_DORRIAN__capsule__cut%20up__06.18.pdf (accessed 24 July 2019).

Becker, R. (2001) '"Hear-and-see radio" in the world of tomorrow: RCA and the presentation of television at the World's Fair, 1939–1940', *Historical Journal of Film, Radio and Television*, 21(4), 361–378.

Beckett, J. and Cherry, B. (1987) *The Edwardian Era*. Oxford: Phaidon.

Beecher, C.E. and Stowe, H.B. (1869) *The American Woman's Home; or, Principles of Domestic Science; Being a Guide to the Formation and Maintenance of Economical, Healthful, Beautiful and Christian Homes*. New York: J. B. Ford and Company; Boston; H.A. Brown & Co.

Blunt, A. and Dowling, R. (2006) *Home*. London: Routledge.

Board of Trade. (1932) *Report of the Committee appointed by the Board of Trade under the Chairmanship of Lord Gorell on the Production and Exhibition of Articles of Good Design and Everyday Use.* London: HMSO.

Bourdieu, P. (1984) *Distinction: A Social Critique of the Judgment of Taste.* Cambridge, MA: Harvard University Press.

Chambers, D.(2019) 'Designing early television for the ideal home: The roles of industrial designers and exhibitions, 1930s–50s', *Journal of Popular Television*, 7(2), 145–159.

Chapman, J. (2014) *Gender, Citizenship and Newspapers: Historical and Transnational Perspectives.* Basingstoke: Palgrave Macmillan.

Curtis, B. (1998) 'Daily Mail Ideal Home Exhibition: The ideal home through the twentieth century', *Journal of Design History*, 11(3), 266–268.

Darling, E. (2007) *Re-Forming Britain: Narratives of Modernity.* London: Routledge.

Davidoff, L. (1986) *The Best Circles: Society, Etiquette and the Season.* London: The Cresset Library.

Davidoff, L. and Hall, C. (2002) *Family Fortunes: Men and Women of the English Middle Class 1780–1850.* London: Routledge.

Duranti, M. (2006) 'Utopia, nostalgia and world war at the 1939–1940 New York World's Fair', *Journal of Contemporary History*, 41(4), 663–683.

Edgerton, G. (2007) *The Columbia History of American Television.* Columbia Histories of Modern American Life. New York: Columbia University Press.

English, D. (1992) Foreword to D. Ryan, *The Ideal Home Through the Twentieth Century.* London: Hazar Publishing.

Forty, A. (1986) *Objects of Desire.* London: Thames & Hudson.

Friedman, M.F. (2003) *Selling Good Design: Promoting the Early Modern Interior.* New York: Rizzoli.

Garvey, E.G. (1996) *The Adman in the Parlor: Magazines and the Gendering of Consumer Culture, 1880s to 1910s.* New York: Oxford University Press.

Garvey, P. (2017) *Unpacking IKEA: Swedish Design for the Purchasing Masses.* London: Routledge.

Gregg, M. (2018) *Counterproductive: Time Management in the Knowledge Economy.* Durham, NC: Duke University Press.

Hamlett, J. (2010) *Material Relations: Domestic Interiors and Middle-class Families in England 1850–1910.* Manchester: Manchester University Press.

Hayden, D. (1981) *The Grand Domestic Revolution: A History of Feminist Designs for American Homes, Neighborhoods, and Cities.* Cambridge, MA: MIT Press.

Hayden, D. (2002) *Redesigning America: The Future of Housing, Work and Family Life.* New York: W.W. Norton.

Hebler, M. (2009) 'The Frankfurt kitchen: The model of modernity and the "madness" of traditional users, 1926–1933', in R. Oldenziel, Z. Zachmann and G. Castillo (eds), *Cold War Kitchen: Americanization, Technology, and European Users.* Cambridge, MA: MIT Press, pp. 163–184.

Jacobson, K.I. (2008) 'Renovating the American woman's home: American domesticity in extreme makeover: Home edition', *Legacy*, 25(1), 105–127.

Jeremiah, D. (2000) *Architecture and Design for the Family in Britain, 1900–1970.* Manchester: Manchester University Press.

Judge, R. (1991) 'May Day and Merrie England', *Folklore*, 102(2), 131–148.

Kellog, A.M. (1904) *Home Furnishing Practical and Artistic.* New York: Frederick A. Stokes Company.

Kristoffersson, S. (2014) *Design by IKEA: A Cultural History.* London: Bloomsbury.

Lara-Betancourt, P. and Hardy, E. (2014) 'Seductive discourses: Design advice for the home: An introduction', *Interiors: Design Architecture Culture*, 5(2), 131–139.

Lindqvist, U. (2009) 'The cultural archive of the IKEA store', *Space and Culture*, 12, 43–62.

Long, H.C. (1993) *The Edwardian House: The Middle-class Home in Britain 1880–1914*. Manchester: Manchester University Press.

Long, H.C. (2002) *Victorian Houses and Their Details: The Role of Publications in Their Building and Decoration*. Oxford: Architectural Press.

McCarthy, F. (1979) *A History of British Design 1830–1970*. London: Allen & Unwin.

Maguire, P.J. (1997) 'Politics and design in post-war Britain', in P.J. Maguire and J.M. Woodham (eds), *Design and Cultural Politics in Postwar Britain: The Britain Can Make It Exhibition of 1946*. London: Leicester University Press, pp. 3–16.

Maloney, R. and Kinkead, E. (1940) 'Trylon, Trylon again', *New Yorker*, 11 May 1940.

Massey, A. (1990) *Interior Design of the Twentieth Century*. London: Thames & Hudson.

McIntosh, D. (1996) 'The lucite box: Futurism, world's fairs, and the Phantom Teleceiver', *Fuse Magazine*, 19(3), 6–11.

Neiswander, J.A. (2008) *The Cosmopolitan Interior: Liberalism and the British Home 1870–1914*. New Haven: Yale University Press.

Quilter, H. (1880) 'The Cornhill on coal-scuttles', *The Spectator*, 17 July, 911–912.

Reiger, K.M. (1985) *The Disenchantment of the Home: Modernising the Australian Family 1880–1940*. Melbourne: Oxford University Press.

Russell, G. (1968) *Designer's Trade: Autobiography of Gordon Russell*. London: Allen & Unwin.

Ryan, D. (1997) *The Ideal Home through the Twentieth Century*. London: Hazar Publishing.

Samuel, L.R. (2007) *The End of the Innocence: The 1964–65 New York World's Fair*. Syracuse, NY: Syracuse University Press.

Sandberg, M.B. (2011) 'The interactivity of the model home', in S.J.A. Ekstrom, F. Lundgren and P. Wisselgren (eds), *History of Participatory Media: Politics and Publics 1750–2000*. New York: Routledge, pp. 63–80.

Schütte-Lihotzky, M. and Zogmayer, K. (2004) *Margarete Schütte-Lihotzky. Warum ich Architektin wurde*. Salzburg, St. Pölten: Residenz Verlag.

Sparke, P. (2008) 'The crafted interior: Else de Wolfe and the construction of gendered identity', in S. Alfoldy and J. Helland (eds), *Craft, Space and Interior Design*. Aldershot: Ashgate, pp. 23–138.

Stewart, S. (1984) *On Longing: Narratives of the Miniature, the Gigantic, the Souvenir, the Collection*. Baltimore: Johns Hopkins University Press.

Tange, A.K. (2008) 'Redesigning femininity: "Miss Marjoribank's drawing-room of opportunity"', *Victorian Literature and Culture*, 36(1), 163–186.

Vallance, A. (1904) 'Good furnishing and decoration of the house: The drawing room', *The Magazine of Art*, 2, 111–118.

Vickery, A. (1993) 'Golden age to separate spheres? A review of the categories and chronology of English women's history', *The Historical Journal*, 36(2), 383–414.

Wasson, H. (2006) 'Every home an art museum: Towards a genealogy of the museum gift shop', in C. Acland (ed.), *Residual Media*. Minneapolis: University of Minnesota Press, pp. 301–344.

Wasson, H. (2015) 'The elastic museum: Cinema within and beyond', in M. Henning (ed.), *The International Handbooks of Museum Studies: Museum Media*, 1st edn. Chichester: John Wiley & Sons, pp. 603–627.

Woodham, J. (2004) 'Design and everyday life at the Britain Can Make It exhibition, 1946: "Stripes, spots, white wood and homespun versus chintzy armchairs and iron bedsteads with brass knobs"', *The Journal of Architecture*, 9(4), 463–476.

3

DOMESTIC MODERNITY IN SUBURBIA

Introduction

In Britain and the United States, substantial post-war developments in housing policies and suburbanisation schemes coincided with dramatic technological and manufacturing advances in household appliances, energy, communications and transport. A re-evaluation of home as a 'modern' but private domestic space was consolidated by the rise of suburban homes designed for the small, nuclear family unit and sustained by a range of appliances that expressed technological progress. This modern home symbolised a new discourse of domestic modernity in the early and mid-twentieth century. At the same time, the rhetoric of domestic modernity encompassed powerful residual ideas about home as a secluded space of stability, self-improvement and moral worth within nineteenth-century domestic cultural values. If the cultural and socio-economic changes underpinning home life involved state and commercial initiatives to improve ordinary homes, they also involved national campaigns that continued to stage home ownership and domestic consumerism as moral virtues. Certain core middle-class values travelled into mid-twentieth-century imaginaries of home which functioned as a showcase of morality, aspiration and wholesome family life.

This chapter traces the rise in home ownership, domestic design awareness and consumerism in mid-twentieth-century Britain and the United States with a focus on the intersecting processes of domestic modernity and suburbanisation. By drawing on a series of illustrative events and developments, the chapter chronicles the wider trends involved in the move from post-World War II reconstructions of home life that lay the foundations giving rise to the social desire for a modern suburban home as a consuming unit. In the durable goods industry, built-in obsolescence in design marked a dramatic shift from earlier attitudes towards the purchases of durable domestic items once viewed as a one-time acquisition.

Underpinned by a discourse of technological progress, this was an era when consumer goods were specifically designed to become rapidly outmoded. The role of the modern housewife was therefore consolidated as a consumer citizen continuously reflecting on the challenges of keeping up with domestic modernisation.

During this period, exhibitions as well as housing policies played a continuing and dramatic role in shaping meanings of home to endorse a distinctive kind of mid-twentieth-century culture. A range of state and commercial interventions and wider cultural tendencies that shaped housing ideals and home cultures in the UK and USA are addressed in this chapter to uncover the role of these cultural agents in shaping distinctive versions of home as national projects. The status of 'home' in the nurturing of mid-twentieth-century national imaginaries, particularly in its guise as a suburban house, corresponded with its prominent role in strengthening national economies (Hayden 2003). The chapter accents the fluctuating imaginaries of the ideal family home and suburban living that perpetuated inequalities of class, gender and race within the organisation of home life as an expression of national pride.

Post-war reconstruction and suburban modernity in the UK

Despite an over-emphasis on post-World War II suburbanisation in the UK and US, research has uncovered a diversity of pre-World War II suburban development dating back as far as the early 1800s (Nicolaides and Wiese 2006; Hanlon et al. 2010; Hayden, 2003). Whether the very first suburbs were eighteenth-century middle-class enclaves near London (Fishman 1987) or mixed-class communities around Boston in the 1820s (Binford 1985), suburban housing spread so dramatically in the early and mid-twentieth century that the suburban home came to typify housing of the twentieth century (Ravetz 1995: 18). Suburbia was a response to middle-class aversions to city 'slums', contagious disease and moral degeneracy (Fogelson 2005). The living conditions of the urban poor and working classes were not only considered dangerous to health. They were judged 'unhomely' – as morally and aesthetically deficient (Blunt and Dowling 2006: 118). By contrast, the suburban home was upheld as the healthy and appropriate place for fostering moral, aesthetic and familial respectability. The drive to eliminate working-class slum housing coincided with strategies of using suburban planning and house design as a model to reform working-class conduct.

Suburban expansion was also associated with privatisation and the growing division between work and leisure, strengthened by the nineteenth-century spatial and moral separation of public and private spheres as correspondingly masculine and feminine spaces (Davidoff and Hall 2002). The realm of work was reconnected to the leisure sphere of suburban home life by the growth in railways and main roads. Conceived as settlements outside the city or village model, suburbs were characterised by straight, regular streets and uniform, mass-produced houses designed as single-family homes separated by lawns or fences. Away from the smoke of the industrial city, the countryside setting of the suburban home was central to home imagery and the distinctive social relations enacted in this space, as a place of middle-class homemaking. The physical form of post-war suburbs corresponded with middle-class aspirations for a privatised, stable yet hierarchical social order. As such, suburbia epitomised middle-class achievement, family-positive lifestyles and desirable moral standards. With this domestic haven came the advantages not only of privacy and space but also property ownership – all requirements that were hard to realise in the urban centres of post-war Britain and America (Spiegel 1992).

While suburbanisation and domestic modernity vary historically and culturally between countries and regions, certain aspects of these processes and developments are shared across nations. A focus on the two national contexts of Britain and the US allows us to consider certain parallels and differences between countries which foreground nationhood as a leading impulse in shaping mid-twentieth-century domestic modernity. The suburban home was 'a dream and function, expression of a utopia and instrument of a convenience' (Barthes 1979: 6). Yet throughout the century, the interconnections between domesticity, class, race and the suburbs have been problematised by critics, with suburbanisation reviled as cultureless or condemned as anti-social (see Fishman 1987; Silverstone 1997).

The growing enthusiasm for suburban development in Britain and the United States was underpinned by visions of a nation recovering from war. In Britain, the experience of post-World War II reconstruction involved years of rationing, acute housing shortages, and a lack of those amenities that were taken for granted by the end of the twentieth century: electricity and modern plumbing. To replace Victorian-built slums after World War I, the British government created the policy of 'Homes fit for Heroes' which coincided with the launch of welfare provision for workers. Working-class soldiers returning from war were entitled to decent housing at affordable prices, enabled by the Housing and Town Planning Act of 1919. This planning of 'Homes Fit for Heroes' was supported by subsidies through a policy of sharing building costs between central government, local councils and tenants. Ongoing post-war legislation that supported the building of 1 million new homes included the construction of council houses and private suburban dwellings. Property ownership had been viewed as a remedy for political instability during an earlier period of economic and political unease in the 1920s and 1930s. At that time, the Conservative government promoted the idea of a property-owning democracy to challenge the rising popularity of socialism and the Labour Party. Importantly, governments offered subsidies to private builders for the construction of private suburban homes as well as subsidies for the building of large council estates (see for example, Daunton 1987; Ball 2017).

Sustained by an expanding supply of mortgages with low interest rates, a housing boom was triggered in 1930s Britain by a growing desire for home ownership among the middle classes. Home ownership reinforced a sense of belonging based on the exclusion of others according to class and race, in both the UK and US. For example, in the UK, mortgages were initially restricted to the more affluent and professional classes in the early twentieth century, with a dramatic increase in home ownership occurring in the 1980s (also see Chapter 5). The aspiration to own a home was a prerequisite for acceptance and reward as respected members of a nation framed by middle-class values of propriety and moral decorum. This social group bought properties in newly built suburbs on the outskirts of large towns and cities. By 1939, home ownership had risen to 27%. However, the outbreak of World War II abruptly ended further investment in housing. An already inadequate supply of liveable accommodation was further compromised by bombing.

The replacement of destroyed or damaged housing stock after World War II became a priority for the government alongside the establishment of a welfare state. This move was implemented by the wartime coalition government's 1942 *Beveridge Report*. However, before the policy could be implemented, the post-war Labour government were faced by numerous challenges including shortages of materials and labour, a massive public debt and the economic crisis of 1947. Yet between 1945 and 1955, a million new council houses were built alongside the slum clearances. A period of prosperity fuelled a rise in home ownership in the 1950s and 1960s, supported by full employment and rising incomes. House-buying was further stimulated by the 1955 Conservative government to create a 'property-owning democracy' by reducing Stamp Duty and lending money to building societies to generate a growth in mortgages. The government-led initiative resulted in a significant rise in home ownership from 29% in 1951 to 45% in 1964. This period of post-war reconstruction is, then, characterised by government interventions in which the revitalisation of domestic life went hand-in-hand with reviving industrial and economic affairs.

British government priorities of replacing destroyed or damaged housing immediately after World War II corresponded with a national drive to return women, who had worked for the war effort, back to the domestic sphere. Housebuilding, rational planning and the promotion of industry, consumerism and modernity were major national interests that depended on elevating the status of the housewife to a 'managerial' and consumer role. This was no easy task since women had played an active and vital role in the war effort, affording personal autonomy and an income. They were therefore reluctant to return to more restricted roles as housewives. Within an expanding post-war consumer economy and the rising affluence of readers, lifestyle magazines such as *Women's Realm* (1958) and radio programmes such as *Women's Hour* consolidated woman's social status and identity as homemaker within a nuclear family discourse.

This contrasted sharply with the way women had been addressed during the war. Lifestyle magazines were politicised in wartime to salute women's national civic participation in the war effort in roles that included factory workers, nurses, farm labourers, air raid wardens, mechanics and drivers of buses and fire engines. For the war's duration, government ministers and officials met with women's magazine editors to publicise wartime policies affecting women's roles. The Ministry of Food directives offered guidance for housewives. These dual wartime roles of women's journals are described as 'both a medium for, and mediators of, British wartime social policy, transmitting messages of sacrifice and hope to women busy keeping both factory wheels turning and home fires burning' (Ferguson 1983: 18). The propaganda value of specialist women's magazines was pursued by both the Churchill and Attlee governments into the 1940s. This wartime formula was sustained after the war in weekly magazines and radio programmes that offered women advice and tips on how to cope with rations and shortages and on 'best buys' to maintain homes during a period of severe austerity.

However, while women were publicly commended for contributing to the war effort, cooperation between government and magazine editors faded by the 1950s. Magazines joined radio programmes and newspapers in urging women to return to the role of housewife and homemaker. As wartime shortages subsided, working-class women were gaining access, for the first time, to consumer durables such as washing machines and steam irons. Women were given chatty advice – whether in print or via the airwaves – on how to purchase and use these new domestic gadgets. Post-war representations of femininity and modes of address to women were now firmly framed within domestic consumerist discourses (Featherstone 1990; Lury 2011). National economic and cultural policies enlisted design aesthetics as a marketing strategy to build new houses and improve mass-produced domestic goods to promote the nation. But most women's organisations were preoccupied with practical household matters rather than aesthetics. This was demonstrated by the launch of an Advisory Committee on Consumer Goods by the National Council of Women in 1945 (Woodham 2004). Notwithstanding, the state's didactic approach to 'good design' for homes was driven by the Council of Industrial Design (COID), founded in 1944 by passionate design reformers under the Board of Trade to foster better British industry standards of design, enhance interior design in homes and elevate the 'housewife'. Yet the COID was overwhelmingly led my men (Woodham 2004).

Post-war exhibitions in the UK

The ideal home was a post-war national issue. By fostering 'good design' to stimulate export trade and cultivate national pride, the COID linked 'good design' with the ideal home and 'good living' as matters of national concern to support Britain's economic recovery. To reach the public, the COID was involved in several publicity exhibitions including the *Daily Herald* newspapers' Post-War Homes Exhibition from 1945 and its Modern Homes Exhibition of 1946. Ambitious national exhibitions such as Britain Can Make It (1946) and the Festival of Britain (1951) followed. This post-war campaign by the COID undertook to improve design quality in both manufacturing and the home. Their objective was to showcase good design for homes by embodying the COID's social idealism (Woodham 2008). By staging the post-war exhibition 'Britain Can Make It' (BCMI) in 1946, the newly formed and confident Labour government conveyed a sense of cultural and political optimism. This was despite widespread and acute social problems linked to shortages in housing, food and raw materials. Held at the Victoria and Albert Museum, the exhibition epitomised initial efforts by the post-war government and design experts to shape public taste. Attracting almost a million and a half visitors, the exhibition was deemed a success by the design establishment. Yet it was marred by severe post-war materials shortages. Most exhibits were either reserved only for export to help pay off the country's war debt to the US or were at the prototype stage and not yet publicly available. The event was soon nicknamed 'Britain Can't Have It' by the press.

The Furnished Rooms Section took up a sizeable space at the exhibition and was influential in offering public spectacles of the modern post-war home. Designed by famous architects and designers, these rooms were modelled for imaginary occupants from specific social classes. Summaries of the fictional dwellers were displayed outside the model rooms with short narratives about their lives to help visitors imagine the occupants' requirements (BCMI Exhibition Catalogue in Woodham 2004). The furnished room that generated most interest was the Kitchen of a Cottage in a Modern Mining Village. The occupants were described as 'Coal miner, middle aged, active trade unionist, member of colliery choir. His wife, a member of Women's Institute …'[1] Part of a Living Room with Kitchen Recess was designed for a family described as 'Storeroom clerk, middle-aged, collects stamps, reads thrillers, regular picture-goer. His wife, same age and interests …'[2] In these ways, the exhibition staged the home as a profoundly classed space by assigning rooms of graded qualities to graded families.

The presentation of numerous ways of designing a room to improve the domestic environment proved to be popular among visitors. A survey by Mass Observation of public responses to the BCMI reveal that more women than men visited the exhibition, mostly representing the 'working class artisanal' class. Yet only 15% of the Councils' Selection Panels for the exhibition were women, and most were assigned to the Fashion and Textile Panels (Woodham 2008). Although the majority of consumer items were either too expensive or not available on the market, Mass Observation confirmed that the exhibition influenced visitors' aspirations for more stylish homes. This was particularly the case among the preponderant 'artisan classes' who, in response to these model rooms, now realised how shabby their own homes were.[3] This engineered dissatisfaction with their own homes. The sense of dissatisfaction with one's own home is a recurring response that runs right through the history of home idealisation, as indicated in the following chapters.

Doing its utmost to influence the design of public and private life, the state was now firmly in the business of constructing new regimes of good taste in the home. Via the COID, architects and industrial designers were at the forefront of the government's attempts to boost Britain's economic performance. Yet the consuming public spurned the moralising and restrained designs of the state backed COID. Such was the public yearning for more cheerful, decorative and stylish designs in reaction to the plain Utility styles after the war, that the Utility Furniture scheme was closed in 1952. In the same year, furniture rationing ended. Remarkably, a major flaw in the COID's approach during this whole period of state-led programmes to improve design and the quality of home interiors was the lack of any in-depth study of the design and furnishings of the British home (Woodham 1996).

Five years after the Britain Can Make It exhibition, the Festival of Britain was launched to achieve a parallel objective. Designed both as a 'tonic to the nation' and 'proclamation of national recovery', the Festival showcased new talent in the arts and sciences. The event conveyed design as an agent for moral guidance. Its aim was to showcase advanced consumer goods and household appliances. The Festival offered popular education in 'culture' by addressing the household as the key site of learning. Although the population was still struggling to recover from post-war austerity and the immediate housing crisis, the 1951 Festival of Britain offered more scope to shape actual consumer practices. To avoid criticisms of the earlier government sponsored exhibitions, visitors could order any items displayed. 'Family' and 'home' continued as key metaphors for the nation at the Festival, conveying a powerful sense of national consensus to circumvent social tensions and inequalities (Atkinson 2012). Model rooms formed major exhibits at the Festival through which family-centred home life was venerated.

The Homes and Gardens Pavilion exhibited model domestic interiors as a major theme to promote an aspirational home-centred lifestyle: comfortable, consumer-oriented, leisure-centred and increasingly privatised. Although exhibits invoked *future* imaginings of home, they were framed by *past* domestic traditions (Langhamer 2005). And this is a cultural strategy that was repeated over and over again to form a theme within the promotion of future homes, as described in the following chapters. Galvanised by concerns about declining birth rates and the need to build families, the government positioned women within the home as 'housewives', as markers of traditional family values yet framed within the 'clean' aesthetics of Modernism. As such, industrial designers were thrust to the forefront of the British government's attempts to introduce regimes of 'good taste' in the home to boost the United Kingdom's economic performance. Yet COID doctrine was impeded by manufacturer unresponsiveness and even hostility towards this government interference. Exhibitions and prizes for good design were therefore thought to be the best approach to coax manufacturers into grasping that 'good design means good business' (Woodham 1996).

Seven parlour rooms were designed as part of the Homes and Gardens by Eden Minns and wife Bianca Minns. But after the Festival started, these initial Minns-designed rooms were rejected as elitist by COID and exhibition organisers because they were furnished with items beyond the reach of the public. Countering COID propaganda, the model parlours were replaced by five redressed rooms. New design teams were appointed to style 'living rooms' for more informal home entertainment (Atkinson 2012: 169). This was a transitional period when the 'parlour' was replaced in many standard homes by a flexible, open-plan living room to provide a sense of space (Madigan and Munro 1999: 63). The five replacement living rooms reflected the Festival organisers' concern to ensure exhibits were accessible to visitors as mass-produced items. Once again, they were delineated along class lines with one luxuriously styled, two for 'lower-class occupants' and two for middle-class occupants. These refurbished rooms emphasised more informal comforts and home-based leisure activities with pianos, gramophones, TV sets and 'hobby corners'. The model home was signified as a retreat from public view 'and a place for the exercise of private dreams and fantasies', yet at the same time, this space was subjected to public scrutiny (Chapman and Hockey 1999: 10). Here, 'good design' was conceived as both a *moral* and *patriotic* endeavour by associating good design with good families as an expression of cultural capital (Bourdieu 1984).

The Festival even built a 'Live Architecture Exhibition' in the East End of London to stage a 'scientifically' constructed housing estate as a sharp contrast to the existing slums of the East End. Travelling exhibitions were also organised throughout the country that included a section on 'People at Home'. Extending its didactic approach, this section of the Festival showed audiences how to solve domestic problems using the expertise of the designer and scientist. And visitors to the Battersea Pleasure Gardens were steered into 'appropriate' consumer habits through the presentation of luxury, well-designed goods. Again, this vision functioned by shaming struggling post-war householders, encouraging them to covet domestic products they could hardly afford in order to improve homes judged by the COID as abject. The role of the professional tastemaker was consolidated but most high Modernist artists, designers, and architects were still men dictating to women as homemakers (Huyssen 1986).

Whilst housewives were approached as 'amateurs', men were deemed as experts. Similarly, while high culture was coded as masculine, mass culture was coded as feminine (Sparke 1995). That said, queer men legitimised, resisted, and intervened in the resolute reconstruction programmes of planners and policymakers that promoted these gendered codes as part of the rebuilding of post-World War II urban environments in cities such as London. Defined by a strong emphasis on civic order and conservative values of national community, the aim of such pro- grammes was to circumscribe citizens' public and private behaviour. These ambi- tions involved a heteronormative coding of public and private space extending from the design of basic public spaces to private living rooms and home décor. Richard Hornsey identifies queer men as a group notably affected by this new, moralistic climate of reformation and renewal. They were targeted by the police, the media and lawmakers as a critical urban problem, marking their lives and desires as criminal and deviant (Hornsey 2010; and see Chapter 7).

The annual Ideal Home Exhibitions, introduced in Chapter 2, formed a vital and well-established mid-twentieth-century commercial medium for displaying model rooms and model homes that advanced this gendered and sexual moral coding of space. But the exhibition contrasted with state-sponsored exhibitions such as the BCMI and Festival of Britain 1951. It was less preoccupied with the state-sponsored 'good taste' campaign. The moralising tone of the COID-led exhibitions was largely absent from the Ideal Home Exhibition. The mid-century Ideal Home Exhibitions expressed modernity within a range of domestic scenarios, but did so through a sense of grand scale, lavishness and choice by celebrating the pleasures of decorativeness, ornamentation and sheer fantasy (Chapman 1999). At a time of great scarcity, after World War II, prefabs and reclamations of old houses turned into flats were on display (Curtis 1998: 267). Yet the exhibition evoked a sense of abundance and modernity. In contrast to COID-led exhibitions, this event played a key role in creating an interactive, collaborative relationship between visitors and displayed domestic artefacts (Ryan 1997).

The Ideal Home Exhibition provided musings on a range of home archetypes to show how the domestic realm can embrace social, economic and technological change. The event generated a creative tension between the functional and fanciful, and between comfort and efficiency. Celebrated projections of a new kind of future relied on an idealisation of the everyday (Chapman 1999). As well as conjuring a fascination with the homes of the wealthy and famous, this idealisation involved a continuing fusion of three apparently contradictory themes: a romanticised past, scientific progress and technologised futurism. As Barry Curtis remarks, 'What could be more mundane and at the same time more unattainable than an Ideal Home? (Curtis 1998: 266). This hybridisation of an idealised past and future, and the veneration of the lives of the glitterati depended on the preservation of traditional relations of gender and family life supported by new technologies and a new 'aestheticisation' of everyday life (Featherstone 1990).

Domestic appliances now reflected scientific management attempts to rationalise the domestic by defining the housewife as 'modern' and homemaking as 'scientific'. However, a key crusade of the mid-twentieth-century Ideal Home Exhibitions was that 'labour saving' devices should convey the idea of home as a *leisured* space and homemaking as a *leisure* activity for women. The servantless house had entered the public imagination even though most visitors to the exhibition could never afford servants. Yet homemaking could be reassigned as a pleasurable activity, even as something glamourous, by offering women a sense of domestic autonomy, consumer choice and expanded leisure time (Nixon 2017). Nonetheless, these exhibitions reveal the expectations and anxieties associated with cultural change in the home. For example, half-timbered villages and the routine salvaging of the idea of the 'Englishman's home as his castle' continued as a powerful narrative that fortified aspirations for the suburban dream.

The American suburban dream

During the late 1950s, the American home ideal was expressed in the imagery of the 'house with the white picket fence' which emerged in the form of suburban sanctuaries beyond metropolitan centres across the US (Jacobs 1961: 122; see Lane 2015). Propelled by American national housing policy, the postwar mass production of suburban houses influenced the physical shape and moral idealisation of suburban housing (Fishman, 2010; see Checkowar 1980). From the mid-nineteenth to the end of the twentieth century, suburban growth and the rise of the American 'dream home' were the outcomes of elaborate alliances between government, developers and residents. Dolores Hayden's critical study of the idealised American suburban home highlights the social ambitions of individualism and privacy associated with romanticised family living (Hayden 2003).

In preference to town or community values, the suburban house functioned to express *national* values of the ideal life. And, as Hayden states, 'the single-family house was invested with church-like symbols as a sacred space where women's work would win a reward in heaven' (Hayden 2003: 6). This echoed the moral tones of earlier advice manuals. Without a tradition of sustained social housing construction of the kind mobilised by the welfare ideology of post-war Britain, the mortgage industry in the US took a separate path. Under the direction of President Herbert Hoover, the federal government of the 1920s fostered private development through taxes, banking and insurance systems. The American suburbs evolved in piecemeal fashion with working-class residences and commercial constructions located along public transit lines by streetcar. Some 'streetcar suburbs' were occupied by recent immigrants who kept hens and tended kitchen gardens. Others were inhabited by middle-class dwellers who managed ornamental gardens and patios (Hayden 2003).

The 1930s American Depression resulting in half a million home repossessions, together with Roosevelt's New Deal prompted radical changes in the regulation and financing of the American mortgage industry. From 1932, the building and loan associations were chartered, regulated and strengthened by a Federal Home Loan Bank System. Between 1933 and 1936, President Roosevelt enacted the New Deal through a series of programmes, public work projects, financial reforms and regulations. The objective was to invigorate the private home building industry and increase the proportion of privately owned homes. The Federal Housing Administration (FHA), created in part by the National Housing Act of 1934, offered government insurance for private residential mortgages. This encouraged home ownership among 'ordinary people'. Long-term, low down-payment mortgage loans were popularised by ensuring mortgages for small, owner-occupied suburban homes. However, collusion between the FHA and builders curbed the buying prospects of non-white families, buttressing the white middle-class ideal of upward social mobility (Jacobs 2015). Following Roosevelt's administration, the federal government implemented several schemes including tax reduction, to extend home ownership for the masses (see Marcuse 2001). 'By 2000, more Americans lived in suburbs than in either central cities or rural areas combined' (Hayden 2003: 10).

The history of home ownership and the rise of suburbia uncovers racialised regulatory frameworks that limit minority groups' opportunities and sustain white privilege. For example, around 70% of the population lived in the Twin Cities metropolis of Minneapolis and St. Paul in 1950. Such was the extent of the migration to the suburbs that by 2010, the population of the metropolis had plummeted to 20%. However, despite the realisation of home ownership among African Americans in St Paul, discrimination and exclusion prompted the later demolition of this housing to build a freeway (see Minnesota Historical Society 2015). While Roosevelt's New Deal involved the allocation of funds to public housing for African Americans, housing polices failed to address issues of housing integration or 'blockbusting'. Blockbusting refers to a practice among US real-estate agents and building developers of persuading white property owners to sell their house at low prices by fuelling fears that racial minorities would move into the neighbourhood. Since then, restricted mortgage lending and racist real-estate practices such as blockbusting have functioned to exclude certain ethnic groups from many specified places (Aalbers and Christophers, 2014). These practices also obstruct a sense of belonging and 'feeling at home' among minority ethnic groups (see Pulido 2000). Related discrimination in the rental market occurs in similar ways, leading to the spatial isolation of certain racialised groups (see Singer et al. 2008).

The revival of the post-war American building industry involved the creation of the household ideal (Jacobs 2015; Dickinson 2015). In the late 1940s and early 1950s, the National Home Builders Association (NHBA) promoted standardised design ideals in styles that ranged from traditional to wooded ranch-style developments to 'colonial' style and split-level modern (Lane 2015). Within this national march towards suburban modernity, real-estate marketing images typically targeted women as the homemaker and caretaker. However, women were generally excluded from decisions about the development and design of suburban homes. Representations of gender roles and family structures in advertisements reminded women of their duties as homemaker and their responsibility for household management and child-rearing (Spigel 1992; Johnson 1993). At the same time, these forms of publicity promoted a domestic modernity that encompassed new technologies such as electricity and labour-saving devices. A 1950s advertisement displayed in the 'Building Suburbia' section of Minnesota History Centre's 'Suburbia' exhibit, announces:

Happiness in her home is the goal of every wife and mother. She ever strives toward harmony, cleanliness, and charm. Eager to save her household funds and accomplish more with less expanded effort, womankind gratefully turns task after task over to electricity, her obedient and faithful servant, and quickly adapts herself to a richer, happier life—the NEW ELECTRIC WAY! (Minnesota Historical Society 2015)

This type of consumerism culminated in the dream of home ownership for the ordinary white middle-class family as part of a discourse of aspiration and upward mobility. For example, in her study of American suburban home interiors after the war, Barbara Miller Lane (2015) captures homebuyers' sense of excitement over new, shiny bathrooms and kitchens brimming with modern equipment.

Subsidised by government loans and low-cost mortgages, the American suburban single-family house is now the archetypal consumer commodity. Lisabeth Cohen demonstrates how the quest for prosperity after World War II transformed American life by provoking a relentless consumer disposition (Cohen 2003: 195). Although mass consumption symbolised patriotism, social equality and the American dream, in practice it fuelled economic inequality and the gendered, classed and racial division of society. While Kenneth Jackson (1985) claims that the appeal of suburbia was fading by the 1980s, Hayden argues that more and more people are moving into 'rural fringes', to this day. These areas tend to be socially and physically isolating (Hayden 2004: 8). Narratives of suburbia have long exposed the fragmentation of community and the isolating effects of the role of housewife resulting from the inward turn towards family and the individual.

Women's negative experiences of suburban privacy were revealed as suburbs were gradually acknowledged to be suffocating and oppressive. In her well-known book, *The Feminine Mystique*, Betty Friedan (1963) wrote about 'the problems that have no name'. With fitted-out kitchens, studies, gardens and new consumption patterns, suburban homes expressed opportunities for women to be agents of modernity (see Hollows 2008). Yet, asked to carry out a survey of her former Smith College classmates for their 15th anniversary reunion, Friedan discovered that many were disappointed with their lives as housewives. This prompted her to extend her interviews to a wider group of suburban housewives alongside a study of advertising, wider popular media and psychology relating to the suburban encounter. Based on her evidence, Friedan disputed the common belief that 'fulfilment as a woman had only one definition for American women after 1949 – the housewife-mother'. Her work served as the foundations of a vital body of feminist knowledge which critiques the ways in which women are 'often objectified, isolated, and sexualised' within the interior of the home (Havenband 2002: 12).

In her feminist study of the gendering of values and the material forms of suburban homes, Hayden emphasises that the housework and maintenance of these homes depended on women's unpaid and unrewarded work. Suburban nuclear family lifestyles actually enlarged women's workload by privatising and individualising domestic tasks (Hayden 2002). With each household shaped by a kitchen and laundry and discrete living zones, and with no communal help, women were forced to supervise their children individually and forgo shared housework or cooking. Women also lacked the support of their mothers and the wider community of women in earlier settlements. This suburban home was entirely contingent on performing countless physical and emotional caring tasks, the planning of children's entertainment, fostering community and kinship ties and negotiating dealings with commercial businesses via shopping, and with the state via schools and medical organisations. Hayden points out that the home may be a haven from work for men but not for women whose work is unpaid.

Highlighting palpable home precarities for women, this encounter with home confirms that it is neither a private space nor an autonomous space. Hayden's feminist critique of the suburban home corresponds with her analysis of the work of American 'material feminists' from the late nineteenth century, mentioned in Chapter 2 (Hayden 1981). Hayden recommends the redesigning of suburban homes and neighbourhoods to include the replacement of individual gardens by collective village greens in order to support communal childcare and the provision of food by gardening (Hayden 2002: 208). In Scandinavian countries such as Sweden and Denmark, apartment houses have been designed to encompass day care centres and restaurants to support working families. As such, Hayden's vision of housing reform represents a prerequisite for gender equality.

Revelations that suburbs are unhomely places for women is mirrored in research on residents' feelings of loneliness and isolation in high-rise apartments. High-rise blocks were typically built by governments in the mid-twentieth century to provide public housing for the working classes in response to the clearance of working-class housing in inner-city communities. The determination to purge cities of inner-city working-class housing, labelled as slums, was in response to fears of disease and low moral standards (Blunt and Dowling 2006: 108). Built to rehouse working-class households, high-rise apartments were cheap and had the capacity to accommodate large numbers of people (Costello 2005). It was assumed that modern buildings would have a civilising effect on its inhabitants. However, it was soon realised that these high-rise blocks triggered or contributed to a range of social problems including family breakdown and crime. It was demonstrated that these environments were unconducive to raising children, deprived residents of privacy and stranded people in their apartments when the lifts broke down.

Domesticity as a Cold War weapon

The post-war mood of 1950s American society was marked by transition. In the process of restoring domestic life after World War II, the American state sought to assert its authority as a superpower. Remarkably, by the 1950s, this aspiration spurred the rise of a new kind of domestic modernity which served as a powerful weapon in the context of the Cold War (a term used to refer to the hostilities between the western powers and the Soviet bloc countries between 1945 and 1991). This process of domestic modernisation was articulated in two key ways: first in terms of designing and manufacturing consumer goods for the home that were derived from and validated a military-industrial complex; and second through the use of an idealised American home as a propaganda tool in the Cold War with the Soviet Union. These events are examined in this section to bring to light the intersection of military and domestic concerns within the design and manufacture of domestic appliances.

American domestic ideals expressed in relation to the remodelling of the post-war home were underpinned by military and space-age initiatives in terms of design and manufacture. For example, in the 1950s and 1960s, the Philco-Ford Corporation, a subsidiary of Ford Motor Company was designing and producing not only radios, phonographs, television receivers, and automobiles but also missiles (see Chapters 4 and 9). This technological range produced by a single corporation reveals a seamless criss-crossing of military, domestic and space-age technology. The Cold War theme also involved the exploitation of domestic consumer goods as a measure of national progress and superiority over other nations. It was in these circumstances that the American home was exploited by the US government as a vital cultural weapon in advancing its propaganda war with the Soviet Union.

In the initial years of the Cold War, the US government specifically drew on American domestic design as a strategy to undermine the Soviet Union by promoting the superiority of American lifestyles as a feature of US political interests. A 'soft power' approach was employed by the US government by propagating information about the 'American way of life' to convince other nations of the authenticity and superiority of its culture in order to cultivate admiration for US culture and generate an affinity with US political objectives (Castillo 2009; see McDonald 2010). Anchored in the American ideal of the suburban dream home and the modern housewife, the modern American kitchen was staged as a central element of this soft war symbolism, exemplified by a famous exchange between the USA and Soviet Union now known as the 'Kitchen debate'. Characterising an ideological battle for Cold War supremacy over the Soviet Union, this exchange occurred in 1959 between Vice-President Richard Nixon and Soviet premier Nikita Khrushev at the American Exhibition in Sokolniki Park, in Moscow.

The purpose of the exhibition was to show the Soviet nation a model American home. The US Vice-President, Richard Nixon visited Moscow in 1959 where an encounter occurred between the two superpowers over the virtues of American appliances. While Premier Nikita Khrushev and Richard Nixon were leaning over the railings of an exhibition display of General Electric's kitchen, Nixon boasted about the merits of American consumer capitalism and its benefits for American women citizens. Nixon deliberately pitted the superior quality of General Electric's canary-yellow kitchen against the lower standards of living endured by ordinary Soviet citizens under a communist regime.[4] The Vice-President proclaimed the American-designed kitchen to be a healthier, more hygienic and labour-saving form of living than Soviet equivalents (Castillo 2009).

Nixon and Khrushchev both understood the political symbolism of the modern kitchen. Situated within a domestic cultural setting, this technological innovation embodied the political system from which it emerged (Castillo 2009). Nonetheless, Soviet exhibition visitors and the wider public were highly ambivalent about the 'American dream kitchen' that Nixon and Khrushchev argued over (Reid 2009). By contrast, in the UK, a British state-subsidised kitchen design was regarded as so advanced and stylish that it was wrongly assumed by the public to be a luxury American product (Holder 2009). The American kitchen became, then, an overtly political issue, propelled by an encounter in Moscow that shaped the kitchen as both ideological construct and material practice (Oldenziel et al. 2009). In this Cold War climate, middle-class affluence was heralded by the US government as a victory even though the Soviet Union had beaten the US in the first stage of the space race by successfully launching Sputnik two years earlier. Through the 'battle of the appliances', the US were determined to generate envy as a cultural strategy to establish their economic and aesthetic superiority over the Soviet Union (Castillo 2009: 10). The American home became a 'mediation junction' (Oldenziel and Bruhe'ze 2008: 9–41) in which politicians, women users, design and producers collaborated in projecting a phantasmagorical expression of American domestic modernity. As Greg Castillo (2009) explains, the American National Exhibition and the Kitchen Debate formed the climax of a prolonged ideological conflict in which refrigerators, televisions, living room-suites and pre-fab homes figured as a cultural battleground. On *both* sides of the Iron Curtain, domestic settings were exploited to stage each regime's superiority (see Oldenziel et al. 2009).

Dream Homes at the New York World's Fair (1964–1965)

The US government's strategy of endorsing the superiority of capitalism culminated at the New York World's Fair of 1964–1965. This was at a time when the Cold War was in full swing. As the largest international exhibition held in the US, this event was designed to showcase mid-twentieth-century American culture and technology. Conceived by a group of New York businessmen at the height of the Great Depression, the New York World's Fair aimed to attract business to New York City and raise the mood of the nation by introducing Americans to the 'World of Tomorrow'. The event was known as the Billion Dollar Fair, with 150 pavilions and exhibits laid out over 640 acres, representing 80 nations. Offering a positive view of the future and attracting more than 51 million visitors, the official theme of the fair was 'Peace through Understanding'. With upbeat visions of 'the world of tomorrow today', the New York World's Fair was a grand consumer spectacle that showcased American products of the period including transportation, domestic living and consumer electronics. Visitors could glimpse the future by encountering flying cars, underwater hotels, and spacecrafts flown 'in orbit' in the Space Park sponsored by NASA, the Department for Defence and the Fair. Remarkably, as Barbrook explains, nuclear weapons, militarised computing, and militarised space were presented at the Fair as expressions of a utopian future and a civilising present (Barbrook 2007).

Among prominent American businesses with a major presence at the Fair were General Electric, Ford, General Motors, Chrysler, IBM, Bell Telephone, US Steel, Pepsi Cola, Seven Up, Dupont, RCA and Westinghouse. A model home called the Formica World's Fair Model Home built by a New Zealand manufacturer was exhibited at the Fair to offer visitors a foretaste of the varied applications of laminate. This ranch house showed how much could be accomplished with Formica: from floors, to tabletops and countertops. Described as a 'dream for tomorrow's living today', a British Pathé film, called 'Showcase for Carefree Living' documents this World's Fair Model Home[5] by providing a walkthrough of the display home. The model home was reviewed in *Good Housekeeping*, in a prominent 14-page article.[6] The spectacular hexagonal shaped 'Better Living Centre' was the third largest pavilion of the Fair built to showcase 'the products, services and ideas that enrich America's standard of living'.[7] It performed as 'the showcase for companies with products and services setting standards for a richer life in six major areas: Fashion, Food, Health, Home, Family security and Leisure'.[8] In the 'Highlights' section of the official guide for the Better Living Centre was an item titled 'House with the most' which declared:

> This exhibit is mainly devoted to the home: what to build it with, how to furnish it. At the center of the floor is a full-sized seven-room dream house fitted out with the last word in modern materials, furnishings and design ideas. The Gallery of Kitchens presents the latest in equipment and appliances for the kitchens of today and tomorrow. The Promenade of Interiors is a

comprehensive exhibition of interior decorating, lively with a variety of new fabric, furniture and lighting ideas.[9]

The idea of the 'dream house' formed a key trope in the promotional discourses that served to idealise the American home.[10] Nearby galleries included kitchens designed by Bette Sanford Roby which showcased products displayed in styles that reflected popular tastes of the time including Mediterranean, Early American, French Regency and Modern. United States Plywood displayed a two-story cut-away house that could be observed from the outside. The interior of the five-room home was designed throughout by Emily Malino. These 'dream homes' were built to save space, with a child's bedroom described by the *New York Times* as: 'A wall bed, built-in shelves, a few pedestal stools and tables used with bright colors and a wood-panelled wall add up to something that could be copied at modest cost for the average home.'[11]

The Cuban missile crisis posed a real danger during the 1960s. A solution offered by the New York World' Fair's was the 'Underground Home'. In addition to the model homes proudly displayed at the 'Better Living Centre', a subterranean dwelling was built as an exhibit that featured a large and luxurious three-bed-roomed home. The Underground Home was designed by a lumber dealer and home builder from Plainview, Texas called Swayze in response to the Cuban missile crisis. This was a time when many Americans were living in dread of an imminent nuclear attack as a palpable experience of home precarity. While families rushed to build fallout shelters, most were featureless and confined. Conceived for 'modern living' the Fair's Underground Home was replete with night and day light settings, candelabras displayed on a Steinway & Sons piano in the living room and even a pipe organ. In previews of the dwelling, the *Herald Tribune* commended the value of living with 'good old earth on all sides' while the *Wall Street Journal* called the dwelling 'a new frontier for family living'. By the time of the Fair's opening, the Underground Home had sparked nationwide debate in the major daily newspapers.

Enfolded in a concrete shell, with its roof only 5 feet underground, the dwelling not only featured a range of furnishings and modern appliances. It even contained an underground 'exterior', featuring a terrace, terrace garden and patio with plastic flowers and artificial wisteria. As well as offering a 'solution' to nuclear war, the exhibit's guides explained during a 20-minute tour that this underground living provided pure air, low noise levels, lower heating and maintenance costs, protection from climate risks and even from radiation fallout (*Official Guide* 1964: 117). The Underground Home boasted several novel features described by Nicholas Hirshon:

> The lighting allowed residents to pick the time of day and the season they wanted with just the turn of a knob—like 'midnight at noon' and 'summer in winter,' as Swayze bragged. He also installed 'dial-a-view,' which let occupants pick the murals they would see through the windows. One of the choices was a knight riding a horse to a castle. (Hirshon 2012)

Drawing attention to the Cold War symbolism of the 'sub-urban' home, Hirshon states: 'A glance at a bookshelf inside the home underscored the chief motivation for buying such a dwelling. One book was titled "Our New Life with the Atom." Another was "Foreign Policy Without Fear".' He quotes the *Miami News* which commented that on the styling of the home's interior by Marilynn Motto: 'Her designs are enough to calm a subterranean dweller during an H-bombing.' Although the Fair's aim was to spread 'peace through understanding', the Underground Home was a troubling reminder of the dangers of the nuclear age and the short-lived nature of peace. This evocation of home precarity was transformed into an exhibition asset. The incentives for and manifestations of domestic modernity and suburbanisation that formed the basis for the invention American dream home were framed in multiple ways by governmental, military and commercial imperatives, confirming the Cold War oriented and wider political nature of mid-twentieth-century American home imaginaries.

Conclusion

This chapter has traced some of the key processes involved in the idealisation of a distinctive kind of middle-class home that emerged after World War II in Britain and America. It provides an important link with the previous chapter for an understanding not only of the prevalent values and sentiments but also the political motives that underpin domestic cultures in the mid-twentieth century. Through the examples of housing policy, design, exhibitions and related social trends in the UK and US, the chapter has identified a series of interconnected socio-cultural trends and social anxieties in the post-war imaginings and manifestations of this idealised home. The state policies of both countries promoted the expansion of the suburbs and a corresponding reinforcement of home ownership as a powerful set of aspirational values among the middle classes. Home ownership became a symbol of good citizenship, echoing past times when only property ownership allowed a subject to vote. However, 'domestic modernity' was expressed and materialised in distinctive as well as overlapping ways in Britain and the US. Nonetheless, despite a stronger welfare-driven course of domestic modernisation in the UK and a more commercially driven path in the US, in both national contexts 'home' functioned to serve implicit and explicit political, economic and cultural interests.

In post-war Britain, the government continued to play an active role in advancing 'good design' as part of its post-war housing schemes. On the one hand, these grand state-led events accompanied other popular mediums in instilling the idea of a universal modern home shaped by 'good taste'. On the other hand, the discursive practices of the commercially led Ideal Home Exhibition sealed imaginaries of the 'ideal home' as a technologically advanced, spacious and glamorous space crammed with domestic appliances. All homes came to be judged by a spectacularised domestic ideal. This 'ideal home' formed a powerful yet fluctuating symbol of mid-twentieth-century modernity as a form of national pride. While this 'ideal home' was projected in the UK in the 1950s, a corresponding 'American dream home' was expressed at exhibitions in the US framed by conspicuous political and military signifiers. Used as a political pawn, this American dream home imaginary invoked ideas of the home as a cultural weapon. Propelled by palpable home precarities associated with the memories and projections of war, this dream home was contrived to promote American propaganda in the Cold War between the US and the Soviet Union. In this Cold War setting, domestic space symbolised the nation as a superpower. As such, the case of the Kitchen Debate epitomises the overtly political nature of home, domestic modernity and middle-class affluence.

Throughout the development and design of suburban homes and domestic appliances in both the UK and US, women were simultaneously heralded and marginalised as modern housewives. They were systematically excluded from decision-making processes. In post-war Britain, women were summoned back into the home as 'housewives', after having contributed significantly to the war effort. Thereafter, within state attempts to modernise the post-war home, design was conveyed as an agent for moral guidance with 'good taste' deployed as both markers of traditional family values and domestic modernity. Yet men continued to predominate as band of artists, designers, and architects who, in their creations of the 'ideal home', not only dictated to women as homemakers but also encouraged hard-up householders to view their homes as shabby and deficient.

The idealisation of home by commercial exhibitions in the UK and US recast homemaking as a leisured, pleasurable and even glamorous activity for women. Yet women's encounters with suburban privacy in both countries indicated that suburbs were stifling and oppressive spaces for women as homemakers. Despite this, women's designated workplace – the modern kitchen – became a symbol of the virtues of American consumer capitalism. The next chapter describes the rise of the 'media home' by tracing the unparalleled impact of television, and then computers, on home life from the mid-twentieth century.

Notes

1 Design Council/ Design Archive, University of Brighton, in Woodham (2004).
2 Dorothy Braddell, design for a BCMI Furnished Room: living room and kitchen with built-in fittings, Council/Design Archive, University of Brighton, in Woodham (2004).
3 ID/903, *Summary of Findings of Mass Observation at Britain Can Make It* (1946) (cited in Woodham 2004).
4 On the 'kitchen debate' see *New York Times*, 25 July 1959, 1; *Daily Mirror*, 25 July 1959, 1; de Grazia 2006; Oldenziel et al. 2009: 3–6 and 59–82; Nolan 2012: 257–260.
5 British Pathé film, 'Showcase for Carefree Living', available at https://www.youtube.com/watch?v=z5FL1mdcc2U (accessed 9 May 2019).
6 See 'Formica' from the *Souvenir Book*, at the 'Website of the 1964–1965 New York World's Fair', available at http://nywf64.com/formica13.shtml (accessed 9 May 2019).
7 Sales brochure, 'Better Living Centre', New York World's Fair website 1964/1965, available at http://www.nywf64.com/betliv01.shtml (accessed 9 May 2019).
8 Visitors' Guide, 'Better Living Centre', New York World's Fair website 1964/1965, available at http://www.nywf64.com/betliv10.shtml (accessed 9 May 2019).
9 Official Guide, 'Better Living Centre', New York World's Fair website 1964/1965, available at http://www.nywf64.com/betliv01.shtml (accessed 9 May 2019).

10 See YouTube film at the New York World's Fair (1964): 'Showcase for Carefree Living: World's Fair Model Home' https://www.youtube.com/watch?v=z5FL1mdcc2U (accessed 27 July 2019).
11 Ibid.

References

Aalbers, M.B., and Christophers, B. (2014) 'Centring housing in political economy', *Housing, Theory and Society*, 31(4), 373–394.

Atkinson, H. (2012) *The Festival of Britain: A Land and its People*. London: I.B.Tauris.

Attfield, J. (2000) *Wild Things: The Material Culture of Everyday Life*. Oxford: Berg.

Ball, M. (2017) *Housing Policy and Economic Power: The Political Power of Owner Occupation*. London: Routledge.

Barbrook, R. (2007) *Imaginary Futures: From Thinking Machines to the Global Village*. London: Pluto Press.

Barthes, R. (1979) *The Eiffel Tower and Other Mythologies*. Berkeley: University of California Press.

Binford, H. (1985) *The First Suburbs: Residential Communities on the Boston Periphery, 1815–1860*. Chicago: Chicago University Press.

Blunt, A. and Dowling, R. (2006) *Home*. London: Routledge.

Bourdieu, P. (1984) *Distinction: A Social Critique of the Judgment of Taste*. Cambridge, MA: Harvard University Press.

Castillo, G. (2009) *Cold War on the Home Front: The Soft Power of Midcentury Design*. Minneapolis: University of Minnesota Press.

Chapman, T. (1999) 'Stage sets for ideal lives: Images of home in contemporary show homes', in T. Chapman and J. Hockey (eds), *Ideal Homes? Social Change and Domestic Life*. London: Routledge, pp. 44–58.

Checkowar, B. (1980) 'Large builders, federal housing programmes, and postwar suburbanization', *International Journal of Urban and Regional Research*, 4(1), 21–45.

Cohen, L. (2003) *A Consumer's Republic*. New York: Vintage Books.

Colomina, B. (2001) *Domesticity at War*. Barcelona: ActarD Inc.

Costello, L. (2005) 'From prisons to penthouses: The changing image of high-rise living in Melbourne', *Housing Studies*, 20(1), 49–62.

Curtis, B. (1998) 'Reviewed work: Daily Mail Ideal Home Exhibition: The Ideal Home: Through the twentieth century by Deborah S. Ryan', *Journal of Design History*, 11(3), 266–268.

Daunton, M.J. (1987) *A Property-owning Democracy? Housing in Britain*. London: Faber & Faber.

Davidoff, L. and Hall, C. (2002) *Family Fortunes: Men and Women of the English Middle Class 1780–1850*. London: Routledge.

de Grazia, V. (2006) *Irresistible Empire: America's Advance Through Twentieth-Century Europe*. Cambridge: Harvard University Press.

Dickinson, G. (2015) *Suburban Dreams: Imagining and Building the Good Life*. Tuscaloosa: University of Alabama Press.

Dovey, K. (1992) *Framing Places, Mediating Power in Built Form*. London: Routledge.

Featherstone, M. (1990) *Consumer Culture and Postmodernism*. London: Sage.

Ferguson, M. (1983) *Forever Feminine: Women's Magazines and the Cult of Femininity*. London: Ashgate.

Fishman, R. (1987) *Bourgeois Utopias: The Rise and Fall of Suburbia*. New York: Basic Books.

Fishman, R. (2010) 'The American metropolis at century's end: Past and future influences', *Housing Policy Debate*, 11(1), 199–213.

Fogelson, R.M. (2005) *Bourgeois Nightmares: Suburbia, 1870–1930*. New Haven: Yale University Press.

Friedan, B. (1963) *The Feminine Mystique*. New York: W.W. Norton.

Hanlon, B., Rennie Short, J. and Vicino, T.J. (2010) *Cities and Suburbs: New Metropolitan Realities in the US*. NewYork: Routledge.

Havenband, L. (2002) 'Looking through the lens of gender: A postmodern critique of a modern housing paradigm', *Journal of Interior Design*, 28(2), 1–14.

Hayden, D. (1981) *The Grand Domestic Revolution: A History of Feminist Designs for American Homes, Neighborhoods, and Cities*. Cambridge, MA: MIT Press.

Hayden, D. (2002) [1984] *Redesigning America: The Future of Housing, Work and Family Life*. New York: W.W. Norton.

Hayden, D. (2003) *Building Suburbia: Green Fields and Urban Growth*. NewYork: Vintage Books.

Hayden, D. (2004) *A Field Guide to Sprawl*. New York: W.W. Norton.

Hirshon, N. (2012) 'The secret spot hidden below New York', *Narratively Hidden History*. https://narratively.com/is-it-down-there/ (accessed 9 May 2019).

Holder, J. (2009) 'The nation state or the United States? The irresistible kitchen of the British Ministry of Works', in R. Oldenziel, Z. Zachmann and G. Castillo (eds), *Cold War Kitchen: Americanization, Technology, and European Users*. Cambridge, MA: MIT Press, pp. 235–258.

Hollows, J. (2008) *Domestic Cultures*. Maidenhead: Open University Press.

Hornsey, R. (2010) *The Spiv and the Architect: Unruly Life in Postwar London*. Minneapolis: University of Minnesota Press.

Huyssen, A. (1986) *After the Great Divide: Modernism, Mass Culture, Postmodernism*. Bloomington: Indiana University Press.

Jackson, K. (1985) *Crabgrass Frontier: The Suburbanization of the United States*. New York: Oxford University Press.

Jacobs, J. (1961) *The Death and Life of Great American Cities*. New York: Random House.

Jacobs, J. (2015) *Detached America: Building Houses in Postwar Suburbia*. Charlottesville: University of Virginia Press.

Johnson, L. (1993) 'Text-ured brick: Speculations on the cultural production of domestic space', *Geographical Research*, 31(2), 201–213.

Lane, B.M. (2015) *Houses for a New World: Builders and Buyers in American Suburbs 1945–1965*. Princeton: Princeton University Press.

Langhamer, C. (2005) 'The meanings of home in postwar Britain', *Journal of Contemporary History*, 40(2), 341–362.

Lury, C. (2011) *Consumer Culture*. Cambridge: Polity Press.

Madigan, R. and Munro, M. (1999) 'Negotiating space in the family home', in I. Cieraad (ed), *At Home: An Anthropology of Domestic Space*. Syracuse, NY: Syracuse University Press.

Marcuse, P. (2001) 'The Liberal/Conservative divide in the history of housing in the United States', *Housing Studies*, 16(6), 717–736.

McDonald, G. (2010) 'The modern American home as soft power: Finland, MoMA and the 'American home 1953', *Exhibition Journal of Design History*, 23(4), 387–408.

Minnesota Historical Society. (2015) 'Pink flamingos and a manicured lawn: The American dream realized?' 'Suburbia' exhibition press release. www.mnhs.org/media/kits/suburbia (accessed 27 July 2019).

Nicolaides, B.M. and Wiese, A. (2006) *The Suburb Reader*. New York: Routledge.

Nixon, S. (2017) 'Life in the kitchen: Television advertising, the housewife and domestic modernity in Britain, 1955–1969', *Contemporary British History*, 31(1), 69–90.

Nolan, M. (2012) *The Transatlantic Century: Europe and the United States, 1890–2010*. Cambridge: Cambridge University Press.

Official Guide. (1964) *New York World's Fair Official Guide 1964–1965*. New York: Time-Life Books.

Official Souvenir Book. (1964) *New York World's Fair, 1964–1965*. New York: Time-Life Books.

Official Souvenir Book. (1965) *New York World's Fair 1964/1965*. New York: Time Life Books.

Oldenziel, R. and de la Bruhe'ze, A.A. (eds) (2008) 'Theorising the mediation junction', in *Manufacturing Technology, Manufacturing Consumers: The Making of Dutch Consumer Society*. Amsterdam: Aksant.

Oldenziel, R., Zachmann, Z. and Castillo, G. (eds) (2009) *Cold War Kitchen: Americanization, Technology, and European Users*. Cambridge, MA: MIT Press.

Pulido, L. (2000) 'Rethinking environmental racism: White privilege and urban development in Southern California', *Annals of the Association of American Geographers*, 90(1), 12–40.

Ravetz, A. (1995) *The Place of Home: English Domestic Environments, 1914–2000*. London: Spon.

Reid, S. (2009) '"Our kitchen is just as good": Soviet responses to the American Kitchen', in R. Oldenziel, Z. Zachmann and G. Castillo (eds), *Cold War Kitchen: Americanization, Technology, and European Users*. Cambridge, MA: MIT Press, pp. 83–112.

Ryan, D.S. (1997) *Daily Mail Ideal Home Exhibition: The Ideal Home: Through the Twentieth Century*. London: Hazar Publishing.

Silverstone, R. (ed.) (1997) *Visions of Suburbia*. London: Routledge.

Singer, A., Hardwick, S. and Brettell, C.B. (2008) *Twenty-First-Century Gateways: Immigrant Incorporation in Suburban American*. Washington, DC: Brookings Institute.

Sparke, P. (1995) *As Long as It's Pink: The Sexual Politics of Taste*. Ontario: Pandora Press.

Spigel, L. (1992) *Make Room for TV: Television and the Family Ideal in Postwar America*. Chicago, IL: University of Chicago Press.

Spigel, L. (2009) *TV by Design: Modern Art and the Rise of Network TV*. Chicago: University of Chicago Press.

West, H. (2016) 'Artisanal food and the cultural economy: Perspectives on craft, heritage, authenticity and reconnection', in J.A. Klein and J.L. Watson (eds), *The Handbook of Food and Anthropology*. London: Bloomsbury.

Woodham, J. (1996) 'Managing British design reform II: The film *Deadly Lampshade*—An ill-fated episode in the politics of "good taste"', *Journal of Design History*, 9(2), 101–115.

Woodham, J. (2004) 'Design and everyday life at the Britain Can Make It exhibition, 1946: "Stripes, spots, white wood and homespun versus chintzy armchairs and iron bedsteads with brass knobs"', *The Journal of Architecture*, 9(4), 463–476.

Woodham, J. (2008) *Twentieth Century Design*. Oxford: Oxford University Press.

4

EARLY MEDIA HOMES

Introduction

From the mid-twentieth century, the movement of media technologies into the home has had one of the most transformational effects on home life. In Britain and America, studies of the cultural history of television's formative years after World War II not only show how television developed as a domestic medium in conveying visual images and narratives of 'normal' family life. Research also confirms how this media technology and its content prompted material changes within the domestic realm from the layout of home interiors to household dynamics (Spigel 1992; Chambers 2016). By tracing the ways in which the home and household relations were reshaped by the introduction of television and then computers into domestic space, this chapter contributes to an understanding of how the home became a key site of media engagement.

The design of television for home use meant that the physical appearance of the equipment that projected programmes, the televison receiver, played a fundamental role in domesticating the medium. Starting with the television set itself, David Morley denaturalises the taken-for-granted status of television as a domestic item by reminding us of the challenging history of its entrance to the home (Morley 2007). The aesthetic and material design of the television set involved the interventions of designers, manufacturers and governments in preparing, shaping and showcasing the television receiver for home consumption. Preceding and coinciding with the phase of television adoption, major efforts to promote and denaturalise the medium and equipment occurred during an imaginary phase: a phase between the 1930s and 1950s. In this period, trade fairs and national exhibitions displayed this new technology to convey powerful ideas about what it could do and how it could be used (Chambers 2016, Chambers 2019). These public events played an essential part in 'normalising' media technology (Ellis 1982: 162).

The chapter maps the broad socio-cultural, political and economic developments involved in the widespread domestic adoption of television in Britain and the US accompanied by a discussion of how the medium, as technology and content, was negotiated by householders. Four intersecting dimensions of early television's domestic adoption are addressed. First, the chapter considers how early analogue television was conceived and designed for domestic space. A case study of the role of designers of TV consoles and exhibitions of TV sets shows how the design and display of early television consoles as furniture in model rooms at exhibitions expressed the technology as a *domestic* item to facilitate its home adoption. Second, it addresses the ways in which televisions' content, via documentaries about homemaking and TV shows about family life, reflected and normalised a nuclear and suburban version of home life. Third, the chapter considers the scheduling of TV programmes, to highlight how they shaped and consolidated domestic routines. A fourth, related issue is how these dynamics instilled in audiences a sense of belonging to a wider national community beyond the home: a sense of belonging to a nation.

The next section considers the entrance of computers into the home, to introduce the theory of *domestication* (Silverstone and Hirsch 1992). Domestication theory offers a way of understanding how media technologies sustain, reflect and transform domestic arrangements by fostering and disrupting family cohesion. Triggered by changing global and personal networks, debates about a dismantling of the boundaries around the home, an erosion of privacy and the encroachment of paid work into the home began in the twentieth century when the television set, and then computer, entered this space. By the twenty-first century, 'home' had become a site of struggle over its role as a place of 'leisure' and a place of 'work' (Spigel 1992; Chambers 2016).

Conceiving the media home

A striking feature of historical accounts about early television's arrival in the home is the complex public deliberations about its prospects: about who should have access to it, how it should be designed and promoted, how it should be used and what kinds of programmes should be broadcast. Early public debates involved scientific and technological discourses of innovation and progress. Yet the main state and commercial institutions engaged in television's inception as a medium and product were concerned to design a *domestic* technology, one conducive to the home and capable of nurturing ideals of family togetherness. Within these parameters, the key challenge facing governments, TV receiver manufacturers and broadcasters was how to stimulate consumer demand for a bulky, alien and expensive product during a period of dramatic social upheaval before and after World War II. As such, television's placement in the home was prefigured and accompanied by public imaginaries of a new type of home: a modern, advanced media home that nonetheless expressed traditional family values.

Although the medium was first launched in the mid-1930s, by the start of the Second World War (1939–1945), televisual broadcasting was suspended in Europe.

A commercially led US television industry took the lead in television adoption in the 1940s while Europe was at war. When resumed in Britain in June 1946, a promotional drive ensured that post-war television came to form a central part of domestic life by the late 1950s. The social turmoil associated with World War II corresponded with changing social attitudes towards women, family life and the relationship between home and the outside world, that is, between domesticity and politics. It was in a climate of social recovery, involving public concerns about how to retrieve 'normal' family life after the war that television was introduced to the home. However, television's introduction was steered by a web of public initiatives as a pivotal feature of national domestic recuperation.

The social need for television broadcasting was underpinned by two apparently contrary tendencies in modern social life referred to by Raymond Williams (1974) as 'mobile privatisation'. These desires for privacy and mobility - both physical and social - feature in home imaginaries throughout the course of the media home's evolution, from analogue to digital settings. The social yearning for *geographical* mobility in the early twentieth century was met through transportation and communication technologies. And the desire for *social* mobility corresponded with the rise of a smaller, nuclear family, suburban living and the veneration of aspirational middle-class values that expressed desires for upward social mobility. At the same time, an accent on domestic privacy was articulated via house building projects, domestic architectural styles and town planning (see Chapter 3).

Alongside more fluid social ties, the rise of separate, privatised home units generated the social need for information to be delivered to the home in order to reconnect this intimate space to the public world of politics, community and nation. Televisual communication enabled this reconnection. William's concept of 'mobile privatisation' also highlights a mediated desire for travel away from the home. Despite being enclosed in domestic retreats, early television gave home-based audiences a feeling of journeying around the world by connecting them with events and entertainment from beyond home (Spigel 2001: 391). Through a flow of news, sport, education and entertainment, television offered householders new opportunities to tie home to the world outside, fundamentally transforming domestic cultures. These demands for both privacy and mobility formed the motives, then, for reorganising the very essence of home as a mediatised space. Through TV programme content and scheduling, this new medium was enlisted to foster women's status as housewives and enhance family togetherness. Yet, at the same time, public debate centred on whether television viewing might undermine family life by distracting women from their housework and caretaking role. To ease these anxieties, television was promoted as a new hearth: a medium that could bring the family together and reclaim traditional family values. Newspapers and women's magazines contained appealing advertisements of white nuclear families gathered round a glowing TV set (Spigel 1992). Images of the 'family circle' inferred that, in the wake of war, television could strengthen family values, values based on a traditional middle-class lifestyle centred on the home as a feminine space.

Exhibiting the TV home

Although television viewing was devised for the intimate sphere of the family home, the technology was first available in kit form during the 1930s, bought largely by men as amateur technical hobbyists and engineers who sought to gain a sense of technical mastery, already established in the context of radio hams, by assembling the equipment. Thereafter, television was feminised and domesticated by relating the medium to dominant ideas of home and family. Initial displays at trade fairs demonstrated how the technology functioned. For example, by 1930 Baird Television's early models were displayed in the UK at trade and consumer-oriented fairs such as at Radiolympia and the Ideal Home Exhibition where visitors themselves could be 'televised' as part of the new media spectacle (Wheatley 2016: 37). The Ideal Home Exhibition played a significant role in promoting television to consumers as a desirable medium and commodity, with six manufacturers exhibiting and demonstrating sets in 1938. BBC television programmes of the Exhibition were broadcast direct from the Olympia site between 14 and 20 April 1938 (*Radio Times* 1938). By explaining how the equipment works, the focus of these early exhibitions of television was on the marvels of the technology.

Before the onset of war, television receivers were treated as a spectacle via exhibitions on both sides of the Atlantic. From 1930, leading television manufacturers in the UK such as Murphy Radio, EKCO and Pye responded to government calls for 'good design' by employing top designers to transform television from a technological marvel to a domestic item. By 1939, about 75% of television consoles were being designed in wood, to convey their dual meaning as technology and 'furniture' (Farr 1955: 72). Some sets were designed with closing doors to conceal the black screen when switched off. Murphy Radio is one example of a company that paid famous furniture designers to style radio and television consoles. Gordon Russell, who led the Utility Furniture Scheme and directed the COID (see Chapter 3), his brother Richard D. Russell, and Eden Minns were architect-trained designers who worked for Murphy by integrating high quality furniture design and craft techniques for near-as-possible mass production. They took on leading roles in shaping the form of the TV set for the British living room.

Television designers dealt with the rise of mass production techniques by adopting the styling of the Modern Movement through the design and display of their wares at national exhibitions. These taste makers performed a vital pedagogical task of shaping consumer aspirations and promoting television as a *legitimate* cultural artefact for the home. By 1939, Britain was leading in sales of TV sets for home consumption against its rivals, the US and Germany. In that year, the radio trade was forecasting that thousands of TV sets would be in homes by Christmas (Moran 2013: 47). Instead, TV broadcasting was closed for the duration of World War II, when less than 1,000 sets were in use among wealthy households that could afford one. The aim was to prevent enemy aircraft homing on the signal transmitted from London and devote engineering and factory production to the advancement of military radio and radar equipment. American manufacturers were able to fill the trade gap and raced ahead as pioneers in television design, exemplified by the 1939–1940 New York World's Fair.

Television technology was introduced to the American public at the vast RCA Pavilion by David Sarnoff, President of RCA (Radio Corporation of America). In a 'Hall of Television' that displayed 13 RCA TRT-12 receivers, visitors could see this new medium in action and also see themselves on television. As a spectacular promotional event, the TRK-12 television set was even taken on board a plane flight and photographed while being watched by passengers four miles above the city (Shapiro 2016: 169). Such was the spectacularisation of the TV set. Television demonstrations also took place at other pavilions such as General Electric's. The RCA Pavilion's television receivers were designed by John Vassos, one of the most influential designers of TV sets in the US and principal consultant designer for RCA from 1932 to 1975 (Schwartz 2006). To convince sceptical visitors that television sets were not a trick, Vassos designed a transparent Lucite plastic case housing a 12-inch TRK-12 receiver for the New York World' Fair which exposed the internal components of the set.

These RCA sets were aimed at the wealthy, conveyed through product styling. By using highly polished wood cabinets made of expensive materials such as walnut, Bakelite, glass and metal, Vassos created luxurious consoles. These designs fused the geometric shapes of Bauhaus functionalism with the softer, popular style of American 'streamlining' (Shapiro 2016: 169). The opulence of these television sets was also signified by high prices from $199.50 to $600 and by sales in New York's luxury department stores: Macy's, Bloomingdale's and Wanamaker's (Schwartz 2006). Advertisements depicted TV viewers sitting at home, or as guests of neighbours' homes, dressed in evening suits and ball gowns. Advertisements also stressed television's link to travel by emphasising that viewers could tour the world from the comfort of the living room. For example, a 1939 advertisement for the TRK-12 proclaims: 'YOU CAN BE IN TWO PLACES AT ONCE WITH RCA VICTOR TELEVISION'.

Alongside advertisements, designers such as Vassos played a major role in guiding potential users in the positioning of this new technology in the home at New York World's Fair. Vassos styled whole living rooms at exhibitions to explain room layout for optimum viewing positions and how to tuck the set away when switched off. Vassos' 'Television Suites' showcased new models in ten different American home settings with television receivers housed in stylish bleached mahogany modular furniture. Vassos also contributed to the 'America at Home' pavilion comprising displays of televisions embedded in model homes. His aim was to use built-in designs in a functional and unobtrusive manner to make the best use of space exemplified by the 'Living Room of the Future', also called the 'Musicorner' by displaying furniture matched with cabinets enclosing the electronic equipment. To appease anxieties about the gaping television eye in the middle of the living room, he designed modular cabinetry in which to slot the television and phonograph. His model living rooms featured indirect lighting and soundproofing, with modern built-in equipment such as combined radio/television/record players all housed in bleached mahogany modular furniture.[1] Imagining the living room as a cosy yet modern media centre, Vassos discarded the now outmoded idea of the formal 'parlour'. These exhibits mark the beginnings of public representations of the ideal *media* home. From now on, the ideal model home at national exhibitions played a major part in endorsing the television's place in the *family* home.

Other major American designers such as Donald Deskey and Russell Wright also performed a promotional and pedagogic role by styling multi-unit display cabinets for the 1939 New York Fair's 'America at Home' pavilion. Together with the work of Vassos, these designs confirmed America's international lead in television set manufacture and sales. Organised as a spectacle, televisions were *publicly domesticated*: contextualised in model home spaces to show potential customers how to organise this new, media home. This media exhibitionism not only marks the celebration of science and technology through domestic styling. With room design now a key strategy for British exhibitions, it also marks the start of the mediatisation of home with designers shaping this technology for the heart of the living room.

Post-war design ideology: designers as moral agents

When TV broadcasting was resumed in Britain in 1946, after World War II in a climate of post-war austerity, British television design was hampered by severe materials shortages. By now, American television product development posed serious competition. Britain's counterattack was the 'good design' movement, endorsed not only by the Arts Council of Great Britain but also the post-war BBC. From 1946, the BBC established an alliance with the COID to promote government design policy via programming. Within a growing commodity culture, television broadcasting and 'good design' became moral agents of national improvement that targeted the family home. In this context, designers mediated between the state, the BBC, the television manufacturers and householders.

In Britain, the challenges were enormous for British broadcasting and manufacturers of consoles. Despite a wealth of pre-war displays of television, the gap in TV broadcasting prompted by the ensuing war meant that the public had forgotten about television and were by now confused about how the machine could be incorporated into home life. Sarah Arnold (2015) offers a fascinating insight into Mass Observation research findings from February 1949 which showed that attitudes towards television sets were mostly negative. This British social research organisation which recorded ordinary working-class people's lives revealed householders' concerns that the console would overcrowd domestic space. It was also commonly assumed that, like cinema, television should be viewed in the dark. Householders were worried that this would prevent audiences from sewing or knitting while watching the screen and would prevent co-present householders from conducting other activities such as reading while fellow householders were watching TV:

A Mrs Barritt cautions as much in her 'housewife's point of view,' whereby she implies that the television set would displace her regular activities (File Report 2903). Alongside viewing conditions, others were concerned about where to situate the television set and how it might compete against other forms of leisure and relaxation. Mary Coates Towers describes a preferred interior design that places the family towards the fireplace and notes that "there just doesn't seem to be anywhere to put it [the television set]." (File Report 1362) The sense in which a television set might overcrowd the domestic space is evident in the remark of Helen Louise Palmer, whose "house is already over full of furniture and anything further would be most unwelcome" (File Report 3418). (Arnold 2015)

Such accounts confirmed the rationale for exhibitions and marketing campaigns to instruct the public about the medium and its benefits.

Leading architects and designers in post-war Britain styled and displayed television receivers at exhibitions and special events such as the 1951 Festival of Britain. Following on from the work of designers such as Vassos at the New York Wold's Fair, famous British designers were not simply involved in designing television for the home. They were also involved in designing model homes for television. Designers of early TV sets such as Wells Coates, as well as Eden Minns, Richard D. Russell and Robin Day became household names through magazine and radio features (Chambers 2019). Robin Day wrote for *Vogue* and *House & Garden* with an April 1949 piece for the latter titled 'Make room for television' which offered advice on how these electronic devices could be incorporated into modern homes. He suggested they could be built into cupboards, bookshelves or disused fireplaces. Consolidating his status as an 'expert' on aesthetics and good taste, he reminded readers that the 'look' of the object was paramount, since the set would be switched off most of the day (Jackson 2001: 74). The combined efforts of these taste makers led to the transformation of television from a machine into a *domestic* cultural item fit for an 'ideal home' (Chambers 2019).

The advent of television in 1950s model living rooms

By 1950, the Ideal Home Exhibition was displaying television consoles in model furnished rooms (Ryan 1997). Yet by now, these bulky sets looked incongruous next to popular, new, spindly 1950s furniture. Designers responded by producing table-top sets with removable spindly legs. Creating a seating problem in the parlour, the question was whether to arrange the chairs around the fireplace or 'electric eye'. One attempt to address the problem at the 1951 Ideal Home Exhibition was a prototype 'fireplace' TV set described as a 'thoroughly modern fireplace, with a single electric fire above which is a built-in television set' (Ryan 1997: 96). The Art Deco styling formed the screen's circular frame, with a tiny electric fire positioned below the screen. Publicised in news and features, post-war Ideal Home Exhibitions' domestic interiors became key platforms for promoting consumer culture.

Earlier trade fairs marketed television to men within established masculine discourses of objective technical rationality. It was approached as a technology for 'boffins' or 'gadget fiends' keen on radios and cars (Hilton 2003: 202). However, the philosophy of the Ideal Home Exhibition accentuated a series of post-war initiatives through which *women* were targeted as new consumer citizens, via design idealism (see Chapters 2 and 3). Whilst men were addressed as rational purchasers of goods, women were addressed as 'good housewives' located in the domestic arena. Women were expected to be concerned with upholding the family's status through material possessions within the post-war rebuilding of family life. As Helen Wheatley states, 'television was at the centre of this narrative of consumer aspiration and affordable luxury at the Ideal Home Exhibition' (Wheatley 2016: 46).

Television figured as a spectacle of modernity at the Festival of Britain in 1951. Advertisements for the medium ensured 'television's placement at the centre of the Festival of Britain's dual aims to celebrate the scientific and cultural achievements of Britain' (Wheatley 2016: 28). More than 20 leading designers and progressive young architects created 'the autobiography of a nation' through a series of themed pavilions including a Television Pavilion. The pavilions' themes formed a story that mapped Britain's past achievements, showing how the nation arrived at today's cutting-edge design and technology. With television receivers displayed in model living rooms in the Homes and Gardens Pavilion as well as the Television Pavilion, this Festival was, then, the first occasion at which many had seen working television sets (Chambers 2019).

Echoing American trends at the time, it was no coincidence that the parlour was replaced by a more informal and flexible open-plan living room in the early 1950s, as mentioned in Chapter 3. This Modernist re-evaluation of the room – originally set aside for receiving guests – coincided with television's arrival in the home. The accent was not only on the equipment's appearance but also on the positioning of the set in this communal room, with viewers gathered around it. Watching television was now conveyed as a resolutely collective, sociable and *modern* family medium experienced in rooms now designed for comfort and set aside for hobbies, radio and gramophone record listening (Chambers, 2016). Emphasising the rise of the 'media home', furniture was now arranged centrally around the TV (Design Council Archive;[2]Jackson 2001: 40–43). Robin Day designed an open-plan living room for the Homes and Garden Pavilion with a Murphy table-top TV placed on a shelf suspended from the wall with '*sectional settee for television viewing*' facing the set (Design Council Archive;[3]Chambers 2019). In this setting, the material shape of early analogue television was staged as an exemplar of science, modernity and good taste in interior décor (Chambers 2019). Yet, paradoxically, women often faced more confinement in this new TV home since, as Spigel indicates in her study of post-war American domestic ideals, the medium was a substitute for public participation (Spigel 1992, 2001).

Domestic television programmes and the scheduling of home life

In the UK, two and a half million private TV sets were in operation by 1953, the year of the Coronation of Queen Elizabeth II. Yet 20 million people watched this major public event on TV (Bussey 1980; Briggs 2000). With so many people gathered in neighbours' homes to watch the ceremony – as well as watching the broadcast in cinemas, church halls, hospitals and other public venues – the televising of the Coronation prompted a boom in the sale of TV sets. The Coronation epitomised the power of television to draw public life into domestic culture and to realign the domestic realm as an integral part of national culture. A decade later, almost every home in the UK housed a TV set with the percentage of TV homes reaching over 80%.[4] Media's arrival into the home allowed intimate access to a public sphere, enabling a sense of national belonging. Together with the scheduling of TV programmes, the televising of national events such as sport and the daily national news, as well as royal ceremonies, facilitated a strong sense of 'nation' and ideas of distant homelands (Morley 1992; Hollows 2008). At the same time, soap operas, sitcoms and programmes on homemaking also invoked traditional and new imaginings of home (Chambers 2016).

In the US, the number of TV homes climbed from 700,000 in 1949 to 26.1 million in 1954 with this number doubling again by 1964. Household viewing in the US rose progressively from 4 hours and 25 minutes per day in 1949 to 5 hours and 25 minutes in 1964 (McGuigan 2015). Spigel develops the term 'home theatre' to explain how television was encountered in mid-1950s America (Spigel 1992). The television screen was habitually characterised as a theatre by broadcasters, advertisers, policymakers, artists, critics, social scientists and engineers. At the same time, home itself was conveyed as a theatrical stage on which family values were performed and perfected through viewing practices that coaxed families to bond together by gathering round the TV 'hearth'. This home theatre comprised, then, a dual interior space: the space of home and the space of the screen projecting programmes about home life from outside the home. Documentaries, sitcoms and soap operas were TV programmes that navigated this double space by projecting images of homemaking and family life by staging 'normal' families and appropriate standards of domestic living organised around middle-class nuclear family values.

Televisual depictions of home life

Radio programme scheduling had already established the routine of creating content that addressed women as housewives after World War II. For example, in the UK, *Woman's Hour*, first broadcast on BBC radio's Light Programme in 1946, invited listeners to decorate and furnish a dream home. Television programmes continued a tradition of joining with women's organisations in a campaign to regard women as experts in their domestic planning. When TV broadcasting was resumed after World War II, the programmes embraced this convention by playing a vital role within homemaking strategies. With no commercial broadcasting until 1955, the BBC commanded the airwaves in the UK, presenting specialist afternoon magazine programmes aimed at women audiences. Programmes such as *Designed for Women* (1947), *For the Housewife* (1948), *Leisure and Pleasure* (1951), *About the Home* (1951) and *Women's Viewpoint* (1951) were devoted to homemaking with advice on household chores, family life and cooking (Chambers 2016).

By addressing women as fulltime housewives, these programmes shared the role of national exhibitions by projecting model homes defined by 'good design' and 'good living' (Irwin 2015; Andrews 2012; Sparke 2004). Some programmes were set in TV studios constructed as middle-class kitchens or living rooms as the back-drop to advice and discussion that fostered middle-class domestic lifestyles centred on consumerism. Marking the beginning of a mediatisation of the home, they coincided with the messages conveyed in women's magazines and home exhibitions by addressing women not just as housewives but as consumer citizens responsible for the array of new appliances designed for the home. Within magazines such as *House and Garden*, this consumerist discourse promoted aspirational living through glimpses of the lifestyles of the rich and famous from members of the royal family to film stars (Irwin 2015: 166). Television programmes also embraced cultural and educational themes in formats that would foreground women's interests as homemakers. For example, architectural programmes offered tributes to 'ideal homes' designed and built in Modernist styles that radiated lav-ishness and affluence during this poignant time of post-war austerity (Irwin 2015). As the following chapters confirm, these early programme themes were the fore-runners of a now well-established tradition of property and lifestyle TV. These TV shows involve a continuous spotlight on home as a context for self-improving lifestyles (Chambers 2016).

In the US, the nuclear family discourse that shaped programming contrasted with broadcasting in the UK. The American media home discourse was centred on commercial imperatives. Spigel explains that television inspired yet also interrupted family ideals and gender roles. Television was akin to 'household cement': it cap-tured the family's attention and rearranged not only the living room furniture but also the family's temporal habits. But television was also blamed for fragmenting families' interests, feminising fathers, and misguiding children (Spigel, 1992). A further public concern was how television was disrupting women's housework tasks. Ambitions for the 'house with the white picket fence' within American suburbia, described in Chapter 3, formed part of a shared national dialogue reflec-ted in television shows and advertising.

With women deemed the archetypal audience, a commercial system of broad-casting in the US involved the sponsorship of advertisements which promoted homemaking as an activity requiring numerous consumer goods. American day-time soap operas slotted into and sustained soap advertisements. As such, large companies such as Procter & Gamble that sold soap and other personal hygiene products at the time had a powerful influence on gendered labour in the home (McGuigan 2015). In these ways, television presented a stylised picture of

American life that served as a key dynamic in the proliferation of middle-class suburban ideals. Through its programming and adverts, this new medium had the capacity to mediate aspirational visions and pervade popular culture. But this daily diet of TV advertisements required time and attention, involving dramatic changes in the social habits of householders.

Soap operas consisted of a succession of brief segments to allow women to watch distractedly while doing housework. Alongside sitcoms, the genre involved narratives of family life that normalised and reinforced women's domestic routines (Spigel 1992). Shows such as *I Love Lucy, The Adventures of Ozzie and Harriet* (1952–1966) and *Father Knows Best* (1954–1960) were organised around notions of a 'family audience' (Haralovich 1992: 111). Television networks and advertisers collaborated in using persuasive visual strategies to shape suburban, middle-class hopes and ambitions. This calculated form of advertising marked the rise of a new kind of media home involving more intensive consumer practices with advertisements and entertainment programmes fuelling aspirations for affluence framed by the psycho-social hegemony of media producers (McCarthy, 2010: 243. Lefebvre, 1984: 91, 122).

Once thought to be based on individual agency, consumer choices were steered by visual commercials displayed in between TV shows, aimed at attuning family audiences to the lifestyles of the characters depicted on the TV shows. TV programmes and advertisements endorsed a particular version of 'family' and 'home' – white and middle-class – as a coveted ideal. Family TV shows also conveyed new cultural values about mid-twentieth-century family life involving new forms of social etiquette. As such, television had a profound influence on the cultural sensitivities and experiences of individuals and families, particularly women as curators of the spatial flows of home life (Spigel 2008:13).

Television scheduling and domestic time

If TV shows altered the way Americans saw the world, they also altered the way Americans viewed themselves on the international stage. Television fostered a sense of nationhood, an awareness of belonging to a nation the heart of home. Benedict Anderson (1991) described this mediated sense of nationhood as an 'imagined community'. In his discussion of the role of newspapers and radio, Anderson explains that the powerful idea of the modern nation state is invoked through the ritual of accessing the news and other nationwide sporting, entertainment and political events from home. A sense of community among anonymous fellow citizens mediated by newspapers and radio engenders a sense of collective consciousness. Similarly, the nationwide spread and arrangement of television broadcasting fostered an awareness of a collective encounter with other audiences – not just by the act of watching but also by the interlinking of TV schedules within household schedules and agendas.

The scheduling of regular programmes such as the news, soap operas and popular dramas in carefully chosen daily and weekly timeslots shaped the routines of households throughout the country to create the sense of a shared domestic identity. This was important, since in television's early years, collective family viewing was not something that emerged spontaneously. As Morley reminds us, 'Not only did the furniture have to be moved around to accommodate TV, but domestic time itself had to be reorganised' (2007: 278). Early television programming was designed to slot into domestic schedules so that programming would reflect or shape daily household rhythms (Scannell 1996; 2000; Gauntlett and Hill 1999). To become a habitual part of domestic life, collective family viewing was carefully coordinated, with meals scheduled to synchronise with TV programme schedules (Gauntlett and Hill 1999). Relating to Anderson's notion of the imagined nation, Paddy Scannell addresses the temporal flow of television to foreground the *dayliness* of its broadcast content. With their emphasis on the 'here and now', news, live sport and other national events were genres organised to integrate with domestic time. Scannell argues that this 'dayliness' of radio and television broadcasting and the liveness of news gives rise to a new kind of *mediated* time, one that fosters nationwide, public and community times.

Early television's temporal characteristics of liveness and regular scheduling ensured that the privatised home came to be structured by a mediated temporal logic that connected viewing to public time. Yet, simultaneously, this daily routine of home-based television viewing established the ordinariness and predictability of broadcasting and the normality of those domestic routines. This temporal ordering of the day, week, month and year through broadcasting schedules became so habitual that its impact on housebound routines went unnoticed (Scannell 2000: 19–21; Gauntlett and Hill 1999). In these ways, television viewing adapted to and shaped household and family routines as part of the spatial dynamics of the home (Chambers 2016). A key question raised in Chapter 6 on the contemporary digital home is whether this temporal logic endures in today's multiscreen living room.

Household dynamics in the TV home

Although 'home' invokes a peaceful retreat from the bustle of the outside world, media technology's entrance into home space was often a troubling and disruptive experience. Television's presence in the living room generated palpable home precarities. If broadcasting offered a sense of 'imagined community' by connecting individual homes together, domestic television was blamed for splintering families within the home itself. Arguments over what to watch and about the repetitive and consuming nature of television, particularly for children, coincided with concerns about the loss of conversation among families. Open-plan kitchens in modern homes from the 1960s onwards provided communal living areas that allowed housewives to keep an eye on children and chat while making family meals (Cieraad 2006; Morley 2007). However, family viewing in open-plan spaces began to generate discord among householders who were engaged in different projects within these communal spaces. The introduction of transistorised portable devices addressed the dilemma. The positioning of smaller and lighter TV sets around the home triggered new viewing habits matched by advances in programmes, scheduling and domestic central heating. The rise in various electronic gadgets in the home during this period accelerated householders' demands to practice more personalised home-based pursuits. Disrupting early television's ideals of shared space, household dynamics shifted from albeit precarious communal activities to individualised activities (Hirsch 1992; Silverstone 1991). Portable TV came to symbolise individual use with the rise of more individualised devices to resolve family fights over programme choice (Cieraad 2006). Home-based access to cable, satellite and video conjured ideas of a decline in family-centred viewing and concerns about the rise of individualised and anti-social media-centred activities (Hirsch 1992; see Chapter 6).

This dispersal of household members into separate rooms sparked anxieties, then, about disrupted communal viewing habits in the living room. Children tended to watch TV in their bedrooms, while parents watched in the living room. By the 1980s, 80% of British households were scattered across separate rooms (Gauntlet and Hill 1999). Initial accounts of TV in advertisements and magazines as a 'harmonising' force were gradually supplanted by imaginaries of individuals entertained separately, as isolated audiences. This was accompanied by criticisms about the unhealthy nature of solitary viewing. Such fears triggered nostalgic memories of an already departed golden age of television and family togetherness. On the one hand, TV was regarded as a wholesome family activity that encouraged children to engage in family time. On the other hand, children were marked out as potentially passive audiences. These concerns revealed the ideological tensions associated with the rise of the media home in the US and UK (Spigel 1992; Chambers 2016).

By the 1980s and 1990s media research confirmed that television can both disperse and also augment family subgroups and subsystems. Studies found that television can foster or cement emotional ties between mothers and daughters, fathers and sons or grandparents and grandchildren (Livingstone and Das 2010; Gillespie 1995; Livingstone 2002). To understand how householders manage this separation and togetherness, James Lull (1990) examined the role of television within householders' domestic routines. Assessing interpersonal engagement with TV, Lull explains that television tends to be used as a form of 'affiliation or avoidance': television viewing can act as a communication facilitator by drawing the family together and sparking dialogue or it can generate tensions among household members (Lull 1990: 36). Householders acquire an awareness of and sensitivity towards each other's domestic television preferences and habits. By consciously planning viewing schedules at separate times or in separate rooms, this awareness of each other's predilections can help avoid frictions about when, what and how to watch television content (see O'Brien and Rodden 1997). Householders generate feelings of collective identity by dividing up and individualising media activities in the home as part of the strategies of living together (Lally 2002). With frictions often arising when a child or adult monopolises the music system or main television screen in the living room, new parent-child dynamics emerge. Householders find new means of coping with the challenges of living together in a media home. These new dynamics led to the rise of children's media-rich bedrooms, home-based video gaming and the entrance of computers into home life.

Domesticating computers

Following television's entrance into domestic space, a new range of media technologies began moving into the home including personal computers (PCs), cable, home video players and video game consoles. A variety of Internet services such as online information, shopping and banking became available from the 1980s and 1990s. The arrival of computer technologies in the home began to upset time-honoured distinctions between work and home life. Indeed, home itself was now defined by the media technologies that inhabited that intimate space (Morley 2007: 214). Towards the end of the twentieth century, these novel media devices were contesting the idea of home as a 'haven from work'. During this period, a research tradition known as domestication theory gained momentum to explain the distinctive stages of media technologies' adoption and domestication in the home. Domestication theory addressed the role media technologies play in home life, the contexts in which they are experienced, and their meanings to householders (see for example, Silverstone and Haddon, 1996; Silverstone and Hirsch, 1992).

The domestication approach explains the acquisition of technologies, and their positioning, uses and adaptation to the dynamics of home living. Studies found that, as part of the process of domestication, householders developed distinctive social habits to negotiate the integration computers and other media equipment into home life (Bakardjieva, 2006; Lally, 2002; Bergman and van Zoonen, 1999; Ward, 2006; Haddon, 2003). Householders make far-reaching decisions about where to place the device, how and when to use it, for what purposes and in what situations. The computer equipment's positioning and repeated use facilitates its ongoing assimilation into householders' daily routines (Silverstone 2006). For householders, media domestication involves a continuous and active process of adjustment. The object appears less alien and more familiar as it is gradually integrated into the daily routines of the household (Haddon 2003; Silverstone and Haddon 1996).

Domestication research revealed close links between the design of media technologies and the reproduction of gendered power relations supported by the ethnographic research of British Cultural Media Studies. For example, studies of family TV viewing practices in the living room by David Morley (1980 and 1986) revealed gender and generational discord and the power dynamics played out in resolving those tensions. Research uncovered family arguments over who gets control over the TV tuner and then the remote control (see, for example, Morley 1986). Morley found gender disparities in decisions about what TV programmes to watch as a family group in the living room. Fathers were inclined to take control of programme selection and commandeer the remote-control device to engage in 'channel hopping'. Underpinned by these findings, studies of information and communication technology uses (ICTs) in the 1990s identified how UK householders used their televisions, landline telephones and how they engaged in paid work supported by computers, referred to as 'teleworking'. The research included studies of how single parents and the young elderly used computers (Silverstone 1999; Haddon 2001). Importantly, Haddon and Silverstone (1995) differentiated the 'home' from 'household' to understand the distinctions between the idea of home as an emotional place of belonging, security or unease and the way that daily routines interrelate with material resources such as media devices. They also identified key stages within the process of domestication that underpin the integration of the media technologies in the home and the ensuing interactions between household members. These stages comprised commodification, appropriation, objectification, incorporation and conversion.

'Commodification' involves a pre-adoption phase when the consumer seeks information about the media device and plans its assignment in the home. 'Appropriation' entails the process of buying the device including the moment when it is placed in the home and starts to be used. The next stage of 'objectification' refers to the point when the technology's various affordances are discovered and the potential of the technology is delved into. The following phase of 'incorporation' is one where the device is integrated into the daily routines and habits of the household through regular use. Finally, 'conversion' involves the following stage when the object becomes commonplace yet, at the same time, functions to augment the households' status, for example, among neighbours or visitors. During this phase, a process of 'continuous negotiation' occurs in which the object's meanings may stabilise as it becomes assimilated into the daily practices of the household. If the device is then linked to another device, it is likely to go through a stage of redefinition as the object is converted by being combined with, say, a computer or smart TV. And if a TV set is moved from the living room to a bedroom, it is redefined as 'older' while a newer and model takes over the living room (Quandt and von Pape 2010).

Silverstone and Haddon (1996) then went on to explain an additional set of processes, of 'double articulation' and 'moral economy' of the household. Double articulation draws attention to the dual qualities of media in the home: both its physical and technological dimensions and its symbolic dimensions of content and programming. This underlines media's role as a material object and conveyor of media messages. The migration of media object from the formal economy of the marketplace to the moral economy of the household involves palpable home precarities. It requires householders to protect their well-being against the continuous risks associated with the media home: from inappropriate content to digital surveillance. The moral principles and values of a household are inevitably affected and often undermined by the introduction of media technologies and content in the home. The layout of the home and choices available for the positioning of media objects such as computers influences their use by children and adults. How these media are positioned and used can transform not only the way we use media equipment but the whole atmosphere of the home. For instance, a device such as a television or gaming console positioned in the shared space of the living room will be domesticated in dramatically different ways from one placed in a child's bedroom or a communal kitchen.

Moral economy refers, then, to the sensitive and often fraught negotiations involved in household decisions about where to place the device, how to use it, who will use it and for how long (Silverstone 1994; Silverstone and Hirsch 1992). For instance, parents experience frustrations in curbing and supervising children and teenagers' uses of TV and computer screen time to safeguard them from inappropriate content and protect school homework time. In their desire to shield children from unsuitable Internet content, parents adopt various strategies to juggle children's education and entertainment uses of media. The negotiations, bargaining and contracts involved can be so relentless that these strategies have transformed late modern parenting practices (see Chambers 2016; Livingstone et al. 2014; Clark 2013). The term 'media parenting' highlights the moral dilemmas underpinning the selection of media equipment suitable for children and patterns of media use adopted by children at home, echoing wider public unease about the potentially disruptive features of today's digital media (also see Chapter 6).

By the 1990s popular media discourses such as lifestyle magazines, newspapers and computer periodicals were depicting images of how computers could be integrated into household agendas. Computers were marketed as devices for working from home, helping to compile household budgets and used as educational tools to help with children's homework (Lally 2002). Importantly, the advent of 'interactive technologies' implied that white-collar workers would work at home (Hamill 2011). The incorporation of computers into the daily routines of the household changed the temporal rhythms of home life. Not only was furniture reorganised around the technology (Lally 2002), but also computers and the Internet extended women's feminine roles of maintaining personal and family networks (Bergman and van Zoonen 1999). Studies of paid office work from home, known as 'teleworking', by Haddon and Silverstone in 1992 uncovered gender differences in use as part of responses to work problems prompted by aspirations to escape commuting, support alternative working patterns or entrepreneurship, and ways of managing redundancy. Women were most likely to adopt teleworking to cope with rising tensions between their domestic and paid work.

Following studies confirmed that technical interests and competences associated with new media technologies are initially ascribed to men, making access to the equipment more problematic for women. Seldom presented as experts, women tend to be portrayed as consumers of the technology. Using computers to work from home initially gave women opportunities to manage their domestic roles so that they could fit their paid work around housework and childcare. But paid work spilled over into home life by eroding personal free time (Haddon and Silverstone 1993, 1995). The technology was given a level of agency that could spark tensions around domestic spatial and temporal routines concerning decisions about such as where to place the computer, how children can use it – whether for gaming or educational purposes – and for how long. Ward (2006) also found that family members assigned status to the computer within a structure of domestic meaning by organising home life around zones of 'work' and 'leisure'. The entrance of computers into the home generally signified 'work' to these families in the sense that computers were perceived as enabling 'home-work'.

In these early days of home computers, it was found that householders used a range of distinctive strategies to cope with ICTs by generating symbolic or spatial zones to differentiate between times and spaces devoted to family, leisure and work. For instance, laptops were often placed in upstairs rooms to reflect their work role while the large TV screen was placed downstairs within a space set aside for leisure. Users often held two separate email addresses, one for work and one for social contacts. This encroachment of work into home life was one of the most significant features of domesticating ICTs. Not only were computers domesticated by the performance of paid work at home. The extension of computer-oriented work experiences into the private sphere also transformed the organisation of wider home life. As well as gendered and generational issues, the use of ICTs by single parents uncovered significant social class issues. It was found that access to media technologies by lone mothers on low incomes was restricted by the high costs of equipment and landline telephone use (Haddon 2001; Haddon and Silverstone 1995). Notwithstanding these constraints of social class and gender, early domestication research on the entrance of computers into the home uncovered the importance of household agency as a central feature of the micro-dynamics of everyday home life.

Conclusion

Chronicling the rise of the media home through the example of television and computers, this chapter demonstrates the multiple and complex ways in which the entry of media equipment into the home reshapes the spatial and temporal flows of home life. In mid-twentieth-century Britain and America, 'home' was reconfigured as a mediatised space in distinctive but overlapping ways, reflecting the cultural dynamics of each country. The rise of the media-rich home coincided with the rise of a post-war consumer society characterised by domestic modernity and suburbanisation. Before television became a taken-for-granted part of everyday life, the aim of governments, industrial designers, manufacturers, exhibitions and broadcasters was to mobilise distinctive imaginaries of a 'television home' in order to persuade householders to adopt the medium.

Home life was reconfigured not only by the design of the technology but also the content of TV programmes that reflected back to family viewers images of 'normal' homes and 'normal' family life. Research on early television reveals the extensive efforts that went into shaping and normalising television as a technology destined for the home. The scheduling of programmes at specific times of the day, week and year was devised to slot into and shape the intricate routines of households. Moreover, by developing a new kind of relationship with the public sphere, television challenged traditional meanings of home as a 'private' space. Affording a connection with public events, from national ceremonies to sports and news events, television generated a sense of national culture, by creating a sense of belonging to a nation. Yet pessimistic views about this new technology were accompanied by concerns that television viewing would weaken family ties, distract women from housework and undermine national pride.

The chapter has also addressed domestication theory by offering a lens through which to consider the allied early introduction of computers into the home. The domestication approach draws attention to householders' agency in the adoption process, by attending to the ways that ICTs were integrated into existing routines. It emphasises the active role played by computer users who worked from home. Not only did computers reshape work life as part of the domestication and organisation of the computer to adapt to home life. The home itself transformed into a new zone of work and entertainment. Research has revealed the moral economy of households by addressing the ensuing tensions generated by computers' presence in the home, resulting from disrupted home routines and the opening up of new relationships between home and work. Taken as a whole, studies of the entrance of early media into the home indicate that these media and communication technologies have both challenged and consolidated ideas about domestic space, traditional domestic routines and household dynamics in distinctive classed, generational and gendered ways. Together, these cultural forces point to the rise of the 'media home'.

Notes

1   See Musicorner room designed by John Vassos displayed at the American at Home Pavilion, 1940 New York World's Fair, Research Collections, Archives of American Art, Smithsonian Institute, available at www.aaa.si.edu/collections/items/detail/musicorner-room-designed-john-vassos-displayed-american-home-pavilion-1940-new-york-worlds-fair-8172 (accessed 17 September 2016).
2   Design Archives, University of Brighton, Festival of Britain 1951, Homes and Gardens Pavilion, THE PARLOUR: designed by Eden Minns F.S.I.A. and Bianca Minns, available at https://vads.ac.uk/large.php?uid=82063&sos=7 (accessed 1 August 2019).
3   Design Archives, University of Brighton, Festival of Britain 1951, Homes and Gardens Pavilion. ENTERTAINMENT AT HOME: Designed by Robin Day, available at https://vads.ac.uk/large.php?uid=82052&sos=8 (accessed 1 August 2019).
4   Broadcasters' Audience Research Board (2019) Television ownership in private domestic households 1956–2018, available at https://www.barb.co.uk/resources/tv-ownership/ (accessed 1 August 2019).

References

Anderson, B. (1991) *Imagined Communities: Reflections on the Origin and Spread of Nationalism*. London: Verso.
Andrews, M.(2012) *Domesticating the Airwaves: Broadcasting, Domesticity and Femininity*. London:Continuum.
Arnold, S. (2015) 'Setting the television set scene', CTS online, 19 November 2015. https://cstonline.net/setting-the-television-set-scene-by-sarah-arnold-2/ (accessed 16 May 2019).
Bakardjieva, M. (2006) 'Domestication running wild: From the moral economy of the household to the mores of a culture', in T. Berker, M. Hartmann, Y. Punie and K. Ward (eds), *Domestication of Media and Technology*. Maidenhead: Open University Press, pp. 62–79.
Bergman, S. and van Zoonen, L. (1999) 'Fishing with false teeth: Women, gender and the internet', in J. Downey and J. McGuigan (eds), *Technocities*. London: Sage, pp. 91–108.
Briggs, A. (1979) *The History of Broadcasting in the United Kingdom, Vol. 4: Sound and Vision*. Oxford: Oxford University Press (Reprinted 2000).

Bussey, G. (1979) *The Story of Pye Wireless, 50th Anniversary: Formation of Pye Radio Limited*. Croydon: Pye Limited and Gordon Bussey.

Castells, M. (1996) *The Rise of the Network Society*. Oxford: Blackwell.

Chambers, D. (2016) *Changing Media, Home and Households: Cultures, Technologies and Meanings*. London: Routledge.

Chambers, D. (2019) 'Designing early television for the ideal home: The roles of industrial designers and exhibitions, 1930s –1950s', *Journal of Popular Television*, 7(2), 145–159.

Cieraad, I. (2006) 'Introduction: Anthropology at home', in I. Cieraad (ed.), *At Home: An Anthropology of Domestic Space*. Syracuse, NY: Syracuse University Press, pp. 1–12.

Clark, L.S. (2013) *The Parent App: Understanding Families in the Digital Age*. Oxford: Oxford University Press.

Council of Industrial Design. (1950) Id Number Current Repository: DCA0147, Ideal Home Exhibition. Brighton: Design Council, Design Archives, University of Brighton Design Archives. www.vads.ac.uk/ large.php?uid=79941&sos=1 (accessed 20 May 2018).

Curtis, B. (1998) 'Daily Mail Ideal Home Exhibition: The ideal home: through the twentieth century', *Journal of Design History*, 11(3), 266–268.

Ellis, J. (1992) *Visible Fictions: Cinema, Television, Video*. London: Routledge.

Fachel Leal, O. (1990) 'Popular taste and erudite repertoire: The place and space of television in Brazil', *Cultural Studies*, 4(1), 19–29.

Farr, M. (1955) *Design in British Industry: A Mid-century Survey*. Cambridge: Cambridge University Press.

Gauntlett, D. and Hill, A. (1999) *TV Living: Television Culture and Everyday Life*. London: Routledge.

Gillespie, M. (1995) Television, Ethnicity and Cultural Change. London:Routledge.

Gregg, M. (2011) *Work's Intimacy*. Malden, MA: Polity Press.

Haddon, L.(2001)Time and ICTs. Paper presented at the workshop 'Researching Time', ESRC Centre for Research on Innovation and Competition (CRIC), University of Manchester, 19 September 2001. http://www.lse.ac.uk/media@lse/whosWho/Academ icStaff/LeslieHaddon/Time.pdf (accessed 7 December 2019).

Haddon, L. (2003) 'Domestication and mobile telephony', in J. Katz (ed.), *Machines that Become Us: The Social Context of Personal Communication Technology*. New Brunswick: Transaction Publishers, pp. 43–56.

Haddon, L. (2006) 'The contribution of domestication research to home computing and media consumption', *The Information Society*, 22(4), 195–203.

Haddon, L. and Silverstone, R. (1993) 'Teleworking in the 1990s: A view from the home'. SPRU/CICT Report Series, No. 10, University of Sussex, Falmer.

Haddon, L. and Silverstone, R. (1995) 'Lone parents and their information and communication technologies'. SPRU/CICT Report Series, No. 12, University of Sussex, Falmer.

Hamill, L. (2011) 'Changing times: Home life and domestic habit', in R. Harper (ed.), *The Connected Home: The Future of Domestic Life*. London: Springer, pp. 29–58.

Haralovich, M.B. (1992) 'Sit-coms and suburbs: Positioning the 1950s homemaker', in L. Spigel and D. Mann (eds), *Private Screenings: Television and the Female Consumer*. Minneapolis: University of Minnesota Press, pp. 111–142.

Hilton, M. (2003) *Consumerism in Twentieth-century Britain: The Search for a Historical Movement*. Cambridge: Cambridge University Press.

Hirsch, E. (1992) 'New technologies and domestic consumption', in R. Silverstone and E. Hirsch (eds), *Consuming Media Technologies: Media and Information in Domestic Spaces*. London: Routledge, pp. 208–226.

Hollows, J. (2008) *Domestic Cultures*. Maidenhead: Open University Press.

Irwin, M.(2015) 'BBC's Wednesday Magazine and Arts televison for women', *Media History*, 21(2), 162–177.

Jackson, L. (2001) *Robin & Lucienne Day: Pioneers of Contemporary Design*. London: Mitchell Beazley.

Lally, E. (2002) *At Home with Computers*. Berg: Oxford.

Lefebvre, H. (1984) *Everyday Life in the Modern World*. New Brunswick: Transaction Publishers.

Livingstone, S. (2002) *Young People and New Media: Childhood and the Changing Media Environment*. London: Sage Publications.

Livingstone, S. (2014) 'Digital media and children's rights', blog post, LSE Media Policy Project. http://blogs.lse.ac.uk/mediapolicyproject/2014/09/12/sonia-livingstonedigital-media-and-childrens-rights/ (accessed 5 December 2015).

Livingstone, S. and Das, R. (with contributions from M. Georgiou, L. Haddon, E. Helsper and Y. Wang) (2010) 'Media, Communication and Information Technologies in the European Family', Working Report (April 2010), Family Platform, Existential Field 8. http://eprints.lse.ac.uk/29788/1/EF8_LSE_MediaFamily_Education.pdf (accessed 7 December 2019).

Lull, J.(1990) *Inside Family Viewing: Ethnographic Research on Television's Audiences*. London: Routledge.

McCarthy, A. (2010) *The Citizen Machine: Governing by Television in 1950s America*. New York: The New Press.

McGuigan, L. (2015) 'Procter & Gamble, mass media, and the making of American life', *Media, Culture & Society*, 37(6), 887–903.

Mellencamp, P. (1990) 'TV time and catastrophe: Or, beyond the pleasure principle of television', in P. Mellencamp (ed.), *Logics of Television: Essays in Cultural Criticism*. London: BFI, pp. 240–266.

Miller, D. (2012) *Tales from Facebook*. Cambridge: Polity Press.

Miller, D. (2018) 'Interior decoration – Offline and online', in A.J. Clarke (ed.), *Design Anthropology: Object Cultures in Transition*. London: Bloomsbury, pp. 169–178.

Moran, J. (2013) *Armchair Nation: An Intimate History of Britain in Front of the TV*. London: Profile books.

Morley, D. (1980) *The 'Nationwide' Audience: Structure and Decoding*. London: BFI.

Morley, D. (1986) *Family Television: Cultural Power and Domestic Leisure*. London: Comedia.

Morley, D. (1992) *Television, Audiences and Cultural Studies*. London: Routledge.

Morley, D. (2007) *Media, Modernity and Technology: The Geography of the New*. London: Routledge.

O'Brien, J. and Rodden, T. (1997) 'Interactive systems in domestic environments', in *Proceedings of the 2nd ACM Conference on Designing Interactive Systems: Processes, Practices, Methods, and Techniques*. New York: Association for Computing Machinery, pp. 247–259.

Quandt, T. and von Pape, T. (2010) 'Living in the mediatope: A multimethod study on the evolution of media technologies in the domestic environment', *The Information Society*, 26(5), 330–345.

Radio Times. (1938) 'Television: 8 to 20 April', pp. 16–21.

Ryan, D. (1997) *The Ideal Home Exhibition through the Twentieth Century*. London: Hazar publishing.

Scannell, P. (1996) *Radio, Television, and Modern Life: A Phenomenological Approach*. Oxford: Blackwell.

Scannell, P. (2000) 'For anyone-as-someone structures', *Media, Culture and Society*, 22(1), 5–24.

Schwartz, D. (2006) 'Modernism for the masses: The industrial design of John Vassos', *Archives of American Art Journal*, 46(1/2), 4–23.

Shapiro, D. (2016) *John Vassos: Industrial Design for Modern life*. Minneapolis: University of Minnesota Press.

Silverstone, R. (1991) *Beneath the Bottom Line: Households and Information and Communication Technologies in the Age of the Consumer*. PICT Policy Research Papers, No. 17. Oxford: PICT.

Silverstone, R. (1994) *Television and Everyday Life*. London: Routledge.

Silverstone, R. (1999) *Why Study the Media?*London: Sage.

Silverstone, R. and Haddon, L. (1996) 'Design and the domestication of information and communication technologies: Technical change and everyday life', in R. Silverstone and R. Mansell (eds), *Communication by Design: The Politics of Information and Communication Technologies*. Oxford: Oxford University Press, pp. 44–74.

Silverstone, R.(2006) 'Domesticating Domestication: Reflections on the Life of a Concept', in T.Berker, M.Hartmann, Y.Punie and K.Ward (eds) *Domestication of Media and Technologies*. Maidenhead:Open University Press, pp. 229–247.

Silverstone, R. and Hirsch, E. (eds) (1992) *Consuming Technologies: Media and Information in Domestic Spaces*. London: Routledge.

Sparke, P.(2004) 'Studying the modern home', *The Journal of Architecture*, 9(4), pp. 413–417.

Spigel, L. (1992) *Make Room for TV: Television and the Family Ideal in Postwar America*. Chicago: University of Chicago Press.

Spigel, L. (2001) *Welcome to the Dreamhouse: Popular Media and Postwar Suburbia*. Durham, NC: Duke University Press.

Spigel, L., Brunsdon, C. and Spigel, L. (eds) (2008). *Feminist Television Criticism: A Reader*, 2nd edn. Maidenhead: McGraw Hill and Open University Press.

Vickery, A. (1993) 'Golden age to separate spheres? A review of the categories and chronology of English women's history', *The Historical Journal*, 36(2), 383–414.

Ward, K. (2006) 'The bald guy just ate an orange: Domestication, work and home', in T. Berker, M. Hartmann, Y. Punie and K. Ward (eds), *Domestication of Media and Technology*. Maidenhead: Open University Press, pp. 145–164.

Wellman, B. and Haythornthwaite, C. (2002) *The Internet in Everyday Life*. Oxford: Blackwell.

Wheatley, H. (2016) 'Television in the ideal home', in R. Moseley, H. Wheatley and H. Wood (eds), *Television for Women*. London: Routledge, pp. 205–222.

Williams, R. (1974) *Television: Technology and Cultural Form*. London: Fontana.

5

PROPERTY DRAMAS AND HOME MAKEOVERS

Introduction

Having addressed the ways in which the early home adoption of media technologies shaped ideas about home and home life, this chapter looks at another dimension of home mediatisation. It examines television programmes and social media networks that, together, idealise 'home' and cast light on home precarities associated with property ownership after the global economic crisis of 2008. The chapter is divided into two sections. First, it assesses how homes are conveyed in lifestyle and property TV programmes relating to house-buying and home makeovers. Second, it considers how homemaking is performed and re-enacted, mainly by women, via social media. Although 'home' has never been a place where we just happen to live, today our ideas about home are now mainly experienced remotely. Presentations of home makeovers and renovations are continually projected into the heart of our living rooms and on our smart devices, fuelling dreams of owning and improving our homes. Home renovations and home improvements within reality TV and lifestyle TV formats form part of today's promotional makeover culture. Programmes about house-buying and interior design were popularised in the 1980s and 1990s. During this period, television emerged as a new gatekeeper for aspirational and transformational domestic living, coinciding with a wider trend of home ownership in countries such as the US, UK, Canada and Australia. This trend raises important questions about how home makeover TV and programmes on home improvements have shaped and affected dominant ideas about home and our everyday experiences of home.

Property TV programmes use subtle yet potent visual signifiers to influence audience views of home ownership and décor aesthetics. This type of lifestyle television conveys a prosperous society where individuals and families have the resources to enact a distinctive kind of self-improvement through reflexive consumption (McElroy 2017: 530). Alongside a range of magazines devoted to style and taste in the home, television became a major catalyst for the rise of middle-class idealism. The arrival of social media in the early twenty-first century then sparked a new, coinciding and complementary layer of communication about the ideal home. This interactive medium offers householders new opportunities to curate ideas from design blogs and social media platforms such as Pinterest and Instagram. However, a key question also concerns how representations of home on lifestyle and property TV have changed after the 2008 recession.

Remarkably, the popularity in property TV intensified after the global financial crash of 2008, at a point when home ownership was actually on the wane. But these programmes changed dramatically in response to the economic crisis of 2008. Foregrounding a subsequent depreciation of real-estate prices, the financial crash triggered a boom in real estate TV shows on lifestyle networks, particularly in homeowning cultures. This trend forms part of what has been referred to as 'the culture of real estate' (Hanan 2010: 177). The chapter examines home makeover and property TV shows before and after the global financial crisis. It asks why and how television became such an influential medium, not only in the evolution of home décor but also after the global economic crisis. Two significant issues are highlighted in this chapter. The first is the culpability of property and lifestyle TV with regard to the financial crisis of 2008. The second is how dreams of home ownership and exploitations of home dispossessions have been projected in gender-bound ways as post-crisis forms of entertainment.

The shift and adaptation of design advice to blogs and social media sites such as Pinterest, Facebook, and Instagram involves photos, written advice, videos and podcasts. These sites highlight the ways in which personal identity is shaped by and expressed via social media to promote the idea of a *curative self*. They foreground the idea of the home as a curative space by drawing on various televisual techniques from lifestyle and home makeover TV programmes including behavioural tests, lifestyle coaching and role modelling. With the help of social media platforms, lifestyle gurus and online microcelebrities, social media users have access to a whole catalogue of ideas, guidance and online groups based on similar lifestyle aspirations. The second section therefore explores the digital logic of 'lifestyle' culture to understand the ways in which the home is approached as a curative space to form part of mediated lifestyles and 'domestic design therapy'.

Lifestyle and property TV

Home decoration and makeover shows form part of a wider set of programmes about food, health and personal grooming that show viewers how to manage and enhance their daily lives through a continuous stream of advice. Television's role in promoting visual home aspirations gathered momentum in the late 1990s when many Americans relied on credit debt to access the trappings of affluence such as expensive cars, furnishings and simulated designer furniture. During this period, chains of domestic merchandise retail stores such as IKEA, Bed Bath & Beyond and

Target took advantage of shrinking middle-class budgets to sell cheap imitations of designer goods. The spread of didactic approaches in TV shows and social media is accompanied by the rise of the celebrity lifestyle guru. Endorsed by their highly visible daily lives, these branded 'experts' have come to take on instructional roles as lifestyle specialists. Celebrity gurus occupy the realm of the 'popular', a public sphere mediated by film, magazines, television and social media where affect is privileged over meaning or information.

Forming part of this wider constellation of lifestyle and makeover TV programmes hosted by celebrity gurus, it is no accident that property TV emerged in Britain, Australia, Canada and the USA where home ownership and residential mobility are comparatively high. Political and media discourse on homes and housing in these regions are underpinned by the enduring idea that a property-owning nation is a democratic nation. Home ownership accords with the rise of consumer culture, DIY and a tradition of renovation and makeover among mainly middle-class homeowners. They adopt the tools and skills of manual and craft work to fulfil the aspirational desires for 'domestic transformation' (Rosenberg 2011: 175). Of course, homeowners' reasons for taking up DIY are varied: some are keen DIYers, others gain a feeling of satisfaction and enhanced sense of identity and many engage in DIY to save money. But most property TV audiences simply watch these programmes for pleasure (Williams 2008).

Although the genre of property TV has distinctive national nuances, it is a global phenomenon signposted by the transnational export of programmes such as the BBC's *Changing Rooms* (1996–2004) and USA's *Trading Places* (2002–2004). Property TV is characterised by the transmission of anxieties and ambiguities associated with changing gender dispositions and post-financial crisis housing conditions (Druick 2017). Makeover reality television uses a problem-solving narrative to makeover or reinvent ordinary people (Hollows 2016: 113–117). Narrative constructions around intimacy and emotion work to appeal to its audiences (Druick 2017; Bruce 2009; Dubrofsky 2009; Skeggs and Wood 2012; and Woods 2014.) Within these narrative strategies, lifestyle gurus host property TV shows by presenting themselves as dependable experts who provide practical advice and emotional support in house-buying and homemaking choices.

In the UK, property TV grew as a genre in response to the housing boom and associated surge in home improvement projects in the 1980s and 1990s. This surge was a response to government policies that promoted the dream of home ownership during the Conservative Thatcher government (1979 to 1990). These policies included the privatising of social housing and widening access to mortgage loans (Heywood, 2011: 3). The 'Right to Buy' scheme introduced in 1980, gave secure tenants of council houses the legal right to buy the council at a large discount (Clarke 2001: 23). Three years later, mortgage interest tax relief was introduced to encourage home ownership, known as MIRAS (mortgage interest relief at source). However, government ambitions of upholding a home ownership democracy have been undermined by low-wage households disadvantaged by insecure tenures and a market of escalating rents (Ronald 2014). Whilst countries in Europe such as

France and Germany offer assured long hold tenancies, UK tenants have shorthold tenancies of six months to a year.

These conditions are likely to be contributing factors in the sustained desire for home ownership in the UK. If the idea of home ownership as personal achievement was fanned by widening access to mortgages and lack of secure renting choices, these schemes also triggered a surge in house prices. The creation of new financial loan schemes and the use of house wealth as collateral for additional consumer spending intensified the commodification of home (Blunt and Dowling 2006). This was accompanied by new uses of household income on home improvements that supported a repertoire of taste cultures. It was in this climate that a new kind of television programming on home improvements emerged. By the 1990s, home improvement and interior design was a well-established part of lifestyle TV. Fuelled by ease of access to mortgages, the rejuvenated demand for home ownership transformed 'home' into a televisual spectacle.

In the US, television also formed an ideological point of reference for attaining the 'American dream' of home ownership by 'dictating the stylistic values of ordinary citizens in ways unimaginable with print and radio' (Akira and Larry Ossei-Mensah 2014: 331). Property and lifestyle reality TV took off with the launch of HGTV, an American basic cable and satellite television channel. Launched in 1994, the HGTV channel itself broadcasts reality programming devoted to lifestyle, home improvements and real estate (Matheson, 2010; Shimpach, 2012). HGTV is part of Scripps Networks Interactive, a multimedia lifestyle network that added five cable stations between 1997 and 2004 including Food Network, the Cooking Channel, the DIY Network, Great American Country and Travel Channel. It defines itself as 'the global leader in lifestyle media'. HGTV is the most successful channel reaching almost 100 million US television homes via basic cable packages with a regular audience of 1–2 million viewers (White 2017). These shows 'demonstrate the rewards of investing time, money, and effort in domestic space, even if that just means watching HGTV' (White 2017: 576).

By the first decade of the twenty-first century, property TV extended to incorporate aspirational real-estate series that emphasised the financial value of the home. As a cultural form, reality entertainment TV works to transform the apparently vulnerable, 'at-risk' citizen into self-directed, conscientious and enterprising individuals (Ouellette and Hay, 2008b). Importantly, the appeal of these programmes extends way beyond those aspiring to buy or renovate a home. The genre taps into and relies on a wider consumer aspirational discourse and sensibility, typifying neoliberal ideas of social mobility, personal aspirations and agency. As these shows became lucrative merchandises, they were traded as formats to a global television market (Moran 2009). For example, in addition to conveying the advice of property experts, property TV programmes rely heavily on online advertising revenue such as Amazon books' *Housebuilder's Bible 12*, retailers, and renovating equipment such as automatic loft ladders.

Significantly, the Scripps TV channels in the US have assembled a range of lifestyle-entertainment media and network branded goods to cater for home décor, design and refurbishment. To tap into the expertise of their TV property and design gurus, the HGTV channel introduced an *HGTV Magazine* in 2011 and licenses a variety of home products with mid-range and high-end market brands from furniture to flooring to tempt audiences to embellish their homes. Bolstered by this array of accompanying merchandise sales, it is in the interests of these property channels to present an optimistic and idealistic vision of residential property ventures. However, in the aftermath of the global economic crisis of 2008, dramatic changes occurred in popular cultural depictions of homes, residential properties and the domestic sphere. Some go so far as to argue that property television programmes augmented the 2008 global economic crisis since it was centred in the US housing market (Akira and Ossei-Mensah 2014).

The 2008 housing market crash

In response to the demand for property in the US, a surge of opportunistic mortgage lenders created new, high-risk loans for both the working and middle classes which led to the crash. These loans were based on lending arrangements that placed the borrowers at a severe disadvantage (Mishkin 2011). Numerous underqualified borrowers who were offered so-called subprime mortgage loans found themselves unable to keep up the payments to settle the debt generated by the high house prices and high interest rates required to buy into the 'American dream' (Akerlof and Shiller, 2009; Akira and Ossei-Mensah 2014). Misled by widespread publicity and misinformation that claimed houses were the best kind of personal investment, ordinary citizens assumed that the value of their property would steadily rise in the same way as they had been since the 1980s. Property prices were inflated, as were the interest rates on the financial loans used to buy the properties. As Akira and Ossei-Mensah put it, 'Desperate for their chance at a quality life, millions of ambitious Americans bought-in to some of the most extensive schemes of fraud and corruption the world has ever seen. Many home buyers could not afford to maintain the fantasies sold to them on the sitcoms they had used as a guide to prosperity'. (Akira and Ossei-Mensah 2014: 346; Chancellor, 2000). The real-estate bubble burst in 2008 with over 5 million American homes repossessed between 2008 and 2011 (Meyers et al., 2011, quoted in Ouellette 2017).

The 2008 financial crisis and ensuing recession exposed palpable home precarities: the dramatic risks of purchasing decisions in a volatile, underregulated and unstable housing market. Remarkably, despite the severe decline in access to mortgages, property TV's logic of property ownership prospered in the aftermath of 2008. Property TV reinvented itself by offering shrewd consumer choices as solutions to housing market problems. During this period, TV shows were reworked in response to the fall in house prices and an explicit allegiance to property was regenerated as the symbol of self-fulfilment and personal success. Consequently, the aspiration for home ownership has persisted after the financial crash since property programming adopted a discursive framing of a new age of austerity (see Bramall 2013; McElroy 2017). The opportunism of earlier aspirational TV series gave way to a new kind of reality TV that stressed prudence, financial caution and ingenuity in recognition of a new era of economic uncertainty. These shows shifted their attention from 2008 onwards to focus on opportunities and strategies of renovating properties bought from previous owners dispossessed by the crash.

A string of television series emerged to offer advice not only on entering or moving up the housing market ladder but also on the purchase and renovations of buy-to-let houses. These included series such as *Property Ladder* (2001–2009), *DIY SOS* (1999–2010), *How to be Mortgage Free* (2017), *£1 For a House* (2018–2019), and *Homes Under the Hammer* (2003 – to date). The highly popular *Homes Under the Hammer* even has a cult following, featuring properties bought at auction in need renovation. These programmes follow a particular pattern where the property bought is valued by an estate agent before and after the renovation to gauge whether the buyer can make a profit. The merit and worth of house ownership are unquestioned within all these programmes (White 2013). Audiences are now given advice on ways to profit from house dispossessions and other people's misfortunes, with an emphasis on DIY restorations and crafting. Various permutations on house purchases and making improvements include the virtuous communal philosophy of *DIY SOS The Big Build* (1999), where members of the local community, including traders, work together to remake the home of deserving families. The risks of potential financial or domestic catastrophe and remedies to save houses with structural damage are observed from the safe distance of an armchair. And, as McElroy explains, Channel 4's *The Restoration Man* (2010–to date) portrays restoration as a moral good. A distinctive moral tone conveys the idea that the restoration of properties concerns a wider kind of restoration: a restoring of the self and of the nation's heritage.

With lifestyle gurus establishing themselves as trustworthy experts who provide practical and emotional counselling, the perceived need for these 'experts' is intensified in a recession climate (Hamad 2014: 224). House-buying and selling is now more competitive and more precarious. Exemplifying this as a palpable home precarity, the term 'Generation Rent' refers to young people in the UK who now live in the private rented sector for extended lengths of time because they cannot access either homeownership or social housing (Hoolachan et al. 2016). And growing numbers of house owners are caught in the trap of negative equity in the UK while first-home prices are inflated by a buy-to-let market and a housing shortage. In these new precarious circumstances, the role of the expert is central, with presenters such as Sarah Beeny in Sarah Beeny's *Selling Houses* (2010- to date), and Kirstie Allsopp and Phil Spencer in *Location, Location, Location* (2000 – to date) guiding viewers to manipulate the new, volatile market. This reinvented breed of experts present themselves as a discerning group of cultural intermediaries who lead new post-recession adaptations of the property genre. The economic climate comprises a mode of home precarity that fuels the popularity and power of lifestyle experts who now set themselves up as 'austerity experts'. These new kinds of expert perform as advocates for recessionary audiences who would otherwise be inclined to reject such tenuous authority (Hamad 2014: 225).

Post-crisis dispossession

In the post-crisis era, the precarious consequences of home ownership continue to be confronted. Programmes about property aired after the 2008 market crash generate a discourse for engaging in and profiting from the numerous dispossessions. Earlier lifestyle TV was associated with and appealed to feminine know-how by coaching women how to care for their families, their homes and their own bodies as a feminine practice (Sender 2012). The property TV of the post-crash period obscures those gender divisions by addressing men as viewers attentive to profit-making from homes and related domestic objects (Esch 2017). For instance, Ouellette (2017) documents the rising number of TV shows in the US such as *Hardcore Pawn, Operation Repo, Storage Wars* and *Flip Men* to explain the emergence of what she calls a 'recessionary entrepreneurialism'. Referring to this as 'bare enterprise', Ouellette explains that these programmes usually evolve around white working-class men looking to profit from other peoples' losses.

'Dispossession TV' differs from much of the reality TV programmes of the early 2000s where needy and vulnerable subjects were improved by their transformation into self-reliant and enterprising individuals. Now, individuals pursue their goals ruthlessly by profiting from the misfortunes of others. The foreclosure of a large number of homes between 2008 and 2011 resulting from the subprime lending crisis fed into American reality TV entertainment. Beginning with *Flip Men* (2011–2012), these programmes were shaped around the idea of dispossession and recessionary entrepreneurialism as a routine and ordinary occurrence. *Flip Men* chronicled people who made offers on foreclosed homes in Salt Lake, Utah with the aim of refurbishing and reselling them for quick profit. This spawned related programmes such as *Property Wars* (2012–2013), *Flipping Vegas* (2011–2014) and *Flip It to Win It* (2013 – to date). *Flip or Flop* (2013–present) involves a husband and wife team who manage their own business of 'flipping' from their home. Flipping is a term used mainly by American real-estate investors to describe buying a revenue-generating asset and then rapidly reselling or 'flipping' it for profit.

A sharp rise in foreclosed homes resulting from the economic recession, caused those experiencing unemployment and rising debts to be trapped by short-term loans with high charges or to suffer dispossession. The dispossessed were forced to sell their home possessions to pawn brokers or place their belongings in storage units, triggering an escalation in the pawnshop business across the US. When the dispossessed were no longer able to pay for the storeroom space, storage companies began auctioning off the contents. This pawn trade formed a mainstream industry as part of the economic recession. After the success of *Pawn Star* (2012–2013), staged in a Las Vegas store, the programme *Storage Wars* began in 2010, elevating viewing ratings. This sparked a series of related programmes focused on the salvage business. A succession of shows emulated the format including *Hardcore Pawn* (2015), *Cajun Pawn Stars* (2012–present), *Hardcore Pawn Chicago* (2013), *Combat Pawn* (2012), *Win, Lose or Pawn* (2013) and *Beverly Hills Pawn* (2013–2015).

Alongside pawnshop and repossession programmes, *Storage Wars* (2010) and *Pickers* (2010) aimed at male viewers now form part of an established range of shows that portray people profiting from dispossession as a normal business practice. The formula of *Storage Wars* is driven by the possibility that buyers of a storage locker might find antiques or other exceptional or valuable objects among the contents. Like other instances of dispossession TV, the story is related from the viewpoint of the person profiteering, the buyer-entrepreneur, with the person unable to pay the storage rent disregarded. This self-serving response to financial hardship exemplifies the neoliberal articulation of property, enterprise and failure (Ouellette 2017). While home renovation TV programmes preceded the financial crisis of 2008, these post-crisis shows exploit foreclosed homes and the forced displacement of occupants as a commercial venture. They present home repossessions as an entrepreneurial recreation that corresponds with neoliberal housing policies. Small-time entrepreneurs who host the shows are conveyed as 'ordinary' TV personalities involved in the redistribution of wealth, forming a significant part of the expansion of predatory industries – payday loans and pawnshops – that pursue the poor and bankrupted (Rivlin 2011). A focus on resourceful, entrepreneurial individuals who gain from dispossession disguises the intricacies of neoliberal capitalism yet also points to the economic vulnerability of the unemployed and working poor as an essential feature of today's palpable home precarities.

If American reality TV has focused on the rehabilitation of needy, vulnerable citizens through systems of self-improvement, dispossession TV has no such motivation. The post-2008 financial crisis has worsened the state neglect of the poor in Western societies, particularly black and minority ethnic groups, prompted by the reversal of public welfare schemes (Giroux 2006, 2012). However, TV programmes such as *Extreme Makeover: Home Edition* (2003–2012) have rallied volunteers such as corporate sponsors and non-profit agencies to help worthy people who suffered from circumstances beyond their control, such as illness or natural disaster. In contrast, dispossession TV dissuades empathy for sufferers to release viewers of any moral obligation to help. This 'cruel entrepreneurialism' relies on the marginalisation of the poor to embolden contempt and abuse (Ouellette 2017).

Financialised and austere femininity

Before the housing market crash, conventional lifestyle shows focused on the feminine management of health and appearance. By contrast, HGTV's Canada programme *Buy Herself* (2012) represents a discourse of self-care and astute financial management. For example, in her analysis of *Buy Herself*, Zoë Druick (2017) chronicles the changing gender dispositions anchored within the post-crisis housing condition. The show emerged as part of a trend that included *Holmes on Homes* (2001–2008), *Property Virgins* (2006–to date) and *Love it or List It* (2008–to date). These shows combine lifestyle, reality TV and real-estate formats. *Buy Herself* presents the narratives of two types of women: those in their 20s and 30s who live with parents and wish to become independent and older women in their 30s and 40s who are divorced, with or without children and 'starting over'. The show's host performs as an expert, as a cultural intermediary and as an 'aspirational stand-in'. As Druick describes, 'In the opening credit sequence, for instance, Rinamato evokes her professional experience: "I've been in real estate for 15 years so I know buying a house can be tough. Buying on your own: even tougher"' (Druick 2017: 564).

While the business of house purchasing has traditionally been presented as an activity confined to men or heterosexual couples, the integration of finance into the daily lives of women through home and domestic activity is now extended to house-buying itself (Allon 2014). *Buy Herself* chronicles the decisions of women determined to become autonomous economic players by investing in real estate. As Druick points out, if houses have triggered passionate ideas of home as a vital part of women's literature such as Jane Austen's *Pride and Prejudice*, the meaning of houses change when viewed as individually owned property. For women, proposing property as a path to independence is an ambiguous solution to the problems of the patriarchal home, highlighted by second-wave feminism. Resonating with nineteenth-century ethics, the domestic realm continues to be regarded as a mythical sanctuary from the sphere of work even though it has become an arena for commercial enterprise. The tenets of neoliberalism mean that for middle-class women, the flight from home has involved a collusion with capitalism's progress by harnessing their labour and outsourcing their domestic work to poor and immigrant women (Druick 2017: 563). This outsourcing of social reproduction generates tensions around experiences of gender that highlight home precarities. But instead of leading to personal autonomy, the privatisation of social provision through home ownership creates the pressures and risks of debt load. Fiona Allon (2014) explains that the drive to deepen women's engagement with mortgages and consumer credit constitutes a 'feminisation of finance'. Women are being offered private residential properties as a financial source across the life-course as part of a process of financial governmentality.

The gendered domestic labour associated with a revived interest in domestic crafts on TV corresponds with the rise of property TV. Traditional craft programmes such as *Kirstie's Homemade Home* (2009 – to date) form part of a new kind of UK lifestyle TV that includes the *Great British Bake Off* (2010 – to date) and the *Great British Sewing Bee* (2013 – to date). As McElroy (2017) explains, this genre is based on a distinctive expression and negotiation of austerity culture. With the focus on interior design, the appropriateness of property ownership is underpinned by the potential for domestic creativity. The expert's gender is imperative. Echoing nineteenth-century advice manuals, a feminine discourse of craft associates aesthetic taste with domesticity, femininity and family which situates women in the home (See Chapter 2). The ease with which presenters of property TV move to craft TV indicates a common ground: the *staging* and *attainment* of home. Kirstie Allsopp, co-host of *Location, Location, Location* (2000 – to date), moves effortlessly into craft TV and is also known for acting as a housing market advisor to the UK Conservative Party. In *Kirstie's Vintage Home* (2012), Allsopp is shown purchasing goods in markets and junk shops in London's Portobello Road as a strategy for coping with 'domestic consumerism in the age of austerity' (McElroy 2017: 540). Allsopp embodies a traditional form of middle-class femininity through her craft work and her screen-couple double act with co-host Phil Spencer on *Location*. She is a shrewd businesswoman and major television celebrity. Yet, significantly, Allsopp foregrounds her identity as a mother and homemaker to validate her proficiency as a lifestyle TV expert. She presents a meticulously classed and racialised social type – white and upper class – one embodying a 'retrosexuality':

> The retrosexual feminine subject is a nostalgic, self-conscious construction of domestic femininity that plays with the supposed innocence of a heritage past with a modern, post-feminist present. It is almost literally a gendered vision of having your cake and eating it! (McElroy 2017: 538)

This kind of lifestyle guru functions, in Western Anglophone contexts, to recuperate crafts and craft production. More than this, as McElroy points out, the feminised gratification gained from homemaking displayed in craft programmes not only invokes the recovery of a distinctive mode of femininity associated with the Arts and Crafts Movement. It also endorses an austerity culture by appealing to a nostalgic wartime emotional response – that is, to rationing and 'making do' (see Chapter 2). While the art of recycling and reusing underpins a 'make do and mend' rationale, it garners a moral response to 'shabby and chic' vintage consumerism. Yet, paradoxically, crafting requires the privilege of leisure time and the funds to pay for materials (Groeneveld 2010). Despite the promise of agency, this craft renaissance in the domestic sphere conveys an idealised feminine past.

Social media and home curation

Social media is making a significant impact on our sense of place, and ideas of home. Social media ensures that 'interior design is no longer limited to professional expertise' (Miller and Sinanan 2014: 4–20). The apparently intimate space of home continues to be on permanent display, performing on a digital stage where we present our aspirational lives. Paradoxically, the processes through which we negotiate this staging become increasingly personalised. Within today's algorithmic culture, the online world is being projected as a social or personalised 'space' where we present a domestic self. In this online/offline world, we now craft and curate not only ourselves but also the home as 'self'.

IKEA and home curation

A popular key strategy involved in online crafting is the 'IKEA hack'. By way of a backdrop to social media home curation, Pauline Garvey (2018) refers to designers as 'creative brokers' who compile, assimilate and recombine knowledge economies in new ways. Interestingly, IKEA consumers describe themselves in similar terms, with respect to the practice of customising and reshaping basic IKEA furniture known as the IKEA hack. The word 'hacking', originates from computer programming, referring to a creative alteration of a programme to change its function. The low cost and modular nature of IKEA furniture has inspired experimentation with individual items of furniture and other IKEA items, with advice and discussion occurring on blogs and social network sites. IKEA hacks involve adapting a standardised, assembly line product by customising it to fit a particular purpose. Simple pieces of furniture or shelving are treated as a blank canvas on which to rework the item into a particular home solution. For example, a wooden chest of drawers can be transformed into a rolling desk, and a plain coffee table's legs can be replaced by wooden tapered legs to create a classic mid-century style. By modifying mass produced objects, these projects foreground creativity, originality and personal taste. By reshaping the aesthetic features of the home, the IKEA hack conveys a sense of transcending class distinctions (Sparke 2009: 92).

Despite its origins as part of a Swedish government-led campaign for inexpensive, rule-bound furniture and kitchen design (addressed in Chapter 2), IKEA became a global furniture retailer in the 1990s, known for its standardised flat pack furniture and accessible design (Hartman 2007). Benefiting from the 1990s bubble economy and despite publicising its long-term support for sustainability, IKEA presented new fashion trends in retail furniture that implied disposability (Reimer and Lesley 2008). During the late twentieth century, the mass media role of educating audiences about design aesthetics was fuelled by an abundance of reasonably priced Modernist-styled consumer goods. As the Sweden managing director of IKEA has advised, 'Our feeling is: It's just furniture. Change it' (Leland 2002; quoted in Ryan 2014).

IKEA fostered a more eclectic sense of style by introducing a new strategy of 'upmarketing downmarket goods'. Trendsetting yet inexpensive and often disposable goods were now projected in the same way as more luxurious, durable upmarket items of furniture and home décor (Ryan 2014). The design narrative that accompanied these goods in the IKEA showrooms, catalogues and advertisements conveyed this Modernist design aesthetic by fusing it with a 'democratising' ethos. Householders on both high and low incomes could now select from a range of artistic and decorative styles to create their own personal sense of style (Spigel 2009). The company offered not only creative storage solutions. IKEA's ethos also emphasised the affordability and availability of 'good design' in furniture that need not be endured for generations. By these means, the company spawned a version of everyday Modernism involving a form of 'aspirational disposability' (Ryan 2014).

Corporations such as IKEA aim to build relationships with consumers by encouraging them to identify with the brand (Garvey 2018). This is done by co-opting their intellectual and affective labour (Zwick et al. 2008). The need to assemble this flat pack furniture works as a key dimension of 'putting the shoppers to work'. As Garvey explains, this 'value co-creation' binds consumers to the company by tapping into consumers' own resourcefulness, creativity and flair. The emotional bond that customers feel for the company also relates to poignant moments in people's lives when they tend to engage in IKEA shopping. IKEA is 'there for us' at the initial stages of setting up home away from parents, attending university, moving in with flatmates or a partner, and after a relationship breakdown (Garvey 2018 112). During these anxious or exciting stages of the lifecycle, inexpensive furniture signifies expectation, freedom or reflection. Referred to as 'brandscaping', and requiring 'atmospherics', the retail store's ambiance is a central part of today's corporate branding process produced by distinctive lighting, design, music and service staff. The aim of the store atmosphere, then, is to charm the senses and generate distinctive types of social interaction in the store (Garvey 2018).

The dual features of IKEA style – as both democratising and disposable – underline and match the curating logic and digital motivations of Pinterest and interior design blogs that supports the philosophy of today's online *curatorial self*. These websites now sustain a curatorial aesthetic of eclecticism that reflects IKEA's ethos: trendsetting yet transient, aspirational yet disposable. Significantly, IKEA has promoted and stimulated this digital makeover culture by fostering IKEA hacking's prominent online presence, allowing viewers and readers to 'hack' material culture to produce what Maureen Ryan refers to as an 'affective domestic space' (Ryan 2014). Within this space, readers engage in what she calls the 'therapeutics of the self' by swapping class mobility for taste. Here, taste becomes a substitute for higher social ranking. Social media platforms such as Pinterest and Instagram, that emphasise image-centric content, showcase IKEA goods and IKEA hacks to celebrate a form of individualism based on agency, choice and a sense of personal control. As Ryan argues, the twin tendencies of 'democratised good design' and a culture of social media curation of eclectic styles merge to form a new kind of neoliberal aesthetics.

Apartment therapy

The Internet offers a profusion of lifestyle blogs such as Apartment Therapy, Design Sponge, Remodelista, Dwell, and Lonny. This genre borrows from the well-established medium of television and lifestyle magazines such as *Homes and Gardens; Country Homes and Interiors, Traditional Home, Ideal Home*. For instance, a blog called Apartment Therapy, attracts 7 million readers per month (Apartment Therapy 2012). The popular following of these blogs is underpinned by an aestheticisation of everyday life aligned with consumer capitalism (Ryan 2014; Postrel 2003). By creating a 'therapy' discourse through consumer practices, Apartment Therapy's blog appeals to a mobile, aspirational group of readers. The label 'placeholder' furniture is used to describe the purchase and use of cheap items of furniture from low-cost retail outlets such as IKEA, until such time as house-holders can save for the 'perfect piece'. The blog's cultural logic is aspirational disposability, in line with IKEA's philosophy: 'the notion that one's domestic space should be personally reflective, uplifting, functional and above all, mutable to allow for upcycling as fashions, tastes, and identities change with time' (Ryan 2014: 69). Fashioning of home as a curative space is anchored in consumer culture. As Ryan confirms: 'In short, aspirational disposability is the imaginative solution Apartment

Therapy presents to commodity capitalism's problems of both overconsumption and conformity' (Ryan 2014: 69). Yet despite an apparent democratisation of taste, these makeover programmes and blogs endorse the superior knowledge of expert taste makers.

Blogs such as Apartment Therapy represent contemporary public taste by offering vintage shopping, eclecticism and mid-century Modernist design as tools to be used in the pursuit of the ideal home and, accordingly, the 'ideal self' (Ryan 2014: 69). The layout of content steers readers to a range of chronologically stored material, serving as a resource archive that provides specialised information for readers to identify solutions to particular domestic problems. The blog features House Tours that showcase real homes refurbished with inexpensive IKEA products to solve home furnishing problems, showing that 'good' home design is something that anyone can achieve. These images present people who have found design solutions to express their personalities by curating a stylish, functional home by engaging with a vernacular Modernism based on aspirational disposability. As Ryan explains, House Tours project images of beautiful living spaces that perform as an affective tool kit, providing material resources and advice for the 'aspiring nester' (Ryan 2014: 73). Occupants may generate cultural capital by adding value to objects through clever sourcing of mid-century modern furniture items via a classified advertisements website and then recontextualising them to create an eclectic style of 'everyday modernism' to reflect their 'personality'.

While the raiding of IKEA products to create a unique and effective domestic home is celebrated on these blogs, audience-participants are warned against cluttering their home with impractical items or becoming conformist in their tastes. The occupant's personal untidiness and disorder is approached as an illness requiring restoration. By these means, then, domestic space is conceived as a reflection and extension of the self. This cautioning resonates with the moral stance of nineteenth-century guidebooks on home decoration (see Chapter 2). Ryan explains that the notion of *therapy* permeates the blog's discourse by offering exemplars of subjecthood centred on class improvement through 'proper' modes of consumption and family life. But these design blogs convey conflicting messages. On the one hand, they foster principles of the hack, re-use, and thriftiness that promote ethics of prudence while creating cultural capital. On the other hand, these principles sit aside posts that recommend new consumer goods and gadgets.

The boundaries between advertisements and advice are obscured on these blogs, not only through the visual and discursive correspondence between the two but also by numerous hyperlinks to online retailers. The work of reading, learning, deliberating and shopping are melded into a consumer-oriented activity. As such, the discourse of self-practice remains individualised and consumerist even though hacking and 'making do' has the potential to conform to environmental principles of reusing and recycling. Here, notions of collectivity and sharing are reduced to the sharing of information on 'how to hack'. If disposability is offered as a solution for problems of taste and aspiration within a ceaseless project of self/home improvement, these websites have enormous potential to support an entirely different kind of lifestyle led by environmental sustainability (see Chapter 10). Soon, we might all be seeking advice on how to transform our homes into environmentally sustainable spaces. But for now, the notion of the IKEA hack offers no more than a temporary cure within a never-ending project of 'lifestylisation'.

Pinterest and digital home curation

Digital homemaking, supported by 'creative brokers' such as popular design blogs and social media platforms, draws audiences into a competitive marketplace as part of a recommendation culture. Social media platforms such as Pinterest and Instagram exemplify the image-centric content and curating quality of this digitised recommendation culture. Interior décor and domestic items are an abundant source for data generation. These social media platforms use algorithms that work as a set of instructions helping the user to search, sort and organise information about home prices, domestic interiors and home décor. Developing the notion of 'algorithmic cultural recommendation', the implications of the algorithms that direct user content on social media sites such as Pinterest are examined by Caroline Wilson-Barnao (2017). She argues that in the era of social media, 'cultural objects are being appropriated to render users compliant with marketing agendas'. Algorithmic cultural recommendation and the digitisation of objects allows media platforms to gain financial value from people's cultural practices.

The expansion of Pinterest as a type of online image-sharing platform enables users to collect and display ideas by saving images to virtual thematic pinboards. Contrasting with the single, centred post or image of Facebook, Twitter or Instagram, Pinterest users 'pin' photos taken on their own smartphones or images from websites beyond Pinterest, or 'repin' images from other Pinterest users' thematic boards. The images are regularly organised around home décor projects, hobbies and inspiration. However, users are more likely to circulate images selected from Pinterest or elsewhere on the web than create their own content (Hall and Zarro, 2012; Moore, 2014; Zarro and Hall, 2012). Nonetheless, as a social networking site, Pinterest fosters interaction (Kaplan and Haenlein, 2010). Users can find new material to pin not only by browsing a category but also by following or browsing others' boards.

Importantly, the design and engineering of Pinterest's website cultivates the inspiration, organisation and performances of gendered subjects (Friz and Gehl 2016). The company expanded in 2011, just a year after its launch. Yet the first users of this rapidly expanding image-sharing online platform were not teenagers – the typical early adopters of most digital services – but adult women. Women soon made up 80% of all US Pinterest users (Moore, 2014). Most of the women users of Pinterest typically search for items associated with home redecoration, wedding events and everyday needs such as recipes and fashion before buying. This American based site is said to have reached 250 million monthly active users as of October 2018 with more than half the company's users being international. Advertisements and linked promotional displays slot into wider domestication discourses and practices aimed at a feminised subject as part of a wider process of gendering technology. Pinterest's attraction to women is shaped by the website's accent on affective interaction, using visual rather than written texts. Emotions are engineered, steered and negotiated via algorithmic affordances. The emphasis is on the curation rather than creation of content, and on cooperation rather than competition with other users - conventions reflecting traditional enactments of femininity. This appeal to women is triggered through the sign-up process. As the website explains: 'Our mission is to help you discover and do what you love' (Pinterest 2018). The sign-up page declares 'Pinterest helps you find ideas to try'.

With the repinning of images from other users' pinboards being the most common activity, Pinterest is identified as a *social curation* website (Duggan and Smith, 2014; Gilbert et al., 2013; Hall and Zarro, 2012; Moore, 2014; Zarro, Hall and Forte, 2013). Digital platforms can refer users back their earlier preferences to commodify their emotional responses by purchasing items. Designers and advertisers that operate marketing agendas then determine the selection of material to present to the user according to users' interests, emotions and likings. Pinterest's curatorial character is reminiscent of the traditional scrapbook craft. Scrapbooking has traditionally enabled women to curate memories (Jones 2016). This practice migrated to digital spaces, with social media versions of crafting activity historically associated with feminised domestic space as a sphere of expertise (see Chapter 2). As such, Pinterest sustains a gender script: 'a script that hails an idealized, feminized user' (Friz and Gehl 2016: 688). This self-construction via consumed products and personal interests fosters identities based on artefacts, styles and hobbies such as an interest in crafts or interior design.

Such tangibles form the pivotal focus underpinning and framing a certain kind of *moral subject*. Like the advertisements and articles in traditional lifestyle magazines, Pinterest uses the word 'love' routinely throughout the site, from its tutorials to its sign-off stage: 'Save all the stuff you love (recipes! articles! travel ideas!) right here on Pinterest'. The emphasis on 'love' as the main affective response is embedded in Etiquette Rule #2: 'We think authenticity – expressing who you really are and what you really like – is more important than getting lots of followers'. By expressing what one feels passionate about or inspired by, the user's affective responses are rewarded as authentic and as part of the self. In these ways, the site appeals to traditionally feminised affective and emotional practices, contrasting with masculinised legal and rational routines (Friz and Gehl 2016: 693–699). The everyday creative activities cherished by Pinterest users such as craft arts, home décor, DIY, cooking and health, are popularised through inspirational quotes, fitness advice, recipes, wedding inspiration, and fashion trends on public boards (Scolere and Humphreys 2016).

The logic of this consumer-oriented digital technology summons consumer/ producers to affirm hyper-individualised experiences that promise individuality through conformity (Manovich 2001; Jones 2016). Designers compose an ideal user that matches a range of gender images or stereotypes to pre-emptively shape user activities and engineer online gender fluidity. Yet this individualised experience involves little more than attaching another user's pin to one's own collection (Hall and Zarro, 2012). The user-generated aspirational content on sites such as Pinterest has been referred to as 'aspirational labour' (Duffy 2014; 2015a, 2015b, Duffy and Hund 2015). Invoked by these social media sites, today's notion of the 'digital housewife' combines the cultural and economic functions of domestic labour with social media labour. But in doing, so it obscures the unpaid labour enacted through social media (Jarrett 2014). Even though this labour occurs for leisure and domestic purposes rather than employment, the hidden labour involved in interior décor forms part of a range of unpaid, invisible domestic work that characterises women's immaterial labour (Campbell, 2011; McRobbie, 2010). By situating Pinterest in these wider conversations about post-industrial, post-feminist digital labour, Jones (2016) foregrounds Pinterest's affective capacity to stimulate a yearning driven by self-surveillance. This post-feminist ideal is depicted as a new mode of entrepreneurial femininity that masks the labour, self-restraint and capital required to live up to these ideals (Duffy and Hund 2015: 2). Nevertheless, while masquerading as leisure, the aspirational labour involved in this unpaid work offers pleasure as a reward. The focus on Pinterest as an example of social media-led home curation highlights the conflicting and ambivalent quality of homemaking as an individual and collective project of identity.

Conclusion

This chapter's exploration of the contemporary dramatisation and aestheticisation of home in the post-financial crash era suggests that television and social media play a decisive role in educating viewers about property ownership and home aesthetics. Via contemporary TV programmes and social media, we are 'amassing a huge number of discourses or "scripts", by which to shape our dreams of living well' (Bawden 2011). As such, social media's promotion of self-enterprise forms a central feature of the 'government of the self'. The transnational spread of property TV shows indicates the varied ways in which capitalism is expressed and sustained through local conditions and identities. This formulaic production model enables a speedy, efficient and low-cost set of programmes. With an accent on consumption, the extraordinary success of these makeover and property shows results from the genre's perfect match with the values and ideals associated with reconstructing both the capitalist economy and the global television industry (Bruce and Druick 2017).

First, the relentlessness of the subgenre of lifestyle, makeover and property TV suggests that this process of normalisation positions non-homers and failed home-owners as deficient members of society (McElroy 2017: 528). Second, as part of the endorsement of a set of neoliberal values, these shows foster the notion of the entrepreneurial self as a distinctive mode of subjectivity adapted to and required by today's consumer society and property market. Here, property ownership is conveyed as both normative *and* privileged. A discourse of the self-reliant consumer citizen as a 'good citizen' disregards alternative, collective versions of social agency by foregrounding individualistic values (McElroy 2017). Lifestyle TV mirrors government policy by promoting the powerful idea that individuals and families can elevate their lives and empower themselves by following the guidance of lifestyle experts. Far from ignoring class divisions, property TV actively helps to justify class divisions by skilfully offering 'middle-classness' as a dream attainable through individual self-determination and consumer choice (McElroy 2017: 526).

This kind of lifestyle television delivers a dramatic popular cultural arena in which neoliberal ideals are expressed, endorsed and sometimes challenged (McElroy 2017). The dramatised home has not only sparked an interest in interior decoration but has also recuperated the nineteenth-century model of creating and shaping self-identity and social status (Akira and Ossei-Mensah 2014). The popular cultural reimagining of home in lifestyle and property TV programmes have, alongside websites such as Pinterest, formed a standard against which audiences assess their refined taste within neoliberal discourses of individual 'responsibilisation' (Rose, 1999). Lifestyle and property TV programmes emphasise a privatised, aspirational culture of home ownership and popularise ways of surmounting the troubling notions of home that comprise today's home precarities. Yet these shows also form part of a network of public scrutiny of personal life (Philips 2005). The trophy home is alive and well: it remains one of the most visually explicit means of presenting one's aspirations to impress the imagined and real public.

Yet the future consequences of home ownership remain palpably precarious in this post-crisis era. The dramatic rise in popular TV programmes dealing with the purchase, sale and renovation of domestic property fuses emotional and domestic labour with market logics. 'Dispossession TV' which relies on the salvaging of dispossessed houses depends on the misfortunes of others. However, the way in which audiences are invited to foster this entrepreneurial self is highly gendered. An austere domesticity is expressed via a craft renaissance that promises agency by referring to an idealised feminine past. By contrast, efforts to draw single women into taking on mortgages and consumer credit represents a 'feminisation of finance' as a form of financial governmentality. These programmes promote the need for self-reliance, resourcefulness and the cultivation of an entrepreneurial self. A web of complex ideological values projects targeted consuming subjects as agents of their own decisions. As part of the mission of reinventing ourselves as good citizens, this discourse of the self-reliant consumer citizen negates alternative versions of social agency by foregrounding individualistic values that deny the possibility of collective identities (McElroy 2017).

The chapter also explains how social media has become influential in shaping gendered perceptions of the domestic sphere. Entire digital economies are now arranged around lifestyle and domestic interior advice. Echoing the guidebooks on home decoration of earlier centuries, homemakers are inspired to choose from a raft of digitally circulated decorative styles to create their own expression of style (Spigel 2009: 304, n.11). The digital mediation of home is signified by social media sites such as Pinterest that facilitate users to transform their homes into personalised sites of self-display. Here, taste becomes a substitute for higher social status. In the age of social media, home is now expressed as deeply intimate and personal yet also managed and presented as profoundly public – now referred to as a hyperpublic space (Friedman 2017). The paired affinities of 'democratised good design' and a culture of 'social media curation' of assorted styles come together to constitute a new form of neoliberal aesthetics. Given its potential to be a supportive online community, Pinterest could be reconfigured to challenge passive curation in favour of an *active* curation to foster and enhance communal and sustainable goals. Likewise, lifestyle TV has the potential for transformation in order to promote dramatically different, environmentally sustainable ways of living to address climate change (see Chapter 10).

References

Akerlof, G.A. and Shiller, R.J. (2009) *Animal Spirits: How Human Psychology Drives the Economy and Why It Matters for Global Capitalism*. Princeton: Princeton University Press.

Akira, S.I. and Ossei-Mensah, L. (2014) 'The construction of taste: Television and American home décor', in D.A. Macey, K.M. Ryan, N.J. Springer (eds), *How Television Shapes Our Worldview: Media Representations of Social Trends and Change*. Plymouth: Lexington Books.

Allon, F. (2008) *Renovation Nation: Our Obsession with Home*. Sydney: UNSW Press.

Allon, F. (2014) 'The feminisation of finance, gender, labour and the limits of inclusion', *Australian Feminist Studies*, 29(79), 12–30.

Andrejevic, M. (2004) *Reality Television: The Work of Being Watched*. London: Rowman & Littlefield.

Apartment Therapy. (2012) 'Apartment Therapy media kit 2012'. http://s3.amazonaws.com/atads/ApartmentTherapy_2012mediakit.pdf (accessed 2 August 2019).

Arvidsson, A. (2006) '"Quality singles": Internet dating and the work of fantasy', *New Media and Society*, 8(4), 671–690.

Atwood, F. (2005) 'Inside out: Men on the "home front"', *Journal of Consumer Culture*, 5(1), 87–107.

Bawden, G. (2011) 'Home theatre: Staging the domestic interior', *Double Dialogues*, 14. www.doubledialogues.com/article/home-theatre-staging-the-domestic-interior/ (accessed 3 June 2019).

Blunt, A. and Dowling, R. (2006) *Home*. London: Routledge.

Bonner, F. (2003) *Ordinary Television: Analyzing popular TV*. London: Sage.

Bonner, F. (2005) 'Whose lifestyle is it anyway?', in D. Bell and J. Hollows (eds), *Ordinary lifestyles: Popular Media, Consumption and Taste*. Maidenhead and New York: Open University Press, pp. 35–46.

Bramall, R. (2013) *The Cultural Politics of Austerity: Past and Present in Austere Times*. Basingstoke: Palgrave Macmillan.

Bruce, J. (2009) 'Home improvement television: Holmes on homes makes it right', *Canadian Journal of Communication*, 34, 79–94.

Bruce, J. and Druick, Z. (2017) 'Haunted houses: Gender and property television after the financial crisis', *European Journal of Cultural Studies*, 20(5), 483–489.

Campbell, J.E. (2011) 'It takes an iVillage: Gender, labor, and community in the age of televisioninternet convergence', *International Journal of Communication*, 5, 492–510.

Chancellor, E. (2000) *Devil Take the Hindmost: A History of Financial Speculation*. New York: Plume.

Corner, J. and Pels, D. (2003) *Media and the Restyling of Politics: Consumerism, Celebrity and Cynicism*. London: Sage.

Daly, K. (2002) 'Time, gender, and the negotiation of family schedules', *Symbolic Interaction*, 25, 323–342. doi:10.1525/si.2002.25.3.323.

Druick, Z. (2017) 'Property TV: Financialized femininity and new forms of domestic labour', *European Journal of Cultural Studies*, 20(5), 560–574.

Dubrofsky, R. (2009) 'Fallen women in reality TV: A pornography of emotion', *Feminist Media Studies*, 9(3), 353–368.

Duffy, B.E. (2014). 'Link love and comment karma: Norms and politics of evaluation in the fashion blogosphere', in H.C. Suhr (ed.), *Online Evaluation of Creativity and the Arts*. New York: Routledge, pp. 41–59.

Duffy, B. (2015a) 'Amateur, autonomous, and collaborative: Myths of aspiring female cultural producers in Web 2.0', *Critical Studies in Media Communication*, 32(1), 48–64. doi:10.1080 /15295036.2014.997832.

Duffy, B.E. (2015b) 'The romance of work: Gender and aspirational labour in the digital culture industries', *International Journal of Cultural Studies*. Advance online publication. doi:10.1177/1367877915572186.

Duffy, B.E. and Hund, E. (2015) '"Having it all" on social media: Entrepreneurial femininity and self-branding among fashion bloggers', *Social Media+ Society*. Advance online publication. doi:10.1177/2056305115604337.

Duggan, M. and Smith, A. (2014, January) Social media update 2013, Pew Research Center. www. pewInternet.org/files/2013/12/PIP_Social-Networking-2013. pdf.

Dyer, R. (1979) *Stars*. London: BFI publishing.

Esch, M. (2017) 'Picking through history: "Mantiques" and masculinity in artifactual entertainment', *European Journal of Cultural Studies*, 20(5), 509–524.

Evans, J. and Hesmondhalgh, D. (eds) (2005) *Understanding Media: Inside Celebrity*. Maidenhead: Open University Press.

Federici, S. (2012) *Revolution at Point Zero*. Oakland: PM Press.

Folbre, N. (2009) *Greed, Lust, and Gender: A History of Economic Ideas*. Oxford: Oxford University Press.

Friedman, A.T. (2017): 'American Glamour 2.0: Architecture, spectacle, and social media', *Consumption Markets & Culture*, 20(6), 575–584.

Friz, A. and Gehl, R.W. (2016) 'Pinning the feminine user: Gender scripts in Pinterest's sign-up interface', *Media, Culture and Society*, 38(5), 686–703.

Garvey, P. (2018) 'Consuming IKEA and inspiration as material form', in A.J. Clarke (ed.), *Design Anthropology: Object Cultures in Transition*. London: Bloomsbury, pp. 101–114.

Gilbert, E., Bakhshi, S., Chang, S. and Terveen, L. (2013) 'I need to try this? A statistical overview of Pinterest', In *Proceedings of the SIGCHI Conference on Human Factors in Computing Systems*. New York: ACM, pp. 2427–2436.

Giroux, H. (2006) 'Reading Hurricane Katrina: Race, class, and the biopolitics of disposability', *College Literature*, 3(3), 171–196.

Giroux, H. (2012) *Twilight of the Social: Resurgent Publics in the Age of Disposability*. Boulder: Paradigm Publishers.

Giroux, H. (2014) *Zombie Politics and Culture in the Age of Casino Capitalism*. New York: Peter Lang.

Green, E., Hebron, S. and Woodward, D. (1990) 'Women's leisure today', in E. Green, S. Hebron and D. Woodward (eds), *A Social History of Women's Leisure*. London: Macmillan.

Groeneveld, E. (2010) 'Join the knitting revolution: Third-wave feminist magazines and the politics of domesticity', *Canadian Review of American Studies*, 40, 259–277.

Hall, C. and Zarro, M. (2012) 'Social curation on the website Pinterest. com.', *Proceedings of the American Society for Information Science and Technology*, 49(1), 1–9. doi:10.1002/meet.4504901189.

Hamad, H. (2014) 'Fairy jobmother to the rescue: Postfeminism and the recessionary cultures of reality TV', in D. Negra and Y. Tasker (eds), *Gendering the Recession: Media and Culture in the Age of Austerity*. London: Duke University Press, pp. 223–245.

Hanan, J.S. (2010) 'Home is where the capital is: The culture of real estate in an era of control societies', *Communication and Critical/Communication Studies*, 7(2), 176–201.

Hartman, T. (2007) 'On the IKEAization of France', *Public Culture*, 19(3), 483–498.

Harvey, D. (1989) 'From managerialism to entrepreneurialism: The transformation in urban governance in late capitalism', *Geografiska Annaler. Series B, Human Geography*, 71(1), 3–17.

Heywood, A. (2011) *The End of the Affair: Implications of Declining Home Ownership*. London: Smith Institute.

Hochschild, A.R. (1983) *The Managed Heart: Commercialization of Human Feeling*. Berkeley: University of California Press.

Hochschild, A.R. with Machung, A. (2000) *The Second Shift*. New York: Avon Books.

Hollows, J. (2003) 'Feeling like a domestic goddess: Postfeminism and cooking', *European Journal of Cultural Studies*, 6(2), 179–202.

Hollows, J. (2016) '"The worst mum in Britain": Class, gender and caring in the campaigning culinary documentary', in J. Leer and K.K. Povlsen (eds), *Food and Media: Practices, Distinctions and Heterotopias*. Abingdon and New York: Routledge.

Hoolachan, J., McKee, J., Moore, T. and Soaita, A.M. (2016) '"Generation rent" and the ability to "settle down": Economic and geographical variation in young people's housing transitions', *Journal of Youth Studies*, 20(1), 63–78.

Ishita, S. (2016) 'Construction of the public memory of celebrities: Celebrity museums in Japan', in P.D. Marshall and S. Redmond (eds), *A Companion to Celebrity*. Chichester: Wiley Blackwell, pp. 135–154.

Jarrett, K. (2014) 'The relevance of "women's work": Social reproduction and immaterial labour in digital media', *Television & New Media*, 15(1), 14–29.

Jones, H.A. (2016) 'New media producing new labor: Pinterest, yearning, and self-surveillance', *Critical Studies in Media Communication*, 33(4), 352–365.

Kaplan, A.M. and Haenlein, M. (2010) 'Users of the world, unite! The challenges and opportunities of social media', *Business Horizons*, 53(1), 59–68.

Kramarae, C. (2001) *The Third shift: Women Learning Online*. Washington, DC: American Association of University Women Educational Foundation.

Lewis, T. (2008) *Smart Living: Lifestyle Media and Popular Expertise*. New York: Peter Lang.

Lewis, T. (2012) '"There grows the neighbourhood": Green citizenship, creativity and life politics on eco-TV', *International Journal of Cultural Studies*, 15(3), 315–326.

Lewis, T. (2015) '"One city block at a time": Researching and cultivating green transformations', *International Journal of Cultural Studies*, 18(3), 347–363.

McElroy, R. (2008) 'Property TV: The (re)making of home on national screens', *European Journal of Cultural Studies*, 11(1), 43–61.

McElroy, R. (2017) 'Mediating home in an age of austerity: The values of property televi-sion', *European Journal of Cultural Studies*, 20(5), 525–542.

McRobbie, A. (2010) 'Reflections on feminism, immaterial labour and the post-Fordist regime', *New Formations*, 70, 60–76.

Manovich, L. (2010). 'Database as a symbolic form convergence', in R. Parry (ed.), *Museums in a Digital Age*. New York: Routledge, pp. 64–71.

Marshall, P.D. (1997) *Celebrity and Power: Fame in Contemporary Society*. Minneapolis: Uni-versity of Minnesota Press.

Matheson, S.A. (2010) Shopping, makeovers, and nationhood: Reality TV and women's programming in Canada, in J. Taddeo (ed.), *The Tube Has Spoken: Reality TV and History*. Lexington: University Press of Kentucky, pp. 145–170.

Meyers, L., Gardella, R. and Schoen, J. (2011) 'No end in sight to foreclosure quagmire', *NBC News*, 9 May. www.nbcnews.com/id/42881365/ns/business-personal_finance/t/no-end-sight-foreclosure-quagmire/#.VMMQVcbJgag.

Miller, D. and Sinanan, J. (2014) *Webcam*. Cambridge: Polity Press.

Mishkin, F.S. (2011) 'Over the cliff: From the subprime to the global financial crisis', *Journal of Economic Perspectives*, 25(1), 50–51.

Moore, R.J. (2014, 7 May) 'Pinners be pinnin: How to justify Pinterest 3.8b valuation' [Web log comments]. http://blog.rjmetrics.com/2014/05/07/pinners-be-pinnin-howto-justify-pinterests-3-8b-valuation/.

Moran, A. (2009) *New Flows in Global TV*. Chicago: University of Chicago Press.

Moseley, R. (2000) 'Makeover takeover on British television', *Screen 41*, 3, 299–314.

Ouellette, L. (2017) 'Bare enterprise: US television and the business of dispossession (post-crisis, gender and property television)', *European Journal of Cultural Studies*, 20(5), 490–508.

Ouellette, L. and Hay, J. (2008a) *Better Living through Reality TV: Television and Post-welfare Citizenship*. Oxford: Blackwell.

Ouellette, L. and Hay, J. (2008b) 'Makeover television, governmentality and the good citi-zen', *Continuum: Journal of Media & Cultural Studies*, 22(4), 471–484.

Palmer, G. (2011) '"The new you": Class and transformation in lifestyle television', in S. Holmes and D. Jermyn (eds), *Understanding Reality Television*. London: Routledge, pp. 173–190.

Philips, D. (2005) 'Transformation scenes: The television interior makeover', *International Journal of Cultural Studies*, 8(2), 213–222.

Postrel, V. (2003) *The Substance of Style: How the Rise of Aesthetic Value is Remaking Commerce, Culture, and Consciousness*. New York: HarperCollins.

Reimer, S. and Lesley, D. (2008) 'Design, national imaginaries and the home furnishings commodity chain', *Growth and Change*, 39(1), 144–171.

Reynolds, B. (2011) *Making Money in Storage Auctions: How to Profit from the Storage Wars and Become a Storage Auction Warrior*. Seattle, WA: Amazon Digital Services.

Rivlin, G. (2011) *Broke USA: From Pawnshops to Poverty, Inc*. New York: HarperBusiness.

Rojek, C. (2001) *Celebrity*. London: Reaktion books.

Ronald, R. (2014) Editorial: Plus ça change. *International Journal of Housing Policy*, 14(1), 1–2.

Rose, N. (1999) *Governing the Soul: The Shaping of the Private Self*, 2nd edn. London: Free Association Books.

Rosenberg, B.C. (2011) 'The our house DIY club amateurs, leisure knowledge and lifestyle media', *International Journal of Cultural Studies*, 14(2), 173–190.

Ryan, M. (2014) 'Apartment Therapy, everyday modernism, and aspirational disposability', *Television & New Media*, 15(1), 68–80.

Ryan, M. (2015) 'Logics of lifestyle and the rise of Scripps network, 1994–2010', *Feminist Media Histories*, 1(2), 37–63.

Scolere, L. and Humphreys, L. (2016) 'Pinning design: The curatorial labor of creative professionals', *Social Media + Society*, doi:2013;March 2016, 1–13.

Sender, K. (2012) *The Makeover: Reality Television and Reflexive Audiences*. London: New York University Press.

Shimpach, S. (2012) 'Realty reality: HGTV and the subprime crisis', *American Quarterly*, 64 (3), 515–542.

Silberman, B. (2013, 19 September). 'Planning for the future'. http://blog.pinterest.com/post/61688351103/ planning-for-the-future.

Skeggs, B. and Wood, H. (2012) *Reacting to Reality Television: Performance, Audience and Value*. London: Routledge.

Sparke, P. (2009) *Designing the Modern Interior: From the Victorians to Today*. Oxford: Berg.

Spigel, L. (2009) *TV by Design: Modern Art and the Rise of Network TV*. Chicago, IL: University of Chicago Press.

Stone, P. (2007) *Opting Out? Why Women Really Quit Careers and Head Home*. Berkeley: University of California Press.

Taylor, L. (2002) 'From ways of life to lifestyle: The "ordinari–ization" of British gardening lifestyle television', *European Journal of Communication*, 17(4), 479–493.

Terranova, T. (2000) 'Free labor: Producing culture for the digital economy', *Social Text*, 18, 33–58.

Turner, G. (2004) *Understanding Celebrity*. London: Sage.

Turner, G. (2010) 'Approaching celebrity studies', *Celebrity Studies*, 1(1), 11–20.

White, M. (2013) 'Gender territories: House hunting on American real estate TV', *Television and New Media*, 14(3), 228–243.

White, M. (2017) 'A house divided', *European Journal of Cultural Studies*, 20(5), 575–591.

Williams, C.C. (2008) 'Re-thinking the motives of do-it-yourself (DIY) consumers', *The International Review of Retail, Distribution and Consumer Research*, 18, 311–323.

Wilson-Barnao, C. (2017) 'How algorithmic cultural recommendation influence the marketing of cultural collections', *Consumption Markets & Culture*. doi:10.1080/10253866.2017.1331910.

Woods, F. (2014) 'Classed femininity, performativity, and camp in British structured reality programming', *Television and New Media*, 15(3), 197–214.

Zarro, M. and Hall, C. (2012) 'Pinterest: Social collecting for# linking# using# sharing', in *Proceedings of the 12th ACM/IEEE-CS Joint Conference on Digital Libraries*. New York: ACM, pp. 417–418.

Zarro, M., Hall, C. and Forte, A. (2013) 'Wedding dresses and wanted criminals: Pinterest.com as an infrastructure for repository building', in *Proceedings of the AAAI Conference on Web and Social Media*, pp. 650–658. www. aai.org/ocs/index.php/ICWSM/ICWSM13/paper/view/6101.

Zborowski, J. (2012) 'Can you see yourself living here? Structures of desire in recent British lifestyle television', *European Journal of Media Studies*, 1(2), 55–76.

Zwick, D., Bonsu, S.K. and Darmody, A. (2008). 'Putting consumers to work: "Co-creation" and new marketing govern-mentality', *Journal of Consumer Culture*, 8(2), 163–196.

6

HOME TIME IN MULTISCREEN HOMES

Introduction

An enduring feature of home life since the 1950s has been the central role of the screen. The early home adoption of analogue television and personal computers opened up new mediated modes of household interaction as described in Chapter 4. Today, technological convergence supports media saturated homes served by multiple smart and mobile screen devices. Ways of accessing media content and home-based viewing practices are being transformed by the growth in mobile media use and the extension of television content from traditional delivery via a TV set, DVDs and DVR systems to Internet streaming and portable devices (Greer and Ferguson 2015). The diverse viewing possibilities offered by today's digital screens, from streaming services to second screen use, prompt an enquiry about the changing conditions of home-based media engagement. Internet access via today's smart TV set opens up multiple opportunities for watching films and programmes on demand while personal devices such as smartphones and tablets facilitate versatile modes of viewing and media sharing. Streaming and video OnDemand television services such as Netflix, Hulu, Amazon Prime and YouTube together with second screen use generate new domestic screen schedules and home routines. These digital viewing technologies re-arrange viewing practices in terms of time shifts. They also introduce new modes of social synchronisation that modify household dynamics and domestic rhythms by affecting levels of concentration and offering new connections within and beyond the home (Chambers 2019).

Debates about the ways in which media affect domestic rhythms and routines confirm that during the early stages of domestic television adoption, the synchronisation of national time and householders' time created significant domestic challenges. Chapter 4 introduced media studies of early television's effects on the temporal rhythms and routines of home life. To reiterate, the liveness of TV news and sport not only intensified and extended our encounter with the present as a *continuous present* as a result of the 'dayliness' of analogue television broadcasting (Scannell 2000). It also invoked the sense of a nationwide, 'public' or 'collective time' structure within the apparently private space of home. This beyond-the-home public community time is crystallised by our routines of watching or accessing the daily news, live sport and other televised public or nationwide events on TV. The idea of a mediated *public time* accessed from home has, then, been central to the ways in which we organise the private, intimate realm of our families and households. The question addressed in this chapter is how this temporal logic changes in today's multiscreen home supported by mobile devices.

New screen activities now form part of emerging domestic routines and household dynamics. Today's digitally mediated domestic spaces generate new experiences of home time shaped by global media networks, involving changing discourses of family, belonging and nation (Morley 2002). Instant and continuous connectivity between home and the 'outside world' not only give rise to dramatic changes in our ideas about home as a bounded space. It also changes our experiences of 'home time'. 'Home' has become a networked, mobile and continuously mutating timespace. Mobile media technologies are triggering new ideas, encounters and configurations of home, privacy and personal life. The ease with which we bring paid work into the home and stretch our personal communications beyond home via digital devices dramatically transforms household interactions by mobilising new mediated encounters.

The changing dynamics of today's multimedia, multiscreen home are addressed in this chapter by exploring the ways that digitalisation and mobilisation of personal and familial relationships shape home life. With its focus on popular cultural reimaginings of home in lifestyle and property TV programmes and via social media curation, Chapter 5 explained the impact of media *content* on our visions of the ideal home. If this media content forms part of home imaginaries, so too does the realisation that home is now a digitally saturated space that affects how we relate with one another at home and how we communicate to outsiders, from home. This chapter's case study of the multiscreen home identifies new routines and temporal arrangements that lead to a new kind of mediated 'home time'.

Media home time

Excessive screen use

As television viewing has long been associated with slothfulness and passiveness, the multiplication of screens in the home fuels public concerns about 'screen excess'. The adoption of mobile media in the home – from laptops to smart phones – triggers public anxieties about solitary and individualised media engagement giving rise to antisocial households. Negative claims have been made that excessive use of home-based media weaken family communication and direct face-to-face interaction, detach children from parents, and disrupt traditional distinctions between home time and work time by allowing the pressures of paid work to intrude on home life (Kayany and Yelsma 2000; Nie et al. 2002). 'Sedentary screen time' has been identified as a related unwelcome condition, particularly among adults and children who lead less physically active and more home-based lives than in previous decades.

Excessive time spent in inactive, screen-based activities has been linked with a rise in childhood obesity and associated health conditions (Hills et al. 2011). For example, a study of changes in school-age children's time use in the UK between 1975 and 2015 by Killian Mullan (2018) explains that concerns for children's safety, technological advancement and a greater emphasis on schoolwork success coincides with children spending less time outdoors and more time at home immersed in screen-based activities. A significant increase in children's screen activities between 2000 and 2015 corresponds with a rise in the total amount of time children spend in home-based indoor activities (Mullan 2018). These anxieties are accelerated by concerns about the ease of children's digital access to strangers and unsuitable content from the privacy of their bedrooms at a young age (Livingstone 2009; Livingstone and Das 2010). Parents face enormous challenges in monitoring the time children and teens spend in front of screens – whether TV shows, films or computer games – to protect them from unsuitable content and the erosion of children's homework time (see Chambers 2016; Clark 2013; Livingstone et al. 2014). Parental uncertainties about how to supervise children's social media use in their media-rich bedrooms are fuelled by fears of cyberbullying, stranger danger and access to pornography. These fears give rise to a new form of media parenting, where parental monitoring involves new kinds of interventions and compromises between parents and their children within efforts to stem children's home-based media use.

The domestication of technology theory, outlined in Chapter 4, provides a contribution to research on media time and the home to explain the integration of media equipment into domestic routines (Lull 1990; Morley 1986; Silverstone 1994). This approach identifies a 'moral economy' of the household to explain the *moral exchanges* and decisions involved in householders' adoption of domestic media equipment. The moral dimension of media adoption and use resonates with public and family anxieties about the temporal chaos or disorder associated with screen excess. Delicate negotiations are part of moral transactions that form household decisions about where the object is to be placed; how it should be used; and when, why, for how long, and who by (Silverstone 1994; Silverstone and Hirsch 1992). How today's second screens and streaming services combine to stabilise or disrupt the rhythms and routines of home life are explored below to highlight a reordering of 'home time'.

Related to the moral exchanges involved in screen use that include media parenting, claims of a late modern 'time crisis' are prompted by assumptions that new digital devices seem to 'waste' time and splinter family life through more solitary screen use. However, householders' engagement with devices in the home are varied and fluctuating. Fears about our excessive dependence on media technologies and misuse of time inferred by notions of 'screen excess' are tempered by research that finds screen-based activities to be important elements in the formation of childhood and youth identity (Livingstone 2009). Television and computer tablets can draw children and parents together by bonding over shared gaming, helping children to learn, and by facilitating relaxation and conversations about programmes and movies (Livingstone and Das 2010). Yet these same devices can be disruptive. They can commandeer or interrupt dialogue, intrude on children's homework and family meals, keep teenagers awake at night, and generate arguments about the amount of time children should use screens. These disruptions lead to complex moral negotiations between parents and children about where and when these devices can be switched on and off.

These moral issues about media parenting, fragmenting families, screen excess including binge-watching, night-time screen activity and home working all raise questions about how the multiscreen home is reorganising and reorganised by 'home time'. Media-oriented temporal shifts in today's digitally oriented home raise important questions about how screen viewing is achieved and experienced in the multimedia home: about what protocols and conventions householders adopt and negotiate to integrate screen viewing into the temporal rhythms of everyday life, and whether the meanings and practices associated with this screen technology engender a new domestic temporal logic.

Losing, making and sharing home time

Leading accounts of digital media and changing temporal routines in late modern societies tend to highlight the unwelcome features of speed, immediacy and the escalating pace of time. Problems of time constraints, associated with the adverse aspects of urbanisation, industrialisation and globalisation, involve pressures of work, consumerism and individualisation as features of the accelerating pace of time (Raso, 2011; Rosa, 2010; Thompson 1967; cf. Glennie and Thrift 2009). These beliefs about a loss or accelerating pace of time coincide with more general and popular convictions that personal, leisure and home time are interrupted, eroded and invaded by the demands of today's frenzied, technology-governed life. For John Tomlinson, modernity is characterised by a 'culture of instantaneity'. Speed has become an essential feature of immediacy with mobile media described as 'impatient' devices that embody instant information access (Tomlinson 2007: 132). Negative accounts of excessive screen activity coincide with fears about the speeding up and loss of time, triggered by anxieties about the repetitive and consuming nature of screen use.

Today's home-based media invoke ideas of disruption and distraction by eroding time-honoured distinctions between home zones and work zones. As Melissa Gregg (2011) argues, new temporal regimes of 'flexible labour', supported by laptops used for work purposes at home, may seem to offer new kinds of neoliberal time-flexibility. Yet they encourage workers, especially women, to extend paid work into domestic time. Being able to 'check in' from the bedroom to the workplace once seemed attractive – conveying a sense of emulating the work styles of business executives. But this allure of mobile technology and imaginaries of the networked home masks the extent to which work life is remoulded to meet the needs of a networked information economy rather the domestic well-being of employees. Even though mobile devices continue to be marketed as symbols of class distinction, they are now compulsory work tools. Compelled to stay connected to the workplace, mothers are susceptible to finding themselves connected to work via mobile devices while engaged in quality time with their children (Gregg 2011: 33). And work tasks now invade intimate phases such as bedtime. Yet, at the other end of the spectrum, today's multiscreen home provides opportunities for customised and personalised viewing and binge-watching.

Although today's multiscreen home is folded into traditional domestic viewing practices, the speed and immediacy enabled by digital media changes the temporal routines of home life. Today's mobile, stream-based, time-shifting and time-stretching multiscreen culture generates a sense of the screen's 'everytime-ness'. Not only are devices available for any purpose, anytime. They also enable a 'stretching' of time through experiences such as binge-watching. In these ways, today's digital screen opens up possibilities of home-based encounters in multiple timescapes. The term 'timescapes', developed by Barbara Adam, enables a conception of time as embedded in cultural practices (Adam 1995: 2004). This approach allows us to consider time not just as something squandered, but as something *produced* through the various routines and practices that we perform. In this sense, time involves more than synchronisation and rhythm. It also involves 'material, emotional, moral and political dimensions' (Shove et al. 2009: 2).

Elizabeth Shove, Frank Trentmann and Richard Wilk emphasise that we 'make time' through the various ways in which we shape our temporal rhythms. They use the term 'multiple temporalities' to foreground the variable and mutually interdependent nature of our daily rhythms and flows, by drawing on Lefebvre's Rhythmanalysis (Lefebvre 2004). The emphasis on *making time* is a useful way to consider how we shape our domestic routines using digital media. Each type of medium, from mobile screen to TV set, involves distinctive yet intersecting temporal orientations or tendencies. While work time can invade home time through our preoccupations with 'checking in', there is another dimension to media use that tends to be overlooked. We have control over media activities to such an extent that we can alter our sense of time passing. Barbara Adam also accentuates the *shared* nature of time as a set of experiences constituted through practice and space. We make time or lose time through our choice of media devices and media content and through our choices about who we decide to share that media time with.

Since today's converged media allow us to manipulate time in multi-layered ways, the multimedia home can be approached as a dynamic site involving a mesh of experienced and shared timescapes. For example, playing an absorbing video game or watching a gripping movie or TV drama are conscious ways in which we shape the quality of our 'made' time. And this mediated temporal experience differs according to who we decide to share that time with, whether alone or with family or friends. As Emily Keightley explains, 'time is not only mediated: our experience of it is always in some way intermediate or produced in our active engagement with these temporal articulations in any given context' (Keightley 2012: 207). Keightley calls these mediated timescapes 'zones of intermediacy' to highlight the various and multiple types of times involved in mediated experiences nowadays. This approach emphasises the growing level of choice involved in our use of mediated time. Keightley considers these zones of intermediacy as ways of *stretching* the present, a present lived through our experiences. This idea of making and sharing time, supported by today's media devices in the home, casts doubt on the idea of time as something diminished by the growing force of immediacy and simultaneity. Rather, it suggests that householders have agency in planning and yielding temporal experiences.

This emphasis on time as practice – on 'making' and 'expanding' time – offers conceptual tools to uncover the temporal dynamics of today's home, as a domestic multiscreen timescape. As mentioned in Chapter 4, earlier research by James Lull (1982, 1990) confirmed that families and householders have always managed separation and togetherness in the household by using television as both modes of 'affiliation' or 'avoidance'. Television can bring people together as a 'communication facilitator' yet also generate conflict about when, where and what programmes to watch. Householders acquire a keen sense of one another's domestic habits and associated media preferences to coordinate family life and avoid tensions related to different media uses in the same rooms. Correspondingly, Elaine Lally (2002: 136) refers to the strategies we use to manage 'living together'. She describes how householders establish feelings of shared identity by dividing up and individualising media-related activities. Our intimate understanding of fellow householders' habits and preferences has enabled families and co-habiting households to synchronise the timing of their home-based daily routines as part of a moral economy of the household (see O'Brien and Rodden 1997).

The temporal dynamics of multiscreen homes

The following case study of the ways in which second screens and streaming services are either interrupting or stabilising the rhythms and routines of home life is based on data about patterns of use of screen devices and streaming services from the UK's communications regulator Ofcom, combined with qualitative studies of media time and domestic screen uses (Chambers 2019). A striking shift in viewing practices away from 'traditional' modes of television viewing was initially reported in 2012 by Google's consumer survey of second screen use in the home (Google 2012). Two years later, it was reported that 'UK adults typically spent eight hours and 41 minutes a day engaging with media such as texting, talking, typing, gaming, listening, or watching' (Ofcom 2014). A 'second screen' usually signifies a portable electronic device – a tablet, computer or smartphone – used while viewing the large TV screen. This second screen enables access to supplementary content or complementary applications. A complementary application (app) facilitates viewer interaction with a TV programme, with the portable screen often referred to as a TV companion device.[1] Second screen broadcasts also coexist with the emergence of portable data delivery through cloud-based software systems, alongside other means of accessing content over wireless platforms.

The advent of the second screen's use in front of the living room's large TV screen suggests a reshaping or 're-making' of the home-based viewing encounter. As well as time-shifting options, screen viewing has recently been transformed into an interactive, real-time activity encompassing immediacy and liveness. Large screens offer a more enhanced viewing experience, particularly for movies and TV programmes. But smartphones and tablet computers are growing in popularity for the purposes of accessing social media and video-sharing websites such as YouTube. Mobile screens are also used at home for pay as-you-go, on-demand and streaming content. Although younger adults are more likely to use these mobile devices to view content, more than half of all adults in the UK value the adaptability of mobile screens for watching content where and when they wish (Ofcom 2017).

However, this kind of home-based media multitasking is not new. It predates the existence of second screens. Before digital convergence, audiences typically read magazines, newspapers or TV schedules to augment viewing. Audience attention wavered for almost half of their viewing time through engagement in dual activities such as eating, reading and chatting (Schmitt et al. 2003). And audiences communicated with broadcasters by writing letters to or participating in phone-in with broadcasters. As John Ellis has explained in his 'glance theory', television narratives have traditionally allowed for the fact that viewers were continually distracted. While reading, chatting or speaking on the phone, viewers would glance at the screen and miss information that came into view then disappeared in an instant as a media event occurring in time not space. As Ellis observes, 'broadcasting presents a continuous set of signals that are either received or missed by their potential audience' (Ellis 1992: 111). Reflecting the ephemeral and evanescent nature of both television broadcasting and the viewing experience, home TV viewing is characterised by partial attention to the screen. Nonetheless, as Elizabeth Evans states: 'The consequences of television's ephemerality and the distractions of the household remain, however now they are becoming mediated as viewer attention is increasingly marshalled across multiple spaces that are framed collectively' (Evans 2015). This habit of *glancing* and *multitasking* creates new opportunities for an interface between audience and broadcasters which are now enfolded in the second screen's digital affordances (Chambers 2019).

Mobile screens used at home while watching the big screen indicate an elaborate interweaving of unrelated, related and semi-related content (Blake 2017; D'heer et al. 2012; D'heer and Courtois 2014; Greer and Ferguson 2015; Wilson 2016). Unrelated content on the second screen refers to the most regular screen use for media tasks such as gaming or extraneous social networking. Fully related second screen use, known as 'meshing', involves the use of the portable screen to enrich the TV viewing experience by retrieving further information about a TV programme. This might include commenting on or engaging in the programme's content as a well as researching further details. This type of browsing is sustained by companion apps that offer complementary content or access to interactive information searches (Dowell et al. 2015). Real-time information can be more interactive by running apps in conjunction with the programme. Downloading a complementary app. facilitates interaction with a TV programme through connection with the second, portable screen. This is also referred to as a 'TV companion' device. As well TV programme-related tasks, second screen activity can involve other kinds of entertainment such as video gaming. Second screens enable interaction with content providers as well as filling moments of main screen inattentiveness. To give an idea of take-up, by 2017, laptops/PCs were used by over half of UK adults to watch TV programmes/films (55%), with tablets and smartphones equally used by just over a third (35% each) (Ofcom 2017).

These evolving screen activities in the home indicate the potential for householders to engage in elaborate synchronisations of time-intervals, downloadable real-time material and time-relevant information. What is rather surprising is that most householders use the second screen for activities unrelated to the broadcast programme, while the main TV set is switched on. Householders are inclined to lose attentiveness on the TV content (Vanattenhoven and Geerts 2012; Blake 2017). This tendency is even noticeable in app interactions when the apps are coordinated with the programmes (Holz et al. 2015). Householders tend to switch from the mobile device to watch the large screen only at strategic moments (Neate and Evans 2017). This kind of second screen use facilitates effortless 'viewing pauses'. In turn, this switching and glancing cultivates a non-immersive viewing experience that generates distracted viewing, referred to as a type of 'mediated glance' (Evans 2015). Significantly, second screen viewing pauses open up possibilities for moments of interaction with co-present household members in the communal space of the living room. Switching between devices is known as 'double attention' in the media industry (Blake 2017: 3), indicating that the second screen, used for web access and smart TV viewing, can foster a new kind of co-presence that can be referred to as 'ambient domestic connectivity' (Chambers 2016).

Personalised screen-viewing schedules facilitated by second screen use, generate new intimate episodes: new ways of watching 'alone together' as a genial habit that allow a *sharing* of home space and time. An important early Flemish study by Evelien D'heer and Courtois (2014) found that secondary screens become embedded within the daily TV viewing routine with household members gathered around the large living room TV screen. Whether alone or in other householders' company, portable screens were regularly picked up and used during an evenings' living room viewing. The device was used for browsing, games, checking emails and so on, to support this intersection between TV and second screens. The rise of this co-present 'alone time' in the shared space of the living room enables digital interaction beyond the home by activating both content-related and unrelated social networking.

In these ways, new screen technologies are offering avenues for negotiating new mediated household interactions and generating new familial dynamics. New modes of home-based interaction are particularly meaningful for families coping with today's 'extended youth' and 'boomerang generation' where young people either spend longer in the parental home or return home after spending some time living alone, to cope with the financial challenges associated with high rents and mortgages (Chambers 2012). Children, teenagers, students and parents are nowadays negotiating household dynamics in intricate and sometimes challenging post-nuclear, cohabiting households. Here, second screens enable a reorganisation of domestic schedules to sustain new or alternative spatial and 'familial' interactions.

Importantly, recent evidence indicates that the large screen TV set is still the most popular screen for viewing TV programmes and movies, at 94% of UK adults. Nevertheless, a significant rise in the use of alternative devices suggests a change in use (Ofcom 2017: 19). Almost a quarter of those who use on-demand and streaming services now view content via iTune store on the TV set. Householders are enhancing or supplanting live broadcast TV viewing with broadcasters' on-demand and streaming services, recorded TV and paid-for streaming services such as Netflix and Amazon Prime Video. Steadily becoming mainstream options, these services offer spatial and temporal flexibility, allowing viewers to 'watching what we want, when we want, wherever we want to watch it' (Ofcom 2017: 12).

Yet watching alone on any screen device remains popular, with nearly half of UK adults doing so daily and over a third several times a week. Householders seek out 'alone time' to watch chosen content, whether live or recorded broadcast TV (55%) or on-demand and streaming services (50%). Teenagers are the most pre-disposed to use social media (53%) or subscription on-demand and streaming services (50%) for watching TV programmes or films alone. Surprisingly, though, is that more than half of adults believe that 'people spend too much time watching alone on their tablets and smartphones nowadays' (Ofcom 2017: 12). This suggests that solitary viewing continues to be regarded as somewhat unsociable, infected by a sense of 'screen excess'. It seems that even though portable screens are now embedded within our domestic lives as a feature of 'home time', anxieties about a mediated detachment from fellow householders continues. Nevertheless, just over a third of householders sit together in the same room watching different content on various screens at least once a week (Ofcom 2017).

Notwithstanding the appeal of portable screens, the large screen in the living room is still used as a *social* screen. It remains the centre of attention in what continues to be communal space. In the UK, a third of adults sit together with family members to watch the same TV or film content together every day while another third does at least once a week. Taken as a whole, this indicates that 70% of householders watch communally, on the same screen, at least once a week and 75% do so at least once a month. This not only demonstrates the value of mediated *shared time* at home in front of the screen. Shared time is also unexpectedly high among teenagers with 88% watching with others on the same devices weekly. Shared viewing continues, then, to be cherished among families and cohabiting households as a form of mediated *family time*. Indeed, Ofcom's survey found that almost 68% of adults and 85% of teens agree that viewing TV programmes and movies 'brings the family together' with all available services now augmenting family viewing (Ofcom 2017: 12). Interestingly, live TV is preferred by just over a third, followed by subscription on-demand and streaming services (31%); with pay TV and broadcasters' on-demand and streaming services at around a quarter. And live TV is also used to 'entertain' children, with over a third of children accessing live broadcast TV as entertainment.

Polymediated timescapes

These diverse forms of synchronised screen activity, shared with co-present householders, generate new temporal practices in shared domestic spaces. Remarkably, then, multiple screens used at home are supporting varied screen practices which suggests the advent of new mediated ways of organising shared time in a new intermedial zone (Keightley 2012). Within the wider temporal setting of 'home time', we create times for being alone and also for interacting in or just sharing the same space. Individualised viewing schedules are generating new patterns of watching 'alone together' as a congenial routine to foster the *sharing* of domestic space and time. Moreover, second screens are not only supporting 'alone time' and 'family time' but also public network or 'communal time'.

It was predicted that a significant rise in the number of domestic screens would fragment and individualise home-based viewing patterns and undermine 'family time' before the arrival of domestic mobile screens (Lull 1982, 1990; Lally 2002). However, new kinds of screen use indicate a contrary pattern. Evidence suggests that second screens and streaming services are facilitating a new form of temporal synchronisation both within and across homes. The concept of 'polymediated timescapes' illuminates a new kind of *home time*, characterised by a new kind of temporal agency among householders that queries conventional assertions of individualised and fragmented domestic viewing activities in today's home ecology. The concept of 'polymediated timescapes' builds on the theory of 'polymedia' developed by Madianou and Miller (2012) which highlights three dimensions of digital media technologies that enlighten our understanding of the ways in which today's home-based screens mediate 'home time'.

First, the term polymedia foregrounds the multiple features of today's digital media and communication technologies involving the affordances of interactivity, temporarily, materiality and storage, replicability, mobility, public/private, information type and social protocols. Second, by supporting the meshing and synchronisation of different screen times, this polymedia environment is transformative. It accentuates user agency by emphasising the personal choices available between various media devices according to householders' circumstances. Householders gain a sense of control in their options about how, where and when to use screens or other media devices around the home. Explaining the significance of this sense of personal agency implicated in the choice of technologies, Madianou and Miller state that one of the major features of polymedia is that 'it shifts the power relationship from one in which the agency of the technology is often paramount towards one in which people have regained much of their control over the technologies, because they now have alternatives' (Madianou and Miller 2012: 137). A third dimension of polymediated timescapes concerns the relational features of individual media devices selected for use in the home. Delicate moral exchanges are implicated in supporting harmonious household routines as part of the temporal dynamics of the multiscreen home. This extends from parental monitoring of children's media use to decisions about which TV programmes or movies to watch together on the large living room screen.

Combined with streaming services, these multiple screens can augment householders' strategies for cohabiting affably. Householders no longer need to use screen devices in separate rooms. Second screens not only enable family members to come together in a communal space but even facilitate conversation through viewing pauses generated by a new kind of distracted viewing. Second screens also offer ways of averting tensions over multiple uses of shared space and viewing preferences (Lull 1990: 36). These second screen affordances confirm that the multiscreen home becomes a polymediated timescape by enabling new, flexible kinds of temporal agency. The term 'polymedia' underlines the ways in which today's digitised screen time is domesticated or 'socialised' through home use (D'heer and Courtois 2014). It draws attention to a sense of choice felt by householders over the devices they select to use, and the possibilities for synchronising content activities involving streaming, time-shifting and 'meshing'. With a heightened awareness of the pacing of time, householders experience time dilation (Coleman 2018). This sense of 'time stretching' transforms the home setting. Generated by multiple media platforms and the emergence of a polymediated domestic 'timescape' (Adam 1995; 2004), 'home' transforms from a setting in which the technology dominates or intrudes, to one in which householders have a sense of control over media technologies and viewing experiences.

Intra- and trans-domestic time

The multiscreen living room is now facilitating new kinds of interaction by enabling more co-located and remote communication within this polymediated timescape. As well as nurturing common talking points, the multiscreen living room forms a domestic space for remote interaction between homes via the web. Two identifiable kinds of polymediated screen time can be described as *intra-* and *trans-domestic temporality*.

First, intra-domestic temporality involves the fostering of new forms of communication between co-present householders, with varying degrees of attentiveness and distractedness. Instead of causing a fragmentation of family time, multiple screen engagement allows householders to share space while involved in various activities, generating a new sense of shared time as *family time*. Second, trans-domestic temporality indicates cross-home interaction that cultivates a wider sharing of time distinguished as *communal time* or public network time. Through relational content-sharing and commenting, this trans-domestic communication involves a collective, national and even transnational synchronisation. Trans-domestic exchange is characterised by the synchronising of media content and time via live and post-programme interactivity as well as one-to one trans-home communication via social media apps such as WhatsApp. As D'heer and colleagues point out, the second screen's capacity for synchronised use of social media and non-immersive interaction with other household members enables a *resocialisation* of the living room through 'outbound affiliation' (D'heer et al. 2012; D'heer and Courtois 2014). This second screen dynamic of enabling householders to communicate with people from a distance, by interconnecting homes, generates a form of 'ambient domestic connectedness' involving new moods and atmospheres in the home (Chambers, 2016).

These qualities of the *social* screen foster the rise of a domestically oriented *communal time* to form a new kind of daily television landscape. Viewers follow hashtags in tandem with live TV programmes, generating online dialogue about events in real-time. Such screen-assisted dialogues enable an expansion or intensification of immediacy, of the 'here-and-now', from the shared space of the living room as a post-live dilation of time. Cross-home second screen dialogues offer a new form of synchronisation and new encounters with the world beyond the home from the heart of the living room by conjoining audience-oriented pursuits with social media engagement. This trans-domestic communal time has great significance for diasporic communities and transnational families whose members regularly keep in contact from across distant parts of the globe. The digital screen augments opportunities to engage in intimate, familial communication across national boundaries, creating a transnational shared time as trans-domestic temporarily.

In terms of the changing experiences of live TV, it is surprising to find that live broadcast TV has an enduring appeal for householders with the choice and flexibility offered by on-demand and mobile content. Despite the availability of time-shifting, live broadcast TV continues to be cherished for its ability to offer a national synchronisation of major events by offering an experience of immediacy through liveness. Live TV continues to be the hub of home-based screen activity. This is confirmed by Ofcom's finding that for 50% of householders, their first action when they switch on the TV is to check what is being broadcast live (Ofcom 2017). Their second action is to go to on-demand subscription services (12%), followed by recorded TV via DVR (11%). Revealingly, UK householders say that they watch live broadcast TV to keep in touch with the news and access information on 'what's happening around them' (Ofcom 2017: 12). And over half (58%) of householders in the UK prefer to watch national events on broadcast TV rather than via on-demand 'because it's good to know everyone is watching at the same time'. Almost half of households in the Ofcom survey (45%) emphasised the same value for sports programmes. It seems then, that 'Broadcast TV dominates as the place to keep up with what's going on in the world and to share important moments with friends, family and the nation' (Ofcom 2017: 25).

The fostering of shared viewing experiences with the nation or a wider community beyond home, supported by live broadcast TV, suggests that 'liveness' remains a strong social force. It facilitates householders' experience of their *home-based* media time as a time shared with others beyond the home, with a wider imagined community. This idea of a 'public realm' accessible from the home through trans-domestic synchronised screen practices recalls Benedict Anderson's notion of the 'imagined nation' (Anderson 1991; see Chapter 4). Even though the multimedia home gives rise to a more fluid domestic multiscreen experience, with more opportunities for time-shifting, multi-viewing and binge-watching, live broadcasting remains central. Liveness fosters symbiotic interconnections between domestic life and public life which shapes and represents domestic cultures as 'national cultures'. We might call this potential a 'trans-domestic' culture, forming part of a new kind of polymediated timescape. It confirms the continued relevance of Scannell's' understanding of the mediation of domestic space in a multiscreen home culture. Scannell explains that 'public events now occur, simultaneously, in two different places: the place of the event itself and that in which it is watched and heard. Broadcasting mediates between these two sites' (Scannell 1996: 76). Live transmissions of large public events such as sport upholds a communal emotional drama, played out in the context of the nation (Chambers 2019).

Binge-watching and 'blue light' activity

Night-time screen activity and watching multiple episodes of a television series in quick succession rather than waiting for the next week's episode is known as 'binge-watching'. This practice invokes excessive or disorderly viewing. Binge-watching is now a normal screen practice that contrasts with the attractiveness of 'liveness'. In the UK, over a third of people binge-watch at least weekly. With four in ten users of Netflix, Amazon Prime and NOW TV in the UK in 2016, Ofcom (2017) discovered that 'More than half (54%) of adults in the UK like the freedom of being able to watch when and where they want on their tablet or smartphone'. Whilst most watch programmes and films on-demand to avoid adverts, binge-watching turns out to be a highly sociable activity with almost half of binge-watchers doing so in the company of family and friends (Ofcom 2017). Binge-watchers explain that it gives them a chance to spend time with others, as well as finding it relaxing and pleasurable. This bonding experience gives householders something to talk about with friends (24%) and brings them closer to family/friends (11%). And 6% of binge-watchers say it gives them a chance to socialise (Ofcom 2017). Rather than fragmenting mediated temporal experiences, this kind of time-shifting and back-to-back viewing offers householders a further sense of shared time, enabling experiences of time dilation (Chambers 2019).

Although scholars foreground the tensions of immediacy, by suggesting that 'presentness' and immediacy involve 'an annihilation of time' Kaun (2015), a study of Netflix by Rebecca Coleman (2018) indicates that the flow offered by these streaming services slows down the pace of time, disrupting the sense of time as sequential and linear. Coleman observes that Netflix's binge-watching 'constitutes specific presents that are simultaneously connected and always-on, and on-going and processual', leading to a 'multiplicity of the present' (Coleman 2018: 615). Resonating with Ofcom's findings, she explains that devices act as 'pacers' of real-time, stating that: 'the production of a present temporality through digital media may also be experienced as a means of making spaces and times for conviviality, pleasure and positive affect' (Coleman 2018: 617). This notion of manipulating the present, by using multiple devices and services to support bingeing, pausing and suspending time indicates a new way of stretching time, a new kind of time dilation that embodies a new form of domestic screen time. This suggests that rather than eroding time or generating a 'disorderly' form of screen excess, second screens and streaming services offer householders new opportunities to control time, generating new kinds of shared time in the communal space of the living room (Chambers 2019).

Yet this striking rise in householders' viewing agency corresponds with an increased embedding of screen activity in conflicting ways. If time-shifting and back-to-back viewing enable more concentrated or immersive viewing, mobile devices also foster distraction and a blurring of traditional distinctions between 'viewing' and 'non-viewing'. This is illustrated by night-time screen engagement. More than a third of UK adults who binge-watch monthly admit to missing out on sleep or feeling tired the next day. And social media use, such as Facebook, tends to peak late at night, from 9.00pm until after midnight (Ofcom 2017). These platforms are used for trans-domestic communication as well as screen entertainment, supporting beyond-home affiliations. Whilst acknowledging the neoliberal regimes of work and self-productivity that motivate night-time screen engagement addressed by Gregg (2011), Dan Hassoun and James Gilmore (2016) point out that this 'bustle of activity' involves *multisensorial* practices. In a study of the intersection of sleep with media technologies, they reveal that night-time's 'blue light' screen activity forms part of individuals' routines, emphasising that engagement with portable devices in between episodes of sleep also blurs the distinctions between viewing and non-viewing. This sense of effortless bedtime screen engagement renders home-based media activity an essential yet invisible and taken-for-granted experience, complicating claims about the screen's addictive qualities.

When asking students about their night-time media habits, Hassoun and Gilmore were struck that participants offered articulate descriptions of their gaming, Netflix, website and app check-ins and about how they hold tablets and place laptops in relation to their bodies in bed. Yet they were unable to offer clear responses about why they undertake these tasks at night in bed, other than 'It's just part of my habit' and 'I don't know'. As Hassoun and Gilmore state: 'it seems more likely that blue light engagement is something that happens from a number of screens and for a number of reasons as part of a larger, ongoing process of drowsing' (Hassoun and Gilmore 2016: 112). They suggest that blue light engagement indicates specific technologies that foster sensations of sleep and relaxation. These media technologies do not simply accelerate life: they may also offer ways of calming down, resonating with examples of sounds and images on video-sharing websites that claim to relax and calm the body (Andersen 2015).

Hassoun and Gilmore suggest that the converged, interactive, mobile, tactile, and intuitive features of today's touchscreens involve affective states that allow an effortless assimilation of mobile screens into domestic routines. If Gregg (2011) foregrounds the ways in which new temporal regimes encroach on intimate episodes such as bedtime, Hassoun and Gilmore (2016) suggest that this night-time screen activity encompasses multisensorial practices. Whilst the process of screen engagement involves moments of potential non-engagement, inattention and distractedness, 'The important point is that the blue light offered by new devices helps to arrange bodies, technologies, and darkness in ways that previous light sensations may not have'. In this sense, habitual night-time engagement with personal screens becomes a multisensorial experience from attention to inattention, from awakened to drowsing states (Hassoun and Gilmore 2016: 108). Although neoliberal systems of work and self-productivity can lure us towards night-time screen use, research on the intersection of sleep and domestic media technologies indicates that 'blue light' activity now forms part of individuals' everyday routines. Yet these technologies do not inevitably accelerate the pace of home life. They might also present ways of relaxing and calming the body (see Andersen 2015), opening up questions about the intriguing relationship between 'drowsing' and screens in a media saturated home ecology.

The language of screen excess as an 'addiction' is now used among certain medical professionals who label prolonged computer gaming and nightly portable screen use as a 'disease'. These notions of addiction, binge-watching and 'blue screen' habits mirror news reports and complaints about screen excess. Concerns about antisocial and harmful screen-based habits are a major site of contention in relation to parental monitoring of children and teenagers' screen engagement. Unease about excessive night-time screen use among young people is exemplified by news reports about 'Vampire Children'. One article in the *Daily Mail* (Carey 2015) quotes danah boyd who argues that young people risk chronic tiredness and parental deception to protect 'me time' during the quiet of the night (boyd 2014). This home-based *personal time*, in the privacy of the bedroom, is often the only interlude in a schedule-packed day when teens can hold intimate, trans-domestic conversations with peers, away from prying adult eyes.

Conclusion

This chapter has addressed shifting meanings of home triggered by the accelerated use of streaming devices and second screens. In the past, it was thought that the spread of screens in the home would prompt a scattering of family members into different rooms. Yet new devices and streaming services indicate dynamic opportunities for active encounters with speeded up media - opportunities which, until now were underestimated. Media imaginaries about home and domestic space now play a fundamental part in defining that space, not only through wider discourses about media but also as a result of the ways in which householders are actively using their screens. Rather than creating a temporal dislocation, the multiscreen home opens up new forms of temporal agency. Second screens and streaming devices support new routines and modes of synchronising that can convert the living room into a flexible temporal space. Today's screen-based dynamics indicate that home time is not simply consumed or squandered but *made* and *expanded* through media practices.

These digital technologies come together to enable not just more 'me time' but also new types of interaction and shared moments in the living room, and new relations beyond home. This multiple medium domestic space has become a polymediated environment that offers households a sense of agency. Domestic screens alter and re-order our concentration, our rhythms and our awareness of schedules through enhanced affordances such as speed and immediacy of access. Instead of just constraining our time, digital screens allow us to subvert and actively reshape temporal routines and the associated needs of work, sleep and timekeeping that characterise late modernity. Today's digital screens open up temporal zones – family time, memory time, alone time, news time, community time and social time – that enable an extension of the present. By stretching the interactive temporalities of the home to create new, multiple forms of personal time and shared time, these temporal circumstances involve new encounters with the present, with the here-and-now.

However, while these polymediated timescapes generate opportunities to reshape or contest distinctions between shared time, personal time, work time, home time, family time and community or collective time, they can also involve distraction, ambient attention and sleep interruption. But they intermingle with certain traditional viewing habits to create a new domestic screen culture in which the home is reconfigured as a site of mobility, agency and change. This new domestic screen culture is distinguished by *intra-domestic* and *trans-domestic* screen-based temporality as two types of time dilation forming part of a new temporal flow. Intra-domestic screen time is supported by portable screens that enable the viewing of different content on second screens in front of the large screen in the living room. The large screen preserves its role of supporting 'family time' or shared household time, through the collective viewing of films, and national events such as sport and news. Trans-domestic screen time indicates a new type of cross-household interaction between viewers. Yet, it also supports a sense of collectivity and shared time not just beyond the home but also through a sense of liveness and immediacy. Liveness can convey a sense of togetherness and community beyond the home, as a form of communal temporality. Second screens supported by companion apps can generate an 'interactive immediacy' relating to popular TV programmes to bring audiences in different homes together. New screen technologies can also open up ways of communicating about screen content by bringing together transnational families and diasporic communities. In this way, the technology can facilitate new transnational intimacies beyond the home, even a new form of 'mobile domesticity' (see Chapter 8).

Note

1 See, for example, on the BBC's Research and Development website, 'Companion Screens: Creating a viewing experience across more than one screen', available at https://www.bbc.co.uk/rd/projects/companion-screens (accessed 1 September 2018).

References

Adam, B. (1995) *Timewatch: The Social Analysis of Time*. Cambridge: Polity Press.

Adam, B. (2004) *Time: Key Concepts*. Cambridge, UK and Malden, MA: Polity Press.

Andersen, J. (2015) 'Now you've got the shiveries: Affect, intimacy, and the ASMR whisper community', *Television & New Media*, 16(8), 683–700.

Anderson, B. (1991) *Imagined Communities: Reflections on the Origin and Spread of Nationalism*. London: Verso.

Blake, J. (2017) *Television and the Second Screen: Interactive TV in the Age of Participation*. London: Routledge.

boyd, d. (2014) *It's Complicated: The Social Lives of Networked Teens*. New Haven: Yale University Press.

Carey, T. (2015) 'The generation dubbed "The vampire children"', *Mail Online*, 4 February 2015. www.dailymail.co.uk/femail/article-2940347/The-generation-dubbed-Vampire-Chil dren-Hooked-iPads-mobiles-late-night-hardly-sleep-experts-reveal-terrifying-toll-takes.html (accessed 3 August 2019).

Chambers, D. (2012) *A Sociology of Family Life*. Cambridge: Polity.

Chambers, D. (2016) *Changing Media, Homes and Households*. London: Routledge.

Chambers, D. (2019) 'Emerging temporalities in the multiscreen home', *Media, Culture and Society* OnlineFirst, 1–19. https://doi.org/10.1177/0163443719867851.

Clark, L.S. (2013) *The Parent App: Understanding Families in the Digital Age*. Oxford: Oxford University Press.

Coleman, R. (2018) 'Theorizing the present: Digital media, pre-emergence and infra-structures of feeling', *Cultural Studies*, 32(4), 600–622.

D'heer, E. and Courtois, C. (2014) 'The changing dynamics of television consumption in the multimedia living room', *Convergence*. doi.org/10.1177/1354856514543451.

D'heer, E., Courtois, C. and Paulussen, S. (2012) 'Everyday life in front of the screen: The consumption of multiple screen technologies in the living room context', in *Proceedings of the 10th European Conference on Interactive TV and Video*. New York: Association for Computing Machinery, pp. 195–198.

Dowell, J., Malacria, S., Kim, H. and Anstead, E. (2015) 'Companion apps for information-rich television programmes: Representation and interaction', *Personal and Ubiquitous Computing*, 19(7), 1215–1228.

Ellis, J. (1992) *Visible Fictions: Cinema, Television, Video*. London: Routledge.

Evans, E. (2015) 'Layering engagement: The temporal dynamics of transmedia television', *Storyworlds: A Journal of Narrative Studies*, 7(2), 111–128.

Glennie, P. and Thrift, N. (2009) *Shaping the Day: A History of Timekeeping in England and Wales 1300–1800*. New York: Oxford University Press.

Google. (2012) 'The new multiscreen world: Understanding cross-platform consumer behaviour'. www.thinkwithgoogle.com/advertising-channels/mobile-marketing/the-new-multi-screen-world-study/ (accessed 9 September 2018).

Greer, C.F. and Ferguson, D.A. (2015) 'Tablet computers and traditional television viewing: Is the iPad replacing TV?', *Convergence*, 21(2), 244–256.

Gregg, M. (2011) *Works' Intimacy*. Cambridge: Polity Press.

Hassoun, D. and Gilmore, J.N. (2016) 'Drowsing: Toward a concept of sleepy screen engagement', *Communication and Critical/Cultural Studies*, 14(2), 103–119.

Hills, A.P., Andersen, L.B. and Byrne, N.M. (2011) 'Physical activity and obesity in children', *British Journal of Sports Medicine*, 45, 866–870.

Holz, C., Bentley, F., Church, K., and Patel, M. (2015) '"I'm just on my phone and they're watching tv": Quantifying mobile device use while watching television', in *Proceedings of the ACM International Conference on Interactive Experiences for TV and Online Video*. New York: TVX '15, ACM, pp. 93–102.

Kaun, A. (2015) 'Regimes of time: media practices of the dispossessed', *Time and Society*, 24(2), 221–243.

Kayany, J.M. and Yelsma, P. (2000) 'Displacement effects of online media in the socio-technical contexts of households', *Journal of Broadcasting & Electronic Media*, 44(2), 215–229.

Keightley, E. (2012) 'Conclusion: Making time – the social temporalities of mediated experience', in *Time, Media and Modernity*. Basingstoke: Palgrave Macmillan, pp. 201–224.

Lally, E. (2002) *At Home with Computers*. Berg: Oxford.

Lefebvre, H. (2004) *Rhythmanalysis: Space, Time and Everyday Life*, trans. S. Elden and G. Moore. New York: Continuum.

Livingstone, S. (2009) 'Half a century of television in the lives of our children', *The Annals of the American Academy of Political and Social Science*, 625, 151–163.

Livingstone, S. and Das, R. (with contributions from Georgiou, M., Haddon, L., Helsper, E. and Wang, Y.) (2010) 'Media, communication and information technologies in the European family working report (April 2010)'. Family Platform, Existential Field 8. http://eprints.lse.ac.uk/29788/1/EF8_LSE_MediaFamily_Education.pdf (accessed 3 August 2019).

Livingstone, S., Mascheroni, G., Ólafsson, K. and Haddon, L. (2014) *Children's Online Risks and Opportunities: Comparative Findings from EU Kids Online and Net Children Go Mobile, LSE*. London: EU Kids Online.

Lull, J. (1982) 'How families select television programs: A mass observational study', *Journal of Broadcasting and Electronic Media*, 26(4), 801–811.

Lull, J. (1990) *Inside Family Viewing: Ethnographic Research on Television's Audiences*. London: Routledge.

Madianou, M. and Miller, D. (2012) *Migration and New Media: Transnational Families and Polymedia*. London: Routledge.

Morley, D. (1986) *Family Television: Cultural Power and Domestic Leisure*. London: Comedia.

Morley, D. (2002) *Home Territories: Media, Mobility and Identity*. London: Routledge.

Mullan, K. (2018) 'A child's day: Trends in time use in the UK from 1975 to 2015', *The British Journal of Sociology*, 1–28. https://doi.org/10.1111/1468-4446.12369.

Neate, T., Jones, M. and Evans, M. (2017) 'Cross-device media: A review of second screening and multi-device television', *Personal and Ubiquitous Computing*, 21(2), 391–405.

Nie, N.H. and Hillygus, D.S. (2002) 'The impact of internet use on sociability: Time-diary findings', *IT & Society*, 1(1), 1–20.

O'Brien, J. and Rodden, T. (1997) 'Interactive systems in domestic environments', in *Proceedings of the 2nd Conference on Designing Interactive Systems: Processes, Practices, Methods, and Techniques, Association for Computing Machinery*. New York: ACM, pp. 247–259.

Ofcom. (2014) 'The communications market report'. www.ofcom.org.uk/data/assets/pdf_file/0031/19498/2014_uk_cmr.pdf (accessed 1 September 2018).

Ofcom. (2017) 'The communications market 2018: Narrative report'. www.ofcom.org.uk/research-and-data/multi-sector-research/cmr/cmr-2018/report (accessed 28 August 2018).

Raso, K. (2011) 'Running out of time at hyper-speed', *Australian Journal of Communication*, 38(3), 179–180.

Rosa, H. (2010) *Alienation and Acceleration: Towards a Critical Theory of Late Modern Temporality*. Malmo: NSU Press.

Scannell, P. (1996) *Radio, Television, and Modern Life: A Phenomenological Approach*. Oxford: Blackwell Publisher.

Scannell, P. (2000) 'For anyone-as-someone structures', *Media, Culture and Society*, 22(1), pp. 5–24.

Schmitt, K.L., Woolf, K.D. and Anderson, D.R. (2003) 'Viewing the viewers: Viewing behaviors by children and adults during television programs and commercials', *Journal of Communication*, 53(2), 265–281.

Shove, E., Trentmann, T. and Wilk, R. (2009) 'Introduction', in E. Shove *et al.* (eds), *Time, Consumption and Everyday Life: Practice, Materiality and Culture*. Oxford: Berg, pp. 1–16.

Silverstone, R. (1994) *Television and Everyday Life*. London: Routledge.

Silverstone, R. and Hirsch, E. (eds) (1992) *Consuming Technologies: Media and Information in Domestic Spaces*. London: Routledge.

Thompson, E.P. (1967) 'Time, work-discipline and industrial capitalism', *Past & Present*, 38 (1), 56–97.

Tomlinson, J. (2007) *The Culture of Speed: The Coming of Immediacy*. London: Sage.

Vanattenhoven, J. and Geerts, D. (2013) *Second-screen Use in the Home: An Ethnographic Study*. Proceedings 3rd International Workshop on Future Television. Berlin: EuroITV 2012, Springer, pp. 162–173.

Wilson, S. (2016) 'In the living room: Second screens and TV audiences', *Television and New Media*, 17(2) 174–191.

7

ALTERNATIVE DOMESTICITIES

Introduction

Dominant discourses of domesticity that present home as a heterosexualised, nuclear family space are reproduced and reinforced through policy, house design and popular media imageries (Blunt and Dowling 2006). As illustrated in earlier chapters, not only are state, commercial and media endorsements of interior designs, styles and spatial layouts of home heterosexualised. So too are normative assumptions about the daily domestic routines involved in maintaining homes and households. For example, most homes are designed for nuclear families by the setting aside of a master bedroom for the heterosexual couple and smaller bedrooms intended for children (Johnston and Longhurst 2010). And studies of the spatial expressions of gendered identities and power confirm that women are normatively associated with domestic and suburban settings, and men with the public sphere of paid work (Duncan 1996; McDowell 1999). Correspondingly, the heterosexualisation of domestic labour is sustained through traditions, arrangements and media representations that fix women's status within the domestic sphere (McDowell 1999; Crompton 2006; Lachance-Grzela and Bouchard 2010). Regardless of a rise in women's educational qualifications, employment and political participation, home continues to be coded as a 'feminine space'. Here, domestic labour and childcare remain gendered, considered to be tasks assigned to women (Crompton 2006). These dominant cultural tendencies involve what is referred to as a 'hegemonic heterosexualisation' of home (Barrett 2015). The habitual, normative behaviour associated with domesticity reflects distinctive ideological commitments to wider patterns of socio-cultural and economic inequality that form part of gendered and sexed histories of managing home life through habit (see Pedwell 2017).

These gender-circumscribed discourses of home set limits on family arrangements, often restricting alternative family and household configurations, demonstrated by the work of Hayden (1981). Such discourses pose challenges for householders in shaping alternative living arrangements that might embrace same-sex couples, extended kin, friends, as well as living alone or coping with home life after divorce. However, these dominant ideologies of home and household life are continually contested and re-formed, often through innovative homemaking practices (Barret 2015). Research suggests that home is now a site for re-organising or sustaining alternative domesticities. Not only can housing cooperatives, co-housing schemes and other modes of shared housing arrangements facilitate diverse living arrangements but also conventional 'heteronormative' homes can at times support diverse experiences such as 'coming out' in the parental home by validating emerging adults' queer identities (Pilkey et al. 2015). As Blunt and Dowling state, 'People's house-based practices illustrate their active engagement with, and recasting of, the social characteristics of home'. (Blunt and Dowling 2006: 89). Nevertheless, LGBTQ[1] people's self-disclosure of their sexual orientation or gender identity can also cause distress, misery and homelessness for those living in an unsupportive home environment (Pilkey 2012).

Changing household types and arrangements, familial values and intimacies have coincided with dramatic transformations in domestic culture. Alternative domesticities encompass a range of identities and domestic arrangements that are often marginalised or ignored in conventional debates about home including homeless people, older LGBTQ people and broken families. This chapter moves beyond the heteronormative ideology of home and domesticity to address modes of home-making that challenge and transform debates. Alternative domesticities are identified that signify struggles and contestations over traditional and new meanings of home in late modernity: from traditional family values to postmodern notions of mobility, agency and change. New domestic living arrangements between householders are considered by chronicling changes in intimate affiliations, for example among lesbian and gay couples, and by assessing how these changes have been mediated by popular media accounts of home. Historical ethnographic and sociological accounts of domestic space are drawn on to foreground the negotiation of alternative home practices. Academic work confirms that the relationship between home and identity is fluid and that they shape one another. Research also demonstrates that identity-affirming homemaking activities can subvert normative discourses of home. This chapter explores, then, the relations between home and identity-construction as themes that characterise studies of alternative domesticities.

Masculinities and domesticities

Early studies of gay male spatiality have attended to gay men's uses of public spaces and the role of gay culture in the gentrification of certain urban quarters, while largely overlooking the significance of home for gay men. Ensuing scholarship on masculinity and the home from the 1990s began by addressing three interconnected social identities: hegemonic heterosexual masculinity, bachelor and gay domesticities (Gorman-Murray 2008a). Within a normative heterosexual nuclear family household shaped by an inequitable gendered division of labour, hegemonic masculinity has traditionally been structured by men's identities as 'breadwinner' and head of household. These designations summon themes such as husbands' control over finances, household decisions and also expectations of being waited on and nurtured (Chambers 2012; Chapman 2004; McDowell 1999). The expression that 'a man's home is his castle' coincides with ideas that home acts as respite from the (masculinised) world of work. Yet, paradoxically, men are also often perceived as largely absent from home. Moreover, a range of scholarship questions these stark oppositions, revealing multiple lived experiences and modes of resistance that challenge these prevailing gendered discourses (Davidoff and Hall 2002; Tosh 2007).

Reinforcing dominant associations between home and femininity, masculine identities tend to be explained in relation to their paid work (Smith and Winchester 1998; McDowell 2005: 19). Yet masculinities are constructed through a multiplicity of institutions and spatial contexts including home, family, school, leisure and sport as well as work (McDowell 2005: 20). Recent research that contests heteronormative ideals of home reveals that the private sphere of the home can facilitate men's negotiation of alternative masculinities, away from the restrictions of paid work that can impose or perpetuate hegemonic models of masculinity. Recognising the home as a significant site of masculine identity practices, scholars argue that masculinity and domesticity are interrelational and co-constitutive (Gorman-Murray 2008a; 2008c; Tosh 1999). Similarly, 'new domestic masculinities' have been identified that deviate from the traditional roles and practices of husbands-in-the-home (Pink 2004: 118). The notion of privacy associated with home supports varied expressions of masculinity in circumstances where emergent domestic masculinities are challenging normative imaginaries of home. Different interactions between men and their homes correspond with different masculine identities and domestic environments.

Bachelor codes

The homes of non-heteronormative residents such as bachelors foregrounds ideological conservatism yet also summons allusions to alternative domesticities. While the cult of the home in nineteenth-century England gives prominence to the status of women and children as described in Chapter 2, Victorian middle-class domestic life was shaped in response to the needs of heterosexual men. This assessment of domesticity was reinforced by the idea of the separation of work and home (Tosh 1999, 2005; Vickery 1993). At the same time, this 'separation of spheres' ensured the home's relevance for masculine identity. Tosh identifies three key themes that question generalisations about familial masculinity as 'breadwinner' and femininity as homemaker and child carer. First, the idea of the companionate marriage formed a key dimension of the Victorian ideal of domesticity. Second, the nurturing role of fatherhood was significant for domestic masculinity. And third, men's roles as the spiritual leaders of their families was bolstered by a religious revival that not only tied men to the home as the appropriate place to foster the family's spiritual well-being but also enabled the family circle to offer the working man a moral compass (Tosh 1999; 2005).

Key research in this field has been further advanced by Andrew Gorman-Murray (2006a), beginning with his consideration of 'bachelor domesticity'. He points to nineteenth-century novels in which the figure of the 'bachelor' living alone and distinguished by his homemaking disrupts normative domestic imaginaries. Defying ideals of nurturing fatherhood that characterise hegemonic notions of domestic masculinity, the single man was marked as immature and self-indulgent. Yet bachelors were also imagined as 'exemplars of domestic life': fastidious in cultivating a stylish and comfortable home (Snyder 1999). Chiming with the work of Richard Hornsey (2010), Gorman-Murray draws attention to the counter-discourse that avowed bachelor domesticity as a masculine virtue, portrayed as a form of domestic refinement. This bachelor code of 'masculine elegance' and domestic selfhood was further elaborated in writings about model bachelor apartments in American films of the 1950s/1960s and magazines such as *Playboy*. Figuring a consuming masculine subject, whose penthouse apartment was filled with sophisticated designer furniture and the latest consumer durables, the model bachelor's home presented an alternative to the suburban nuclear family dwelling, free from familial responsibilities (Cohan 1996; Osgerby 2005). In a study of modern bachelors in England and Spain, Sarah Pink (2004) found echoes of this ethos. Many of her interviewees described their homemaking as narratives of self-identity and some men said that their domestic practices defied prevailing domestic ideologies and traditional family values associated with home.

An alternative type of domestic arrangement that can also be categorised as bachelor domesticity is all-male shared houses comprising cohabiting groups of men (Gorman-Murray 2008a). Deviating from the 'playboy' image, these forms of bachelor share-housing emerged in television programmes like *The Odd Couple* (1970–1975), *Friends* (1994–2004), *Last Man Standing* (2011–2017) and *My Name is Earl* (2005–2009) (Natalier 2003; McNamara & Connell 2007). As Gorman-Murray points out, this genre highlights the need to move beyond the singular bachelor 'lifestyle' stereotype characterised by single occupancy and stylish consumption. Importantly, these presentations and practices of alternative domestic arrangements indicate shifting meanings of home and changing masculine identities. In his consideration of the ways in which Australian gay have used homes to shape and affirm their identities, Gorman-Murray (2006b) found that gay men use 'private' homes in ways that differ from traditional 'homely' homes. External activities, identities and discourses are invited into the home with the aim of 'queering' domestic space and activating non-heteronormative modes of socialisation including nurturing queer identities. Understood as 'private' spaces, homes interconnect with and spread into 'public' sites and expressions of subcultural sexual identities in ways that 'stretch' home and reconfigure public spaces as 'homelike'. In these ways, gay men's 'queered homes' extend beyond the physical threshold of home to reveal the ways in which home is at one and the same time private and public.

How spaces are shaped by sexuality and encrypted with sexual meanings has been studied since the 1990s (Colomina 1996). For example, Matt Cook tracks the meaning of 'queer' in London from the early nineteenth century when the term was associated with 'oddity, badness, malformation or foreignness' (Cook 2014: 7). This negative connotation endured in the late nineteenth to early twentieth century until its meaning changed to describe 'eccentricity, Bohemianism, and exoticism' (Cook 2014: 7). As Scicluna (2015) points out, the historical notion of 'queer' refers mainly to men. The word 'queer' was then adopted within everyday language to denote homosexual difference, often to refer to people, their values and practices. The term has since been adopted within sexuality and gender scholarship to refer to sexual fluidity and allude to other categories of identity. Whilst endorsing contemporary uses of the term 'queer', Cook points to the fluctuating and elusive nature of the concept. He exploits the ambiguity and openness of the term to emphasise its multiple meanings over time, particularly in relation to the twentieth-century homemaking practices of homosexuals in London. In this way, the word 'queer' draws attention to the complexities of everyday life. It seldom fits and therefore challenges the neat categories, conventions and stereotypes surrounding heterosexuality, homosexuality or transsexuality.

However, the notion of 'queering home' is a recent conceptualisation advanced in studies of alternative domesticities and exploited in the popular media to refer, for example, to gay men's skills as makeover show hosts. A series of case studies by Gorman-Murray, addressed in this chapter, has spearheaded explorations of the 'queering' of home and domesticities. For example, his study of middle-class lesbians and gay men in urban Australia show that gay/lesbian meanings of home correspond with and yet also subvert normative meanings of home. His participants invoked a series of traditional values but have translated them through the lens of gay or lesbian experiences (Gorman-Murray 2007b). Paradoxically, then, established norms that underpin homely values are drawn on by members of gay and lesbian households that actually sustain and endorse sexual difference. Gorman-Murray describes two key processes through which the 'queering home' occurs through home activities: first, though the uses of home activities and second, by making changes to the materiality of domestic space within homemaking practices. His work confirms that gay and lesbian identities and relationships are 'embedded' in the material environment of home.

Gay stereotypes on home makeover TV shows

Studies of gay domesticity point to the link between gay men and desirable domestic style established by their portrayal as 'design experts' in lifestyle television programmes (Attwood 2005; Gorman-Murray 2008a; Hart 2004). Such research offers a useful lens through which to explore mainstream accounts of gay domesticity, their popular appeal and the constraints they involve. While hegemonic masculinity tends to be dissociated from domesticity as a means of upholding patriarchal privilege, cultural discourses tend to associate gay men with domesticity as a feature of the feminine realm (van Hoven and Horschelmann 2005: 8). Since 2000, a growing number of studies interrogate the association of gay stereotypes and domestic sensibility conveyed in the media (e.g. Meyer and Kelley 2004; Gorman-Murray 2006a: 230; Pilkey 2015). A rise in magazine and newsprint depictions of the design and styling of gay men's homes are exemplified by Toronto's 2012 Annual Tour of Homes in the city's historic Cabbagetown district where most displayed homes were owned by male same-sex couples (Potvin 2013). Post-war Hollywood films and TV programmes have regularly stereotyped gay men as effeminate and as pursuers of feminine interests such as domestic styling. Nevertheless, they do so by presenting frivolous gay interior designers confined to the home, contrasted with the progressive force of 'macho' heterosexual male architect (Sanders 2002). However, gay domesticity became a venerated media spectacle when lifestyle television programmes about homemaking figured gay men as experts.

In 2003 *Queer Eye for the Straight Guy* (2003–2007) was introduced on the cable TV network Bravo and later the title was shortened to *Queer Eye*. This lifestyle programme draws on the stereotype of gay men (queer) as inherent experts in interior design, fashion and personal grooming. Each episode features a team called the 'Fab Five' who carry out a home makeover for a heterosexual (straight) man by providing advice based on a queer sensibility. Gaining high ratings within two months, *Queer Eye* was an immediate and unexpected success. It won an Emmy Award for Outstanding Reality Programme in 2004. Television networks in many countries syndicated the American episodes and the concept was franchised across Anglophone nations. In this respect, the figure of the gay man performs a key role in present-day consumer culture by challenging the exclusive association of fashion, beauty and the home with feminine worlds (Attwood 2005: 97).

Analysts have offered varying accounts of representations of stereotypical gay characters on lifestyle television. Some have criticised *Queer Eye* for its generalisations about gay men as innately more fashionable and stylish than straight men, and by associating gay masculinity with femininity (Meyer and Kelley 2004; Ramsey and Santiago 2004). Several examples of representations of gay identity on television preserve heteronormativity. *Queer Eye*, for instance, employs a gay domestic expert to support the straight guy in refashioning and enhancing his home and lifestyle in order to enhance his heterosexuality (Gallagher 2004: 225; Gorman-Murray 2006a: 231). Sanctioned by a feminine aesthetic, this stereotype is welcomed by Fellows (2004: 27) as a way of justifying gay men's deep appreciation of houses and domesticity. Although the show typecasts gay men, Fellows' intention is to foreground the ways in which they are empowered while emphasising their skills in feminine domestic practices. Others argue that these programmes' depictions of gay domesticity disrupt dominant discourses of home as a heteronormative space. As Pearson and Reich state, 'By queering mundane objects, the Fab 5 redistribute space, thereby creating "play" within the hetero-order' (Pearson and Reich 2004: 230). Certain analysts bring together opposing accounts by arguing that programmes such as *Queer as Folk* (1999–2000) destabilise dominant views yet, at the same time, also foster conservative attitudes of 'us' and 'them'. In his study of reality home renovation shows, Gorman-Murray argues that heterosexual family-based ideology of home is queered by the presence and homemaking practices of gay male couples in the shows (Gorman-Murray 2006a).

Notwithstanding these assessments of the depiction of gay identities on lifestyle TV, a group of scholars maintain that gay men have a strong commitment to home that differs from popular media images of the interior decorator or 'trendy gentrifier'. Given the continued marginalisation of gay identities and higher rates of assaults on gay men than heterosexual men in public spaces, gay men's homes become significant and relatively safe sites for affirming gay masculinity (Gorman-Murray 2006a,b,c, 2007a,b, 2008a,b; Waitt & Gorman-Murray 2007). Nevertheless, it is observed that gay men's domestic skills are based on their feminisation in the sense that the gay home is appealing only when it endorses feminised homemaking ideals (Gorman-Murray 2011: 440, 449). In his assessment of an Australian reality television series, Gorman-Murray highlights two contrasting domestic styles by gay couples on *The Block* (2003–2004; 2010 to the present). He points out that conventional attitudes about gay domesticity are regulated by conventional discourses of gender and sexuality. Gay domesticity is regarded as acceptable when defined in feminine or familial terms yet deemed unacceptable if it challenges heteronormativity through a more public masculine bachelor domesticity (Gorman-Murray 2011: 448).

Pilkey contends that ordinary contemporary LGBTQ identities and home-spaces are framed in multiple ways in response to the stereotypes presented in 'queer domestic aesthetic discourse' (Pilkey 2015). He locates the stereotyping of gay men's domestic styling skills through a joke referenced by Robin Williams: 'We had gay burglars the other night. They broke in and rearranged the furniture' (Pilkey 2015: 213). Pilkey draws on qualitative research with LGBTQ London residents to argue that this widespread queer aesthetic influences everyday space by shaping people's attitudes and relationships to home in complicated ways that affect daily domestic living.

The queering of home

In response to earlier over-emphases on studies of public and metropolitan spaces associated with sexual minority identities, calls have been made to attend to LGBTQ domesticity and homemaking meanings and practices (Cook 2014; Gabb 2005; Halperin 2012). For example, interest in home and domesticity across geography and related disciplines has accented the relationship between home, domesticity, and various identity categories, including gender, race, class, age, disability and sexuality. Drawing attention to the diverse homemaking and domestic experiences of gay and lesbian ordinary lives, many studies about LGBTQ experiences of home and domesticity aim to subvert hegemonic domestic practices. A growing body of research on alternative domestic experiences also confirms the complexity of identity formation. As Pilkey et al. (2015) explain, the term 'alternative' in the study of new domesticities foregrounds the multiple dimensions of identity across the life course that disrupt neat, linear categories. Correspondingly, hegemonic heteronormative domesticity has been challenged by studies on polyamorous relationships (Gorman-Murray 2015; Johnston and Longhurst 2010), trans residents and domesticities (Felsenthal 2009; Halberstam 2005), and also unrelated people living together (McNamara and Connell 2007). Conventional discourses about gender and home tend to neglect young men's experiences of home. However, a range of work advances debates in the field by exploring the role of domesticity in the shaping of queer identities and domestic norms.

In a study of the meanings of home and homemaking practices of young men aged 18 to 25, Gorman-Murray (2015) draws attention to the multiplicity of 'youthful masculine domesticities' within the gender dynamics of contemporary domestic life. Using the term 'twentagers' to describe young men in their late teens and early 20s who are spending longer periods living in or returning to their parental homes, he identifies three masculine-domestic relations that highlight modes of shared housing that challenge the conventional focus on heterosexual couple family homes in domestic imaginaries: young men in parental homes, share-housing and 'alternative' family homes. The study is enlightening, with close, detailed ethnographic observations that show how masculinities and homes are co-constructed in the sense that they are embedded in various social and material practices. These practices involve 'intimate relations; care for partners, parents, siblings, housemates and friends; chores, housework and cooking; sociality and hospitality; decoration; place-attachment; utilising private/common spaces' (Gorman-Murray 2015: 435). These varied home-based practices encompass frictions as well as bonding activities. For instance, domestic labour and care-related tasks in the family home and in shared houses reveal the challenges involved in young men's homemaking.

For two of these young men, taking responsibility for domestic chores and errands for their heterosexual parents strengthened family bonding and homemaking. Yet explanations of their domestic situations revealed a continuous gendering of accounts of their domestic labour:

> Both framed their domestic activities in terms of 'helping Mum', 'taking the stress off Mum' and 'giving Mum a break', suggesting housework is an expected part of mothering work. Note, then, they did not suggest they were 'helping Dad' or 'giving Dad a break'; domestic work was not linked to fathering and men's domestic roles. (Gorman-Murray 2015: 429)

Here, the domestic routines of these young men indicate strong attachments to the parental home where their domestic practices influence their masculine identities in terms of family bonding and care work. Yet they still regard homemaking as an essentially feminine set of practices.

Young men in inner city rented shared housing with other men and with opposite sex partners deviate from the norm of nuclear, owner-occupier suburban dwelling in a different way. Those interviewed by Gorman-Murray questioned the notion that shared housing was 'unhomely'. This echoes earlier research on shared homes in Britain and Australia, revealing that shared homes can be as homely as conventional heteronormative household arrangements (Heath and Cleaver 2003; and Connell 2007). For these young men, engagement in a range of domestic practices contributed directly to this sense of homeliness. Relating to the work of McNamara and Connell 2007, Gorman-Murray explains that the friendship between household members takes on quasi-family qualities reinforced through domestic labour as well as leisure activities. He states:

> Housemate-friends cook and clean for each other, and in these share-houses this means young men do care work for other, unrelated young men and women. This subverts normalised understandings of domestic labour as the care work of wives-and-mothers in family homes. Domestic labour, care and intimacy are equally significant in making young men's share-houses into homes. (Gorman-Murray 2015: 431)

This intra-household sociality contrasts with the dynamics of 'stranger houses' where residents do not know each other or share time together (Heath and Cleaver 2003). The domestic practices that generate family-like qualities of masculine domesticities that transform shared houses into 'homes' are activities that stretch beyond home. These young house-sharers extend hospitality to visiting friends through the preparation of food for guests as vital features of homemaking. Once again, the homemaking ideals of nuclear family homes are challenged by these kinds of practices where young men act as domestic hosts and extend bonds of intimacy beyond home and family members by engaging in 'extra-household hospitality'. Nevertheless, tensions are generated when disputes arise between householders over levels of cleanliness and tidiness relating to domestic tasks. These disputes indicate that such care work involves the kinds of problems displayed in unequal nuclear family contexts. This finding concurs with related research on housework in all-male share houses which suggests that gender power is present where some men take on traditional masculine roles of avoiding housework tasks (Natalier 2003). Nevertheless, men who adopt a less traditional approach to homemaking are developing 'a masculine subjectivity embedded in domestic spaces and the labour invested in their upkeep' (Gorman-Murray 2015: 432).

'Alternative' domesticities such as share-housing are generally considered to be temporary and inferior to the ideal of the heterosexual couple family home unless they form part of a young person's transition from parental home to partnered relations in newly set-up homes as a defining feature of the transition from youth to adulthood. However, these assumptions ignore the variability and unevenness of life course transitions (Heath and Cleaver 2003). Gorman-Murray describes a cohabiting arrangement involving polyamorous partners where a gay man, Ian, lives with two same-sex partners in a house owned by one of the partners. Ian moved straight from his parental home to a partnered family home, as a conventional housing career transition. Yet the new living arrangement was atypical: an 'alternative' family home, described by Gorman-Murray as a polyamorous same-sex family home.

This housing transition signified Ian's identity as a gay man. His move away from his parental home was triggered by a feeling of awkwardness at coming out. Importantly, moving to polyamorous same-sex family home offered a home space that affirmed physical expressions of intimacy such as the hugging and kissing of greetings and farewells and demonstrations of love and care between same-sex partners. Related to expressions of intimacy are practical dimensions of familial homemaking such as preparing meals and shopping that also generate mutuality. Yet again, taking on these tasks was interpreted through a gendered lens as 'housewifely' tasks signalling power differences and a sense of being undervalued. This reminds us that gendered power relations continue to play out even in all-male households. These dynamics coincide with and may sometimes be articulated in relation to age ranking (Natalier 2003; Carrington 1999). In these respects, Ian's masculinity was simultaneously endorsed and undermined through his home-making practices. Nevertheless, these studies on domestic masculinities challenge the normalisation of heterosexual couple family homes. They cast light on the ways in which alternative family homes and diverse domestic practices may offer meaningful contexts to support a sense of masculine self. Emphasising the persistent association of housework with femininity, this work also challenges often invisible gendered power relations and provides clues about the emotional costs to many women in terms of sense of a feminine sense of self.

Lesbian and queer domesticities

A tendency to focus on public settings and commercial gay assemblies associated with gay identities has allowed male-to-male same-sex intimacy to overshadow other kinds of same-sex intimacies in relation to home cultures. In the past, few women have had the financial resources to design and build the homes in which they live. However, atypical examples of women who commissioned new houses for female-headed households in the US have been identified by Alice Friedman (2015). Whether because they were widowed, divorced, lesbian or desired to remain single, certain women created architecturally original houses such as Frank Lloyd Wright's Susan Lawrence Dana House (1904), his Aline Barnsdall 'Hollyhock House' (1921), and Mies van der Rohe's Farnsworth House (1951) (Friedman 2015). Friedman's historical and archival study of lesbian experiences of queering the heteronormative home describes the 1907 home of Katharine Lee Bates and her partner Katharine Coman. Friedman explains how the domestic architecture of their home, 'The Scarab', challenged domestic conventions in terms of its plan, programme, use and occupation. Here, the women experienced love and companionship, while 'hiding in plain sight' in suburban Wellesley, Massachusetts despite radically queering early-twentieth-century domesticity. Friedman describes the sprawling, Shingle-style house of poet and professor Katharine Lee Bates who built the Scarab for herself and partner Katharine Coman, a labour activist and social economist. They had previously both lived and taught at Wellesley College in 1870, a single-sex higher educational establishment.

Acknowledging that these were privileged middle-class women, Friedman's research nevertheless uncovers the intersection of historic domestic architecture and queer identity within a setting framed by gendered, classed and sexed expectations. She shows how women negotiate their non-heterosexual identities, same-sex relationships, families and work experiences. The inhabitants of the Scarab formed an animated and dynamic community of women by gathering around them a group of friends, family, colleagues and students. Although departing from domestic conventions, 'The Scarab' was a fairly typical example of a suburban, single-family home. It blended into its leafy suburban neighbourhood, demonstrating that 'this committed couple could "hide in plain sight" while radically queering the terms of early-twentieth-century domesticity' (Friedman 2015: 143).

Whilst this historical work uncovers alternative domesticities, sociological studies among LGBTQ families reveal a gendering of domestic labour (Dunne 1997, 2000; Oerton 1997, 1998; Carrington 1999; Kamano 2009; Kentlyn, 2008; Rawsthorne and Costello 2010). Household and childcare tasks in same-sex households often revert to conventional gender roles. And although often justified in terms of fairness or personal preferences, they tend to reflect power differences between couples defined by waged work (Carrington 1999). These challenges suggest that the aspiration towards a fair distribution of domestic tasks among LGBTQ couples can be difficult to put into practice. But research on domestic labour in lesbian and gay households in Australia by Kentlyn (2008) indicates the correspondence between performing household chores and 'doing' femininity by explaining that the queer home can work to disrupt gender norms. Here, domestic labour refers to household management and physical domestic tasks that support the daily lives of child and adult householders (Barrett 2015; Lachance-Grzela and Bouchard 2010). Christopher Carrington (1999) found that gay men who take on most of the household chores, and lesbians who undertake very little domestic labour can suffer stigma for disrupting home-based gender norms. This indicates that domestic encounters are signified by householders' status as gendered subjects. Contrasting studies suggest that the avoidance of conventional gender scripts within LGBTQ homes and the conscious adoption of principles of parity can support more equitable sharing of domestic tasks (Rawsthorne and Costello 2010).

Related studies on the division of housework labour and childcare among lesbian and gay couples suggest that they have more flexibility and choice over the allocation of domestic tasks and childcare responsibilities, as exemplified by studies in Australia (Rawsthorne and Costello 2010), Japan (Kamano 2009), Israel (Shechory and Ziv 2007) and England (Dunne 2000). This is because there is no prevailing social standard to govern the domestic roles within lesbian and gay relationships (Barrett 2015). Yet the deep-seated heterosexualisation of domestic tasks, and lack of alternative models to support lesbian and gay homes can lead to the expression of divisions of labour in the home through heteronormative ideals. Within a heteronormative culture, beliefs about conventionally gendered roles run so deep that it is often implied that these responsibilities and practices can simply be transferred to gay and lesbian homes as a norm (Barrett 2015).

This body of research echoes the findings of Sarah Green (1999) who chronicled the lives of (radical) lesbian feminists whose aim was to create a safe space within the metropolis of London while building diverse ways of relating to others. The ideas about gender and sexuality that framed their political beliefs prompted the women to reassess relationships with their male partners and wider institutions, to embrace the ideology of the 'personal is political'. Some women elected to work and dwell in women-only workplaces and households with the aim of following such political beliefs. In doing so, they contested prescribed norms about how to perform family and gender relations. Green emphasises that, at the time, (radical) lesbian feminists sought ways to create a safe space within the metropolis at the same time as constructing different ways of relating to others. This required women to reconsider their relationships with their male partners and wider institutions, and to live through the ideology of the 'personal is political'. Some women even chose to live and work in women-only workplaces and households in order to abide by such political beliefs (Green 1999).

In a related study conducted more than a decade and a half later, Rachael Scicluna (2015) reflects on meanings of home and domestic space in her ethnographic study of a group of older lesbians, mainly feminist activists, who have pursued alternative public and intimate living spaces. She highlights the wider social issues of institutionalised homophobia, the traditional nuclear family and housing issues such as living in squats. These 'home' settings are ones in which domestic relations emerge as a form of direct resistance to dominant ideologies about home, contributing to ambivalent sentiments associated with the domestic kitchen as an emotional space. Scicluna demonstrates how sexual life stories can change across the life course. Chronicling the life experiences of 'making a home' among older lesbians in contemporary London, Scicluna finds that the kitchen 'emerges as a contested, transformative, and political domestic space' (Scicluna 2015: 169). Such domestic narratives show how the kitchen, as a physical and metaphorical space, becomes a resource for breaking down conservative ideals and rigid boundaries by introducing distinctive intimate practices and lesbian-feminist politics. Scicluna refers to a study of kinship and memory by anthropologist Janet Carsten (2004) which highlights the central role played by the kitchen within 'house memories' of her parents' house. Carsen remembers how her parents treated kitchen-based objects that carried memories of their earlier lives before they were exiled from their previous homes.

While the kitchen often sparks childhood memories, particularly regarding stories of mother-centred kitchens, the women in Scicluna's research not only challenge normative gender stereotypes in these domestic spaces but also actively digress from family norms, often as a political act. Scicluna argues that 'the domestic' does not necessarily refer to a fixed space like the home. Instead, she approaches the domestic as syncretic and subversive: 'The domestic is like a melting pot, where it becomes one of the greatest powers of and for integration and becomes a symbol of pluralisms within society at large' (Scicluna 2015: 175). In her work, Scicluna draws on the term 'queer' to emphasis its fluid and porous qualities in relation to domesticity. This allows the term to be linked to and juxtaposed with domestic space to highlight both the syncretic and subversive meanings of home. However, as Scicluna points out, the historical concept of 'queer' refers mainly to men and has not been a term widely used by women to describe their identities.

Drawing on in-depth interviews in England, Carla Barrett (2015) considers how a group of lesbian and gay couples organise and carry out domestic tasks. Their domestic lives seem to correspond with yet also contest the heteronormative assumptions about gendered households prevalent in dominant discourses of the home. Barrett explains how these couples subvert heteronormative household practices through their attitudes towards and organisation of domestic labour and parenting. Lesbian and gay couples disrupt conventional domestic gender roles and queer the spaces of the home in complex ways through the seemingly ordinary, mundane practices and negotiations of domestic labour and childcare. Several of Barratt's participants highlight the lack of social scripts for lesbian and gay couples in negotiating domestic labour. They all refuse the notion that domestic labour should be divided in terms of one partner taking responsibility for those domestic tasks traditionally perceived as feminine, such as washing and cleaning, while the other partner takes on the DIY jobs and car maintenance. Barrett's participants resist the idea that domestic labour is a feminised task. In fact, domestic labour itself is transformed into a queer activity, through which to subvert gender norms and support a queer identity within the space of home. Striving to avoid any divisions based on hierarchical gender roles, most of the couples explain that they consciously base the organisation of domestic labour around principles of equality or fairness.

In households with children, childcare also expresses queer homes and identities by interrupting the heterosexual rationale surrounding conventional understandings of childcare. The queering of parenting is exemplified by a gay couple who had four-month-old twin boys. However, in addition to sharing the childcaring equally, they could afford to pay for a live-in nanny and had flexible working arrangements allowing them to work from home (Barrett 2015). These arrangements show that childcare forms a key activity in which heteronormative gender scripts can be resisted, highlighting the importance of discussion and negotiation between partners. But it also demonstrates the advantages of middle-class incomes and cultural capital in resisting normative gender scripts and negotiating alternative domesticities that support the queering of home. Nevertheless, just as the home can be queered, so too can childcare as an activity: by subverting gender norms and upholding their lesbian and gay identities. Barrett's research mirrors earlier studies that conclude that lesbian and gay parenting can challenge the heteronormativity of dominant discourses of childcaring and parenting (Dunne 2000; Ciano-Boyce and Shelley-Sireci 2002; Rawsthorne and Costello 2010; Patterson and Farr 2011).

'Queering' the parental home and multiple domesticities

While home precarities are not inevitably linked with LGBTQ identities or communities, the heterosexual nuclear home may be a distressing and uncomfortable environment for gay and lesbian youth. In his study of disclosure at home, Andrew Gorman-Murray (2008b) reassesses the experience of the nuclear family home for well supported LGBT youth to resist the normalisation of homophobic heterosexual nuclear homes. Drawing on autobiographies, he demonstrates that family homes can be sites of resistance against broader heterosexist practices, with the backing and assistance of parents and siblings for LGBT youth. Gorman-Murray argues that because some heterosexual parents and siblings embrace and nurture sexual difference, this generates a 'queering' of the family home by providing a space for the 'fluorescence of non-heterosexuality' in what appears to be a heteronormative site. A range of studies have considered the effects of a heteronormative home for gay and lesbian people. Among early work in the field, Gill Valentine (1993) observes that home can feel alienating or oppressive for lesbians and young gay men living in the parental home. Enforced heterosexual norms and assumptions can render the parental home a place in which they are unable to feel at home. Assessing the repercussions for lesbians and gay young people of "coming out" to their parents, she argues that parental homophobia poses a particular risk for those with families intolerant of lesbian or gay family members. For those anxious about coming out, home can often be viewed as a closet, an uncomfortable and isolating place to be escaped in order to avoid negative parental responses which may involve verbal abuse, physical violence and estrangement.

Although some lesbian, gay or bisexual young people encounter homophobia, others gain positive reactions and support when they come out at home. Gorman-Murray (2008b) has found that these affirmative responses can queer the family home by transforming home into a space that endorses non-heterosexual identities. Research in urban parts of the US by Elwood (2000) shows how lesbians can experience home as a place of safety yet also one of scrutiny. While lesbians may articulate their sexual identity through lesbian emblems such as rainbow flags and posters, some experience hostile responses to these motifs from neighbours or callers. Her study confirms that this apparently private space is exposed to public surveillance. But the home may be transformed into a queer space supported by the gathering of lesbian and gay guests and display of objects that endorse and celebrate their sexual identities (Gorman-Murray 2006a, 2006b).

However, for young people who find the parental home to be an oppressive place, home can be a precarious space leading to homelessness. While ethnographic case studies perform a vital role in contributing to research on alternative and queer domesticities, much research focuses on the meanings and values of home for middle-class gay men and lesbians. More recently, in her ethnographic study of the lived realities of homeless LGBT youth, Carin Tunåker (2015) offsets this tendency. Confirming the palpable home precarities involved in struggles to perform alternative domesticities, Tunåker considers the role of minority sexuality as a factor contributing to homelessness. Associated with a homelessness charity in southeast England and based on the personal narratives of homeless young people, Tunåker explains how social exclusion functions within and beyond the home and disrupts the powerful imaginary of domestic space as a refuge. Aged between 16 and 25, young people who identify as LGB or T are often subject to hate crime, bullying, harassment, violence, oppression and social exclusion in the home, in schools and the wider community.

This level of homophobia persists despite the UK government's same-sex marriage Act (2014), and the regular presence of gay couples in popular television dramas which imply that being LGBT in today's Britain is unproblematic. The disclosure of a young person's sexual orientation or gender identity to family members can spark conflicts in the parental home, resulting in the young person having to walk out of the family home, and then become homeless. While most minority groups gain emotional help from families and wider kin to cope with discrimination, LGBT youth are often spurned by parents and wider relatives. Without these support mechanisms, it is unsurprising that levels of depression and self-harm are much higher among LGBT youth than among their peers. Research indicates that for young people, 'coming out' to their families can involve palpable home precarities by resulting in leaving home at a young age (Valentine et al. 2003). Yet the subject matter of homelessness tends to be eclipsed by concerns with mental health issues. Tunåker argues that the idea of 'home' as a caring and intimate space is alien for young people who are 'homeless' and estranged from their families due to their sexual orientation.

Tunåker approaches home as a liminal space, arguing that homeless youth, particularly LGBT young people, can 'find themselves' (Tunåker 2015: 243). After the relationship breakdowns with parents or guardians, they move for various lengths of time between friends' sofas, youth hostels, social service placements and foster homes. Because few actually sleep rough, on the streets, they do not conform to conventional images of homelessness associated with drug use, alcoholism and begging. For most of the residents of Young Persons' Services (YPS) interviewed by Tunåker, 'home' meant safety. While they were unsure whether the hostel would be characterised as their home, most were certain that they were not 'home-less'. For these young people, 'Home is connected to notions of family life, and a past with a mother, father, siblings, or other relatives' (Tunåker 2015: 246).

The young people at the YPS, resided in a space that they called a home of sorts, but it did not reflect as much of a home compared to the space they inhabited with a family of origin. Yet the hostel becomes a 'principle for social organization' (Joyce and Gillespie 2000) where residents view one another as a family, invoked by feelings of belonging to a particular physical space. The friendships forged with fellow residents also creates another sort of 'family', based on 'soil' rather than 'blood'. These young people enter a phase of liminality where forged friendships can lead to a new family. For homeless LGBT youth, 'home' and 'homelessness' reflect complex ideas of family, identity and belonging where the 'rituals of adolescence' become blurred. Tunåker confirms that notions of home and homelessness experienced by homeless LGBT youth are complex and intricate. This mirrors scholarship that emphasises the multiple meanings of home generated by several diverse experiences (see for example Douglas 1991; Elwood 2000; Blunt and Dowling 2006; Das et al. 2008). As such, Tunåker concurs with Blunt and Dowling that 'home' constitutes a process that conveys a range of 'lived as well as imagined' (2006: 254) feelings interwoven with visions of an ideal home, which for the young people Tunåker encountered involves a yearning for the thing they do not have: a loving family.

To consider domestic practices that subvert normative ideas of home, Susan Thompson (2007) also uses an ethnographic approach by addressing a different social group, one which also questions dominant nuclear family values. In an Australian study, she examines meanings of home after relationship breakdown for heterosexual couples. The deterioration of a couple's relationship are reflected in the material state of the home, once a shared space where domestic routines were part of self-identity and personal expression and where homely connections and links with the local neighbourhood are involved. The privacy and personalisation established in the home, including memories associated with rooms and objects, underscore the emotional dimensions of relationship collapse. The financial aspects of home and the need to maintain continuity for children mean that the loss of the physical dwelling highlights a particular kind of home precarity that reflects a loss of security as well as the loss of the comforts of daily home-based routines and a shared future, into old age. Thompson quotes one of her respondents, a woman who said:

> And that home became the symbol of our fight... a symbol of how closely glued we were together... And I think that's why we had such enormous difficulty breaking up because the house actually held us together in some way ... it was as though the house was a sort of a binding force of the relationship. (Thompson 2007: 19)

The house symbolised both the unity and the deteriorating relationships of her participants. Thompson identifies the hope involved in the newly adopted homes which become a springboard for empowerment for individual former partners. Despite the feelings of grief and loss conveyed by individuals, involving relationship disputes, new meanings of home emerge during the major life transition after separation and divorce. And although divorce involves feelings of failure and disappointment, later acknowledgements that the break-up was beneficial often accompanies ex-partners' feelings of an improved quality of life. In these ways, such studies cast light on how multidimensional meanings of home change. Thompson draws attention to the transformative journey involved: 'from the devastation of the initial loss to an eventual redefining of home across its symbolic, psychological and physical constructs' (Thompson 2007: 55).

The term 'multiple domesticities' has been developed in relation to contemporary ethnographic fieldwork with marginalised groups of African American and Caribbean families in the United States, in Miami, Florida, and Baltimore, Maryland (Das et al. 2008). The families, mainly living in public housing, include HIV-positive adolescents and children from transnational families abused by their kin. The term 'multiple domesticities' describes both the intimacy and alienation experienced by women who repeatedly move between households and also to and from home and institutional 'households' such as prisons. The researchers reveal that the kinship relations among these marginalised groups are negotiated in relation to state actors whom they are obliged to interact with (Das et al. 2008: 352). Through these experiences, 'the domestic' is shaped not only by kinship structures but also by recurring movements between the house and penal, custodial or correctional institutions. The authors explain that the intimacy and alienation dyad imbue these interactions with 'fugitive emotions' (Das et al. 2008: 352).

In this respect, 'the domestic' is lived not through the stable notion of home but precariously through the interstices of the house, the street, prison and clinic. The framework of multiple domesticities is not inevitably viewed as related to or equivalent to family and household. Rather, the term 'home' can stand for or extend to several types of domesticities. Work on lesbian motherhood by Jacqui Gabb (2005) also addresses this form of fugitive and precarious experience of home. Her study of lesbian mothers and their children in Britain bring to light fugitive and precarious encounters with home relating to their children's schools and their sexual identities. She describes how some lesbian mothers even felt awkward in the apparently private space of the home. Some closed their curtains to avert the heteronormative gaze.

Conclusion

The series of studies and range of issues addressed in this chapter confirm the significance of new arrangements and meanings of domestic living as part of a queering of home as a *space* and therefore as a site of study. This body of research provides a series of instances that indicate how alternative household dynamics have been shaped by mass-mediated home imaginaries and by changing intimate relationships. As such, these studies underline the question of *what homes are for*, as places to dwell and engage with productively. They also emphasise the differences in meanings of home and the domestic, confirming the vital importance of critiquing dominant discourses of home, conventional domesticities and heteronormative living arrangements. Competing notions of the purpose of the home relate to competing notions of social and cultural life. Importantly, the breadth and inclusiveness of the term 'alternative domesticities' highlights the diverse domestic scenarios associated with 'home'. At the same time, by contesting normative notions of domesticity, the emphasis on *alternative* domesticities opens up the possibilities of considering plural domesticities (Pilkey et al. 2015; see Das et al. 2008). The notion of the 'queering of home' can be extended to all social groups subordinated or judged as 'failures' by traditional norms associated with home as a nuclear, heterosexualised, family space.

Anne-Marie Fortier (1999) refers to 'queer diasporas' to explain how gays and lesbians migrate to 'terrains of belonging' as migratory subjects and how the 'queer' concept of home is a hoped-for destination that re-claims the home as a new source and a new kind of ideal (Fortier 1999; 2001; 2002). The concept of 'diaspora' invokes the idea of a universal queer subject and challenges nation-centred notions of identity. At the same time, the discourse of migration underlines ideas of homecoming rather than home leaving which circumvent the notion of 'home' as a space created by and for a heterosexual family (Fortier 2002: 188). Correspondingly, Alan Sinfield identifies a Black queer diaspora to foreground the idea of 'coming out' as a moment of emergence that contrasts with the idea of alternative homelands to suggest that 'we never quite arrive' (Sinfield 2000: 188). This association between 'queer' and 'diaspora' generates a framework in which scholars can reimagine alternative sites and conceptualisations of home (Bryant 2015).

Jason Bryant refers to Avtar Brah's term, 'homing desire', which challenges the idea of home as a self-evidently insular place. For Brah, the concept of diaspora allows the discourses of 'home' and 'dispersion' to be placed in a creative tension by foregrounding a 'homing desire' at the same time as questioning discourses of fixed origins (Brah 1996: 192–193). As Bryant points out, this draws attention to 'in-betweenness' as a condition of homemaking which can complement notions of queering home. Bryant argues that by invoking the idea of a *queer diaspora*, experiences of diaspora can serve to destabilise dominant conceptualisations of home. But this can only occur if the particularities of race and class inferred by claims of diasporic subjectivity are resisted (Bryant 2015: 272). This emphasis on the in-betweeness and ambiguities associated with home, origins and identities leads us to the theme of the next chapter which explores experiences of identity and belonging in the context of home mobility, migration and diasporas.

Note

1 Lesbian, gay, bisexual, transgender, queer.

References

Attwood, F. (2005) 'Inside out: Men on the "home front"', *Journal of Consumer Culture*, 5, 87–107.
Barrett, C. (2015) 'Queering the home', *Home Cultures*, 12(2), 193–211.
Blunt, A. and Dowling, R. (2006) *Home*. London: Routledge.
Brah, A. (1996) *Cartographies of Desire: Contesting Identities*. New York: Routledge.
Brown, G. (2008) 'Urban (homo)sexualities: Ordinary cities and ordinary sexualities', *Geography Compass*, 2(4), 1215–1231.
Bryant, J. (2015) 'The meaning of queer home', *Home Cultures*, 12(3), 261–289.
Carrington, C. (1999) *No Place like Home: Relationships and Family Life among Lesbians and Gay Men*. Chicago: University of Chicago Press.
Chambers, D. (2012) *A Sociology of Family Life*. Cambridge: Polity.
Chapman, T. (2004) *Gender and Domestic Life: Changing Practices in Families and Households*. Palgrave Macmillan, London.

Cohan, S. (1996) 'So functional for its purposes: The bachelor apartment in pillow talk', in J. Sanders (ed.), *Stud: Architectures of Masculinity*. New York: Princeton Architectural Press, pp. 28–41.

Colomina, B. (1996) *Sexuality & Space* (Princeton Papers on Architecture), 4th edn. New York: Princeton Architectural Press.

Cook, M. (2014) *Queer Domesticities: Homosexuality and Home Life in Twentieth-century London*. Basingstoke: Palgrave Macmillan.

Crompton, R. (2006) *Employment and the Family: The Reconfiguration of Work and Family Life in Contemporary Societies*. New York: Cambridge University Press.

Das, V., Ellen, J. and Leonard, L. (2008) 'On the modalities of the domestic', *Home Cultures*, 5(3), 348–372.

Davidoff, L. and Hall, C. (2002) *Family Fortunes: Men and Women of the English Middle Class 1780–1850*. London: Routledge.

Douglas, M. (1991) 'The idea of home: A kind of space', *Social Research*, 58(1), 287–307.

Duncan, N. (ed.) (1996) *BodySpace: Destabilizing Geographies of Gender and Sexuality*. London: Routledge.

Dunne, G. (1997) *Lesbian Lifestyles: Women's Work and the Politics of Sexuality*. London: Macmillan.

Dunne, G. (2000) 'Opting into motherhood: Lesbians blurring the boundaries and transforming the meaning of parenthood and kinship', *Gender and Society*, 14(1), 11–35.

Eichler, M. and Albanese, P. (2007) 'What is household work? A critique of assumptions underlying empirical studies of housework and an alternative approach', *Canadian Journal of Sociology*, 32(2), 227–258.

Elwood, S.A. (2000) 'Lesbian living spaces', *Journal of Lesbian Studies*, 4(1), 11–27.

Fellows, W. (2004) *A Passion to Preserve: Gay Men as Keepers of Culture*. Madison, WI: University of Wisconsin Press.

Felsenthal, K. (2009) 'Creating the queendom: A lens on Transy House', *Home Cultures*, 6 (3), 243–260.

Fortier, A.-M. (1999) 'Re-membering places and the performance of belonging(s)', *Theory, Culture & Society*, 16(2), 41–64.

Fortier, A-M. (2001) '"Coming home": Queer migrations and multiple evocations of home', *European Journal of Cultural Studies*, 4(4), 405–424.

Fortier, A-M. (2002) 'Queer diaspora', in D. Richardson and S. Seidman (eds), *The Handbook of Lesbian and Gay Studies*. Thousand Oaks: Sage, pp. 183–197.

Friedman, A.T. (2015) 'Hiding in plain sight', *Home Cultures*, 12(2), 139–167.

Gabb, J. (2005) 'Lesbian m/otherhood: Strategies of familial-linguistic management in lesbian parent families', *Sociology*, 39(4), 585–603.

Gallagher, M. (2004) 'Queer eye for the heterosexual couple', *Feminist Media Studies*, 4(2), 223–225.

Gill, R. (2003) 'Power and the production f subjects: A genealogy of the new man and the new lad', *The Sociological Review*, 51(1), 34–56.

Green, S. (1999) *Urban Amazons: Lesbian Feminism and beyond in the Gender, Sexuality and Identity Battles of: Lesbian Feminism and beyond in the Gender, Sexuality and Identity Battles of London*. Basingstoke: Palgrave Macmillan.

Gorman-Murray, A. (2006a) 'Queering home or domesticating deviance? Interrogating gay domesticity through lifestyle television', *International Journal of Cultural Studies*, 9, 227–247.

Gorman-Murray, A. (2006b) 'Homeboys: Uses of home by gay Australian men', *Social and Cultural Geography*, 7, 53–69.

Gorman-Murray, A. (2006c) 'Gay and lesbian couples at home: Identity work in domestic space', *Home Cultures*, 3(2), 145–168.

Gorman-Murray, A. (2007a) 'Contesting domestic ideals: Queering the Australian home', *Aust Geogr*, 38, 195–213.

Gorman-Murray, A. (2007b) 'Reconfiguring domestic values: Meanings of home for gay men and lesbians', *Housing, Theory and Society*, 24, 229–246.

Gorman-Murray, A. (2008a) 'Masculinity and the home: A critical review and conceptual framework', *Aust Geogr*, 39(3), 367–379.

Gorman-Murray, A. (2008b) 'Queering the family home: Narratives from gay, lesbian and bisexual youth coming out in supportive family homes in Australia', *Gender, Place and Culture*, 15, 31–44.

Gorman-Murray, A. (2008c) 'Reconciling self: Gay men and lesbians using domestic materiality for identity management', *Social and Cultural Geography*, 9, 285–303.

Gorman-Murray, A (2011) '"This is disco-wonderland!" Gender, sexuality and the limits of gay domesticity on The Block', *Social & Cultural Geography*, 12(5), 435–453.

Gorman-Murray, A. (2013) 'Urban homebodies: Embodiment, masculinity, and domesticity in inner Sydney', *Geographical Research*, 51(2), 137–144.

Gorman-Murray, A. (2015) 'Twentysomethings and twentagers: Subjectivities, spaces and young men at home', *Gender, Place & Culture*, 22(3), 422–439.

Halberstam, J. (2005) *A Queer Time and Place: Transgender Bodies, Subcultural Lives*. New York: New York University Press.

Halperin, D. (2012) *How to Be Gay*. Cambridge MA: Harvard University Press.

Hart, K.P. (2004) 'We're here, we're queer – and we're better than you: The representational superiority of gay men to heterosexuals on Queer Eye for the Straight Guy', *Journal of Men's Studies*, 12(3), 241–253.

Hayden, D. (1981) *The Grand Domestic Revolution: A History of Feminist Designs for American Homes, Neighborhoods, and Cities*. Cambridge, MA: MIT Press.

Heath, S., and Cleaver, E. (2003) *Young, Free and Single? Twenty-Somethings and Household Change*. Basingstoke: Palgrave Macmillan.

Hollows, J. (2003) 'Oliver's twist: Leisure, labour and domestic masculinity in The Naked Chef', *International Journal of Cultural Studies*, 6, 229–248.

Hornsey, R. (2010) *The Spiv and the Architect: Unruly Life in Postwar London*. Minneapolis: University of Minnesota Press.

Jackson, P., Stevenson, N. and Brookes, K. (2001) *Making Sense of Men's Magazines*. Cambridge: Polity Press.

Johnston, L. and Longhurst, R. (2010) *Space, Place, and Sex: Geographies of Sexualities*. Lanham: Rowman & Littlefield.

Johnston, L. and Valentine, G. (1995) 'Wherever I lay my girlfriend, that's my home', in D. Bell and G. Valentine (eds), *Mapping Desire: Geographies of Sexualities*. New York: Routledge, pp. 88–103.

Joyce, R. and Gillespie, S. (2000) *Beyond Kinship: Social and Material Reproduction in House Societies*. Philadelphia: University of Pennsylvania Press.

Kamano, S. (2009). 'Housework and lesbian couples in Japan: Division, negotiation and interpretation', *Women's Studies International Forum*, 32(2), 130–141.

Kentlyn, S. (2008) 'The radically subversive space of the queer home: "Safety house" and "neighbourhood watch"', *Aust Geogr*, 39(3), 327–337.

Kosofsky Sedgwick, E. (1990) *Epistemology of the Closet*. Berkeley, CA: University of California Press.

Lachance-Grzela, M. and Bouchard, G. (2010) 'Why do women do the lion's share of housework? A decade of research', *Sex Roles*, 63, 767–780.

McDowell, L. (1999) *Gender, Identity and Place: Understanding Feminist Geographies*. Cambridge: Polity.

McDowell, L. (2005) 'The men and the boys: Bankers, burger makers and barmen', in B. van Hoven and K. Horschelmann (eds), *Spaces of Masculinities*. London: Routledge, pp. 19–30.

McNamara, S., and Connell, J. (2007) 'Homeward bound? Searching for home in inner Sydney's share houses', *Aust Geogr*, 38, 71–91.

Meyer, M. and Kelley, J. (2004) 'Queering the eye? The politics of gay white men and gender (in)visibility', *Feminist Media Studies*, 4(2), 214–217.

Mort, F. (1988) 'Boys own? Masculinity, style and popular culture', in R. Chapman and J. Rutherford (eds), *Male Order: Unwrapping Masculinities*. London: Routledge.

Namara, S. and Connell, J. (2007) 'Homeward bound? Searching for home in inner Sydney's share houses', *Aust Geogr*, 38, 71–91.

Natalier, K. (2003) '"I'm not his wife": Doing gender and doing housework in the absence of women', *Journal of Sociology*, 39, 253–269.

Nixon, S. (2001) 'Re-signifying masculinity: from "new man" to "new lad"', in D. Morley and K. Robins (eds), *British Cultural Studies*. Oxford: Oxford University Press.

Oerton, S. (1997) '"Queer housewives?" Some problems in theorising the division of domestic labour in lesbian and gay households', *Women's Studies International Forum*, 20(3), 421–430.

Oerton, S. (1998) 'Reclaiming the "housewife"?', *Journal of Lesbian Studies*, 2(4), 69–83.

Osgerby, B. (2005) 'The bachelor pad as cultural icon: Masculinity, consumption and interior design in American men's magazines, 1930-65', *Journal of Design History*, 18, 99–113.

Patterson, C.J. (2000) 'Family relationships of lesbians and gay men', *Journal of Marriage and the Family*, 62, 1052–1069.

Patterson, C.J. and Farr, R.H. (2011). 'Coparenting among lesbian and gay couples', in J. McHale and K. Lindahl (eds), *Coparenting: Theory, Research, and Clinical Applications*. Washington, DC: American Psychological Association, pp. 127–146.

Pearson, K. and Reich, N. (2004) 'Queer Eye fairytale: Changing the world one manicure at a time', *Feminist Media Studies*, 4(2), 229–231.

Pedwell, C. (2017) 'Habit and the politics of social change: A comparison of nudge theory and pragmatist philosophy', *Body and Society*, 23(4) 59–94.

Perlesz, A., Power, J., Brown, R., McNair, R., Schofield, M., Pitts, M., Barrett A. and Bickerdike, A. (2010) 'Organising work and home in same-sex parented families: Findings from the work love play study', *Australian and New Zealand Journal of Family Therapy* 31(4), 374–391.

Pilkey, B. (2012) 'LGBT homemaking in London, UK: The embodiment of mobile homemaking imaginaries', *Geographical Research*, 51(2), 159–165.

Pilkey, B. (2015) 'Reading the queer domestic aesthetic discourse', *Home Cultures*, 12(2), 213–239.

Pilkey, B., Scicluna, R.M. and Gorman-Murray, G. (2015) 'Alternative domesticities', *Home Cultures*, 12(2), 127–138.

Pink, S. (2004) *Home Truths: Gender, Domestic Objects and Everyday Life*. Oxford: Berg.

Potvin, J. (2013) 'Guilty by design/guilty by desire: Queering bourgeois domesticity', in G. Brooker and L. Weinthal (eds), *The Handbook of Interior Architecture and Design*. London: Bloomsbury, pp. 291–303.

Ramsey, E.M. and Santiago, G. (2004) 'The conflation of male homosexuality and femininity in queer eye for the straight guy', *Feminist Media Studies*, 4(3), 353–355.

Rawsthorne, M. and M. Costello (2010) 'Cleaning the sink: Exploring the experiences of Australian lesbian parents reconciling work/ family responsibilities', *Community, Work and Family*, 13(2), 189–204.

Sanders, J. (2002) 'Curtain wars: Architects, decorators, and the twentieth century domestic interior', *Harvard Design Magazine*, 16. www.gsd.harvard.edu/research/ publications/hdm/back/16sanders.html.

Scicluna, R. (2015) 'Thinking through domestic pluralities', *Home Cultures*, 12(2), 169–191.

Shechory, M. and Ziv, R. (2007) 'Relationships between gender role attitudes, role division, and perception of equity among heterosexual, gay and lesbian couples', *Sex Roles*, 56(9–10), 629–638.

Sinfield, A. (2000) 'Diaspora and hybridity: Queer identities and the ethnicity model', in N. Mirzoeff (ed.), *Diaspora and Visual Culture: Representing Africans and Jews*. New York: Routledge, pp. 95–114.

Smith, G. and Winchester, H. (1998) 'Negotiating space: Alternative masculinities at the work/home boundary', *Aust Geogr*, 29, 327–339.

Snyder, K.V. (1999) *Bachelors, Manhood, and the Novel*. Cambridge: Cambridge University Press.

Thompson, S. (2007, August) 'Home and loss: Renegotiating meanings of home in the wake of relationship breakdown', *M/C Journal*, 10(4). http://journal.media-culture.org.au/0708/07-thompson.php.

Tosh, J. (1996) 'New men? The bourgeois cult of home', *History Today*, 46, 915.

Tosh, J. (1999) *A Man's Place: Masculinity and the Middle-class Home in Victorian England*. New Haven: Yale University Press.

Tosh, J. (2005) *Manliness and Masculinities in Nineteenth-century Britain: Essays on Gender, Family and Empire*. Harlow: Pearson Longman.

Tosh, J. (2007) *A Man's Place: Masculinity and the Middle-Class Home in Victorian England*. New Haven: Yale University Press.

Tunåker, C. (2015) 'No place like home?', *Home Cultures*, 12(2), 241–259.

Valentine, G. (1993) '(Hetero)sexing space: Lesbian perceptions and experiences of everyday spaces', *Environment and Planning D: Society and Space*, 11, 395–413.

Valentine, G. Skelton, T. and Butler, R. (2003) 'Coming out and outcomes: Negotiating lesbian and gay identities with, and in, the family', *Environment and Planning D: Society and Space*, 21(4), 479–499.

van Hoven, B. and Horschelmann, K. (2005) 'Introduction: From geographies of men to geographies of women and back again?', in B. van Hoven and K. Horschelmann (eds), *Spaces of Masculinities*. London: Routledge, pp. 1–16.

Vickery, A. (1993) 'Golden age to separate spheres? A review of the categories and chronology of English women's history', *The Historical Journal*, 36(2), 383–414.

Waitt, G. and Gorman-Murray, A. (2007) 'Homemaking and mature-age gay men "down under": Paradox, intimacy, subjectivities, spatialities, and scale', *Gender, Place and Culture*, 14, 569–584.

8

HOME MOBILITIES AND MIGRATION

Introduction

The theme of home now forms a key dimension of research within studies of mobility, migration, transnational families, diaspora and attachments to distant homes. The prominence and recent intensification of mobility, migration, displacement and diaspora communities as features of globalisation have provoked a reassessment of the fixity of home. In the face of increasing mobility and displacement, these trends challenge the notion of a static, fixed home (Chambers 1994; Clifford 1997; Morley 2000; Rapport and Dawson 1998). This research emphasis allows mobility, as geographical movement, to become a central theme in enquiries about the meaning of home. It foregrounds national and transnational meanings of home involving affinities with homeland and belonging.

This chapter considers complex meanings of home within processes of identity and belonging by addressing the ways that home cultures are connected to wider identities and meanings about belonging and marginalisation. How migrant's visions of home are shaped by gender, life experience, religion and related socio-cultural circumstances are considered as key elements of these processes. The first section examines experiences of transnational migrant movement in relation to ideas of home and belonging. This includes an exploration of homemaking activities and material culture. The second section considers mediated home mobilities. Here, the harnessing of media and communication technologies to facilitate migrant families' connections with their home country are explored as transnational features of today's mediatised home.

Belonging, home and transnational migration

Collective migration activities, facilitated by globalisation and inter-state relations, generate transnational communities involving sustained networks of people, information and goods. Recent academic work has therefore approached home as a flexible entity that adapts to changing time and space (Appadurai 1996; Bauman 2001; Chambers 1994; Clifford 1997). This emphasis corresponds with anthropological theories of place and identity that describe home as 'transportable' (Rapport and Dawson 1998: 26). The notion of the transportable home encompasses not only ideas of home as movement but ideas of movement that *express* home (Chambers 1994: 24). Articulated in terms that invoke fluidity and mutability, migrants' ideas of mobile homes suggest that identities are constructed while 'on the move' as well as through a sense of fixed space (Ward 2003: 80). For migrants, home functions as a vital expression of identity closely related to notions of belonging. While homemaking is about the attainment of a kind of 'ontological security' (Giddens 1991), circumstances of migration involve the continuous 'reprocessing' of the home of origin as one's personal identity grows and changes.

By identifying strategies of homemaking via interviews and an assessment of the online narratives of long-term global travellers, Germann Molz (2008) develops the term 'global abode' to denote an idea of home encapsulated in the opposition between stasis and mobility. Germann Molz explains that continuity and cohesion always intersect with one another through homemaking practices. She emphasises that cosmopolitan travellers can create home in and through mobility as a privileged group protected by financial security and the recognition that they will return in the future. Yet Germann Molz also sees home as a series of exportable practices to the extent that for some individuals, travel itself can develop into a situation that *feels like home*. Through a continuous interplay of travel and destinations, cosmopolitans galvanise material objects and domestic activities to support feelings of 'at home-ness' facilitated by the enactment of familiar routines. An example might be the selection and cooking of familiar foods and dishes from the home country to bring a version of 'home' to the new country in which migrants have settled. Social media is recognised as a vital means for coping with and living through the unpredictability of this continued travel. Continuous contact using social media such as Facetime, Skype, and email can provide a stable and constant site where travellers can construct a familiar space through which to call on and nurture networks with relatives and friends, as discussed below.

However, home movement activities among privileged and mobile middle-class cosmopolitans are poles apart from the experiences of refugees and many displaced transnational migrants. Key differences in meanings of home also emerge between migrants who have moved voluntarily, and refugees who have been forced to move from their country of origin (Gram-Hanssen and Bech-Danielsen 2007). Levels and qualities of settlement in the receiving region or country are affected by the depth of emotional and economic ties to settlers' home country and the quality of reception and new ties in the host country. Refugees forced to flee their homes leave behind not only their dwelling but also the community, neighbourhood and social relationships associated with home as place. Reception in the new country is often hostile.

For cosmopolitans, with the choice and resources to make comfortable 'homely' homes in multiple places, physical mobility can be an adventure rather than a form of suffering. Indeed, we are reminded of the underlying meaning of the term 'cosmopolitan' by Mica Nava (2007) in her exploration of everyday urban cosmopolitanism in early twentieth-century Britain. Nava points to the gendered, imaginative and empathetic aspects of positive engagement with cultural and racial difference. In urban settings such as London, the diffusion of middle and working classes, foreigners and natives, and processes of gentrification offered a cultural context of intimate proximity and familiarity by affording spaces for interconnections, everyday participation, political mobilisation and enactments of 'mutuality'. Before World War I, cosmopolitanism was promoted as a consumer culture by the iconic London department store, Selfridges. This celebration and normalisation of racial and cultural difference has been severely disrupted by the twenty-first-century spread of popular nationalism across Western contexts.

Among refugees, physical mobility is often marked by tragedy. The loss of place, as a central constituent of refugee identities, involves adversity in terms of level of physical security and economic attainment (Zetter 1999, Stefansson 2006). Referring to the condition of statelessness experienced by refugees who are forced to flee their country of origin, Nicholas Gill (2010) highlights the role of the nation state in shaping refugees' predicaments. In circumstances where nation states generate conditions of refugeeism, 'home' is controlled at a state level. Such circumstances foreground the intents of nation states to rule the *nation as a home*, as a domicile symbolised as a form of belonging to a distinct group based on the premise of excluding others (Walters 2004). Such practices of exclusion structure the international order when reactions to the displacement of people becomes a vital catalyst in popularist appeals to 'nationhood'. David Morley (2017) exposes the power and geopolitics of material mobility which – by controlling the mobility of people, information and commodities – designate certain subjects as legitimate 'insiders' and others, such refugees and asylum seekers, as illegitimate 'outsiders'. Foregrounding issues of palpable home precarity, these socioeconomic and political processes that shape ideas of home operate within complex new 'ethnoscapes' (Appadurai 1996).

Precarious circumstances in their countries of origin compel refugees to 'reinvent home' in different locations without prospects of immediate material improvement (Cieraad 2010). For refugees, this reinvention of home involves the preservation of a sense of a 'real' home as a valid and authentic place in the country of origin. Yet, at the same time, this preserved sense of home is often located within a place of marginalisation (Azmi and Lund 2009; Gill 2010; Fenster 2013). Expressed as a yearning to return to their country of origin, this alignment of 'home' frequently leads refugees and settled diasporic communities to define home more fervently as a bounded geographical place. As such, 'diaspora' infers not only journeying and movement but also the forming of 'collective homes away from home' (Clifford 1994: 317). The inexorable desire for a home and homemaking is, then, central to diasporic politics and strategies of belonging (Martin and Mohanty 1986; Rapport and Dawson 1998) and, at the same time, highlights the precarious nature of 'home'.

The concept of transnationalism contributes to an understanding of how ideas of mobility, belonging and attachment are shaped by complex interconnections between global networks and physical movement. Transnational encounters of home involve experiences of being 'stretched between' two countries or 'dually located' (Guarnizo and Smith, 1998; Smith 2001). In this respect, the social worlds of individuals and families are intimately woven into two physical places and communities, across nation states (Vertovec 2001). The 'in-between' nature of transnational migrants' everyday lives generates new kinds of social adjustment and forms of belonging (Alexandrova and Lyon 2010). This dual, in-between quality may involve divided claims and loyalties within diasporas (Sheffer 1996). Depending on the nature and motives for the movement of home, the crossing of national boundaries can generate intensified longings for home, invoked by feelings of distance from family members, friendship and wider social networks that once gave a sense of familiarity and security.

Diasporic identities are shaped by migrants' sense of attachment to a special place they call 'home'. It is the very sense of loss and distance that shapes such identities. Indeed, transmigration suggests that meanings of home are acquired precisely by *journeying away* from home (Case 1996). Referred to as a deterritorialised space, this absent 'home place' can bring forth a sense of heritage and feelings of being rooted elsewhere even though individuals and communities may have resided in the host country for more than one generation (Olwig and Hastrup 1997; Smith 2014). For example, in Sarah Ahmed's study of narratives of migration and estrangement among two very different nomadic or migrant communities – a community of Asian women writers in the UK and internationally mobile families and individuals referred to as the Global Nomads International – she shows how the migrant experience draws attention to the change, uprooting and repositioning involved in homemaking. Ahmed refers to the material and sensory 'experience of locality' that comprise places: 'it is sentimentalized as a space of belonging ("home is where the heart is")' (Ahmed 1999: 341). Home is not necessarily one place – the place one inhabits – but often involves 'the roots or routes of one's destination'. Calling attention to representational and embodied aspects of home movement, Ahmed highlights the importance of stories about departed homes for transnational subjects: the journey, remembering the past and dislocation within 'communities of strangers' (Ahmed 1999: 345). The sharing of these narratives helps build a foundation on which to assemble a new sense of home wherein an encounter with a new place gradually enables a supplanting of nostalgic memories of past spatial belonging.

A focus on Scottish migrant family histories in Australia by Basu (2007) provides an example of how certain communities consider themselves as members of a 'victim diaspora'. The Scottish 'homecomers' self-conception refers to the Highland Clearances in the nineteenth century, where Scottish people were callously ejected from their homes to clear land for large-scale agricultural development. The narratives analysed by Basu reveal that the Clearances are often compared to other historical violence events, such as slavery, colonial genocide or the Jewish diasporic experience. In this regard, homecoming is expressed by these 'imagi-neered' Scots as a form of healing and often articulated as a pilgrimage. For Basu, the popular identification with exile and victimhood stems mainly from the present and privileged status of white middle-class people in former settler colonies. Yet given that the exodus triggered the oppression of Aboriginal communities in Aus-tralia, these representations of homecoming often overlook the colonial or eco-nomic aspirations that characterise the Scottish diaspora as an 'imperial diaspora' or 'trade diaspora'. In their search for 'uncomplicated belonging', Basus's Scottish participants invoke 'a moral rhetoric of exile' as a strategy for navigating 'a morally ambiguous history of emigration and colonization' (Basu 2007: 193).

In this way, the ambiguity and multidimensional nature of the homecoming ambition is revealed in Basu's study of Scottish migrant family histories in Australia. His interpretation of this yearning to return to an imagined 'wholeness' contests mainstream academic ideas of 'identity' as something inherently fragmented and continually re-formed 'on the move'. Instead, Basu, foregrounds the need for 'ontological security', in the sense used by Giddens (1991), to explain that 'home' 'is not to be found *either* in movement *or* in stasis but in the articulation of both' (Basu 2007: 8, original emphasis). The metaphors of ancestral kinship and territorial attachment drawn on by these diasporic Scots exploit notions of home precarity by summoning 'homecoming' as a form of identity formation. As such, Basu highlights the growing practice of homecoming or 'roots tourism' in the late twentieth century as an impulse that extends beyond people of Scottish heritage: 'The quest for roots is a quest for origins: a journey to the "source"' (Basu 2007: xi).

Transient modes of dwelling and belonging

We find, then, that the term 'belonging' is multi-scalar. It extends from persona-lised feelings of attachment to the dwelling, to a community and to wider and sometimes more complicated politics of belonging that relates to dominant or oppositional discourses of integration or rejection (Christou 2011). Within con-ceptualisations of home relating to migration and diasporas, a focus on geographical mobility and belonging foregrounds the imaginaries as well as the material strategies employed by individuals and families to move and resettle. Research also indicates that despite the fluctuating and mobile meanings of home for migrants, a remark-able affective resilience can underscore home mobilities suggesting that today's mobile identities are underpinned or framed by stable, fixed and bounded accounts of home (Ralph and Staeheli 2011). The following examples of research on home mobilities reveal the scope, diversity and complexities involved in the varied ima-ginings of home for geographically mobile social groups.

Studies of the home cultures of migrants tend to distinguish between 'recent' and 'settled' migrants, defined in relation to intentions to return or not to return back to the country of origin. While settled migrants have committed to staying and making their life in the new country, recent migrants are still considering whether to settle in the host country. New migrants often face disadvantages in finding accommodation, compared to the rest of the population. This relates to lack of resources, low income and discrimination. New economic migrants may live in private rented accommodation or with friends or relatives (Pillai et al. 2007). Alternatively, they may have accommodation linked to their work, as live-in domestic workers or au-pairs (Spencer et al. 2007). With less likelihood of becoming homeowners compared to long-term stayers, new migrants often encounter poor living conditions or overcrowding in multiple occupancy housing shared with other migrant workers. Most converge in the private rented sector which has some of the poorest conditions and short-term tenancies (Garvie 2001). Poor housing standards and unstable tenancies contribute to a sense of vulnerability for migrants who often experience home precarities by feeling at risk of home-lessness. Without access to social housing, these conditions can lead to feelings of stress, depression and isolation (Carter and El-Hassan 2003).

An example of the dynamics associated with temporary and permanent experi-ences of settlement is illustrated by an ethnographic study of Turkish people in Vienna by Savaş (2010). Her research shows how migrants can create a collective sense of belonging in a new place expressed through the materiality and aesthetics of their homes. Savaş found that Turkish homes in Vienna are conceived through a distinctive aesthetic that produces and reproduces a communal Turkish narrative of migration to the host city. Savaş identified differences between 'aesthetically indif-ferent homes' and 'the beautiful Turkish home' as new cultural forms that arise from specific biographies and experiences of migration and resettlement that gen-erate particular ways of engaging with material objects (Savaş 2010: 336). Oriented towards life in Turkey, guest workers initially viewed their Vienna homes as tem-porary. The 'myth of return', held by most Turkish people in Vienna until around the early 1990s reflected the intention to save enough money in the new setting in order to return to the home country after several years and buy land, a house or at least a tractor back in Turkey. This generated an 'indifference to aesthetics' within their migrant homes in Vienna. Aesthetic indifference is a response to the tem-porary nature of home in Vienna where the Turkish migrants felt 'suspended between return and settlement'. Galvanised by the myth of return and an asso-ciated reluctance to spend money, the guest workers from Turkey experienced real or ritualistic poverty. Savaş calls this a 'custom of poverty', where the guest workers avoid shopping in Vienna (Savaş 2010: 332).

More recently, Turkish residents with Austrian citizenship moved to more spa-cious apartments, in state housing. Their decision to settle permanently in Vienna has coincided with the establishment of Turkish shops, a sense of Turkish space in Vienna and the adoption of new domestic aesthetic practices. Women without paid jobs were initially confined to their homes, but the creation of a spatial community in Vienna facilitates their movement beyond home. In a location viewed as unfriendly, migrants gain a sense of controlling and claiming certain urban areas by re-signifying these spaces as *Turkish* places that foster a sense of belonging and support for diasporic identities (also see D'Alisera 2001; Ehrkamp 2005). The more recent homes of migrants who adopted Austrian citizenship are typically furnished with beautiful Turkish furniture from Turkish shops in Vienna. This typical 'beautiful Turkish home' comprises a shared aesthetic that expresses the unity of the Turkish community, forming a shared domestic material culture (Savaş 2010: 334)

How migrants actively develop connections between their old life and new environment is also considered in an intriguing ethnographic study of a Moroccan family who lived in a collective squat in the centre of Rome. Sabina Giorgi and Alessandra Fasulo (2013) concentrate on one family from Casablanca by considering two aspects of the material home within this migrant family's experience. Giorgi and Fasulo point out that squatters' characteristics and aims often change over time, particularly given that a squat is an unoccupied and unmarked territory in terms of official urban planning. Such urban spaces are 'transgressive zones'. These marginal spaces become occupied by marginal communities such as the homeless, ravers or protesters. The persistent threat of evacuation shapes the activities, materials, identities and politics that characterise squats (Novy and Colomb 2012). Giorgi and Fasulo (2013) discovered the important role played by the materiality of home in migrants' psychological adjustment to their new setting. At the time, in 2012, migrants from Morocco comprised the largest groups of migrants to Italy. Of all migrants, around 40–50,000 (3%) were living in unhealthy and overcrowded housing (Giorgi and Fasulo 2013: 119). The mothers' squatting experience led her to join the Citizen's Movement for the Fight for Housing to campaign for the right to a home. Her daughter, Samia, also took part in political action to support migrants' rights and went on to become a sociology student at the University of Rome, to advance the cause of migrants.

Living among a community of squatters, the family 'cleaned' a grey, stressful military building they occupied in Porto Fluviale. They restored the living space through traditional Moroccan style furnishings with pot plants and chairs outside to conserve their cultural identity and accustom the children to traditional uses of space. Reflecting on the building, Fatima says, 'this place has come alive and it listens to us' (Giorgi and Fasulo 2013: 125). Rather than investing in costly furniture, the squat dwellers assembled and recycled salvaged items, emphasising the transient quality of the communal home. The family were able to express their identity as Moroccans by reinterpreting the traditional Moroccan living room with objects mostly obtained in the new environment and by expressing the ambiguities and the precarious experience of migration. This family's personal history and identity was 'supported by the possession of a space that affords syncretic choices in object display and furniture arrangement' (Giorgi and Fasulo 2013: 126). Such studies suggest that home precarities can trigger a strong sense of agency.

Transferrable habits, customs and materialities of home

Research on the role of the materiality of home for migrants confirm that material objects support migrants' shared memories and identities. Notions of home can either be connected to and expressed through their material dimensions or, by contrast, de-coupled from home's materiality to become a set of transferrable habits and customs. A range of cultural strategies are used by migrants to create a sense of home that often involves the replication of familial ties back home, multi-scalar meanings of home and fluctuating emotions about belonging and acceptance. For example, Turan (2010) proposes that objects form a 'facilitating environment' to support feelings of cultural continuity between the past life and present migratory life. Such uses of material objects extend to desires to reconstruct the familiar shapes of homes of origin in the new host country (Lozanovska 2009; Sinatti 2009). These expressions of home mobilities and relocation also entail an active shaping of home: an active form of home living.

The importance of family ties and family-like attachments within meanings of home among migrants is illustrated by Becker (2003) who studied three groups of older immigrants – Latinos, Filipinos and Cambodians – living in northern California. The conditions of overcrowding experienced by these migrants was decried yet tolerated because they drew on familial metaphors as means of bonding. For example, those migrants accompanied by their families to California tended to have around six people living together in two-bedroom apartments. Here, elderly relatives shared rooms with their grandchildren or slept in a bed set in the corner of the living area. Becker's participants both complained about yet valued the close contact afforded by this living arrangement because it emulated extended family relations traditional to their homeland. The daily interactions involved in this sharing supported elderly migrants' feelings of belonging, in the new context of North America. As Becker explains, positive meanings associated with the migrants' new homes in the host country were cultivated by the company of family and friends which compensated for absent families back home. Becker's findings exemplify the importance of preserving extended family values through migrant living arrangements as a strategy for adjusting to migration.

However, research on migrants' meanings of home also indicate how the home's physicality facilitates settlement. A series of Australian studies confirm that 'home' as a material entity can symbolise feelings of belonging and acceptance in the host country and a continuing connection with the country of origin. For instance, Becky Thompson (1994, 2005) explored meanings of home among Arabic, Greek and Vietnamese migrant women who moved to Sydney, revealing that home can be a space of empowerment in an unfamiliar Australian culture. The migrant's home compensates for feelings of cultural loss by helping them to cope with an alien culture. Referred to as a form of atonement, the migrant home becomes a sign of achievement, a display of difference, and a secure place where one's first language can be comfortably used. The migrant fashions a space where the interior décor, veranda and garden can express the customs and traditions of the migrants' homeland and convey the family's success in establishing themselves in the host country through perseverance and hard work.

An enquiry into Italian migrants' meanings of home in Melbourne by Mariastella Pulvirenti (2000) addresses meanings of home ownership among first generation migrants from Southern Italy. To own a house in Australia was the moral priority that attracted the migrants from Italy. In addition to security, independence, autonomy and a sense of success, Pulvirenti found that home ownership also means responsibility: the task of maintaining and looking after the home. Pulvirenti refers to the Italian notion of 'sistemazione' (to settle, to establish oneself) to describe the move from their homeland and the hope of new prospects in Australia for themselves and their offspring. Home ownership in the new, host country was a powerful symbol of having established oneself and one's family.

A further study by Laura Faggion and Raffaello Furlan (2018) of the material aspects of post-World War II homes built in Brisbane, Australia by a group of Italian migrants relates home as a symbolic place for elderly Italian migrants. The large movement of Italian economic migrants from the Veneto region of Italy to Australia in the 1950s was enabled by an assisted passage scheme sponsored by the Italian and Australian governments. Forming part of Australia's multicultural nation, these migrants made a significant contribution to the distinctiveness of Australian domestic architectural development. Faggion and Furlan found that their Italian migrants relate home to two specific locations defined as 'here' and 'there'. 'There' refers to the hometown in Italy and 'here' denotes the Brisbane home. 'Home' is linked to the migrants' roots yet, at the same time, 'home' also refers to the house where they live now, in Brisbane, signifying the divergent locality and scalarity of home.

Faggion and Furlan highlight the complex and multifaceted meanings associated with the homes built by the Italian migrants. They identify five distinctive meanings of home corresponding with the 'here', the house in Brisbane: 'sistemazione', meaning to settle (in Australia); hard work; pride in their culture; place of reference for the family; and feeling of security. Faggion and Furlan explain that some of these meanings are 'multi-scalar and plurilocal', some affected by social or cultural factors, some influenced by gender, age or lifestyle factors and others are shaped by specific historic, economic and political circumstances associated with the country of origin and host countries during the migration process. As a variable, the Italian architectonic elements continue to influence the way in which the informants view their world, leading Faggion and Furlan to conclude that 'These meanings are rooted in the experience of migration, in the culture of the country of origin and in the acceptance by the dominant culture' (Faggion and Furlan 2018: 5).

Alana Smith (2014) contributes to migration research in Ireland by examining how Polish migrants in Dublin interpret home after leaving Poland. She chronicles their ambitions, predilections and customs by relating their migration encounters to their perceptions of 'feeling at home in the world' to understand the discourse of transnationalism. Smith's study began in 2008, when Ireland was one of the most flourishing economies of the world, forming a new destination for immigrants. The country's prosperity involved returning Irish citizens and migrants from accession states of the European Union. Polish emigration has been triggered by limited employment opportunities, poor housing and household structures in Poland (Kicinger and Weinar 2007; Kaczmarczyk and Okólski 2008). Although economic factors often initiate decisions to migrate, these considerations decline in importance the longer migrants remain abroad. As well as seeking a better life and better employment opportunities, access to friends and informal networks in the host country are vital factors that sustain Polish labour migration (Waldinger and Lichter 2003). Finding that the lives of her Polish migrant informants were marked by the intersection between home and mobility, Smith identified three overlapping interpretations of home within their narratives of home: the 'centred home', the 'sentimental home' and the 'transportable home'. Those Polish migrants who expressed a centred home had a pragmatic rather than an emotional view of home: as a geographically fixed place of bricks and mortar.

With regard to the sentimental home, informants conveyed an emotional sense of home and place based on a perspective of change, involving a past time and place in Poland that no longer exists. This sentimentality conveyed a nostalgia that carried memories of affection or longing for a bygone, idyllic homeland. One informant, who now had young children and was far from her parents, had trouble describing 'home' but then recalled the reasons her family moved to Ireland:

> I try to focus on the fact that home doesn't mean walls. I think once you're away you miss your country and it becomes such a wonderful place, like wonderland. You forget about everything that was bad. (Smith 2014: 114)

Some of Smith's informants who expressed a transportable sense of home articulated what she calls a 'meso-form' of transnational residency by referring to home in terms of a mental geography. For example, one informant regularly travelled between Ireland and Poland, skyped with her family back in Poland, and said how she missed Dublin when with her mother in Krakow. Representing this intermediate or meso-form of transnational residency, Anna, one of Smith's informants expressed her homesickness:

> Home is a very weird notion that fluctuates. It changes. It doesn't have one meaning to me anymore. I have this sense of home being Krakow (not my hometown, but Krakow; my mum lives close to Krakow as well), and then, when I'm there, I refer to Dublin as home. So home is really kind of an open notion really. Not a closed idea. (Smith 2014: 116)

Confirming the multi-scalarity of home imaginings, Smith explains: 'Here, home is transportable and may stretch across several planes of time and different places, an idea facilitated by advances in communication, technology, and transportation' (Smith 2014: 116). Her Polish migrants navigated movement through attachment and emotion, managing their sense of belonging through multiple interconnecting movements of technology, culture, images and objects.

Anthropological and sociological studies of settled migrants' homes have uncovered the ways in which migrants assemble objects in the homes and how these objects express their identities (see for example, Csikszentmihalyi and Rochberg-Halton 1981; Miller 1998, 2001, 2008, 2010). In the *Comfort of Things*, anthropologist Daniel Miller (2008) studies families who have moved thousands of miles from 'home' to consider the role of objects in generating new stories as people traverse cultural spaces. Sustaining a wider approach to home as both physical and emblematic, the theme and experience of moving home is intertwined with material culture whether through photos, mementoes, furniture or food. Domestic material cultures associated with diasporic and migratory resettlement have therefore been studied in relation to memorialising and preserving connections with former lives and domiciles. Research suggests that migrants' homes tend to be characterised by a combination of two distinct kinds of material objects. One type is connected to the current domicile while the other is linked to the country of origin. Material objects in the home are a vital aspect of the process of shaping memories and a sense of belonging as part of the formation of new political and gendered identities (Datta 2009).

Ruba Salih (2002; 2003) presents a gendered account of transnational migration through the study of home, longing and narratives of displacement and belonging among Moroccan migrant women in Italy. Moroccan homes in Italy are adorned with a combination of Italian and Moroccan objects, suggesting feelings of 'double belonging', feelings that reflect plural identities. The qualities associated with these two distinct kinds of material objects, from Italy and Morocco, can be understood as having a 'bridging' effect, echoing aspects of the above account of adapting to a squat. Clifford (1997) suggests, for example, that objects can act as a 'contact zone' by bridging differing experiences across cultures and taking on new meanings in new settings. Objects in homes have been approached as traces of identity narratives and as mediators of identity reiterated through stories. Correspondingly, a study of British domestic culture by Hurdley (2006) explores the provenance and meaning of objects through stories of home. Her study confirms that representations of home objects are mediated by the ways which they are displayed and the way they are narrated. The re-experience of notions of home through relationships with objects is also explained using the concept of *sensory memory* in work by Sarah Pink (2004; 2009). Using sensory ethnography to understand how people experience, remember and imagine place, Pink explains how time is organised and experienced through the living out of everyday life in the intimate, sensory and affective context of the domestic home

Highlighting a 'materialist' approach, Tolia-Kelly (2004a,b,c) explores the visual and material cultures of British South Asian homes in the UK to form part of postcolonial studies of home. The 'fluid citizenry' experienced by British South Asians is shaped by British colonial rule and expressed through domesticity. In the host country, the South Asian women cultivate a postcolonial identity by furnishing the new domestic space with familiar paintings and photos from 'back home'. Objects selected by the women to decorate their home elicit memories that recount past experiences as individual and collective histories. By triggering memories, these objects perform as dialogic connectors with social memory in postcolonial contexts (Tolia-Kelly 2004b). Private mementoes regarded as *transitional* objects also perform a key role in narratives of forced displacement (Parkin 1999).

It is worth recalling, here, that the terms 'transitional object' and 'transitional phenomena', originally introduced by D.W. Winnicott (1953), explain the way we use certain objects as a 'security blanket' or 'comfort blanket' to provide psychological comfort particularly in unusual situations (see Kuhn 2013).

In the case of forced displacement, mementoes may even stand in for personal interactions by acting as an archive of emotional memories and reflections. As Tolia-Kelly explains, the material dimensions of domesticity support associations with pre-migratory places.

The significance of home as a site of socialisation appears even more pronounced in the context of migration as demonstrated by an ethnographic study of the homes of Sikhs in Finland by Laura Hirvi (2016). Alongside the Internet and cultural occasions and places of religious activity, the home offers one of the few contexts where children in their new homeland learn about the cultural traditions of their parents. As such, Hirvi describes migrant's homes as a 'cosmos of senses' shaped by its occupants' everyday practices. At home, elder generations convey religious teachings to young members of the family directly through religious lessons. They inspire the children to pray and acquaint children with tangible religious objects from pictures of the Golden Temple to those displayed on the home altar. Home becomes a site through which parents and other relatives impart to children a sense of their parents' religion in tacit ways ranging from the taste and smell of food, to the sound of kirtan (devotional music) broadcast on a Finnish television channel. This kind of engagement with transnational media supports the socialisation of young Sikhs growing up in Helsinki away from the Punjab into their parents' religious culture. In these implicit ways, Sikh children growing up in Finland are socialised via the culture of the home in a manner that enable them to become more familiar with the Sikh religion.

Home mobilities as mediated spaces

Media play a vital role in householders' experiences of home through global media flows enabling householders to experience a sense of place and belonging through a trans-spatial lens. Mediated interactions with people and events beyond home and national borders allow householders to experience home as a fluid, mobile space. Facilitated by improvements in communication technology, home mobility is mediated at several levels. Among these levels we can identify first, the mediated connection and reconnection of transnational families and friends; second, the mediated journeying beyond the borders of home and nation by accessing media content about distant or past home cultures, events and ideas in different parts of the world; and third, the use of mobile media while on the move. Basu's study of Scottish migrant family histories in Australia, mentioned above, reveals that local and global references to the Scottish Highlands are communicated through social media, online news and advertisements, travel blogs and email discussion lists that sustain globally networked clan societies as well as local heritage museums, souvenirs, and the organisation of personal and package tours (Basu 2007). This confirms that the quest for homecoming is supported by a 'semantic migration' of concepts and meanings that traverse online/offline boundaries (Basu 2007: 188). These modes of virtual and embodied mobility comprise thick, complex network geographies (Morley 2017).

Home as a virtual living space

Studies of social media in the last decade have prompted a radical reassessment of the way new media are approached and conceived in relation to place. Social media use by diasporic migrants demonstrates that one of the most significant impacts of new media is the way it connects people living in distant homes (see for example Fortunati et al. 2011). Daniel Miller and Jolynna Sinanan (2012) provide a range of examples that indicate the multiple ways in which new media 'destabilise' traditional ideas of home as a bounded space. They state:

> Instead of seeing the media as connecting separate location, we may now have reached the point where we should start to think of new media as places within which people in some sense live. A third place distinct from the two offline locations. (Miller and Sinanan (2012: 6)

In other words, the *online* world can be encountered as a living space that represents home. Miller and Sinanan (2018) identify three factors or media dynamics that contribute to this radical reassessment of the relationship between media and place, supported by distinctive features of digital technology. First is the creation of a temporary mobile space using smart phone technology. Through this use, specific locations are no longer of defining consequence. A second media dynamic is the creation of an online identity through social media use. A third factor is exemplified by living together in the same space through, for example, webcam. Miller and Sinanan explain these dynamics through a range of examples of digital media use. The first example, regarding the creation of a temporary mobile space, is about how we use mobile smart phones. Our range of uses of this device suggests that specific location is not the defining feature or consequence. The emphasis is less on located individuals and more on connecting people through the medium itself which performs as a temporary mobile space.

A second instance is that young social media users go to great lengths to manage the appearance and style of their online presence. Horst (2009) demonstrates that the aesthetics of teenagers' online identities reflect the aesthetics of teenagers' bedrooms, through photos and other kinds of symbols. Referring to Horst's work, Miller and Sinanan state: 'But if instead of seeing Facebook as merely a mode of communication it was designated as the place in which you lived then this transforms our perception of such activity' (Miller and Sinanan 2012: 6). This is demonstrated by Miller in his study of Facebook in Trinidad through a series of personal vignettes (Miller 2011). He argues that social media sites such as Facebook are not simply a cipher for 'real' social interactions. Loyalty, kinship, friendship and relationships reconstructed in the space of Facebook are positively reinforced by the platform. The technology intersects with local cultural idioms and understandings of national identity, and national anxiety. This localisation or domestication of Facebook evolves and extends to become a living space organised around the various devices and platforms used. Miller illustrates this with the example of a participant called Malcom whose relationship to his laptop was so intense that his living space was organised around the device. With his work moving back and forth between Australia and the UK, Malcom regarded his email address as his permanent home address, describing his laptop as the 'nearest thing to home' (Miller 2011). The recurrent updating and rearrangement of his emails comprised the updating of his social relationships.

The perception of online activity as a living space is also exemplified by the ways in which dispersed family members forge ties by using mobile devices to create a communicative space through which they organise daily needs and generate feelings of being at home. Homemaking practices enabled by mobile device use are shaped by gender dynamics (Elliott and Urry, 2010; Hjorth, 2009; Lim, 2016; Ling and Horst, 2011; Madianou and Miller, 2012; Parreñas, 2005). For example, among Filipina families, social media reunites families divided by migration by reconnecting Filipina mothers in the UK with their children left behind in the Philippines (Francisco, 2015; Madianou and Miller, 2011, 2012; Parreñas, 2001, 2005b; San Pascual, 2016). In a study of transnational parenting, Madianou and Miller (2012) describe a young Filipino woman working in London for more than two years as a cleaner and carer for the elderly. To save money to send back home, she never went to the cinema, pubs or other public sites of entertainment in London. Instead, she spent her time working and then returned to her accommodation shared with another Filipino woman, made up of bunkbeds. However, her spare time was spent communicating with her family on social media, first on Friendster and then Facebook, within a polymedia ecology (see Chapter 6). As Miller states, 'One could say that she works in London, also that she sleeps and eats on London, but in many respects, she lives with her family not in the Philippines but really and truly on Facebook' (Miller 2018: 174). In this respect, Facebook not only brought these two physical spaces back into relation with one another, it became her home.

By approaching Facebook as a designated place where a person lives rather than simply a device through which a person communicates, Miller explains that this dramatically changes our understanding of social media engagement in the home. This mediated form of transnational communication generates variant lived experiences of being 'at home' (Lim, 2016; Madianou and Miller, 2012). It enables the coordination of domestic activities by family members including a form of 'remote control' for parents to track their distant children's locations and activities (Matsuda, 2009; Madianou and Miller, 2012). In these ways, digital mobile media dissolve the distinction between digital and physical places to produces 'hybridised spaces' (De Souza e Silva, 2006).

A third factor which prompts a radical reconsideration of the relationship between media and place relates to webcam, a generic term for a video camera connected to a computer, allowing its images to be seen by Internet users and exemplified by Skype. This technology is perceived as 'always on'. Rather than emphasising features of media mobility, webcam's affordances offer the possibility of living together in the same space, a joined space formed by the technology itself: 'A couple lives in the join created by webcam as much as in the places that are joined' (Miller and Sinanan 2012: 7). In their book titled *Webcam*, Miller and Sinanan (2014) take a sociological approach to 'webcamming', a term they use to refer to conversations via Skype or any other Internet solution for communicating across distances using sound and images. Through ethnographic research in the small Trinidadian town of El Mirador, they explored the everyday uses of the webcam from several viewpoints, including how the technology has come to alter not only notions of self-consciousness, intimacy and interpersonal relationships but also a sense of place. A woman from Trinidad talked about the way she maintained a connection via Skype with her sister in Texas who lived on a US military base. With no close friends there, her sister's social life was restricted to her Skype interactions with her family back in Trinidad. This included some of her cousins whom she had never seen in person. Skype helped establish a more significant relationship with her cousins than those she experienced with people on the military base Miller and Sinanan (2014).

It became apparent to Miller and Sinanan that the webcam has fulfilled the human desire of long-distant communication through face-to-face social engagement. As strangers or divorcing couples who live in shared accommodation find, physical space alone does not act as a bonding mechanism. Yet the use of audio-visual devices to sustain long distance relationships reveals how both 'always-on' and scheduled engagement can re-connect imaginaries and feelings of intimate space with interpersonal affiliations. Face-to-face time and co-produced or co-present domestic practices such as watching television together or simply being in each other's presence are now sustainable using today's digital audio-visual screen. Video cameras connected to Internet smart devices such as laptops and smart phones now characterise the multiscreen home (Miller and Sinanan 2014; see Chapter 6). Second screens enable trans-domestic communication by the digital creation of a 'space' in which partners, families and friends living apart from each other can meet, renew contact, check that their relationship is stable, reaffirm bonds and share time and space together.

For family members separated by migration, encounters with domestic space are enabled by second screens and networked communications platforms. These screens are now used to sustain family ties as well as friendships and romantic relationships, as a matter of routine. Whether they are at the other end of the world or a few miles away, grandparents may meet their grandchildren for the very first time via Skype and go on to develop a relationship with their grandchildren via screen devices, watching them grow up on a computer camera. Parents use webcams to check on children and ensure they're safe and whole families gather together to celebrate birthdays and anniversaries via Skype. Some use the camera not just to reinforce bonds through face-to-face encounters but also to connect physically absent friends and family to their domestic space by showing them how they have decorated or rearranged their homes and gardens, or by asking for advice on aspects of material home life. And as shown in Chapter 6, the temporal dynamics of the multiscreen home enable householders to shape trans-domestic media encounters. This includes communicating with distant households while watching TV programmes or movies 'together' in domestic spaces separated by distance but not time. As Miller and Sinanan (2014) observe, because such devices enable *visibility* to others and offer a sense of actual presence, the interaction appears to be more immediate and more authentic (even though digital images can be falsified). As a result, Skype and related audio-visual mobile screens facilitate a complex interweaving of physically distant spaces. Space is no longer the main factor in social relationships. Instead, home space has been elevated, rehabilitated and supplanted by online networks. In this respect, then, home as a physical space has dual qualities: it exists in both a physical and *virtual* place.

As part of this radical reconsideration of the relationship between media and place, Miller and Sinanan explain the transformative social impact of this audio-visual feature of computer technology by developing a theory of attainment. The 'humanisation' of information and communications technologies is explained by foregrounding how these technologies are used to actively define our identities as a vital part of social interaction. Miller and Sinanan argue that it is misleading to view new technology as disruptive of some previous utopian, holistic or ideal state. Rather, 'attainment' emphasises that with this digital audio-visual technology, we can achieve what has been latent within humans but was not previously realisable (Miller and Sinanan 2014).

Today's home mobilities are now organised, then, around audio-visual domestic devices as powerful ways of managing intimate attachments and sustaining homeliness across distance. Becoming a key feature of the mediatisation of home mobilities, these devices *re-stage* home living by facilitating a sense of mediated co-presence (Madianou and Miller, 2012) and a mediated sense of belonging (Cabalquinto 2018). The anthropological reassessment of the relationship between media and space articulated through Miller and Sinanan's theory of attainment can be brought together with the notion of polymediated timescapes discussed in relation to the multiscreen home, to highlight the transformative nature of today's home as a trans-domestic timescapes. We can say that contemporary home mobilities arecharacterised by a new kind of mobility, a mediated and virtual home mobility that comprises a *virtualisation* of home generated by a digital materialisation of the homescape. Supported by householders' engagement with multiple digital screens in a polymedia ecology, the virtualisation of home signifies a mediated expression and management of home This virtual home mobility entails a re-construction or re-making of home's transient and nomadic tendencies involving a digitally retrieved and restored home as a space *imaginatively fixed, stable and holistic*. As a feature of home mediatisation, digital screens play a fundamental role, then, in managing home mobilities as mediatised spaces.

Mobile audio-visual devices not only enable imagined home fixity but also the possibility of travel to places without moving physically (Urry, 2000: 70). This notion of a virtualised home therefore also confirms the vital role of mobile technologies, from mobile phones to webcams, in creating a sense of home while on the move. For new migrants and refugees, smart phones confer a sense of normality by supporting familiar and intimate connections 'back home' while they navigate their way through an unfamiliar and alien space. These personal mobile devices help them to overcome feelings of isolation and loneliness (Bonini 2011: Horst 2006). By communicating at a distance while on the move, the 'habitual' use of smart phones offer migrants connections with loved ones left behind (Moores, 2012). In this respect, 'being at home' can be experienced outside the boundaries of the family home (Hjorth, 2009; Meyrowitz, 1985; Morley, 2006). This mobility approach opens up 'home' as a travelling space (Sheller and Urry, 2006), suggesting that individuals' relationships to their mobile devices generates a form of *mobile domestication* to negotiate and cope with the challenges of being on the move and settling in a new country.

Family rituals via mobile devices

While mobile devices can offer a sense of mobile domesticity, at the same time, the complex and intertwined movements of users, objects and data can generate a disruption and dislocation of domesticity (Morley 2007). A study by Earvin Cabalquinto (2018) shows how the use of mobile devices 'reworks domestic spaces' by stretching familial relationships across continents. Using various mobile media, overseas Filipino workers in Melbourne, Australia connect with their left-behind families, enabling them to re-stage, experience and negotiate home. Using mobile devices, dispersed family members constantly negotiate feelings of being at home by deploying various strategies that reconstruct a sense of home. These transnational families set up a 'digital hub' within their physical places of dwelling. As most overseas Filipino workers rent a shared house or apartment, they arrange a space in their private bedroom where digital devices are placed. In the Philippines, digital devices are positioned in shared spaces such as the living room or in the bedroom.

Drawing on Kitchin and Dodge (2005), Cabalquinto explains that domestic and physical spaces are therefore transformed into 'transduce space' by creating new spatial forms generated via mobile social computing. This transformation is enacted through ritualic practices, gender roles and socioeconomic conditions based on videoconferencing as a regular form of synchronised communication. Some of Cabalquinto's participants use Skype while moving around inside the household or in a private bedroom, while others access Skype via a desktop computer. They prefer to communicate in indoor spaces for safety reasons, to avoid the theft of mobile phones in public spaces. The performance of everyday family rituals is an important way of forging family bonding and strengthening relationships. One overseas worker in Melbourne conducted 'jamming' sessions with his distant family using Skype via his laptop place by placing his laptop in the living room. Another worker would 'move around in the kitchen while videoconferencing with his loved ones in the Philippines' (Cabalquinto 2018: 804).

However, enacting family rituals through mobile devices reinforces gender roles by contributing to the idealised gendered images of the domestic home. Restrictive gender ideologies influence transnational communication in the Philippines. The gendering of domestic spaces is reinforced though 'remote mothering' from Melbourne exemplified by mothers urging their children to complete homework. Relatedly, overseas fathers also use Skype to discipline their children, uphold authority and establish presence over family rituals. Reflecting differing levels of digital literacy, Cabalquinto has also found that younger adult participants use multiple platforms and devices to maintain continuous mobile, interactive, and highly personalised communication that include group texts to facilitate an 'ambient co-presence' (Madianou, 2016).

While a sense of dwelling is recreated through family rituals which is gendered and stratified through mobile device use, Cabalquinto also found that mediated mobilities experienced by transnational families can be constrained, exclusionary and frustrating. Structural and infrastructural forces marginalise transnational families in a mobile society. Some left-behind family members in the Philippines have limited broadband connection at home and find that the credit of prepaid broadband external USB could run out. One participant had to eat in a restaurant to access Wi-Fi, there being no Wi-Fi at home. As Cabalquinto states, 'the interrupted mediated mobilities experienced by the transnational Filipino family reinforce the social inequalities within the operations of global capitalism' (Cabalquinto 2018: 808). Family group chat exacerbates pre-existing family divisions by further fragmenting dispersed living arrangements through the exclusion of certain family members from group chats. And the normative expectations of physical co-presence often make some absent mothers feel frustrated because the only way they can show their affection or enact their caring role is via the mobile phone. Yet their children often ignore their mothers' distant advice or attempts to discipline them. Using a critical mobilities lens, Cabalquinto explains that these social structures and technological divisions indicate hidden social inequalities in a digital society. As Cabalquinto states,

> to fully experience comfort and at-homeness in alternative spaces of dwelling is not as straightforward as connecting to the Internet, running mobile applications and clicking a button. Logging onto and logging off these networked and multimedia-based environments are perpetually struggled over and negotiated to ensure the organisation and maintenance of a home away from home. (Cabalquinto 2018: 812)

Conclusion

Complex emotions of loss and gain are involved in migrant, mobile and diasporic imagining of home as a place. For migrants, home can be managed as a temporary or a permanent resettlement, and the place of relocation can be encountered as a site of inclusion and exclusion. When negotiating social fields of transnationalism, migrants' conceptualisations of home involve the challenges of new meanings of time, space and place (Smith 2014). These challenges and multiple experiences comprise a central feature of late modern home precarities.

Yet research also suggests that despite the fluctuating and mobile meanings of home for migrants, a remarkable affective endurance underpins these home mobilities, suggesting that today's mobile identities are often driven by stable, fixed and bounded imaginaries and accounts of home. For transnational migrants and members of diasporas, home imaginaries involve home precarities that centre around feelings of absence, distance and disruption. The longed-for home may be as important as the 'real' in influencing where migrants place home (Ralph and Staeheli 2011). Nevertheless, the material culture perspective that characterises several of the above research findings contributes to an understanding of how migrants manage resettlement by recreating a domestic space that involves a fluid set of encounters. These reformations are expressed by deploying and integrating objects, architecture, spaces, technologies and creating familial or family-like groupings. Such studies highlight migrants' *active agency* in negotiating encounters of belonging and attachment by creating 'home' in precarious new circumstances to evoke the familiar shapes and meanings of homes of origin in the new host country.

Although physical mobility organises contemporary experiences of belonging (Appadurai, 1996; Morley 2000), imaginaries of immobility and of a fixed and stable home serve as a vital orientation in contemporary transnational and transregional cultures. Studies of home mobilities highlight the situated and contextualised nature of migrant individuals' and families' negotiations of home and attachment. Yet the emphasis on home as an intimate, symbolic, private space has been both complicated and enhanced by technologies of communication from Skype to mobile phone for maintaining transnational intimate contact. The varied uses of audio-visual mobile devices to maintain contact with distant relatives and friends, while immobile or on the move, reveal that perceptions of home are not only encountered as physical space but can be experienced as a hybridised, digital space.

We find that experiences of home are now shaped by flows and movements that involve digital communication technologies which support the creation of a *virtual home* which forms part of the mediatisation of home imaginaries. This virtual home performs on two levels: first, the technology itself can become 'home' and second, the virtual interaction can generate a sense of homeliness. Computer screens that support face-to-face and real time encounters enable the creation of home as a stable, holistic place through interaction within a shared virtual space to fulfil the needs of intimacy, constancy and 'ontological security'. As such, 'home' as a physical space has multiple qualities. It is experienced as a physical setting yet also an imagined space, one yearned-for as a memory or recreated as welcoming mediated place. In effect, mobile communication devices *re-stage* home living by generating an awareness of a mediated shared presence (Madianou and Miller, 2012) and a sense of belonging (Cabalquinto 2018). As a key feature of the mediatisation of home mobilities, today's home mobilities are, then, coordinated around audio-visual domestic media devices as potent strategies for maintaining intimate attachments and sustaining a sense of homeliness across distance.

References

Ahmed, S. (1999) 'Home and away: Narrative of migration and estrangement', *International Journal of Cultural Studies*, 2(3), 329–347.

Alexandrova, N. and Lyon, D. (2010) 'Imaginary geographies: Border places and "home" in the narratives of migrant women', in E. Capussotti, I. Laliotou, D. Lyon and L. Passerini (eds), *Women Migrants from East to West: Gender, Mobility and Belonging in Contemporary Europe*. Oxford: Berghahn, pp. 95–110.

Appadurai, A. (1996) *Modernity at Large: Cultural Dimensions of Globalization*. Minneapolis: University of Minnesota Press.

Axel, B.K. (2001) *The Nation's Tortured Body: Violence, Representation and the Formation of a Sikh 'Diaspora'*. Durham, NC: Duke University Press.

Azmi, F. and Lund, R. (2009) 'Shifting geographies of house and home female migrants making home in rural Sri Lanka', *Journal of Geographical Science*, 57, 33–54.

Basu, P. (2007) *Highland Homecomings: Genealogy and Heritage Tourism in the Scottish Diaspora*. London: Routledge.

Bauman, Z. (2001) *Community: In Search of Security in a Hostile World*. Cambridge: Polity Press.

Becker, G. (2003) 'Meanings of place and displacement in three groups of older immigrants', *Journal of Aging Studies*, 17(2), 129–149.

Blunt, A. and Dowling, R. (2006) *Home*. London: Routledge.

Bonini, T. (2011) 'The media as "home-making" tools: Life story of a Filipino migrant in Milan', *Media, Culture and Society*, 33(6) 869–883.

Cabalquinto, E.C. (2018) 'Home on the move: Negotiating differential domesticity in family life at a distance', *Media, Culture & Society*, 40(6), 795–816.

Carter, M. and El-Hassan, A. (2003) *Between NASS and a Hard Place*. London: Housing Action Charitable Trust.

Case, D. (1996) 'Contributions of journeys away to the definition of home: An empirical study of a dialectical process', *Journal of Environmental Psychology*, 16(1), 1–15.

Chambers, I. (1994) *Migrancy, Culture and Identity*. London and New York: Routledge.

Christou, A. (2011) 'Narrating lives in (e)motion: Embodiment, belongingness and displacement in diasporic spaces of home and return', *Emotion, Space and Society*, 4(4), 249–257.

Cieraad I. (2010) 'Homes from home: Memories and projections', *Home Cultures*, 7(1), 85–102.

Clifford, J. (1994) 'Diasporas', *Cultural Anthropology*, 9(3), 302–338.

Clifford, J. (1997) *Routes: Travel and Translation in the Late Twentieth Century*. Cambridge MA: Harvard University Press.

Csikszentmihalyi, M. and Rochberg-Halton, E. (1981) *The Meaning of Things: Domestic Symbols and the Self*. Cambridge: Cambridge University Press.

D'Alisera, J. (2001) 'I ♥ Islam: Popular religious commodities, sites of inscription, and transnational Sierra Leonean identity', *Journal of Material Culture*, 6(1), 91–110.

Datta, A. (2009) 'Editorial: Home, migration and the city', *Open House International*, 34(3), 4–7.

De Souza e Silva, A. (2006) 'From cyber to hybrid: Mobile technologies as interfaces of hybrid spaces', *Space and Culture*, 9, 261–278.

Ehrkamp, P. (2005) 'Placing identities: Transnational practices and local attachments of Turkish immigrants in Germany', *Journal of Ethnic and Migration Studies*, 31(2), 345–364.

Elliott, A. and Urry, J. (2010) *Mobile Lives*. London: Routledge.

Faggion, L. and Furlan, R. (2018), 'The symbolic realm of Italian migrants' post-WWII houses in Australia', *Home Cultures*. doi:10.1080/17406315.2018.1507738.

Fenster, T. (2013) 'Moving between addresses', *Home Cultures*, 10(2), 159–187.

Fortunati, L., Pertierra, R. and Vincent, J. (2011) *Migration, Diaspora, and Information: Technology in Global Societies*. New York: Routledge.

Francisco, V. (2015) '"The internet is magic": Technology, intimacy and transnational families', *Critical Sociology*, 41, 173–190.

Garvie, D. (2001) *Far from Home: The Housing of Asylum Seekers in Private Rented Accommodation*. London: Shelter.

Germann Molz, J. (2008) 'Global abode: Home and mobility in narratives of round-the-world travel', *Space and Culture*, 11(4), 325–342.

Giddens, A. (1991) *Modernity and Self-identity*. Cambridge: Polity Press.

Gill, N. (2010) 'New state-theoretic approaches to asylum and refugee geographies', *Progress in Human Geography*, 34, 626–645.

Giorgi, S. and Fasulo, A. (2013) 'Transformative homes', *Home Cultures*, 10(2), 111–133.

Gram-Hanssen, K. and Bech-Danielsen, C. (2007) 'Housing and immigrants – consumer aspects of the meaning of the home', in P. Repo and E. Pylvänäinen (eds), *Proceedings of the Nordic Consumer Policy Research Conference Nordic Council of Ministers; Ministry of Trade and Industry; National Consumer Research Centre.* https://vbn.aau.dk/ws/portalfiles/portal/12812770/housing11-_20Gram-Hanssen.pdf (accessed 8 December 2019).

Guarnizo, L.E. and Smith, M.P. (1998) *Transnationalism from Below*. Piscataway: Transaction Publishers.

Hage, G. (1997) 'At home in the entrails of the West: Multiculturalism, ethnic food and migrant home-building', in H. Grace, G. Hage, L. Johnson, J. Langsworth and M. Symonds (eds), *Home/World: Space, Community and Marginality in Sydney's West*. Annandale, NSW: Pluto Press, pp. 99–153.

Hall, K.D. (2002) *Lives in Translation: Sikh Youth as British Citizens*. Philadelphia: University of Pennsylvania Press.

Hamdan, H. and Fenster, T. (2012) 'Tactics and strategies of power of Palestinian women in Jaffa-Tel Aviv: A new understanding of spaces of belonging', *Women's Studies International Forum*, 35, 203–213.

Hirvi, L. (2015) 'Young Sikhs in Finland: Feeling at home nowhere, everywhere, in between and beyond', in K. Myrvold and K.A. Jacobsen (eds.), *Young Sikhs in a Global World: Negotiating Traditions, Identities and Authorities*. Farnham: Ashgate, pp. 35–50.

Hirvi, L. (2016) 'Exploring the domestic homes of Sikhs in Finland as a "cosmos of senses"', *Home Cultures*, 13(1), 23–37.

Hjorth, L. (2009) *Mobile Media in the Asia-Pacific: Gender and the Art of Being Mobile*. London: Routledge.

Horst, H. (2006) 'The blessings and burdens of communication: Cell phones in Jamaican transnational social fields', *Global Networks*, 6(2), 143–159.

Horst, H. (2009) 'Aesthetics of the self digital mediations', in D. Miller (ed.), *Anthropology and the Individual*. Oxford: Berg.

Hurdley, R. (2006) 'Dismantling mantelpieces: Narrating identities and materializing culture in the home', *Sociology*, 40(4), 717–733.

Kaczmarczyk, P. and Okólski, M. (2008) 'Demographic and labour market impacts of migration on Poland', *Oxford Review of Economic Policy*, 24(3), 599–624.

Kicinger, A. and Weinar, A. (2007) *State of the Art of the Migration Research in Poland*. Amsterdam: IMISCOE.

Kitchin, R. and Dodge, M. (2005) 'Code and the transduction of space', *Annals of the Association of American Geographers*, 95, 162–180.

Kuhn, A. (ed.) (2013) *Little Madnesses: Winnicott, Transitional Phenomena and Cultural Experience*. London: I.B.Tauris.

Lim, S.S. (2016) 'Asymmetries in Asian families' domestication of mobile communication', in S.S. Lim (ed.), *Mobile Communication and the Family: Asian Experiences in Technology Domestication*. London: Springer, pp. 1–12.

Ling, R.S. and Horst, H.A. (2011) 'Mobile communication in the global south', *New Media & Society*, 13, 363–374.

Lozanovska, M. (2009) 'Migrant housing in the city and the village: From Melbourne to Zavoj', *Open House International*, 34(3), 39–47.

Lundgren, M. (2016) 'Boundaries of displacement: Belonging and return among forcibly displaced young Georgians from Abkhazia'. www.academia.edu/28887029/BOUND ARIES_OF_DISPLACEMENT_Belonging_and_Return_among_Forcibly_Displaced_ Young_Georgians_from_Abkhazia.

Madianou, M. (2016) 'Ambient co-presence: Transnational family practices in polymedia environments', *Global Networks*, 16, 183–201.

Madianou, M. and Miller, D. (2011) 'Mobile phone parenting: Reconfiguring relationships between Filipina migrant mothers and their left-behind children', *New Media & Society*, 13, 457–470.

Madianou, M. and Miller, D. (2012) *Migration and New Media: Transnational Families and Polymedia*. Abingdon: Routledge.

Martin, B. and Mohanty, C.T. (1986) 'Feminist politics: What's home got to do with it?', in T. de Lauretis (ed.), *Feminist Studies/Critical Studies: Language, Discourse, Society*. London: Palgrave Macmillan.

Matsuda, M. (2009) 'Mobile media and the transformation of family', in G. Goggin and L. Hjorth (eds), *Mobile Technologies: From Telecommunications to Media*. New York: Routledge, pp. 62–72.

Meyrowitz, J. (1985) *No Sense of Place: The Impact of Electronic Media on Social Behavior*. New York: Oxford University Press.

Miller, D. (1998) *The Comfort of Things*. Cambridge: Polity Press.

Miller, D. (2001) *Home Possessions: Material Culture behind Closed Doors*. Oxford: Berg.

Miller, D. (2008) 'Migration, material culture and tragedy: Four moments in Caribbean migration 1', *Mobilities*, 3(3), 397–413.

Miller, D. (2010) 'Anthropology in blue jeans', *American Ethnologist*, 37(3), 415–428.

Miller, D. (2011) *Tales from Facebook*. Cambridge: Polity Press.

Miller, D. (2018) 'Individuals and the aesthetic of order', in D. Miller (ed), *Anthropology and the Individual: A Material Culture Perspective*. Oxford: Berg, pp. 3–24.

Miller, D. and Sinanan, J. (2012) 'Webcam and the theory of attainment'. Working Paper for the EASA Media Anthropology Network's 41st e-Seminar, 9–23 October 2012. file:///C:/Users/User/Documents/a%20a%20HOME%20BOOK%203/Miller_sinanan_ webcam.pdf (accessed 16 February 2019).

Miller, D. and Sinanan, J. (2014) *Webcam*. Cambridge: Polity Press.

Moores, S. (2012) *Media, Place and Mobility*. New York: Palgrave Macmillan.

Morley, D. (2000) *Home Territories: Media, Mobility and Identity*. London: Routledge.

Morley, D. (2006) 'What's 'home' got to do with it? Contradictory dynamics in the domestication of technology and the dislocation of domesticity', in M. Hartmann, T. Berker, Y. Punie et al. (eds), *Domestication of Media and Technology*. Maidenhead: Open University Press, pp. 21–39.

Morley, D. (2007) *Media, Modernity and Technology: The Geography of the New*. London: Routledge.

Morley, D. (2017) *Communications and Mobility: The Migrant, the Mobile Phone and the Container Box*. Oxford: Wiley Blackwell.

Nava, M. (2007) *Visceral Cosmopolitanism: Gender, Culture and the Normalisation of Difference*. Oxford: Berg.

Novy, J. and Colomb, C. (2012) 'Struggling for the right to the (creative) city in Berlin and Hamburg: New urban social movements, new "spaces of hope"?', *International Journal of Urban and Regional Research*. http://dx.doi.org/10.1111/j.1468-2427. 2012.01115.x (accessed 24 November 2012).

Olwig, K.F. and Hastrup, K. (1997) *Siting Culture: The Shifting Anthropological Project*. London: Routledge.

Parkin, D. (1999) 'Mementoes as transitional objects in human displacement', *Journal of Material Culture*, 4(3), 303–320.

Parreñas, R.S. (2001) 'Mothering from a distance: Emotions, gender, and intergenerational relations in Filipino transnational families', *Feminist Studies*, 27, 361–390.

Parreñas, R.S. (2005) 'Long distance intimacy: Class, gender and intergenerational relations between mothers and children in Filipino transnational families', *Global Networks*, 5, 317–336.

Parutis, V. (2011) '"Home" for now or "home" for good?', *Home Cultures*, 8(3), 265–296.

Pillai, R., Kyambi, S., Nowacka, K. and Sriskandarajah, D. (2007) 'The reception and integration of new migrant communities', Institute for Public Policy Research. www.ippr.org/ publicationsandreports/publication.asp?id=536 (accessed 14 May 2008).

Pink, S. (2004) *Home Truths: Gender, Domestic Objects and Everyday Life*. Oxford: Berg.

Pink, S. (2009) *Doing Sensory Ethnography*. London: Sage.

Pruijt, H. (2012) 'The logic of urban squatting', *International Journal of Urban and Regional Research*, 37(1), 19–45. http://dx.doi.org/ 10.1111/j.1468-2427.2012.01116.x (accessed 24 November 2012).

Pulvirenti, M. (2000) 'The morality of immigrant home ownership: Gender, work, and Italian Australian sistemazione', *Aust Geogr*, 31(2), 237–249.

Ralph, D. and Staeheli, L. (2011) 'Home and migration: Mobilities, belongings and identities', *Geography Compass*, 5(7), 517–530.

Rappaport, N. and Dawson, A. (eds) (1998) *Migrants of Identity: Perceptions of Home in a World of Movement*. Oxford: Berg.

Salih, R. (2002) 'Reformulating tradition and modernity: Moroccan migrant women and the trasnantional division of ritual space', *Global Networks*, 2(3), 219–232.

Salih, R. (2003) *Gender in Transnationalism: Home, Longing and Belonging among Moroccan Migrant Women*. London and New York: Routledge.

San Pascual, M.R. (2016) 'Paradoxes in the mobile parenting experiences of Filipino mothers in diaspora', in S.S. Lim (ed.), *Mobile Communication and the Family: Asian Experiences in Technology Domestication*. London: Springer, pp. 147–164.

Savaş, O. (2010) 'The collective Turkish home in Vienna: Aesthetic narratives of migration and belonging', *Home Cultures*, 7(3), 313–340.

Sheffer, G. (1996) 'Israeli-diaspora relations in comparative perspective', in M.J. Barnett (ed.), *Israel in Comparative Perspective*. New York: SUNY Press, pp. 53–84.

Sheller, M. and Urry, J. (2006) 'The new mobilities paradigm', *Environment and Planning A*, 38, 207–226.

Sinatti, G. (2009) 'Home is where the heart abides: Migration, return and housing in Dakar, Senegal', *Open House International*, 34(3), 49–56.

Smith, A. (2014) 'Interpreting home in the transnational discourse', *Home Cultures*, 11(1), 103–122. doi:10.2752/175174214X13807024690783.

Smith, M.P. (2001) *Transnational Urbanism: Locating Globalization*. Oxford: Blackwell.

Spencer, S., Ruhs, M., Anderson, B. and Rogaly, B. (2007) 'Migrants' lives beyond workplace: The experiences of central and eastern Europeans in the UK'. COMPAS. www.jrf.org.uk/bookshop/ eBooks/2045-migrants-experiences-UK.pdf (accessed 18 September 2008).

Stefansson, A. (2006) 'Homes in the making: Property reinstitution, refugee return and senses of belonging in a post-war Bosnian town', *International Migration*, 44(3), 115–139.

Taylor, A. (2000) 'The sun always shines in Perth: A post-colonial geography of identity, memory and place', *Australian Geographical Studies*, 38(1), 27–35.

Thompson, S. (1994) 'Suburbs of opportunity: The power of home for migrant women', in K. Gibsonand S. Watson (eds), *Metropolis Now: Planning and the Urban in Contemporary Australia*. Leichhardt, NSW: Pluto Press, pp. 33–45.

Thompson, S. (2005) 'Digestible difference: Food, ethnicity and spatial claims in the city', in E. Guildand J. van Selm (eds), *International Migration and Security: Opportunities and Challenges*. London: Routledge, pp. 217–237.

Tolia-Kelly, D. (2004a) 'Landscape, race and memory: Biographical mapping of the routes of British Asian landscape values', *Landscape Research*, 29(3), 277–292.

Tolia-Kelly, D. (2004b) 'Locating processes of identification: Studying the precipitates of re-memory through artefacts in the British Asian home', *Transactions of the Institute of British Geographers* (New Series), 29, 314–329.

Tolia-Kelly, D. (2004c) 'Materializing post-colonial geographies: Examining the textural landscapes of migration in the South Asian homes', *Geoforum*, 35, 675–688.

Tolia-Kelly, D. (2006) 'Mobility/stability: British Asian cultures of 'landscape and English-ness', *Environment and Planning A*, 38(2), 341–358.

Turan, Z. (2010) 'Material objects as facilitating environments: The Palestinian diaspora', *Home Cultures*, 7(1), 43–56.

Urry, J. (2000) *Sociology beyond Societies: Mobilities for the Twenty-First Century*. London: Routledge.

Urry, J. (2007) *Mobilities*. Cambridge: Polity.

Vertovec, S. (2001) 'Transnationalism and identity', *Journal of Ethnic and Migration Studies*, 27 (4), 573–582.

Waldinger, R. and Lichter, M.I. (2003) *How the Other Half Works: Immigration and Social Organization*. Berkeley: University of California Press.

Walters, W. (2004) 'Secure borders, safe haven, domopolitics', *Citizenship Studies*, 8(3), 237–260.

Ward, S. (2003) 'On shifting ground: Changing formulations of place in anthropology', *The Australian Journal of Anthropology*, 14(1), 80–96.

Westwood, S. (1995) 'Gendering diaspora: Space, politics, and South Asian masculinities in Britain', in P. van der Veer (ed.), *Nation and Migration: The Politics of Space in the South Asian Diaspora*. Philadelphia: University of Philadelphia Press, pp. 197–221.

Winnicott, W.D. (1953) 'Transitional objects and transitional phenomena: A study of the first not-me possession', *International Journal of Psycho-Analysis*, 34, Part 2, 89–97.

Zetter, R. (1999) 'Reconcetualizing the myth of return: Continuity and transition among the Greek-Cypriot refugees of 1974', *Journal of Refugee Studies*, 12(1), 1–22.

9

HOMES OF THE FUTURE

Introduction

The enthusiasm for 'modern' living in the early and mid-twentieth century led to novel ways of imagining the home through initiatives such as 'homes of tomorrow' and 'smart homes'. This trend extended the meaning of home from a place of sanctuary to a symbol of scientific progress that expressed a technologically efficient space for multiple leisure and work-related tasks. Early future homes were named 'homes of tomorrow' or 'homes of the future'. By the late twentieth and early twenty-first century, they were increasingly referred to as 'smart homes'. At a technical level, today's smart home refers to a residence designed to integrate advanced automation systems with sensors, multimedia devices, communication protocols, and computational systems to promote comfort, convenience, security and entertainment. While most research on 'smart homes' has focused on their architectural designs or technical features, these dwellings are much more than that. Inspired by science fiction and digital expectations, at a cultural level these homes of the future are inscribed with utopian visions of a technology-driven existence (see Aldrich 2003; Chambers 2016; 2020; Morley 2007; Spigel 2005, 2010). They also harbour dystopian anxieties about the meaning of the 'modern home' in terms of privacy, security and control.

This chapter explores the motives and discourses underlying 'homes of the future'. By tracing their history and contemporary formulations, it considers their cultural antecedents and current implications. The first section considers visions of smart home futures in the early, mid and late twentieth century that symbolised progress and national prowess. The second section deals with contemporary transformations in smart home technologies including the impact of the Internet of Things on domestic life. The chapter provides a case study of corporate films and videos of the 'future home' from the 1950s to the present to assess dominant corporate motives and narratives that sustain 'future home' prophecies (see also Chambers 2019). In addition to exhibitions, trade shows and media accounts, these corporate-made speculative films and videos of the 'future home' have played a major part in anticipating and popularising what we can call 'home futurism'. Concerns associated with smart home security, the datafication of home and associated breaches of privacy are then addressed in the third section. The gender implications of smart homes are examined by foregrounding the disappointing track record of smart homes in lightening housework loads. The chapter draws attention to gendered power relations reproduced by a masculine discourse of smart expertise configured around the digital maintenance needed to sustain a smart home.

Homes of tomorrow

'Homes of tomorrow' exhibited at world fairs resonated with certain aspects of these innovations as expressions of early twentieth-century modernity. Many futurist houses of this period were designed as experiments to showcase modern home conveniences and promote the companies and architects who staged innovated materials such as concrete, glass, electricity and pre-fabrication. For example, at the Chicago World's Fair of 1933 in the US, the 'Homes of Tomorrow Exhibition' was featured with the theme of 'A Century of Progress'. This World's Fair was characterised by advances in science, technology and transportation to boost national optimism during the Great Depression's bleakest years. The Fair's rationale was that progress rests on technological innovation and consumerism by harnessing science and technology to everyday life towards an optimistic future (Ganz 2012). The uncompromising motto of the Fair, 'Science Finds, Industry Applies, Man Conforms' reflected the business-military-engineering approach of its organisers who were mostly former military men.

A dozen model homes in art deco and other modern designs were built on site at the Chicago World Fair, with the latest technology and materials together with futuristic furnishings and accessories. These showcased model homes included the House of Tomorrow, with glass walls and even its own aeroplane hangar, designed by architect George Fred Keck. This was accompanied by the Weibolt-Rostone House designed by Walter Schuler, framed in steel and artificial stone cladding made by Rostone Inc. Another model home was the Florida Tropical House commissioned by the state of Florida to attract tourists to Florida, designed in the Modernist style by Robert Law Weed. Built by the Deigaard & Preston construction firm, the Florida Tropical House was designed in such a way that the inside and outside environments blended into one another (A Century of Progress International Exposition 1933–1934). When the Chicago World's Fair ended, these exhibited 'homes of tomorrow' were all bought by real-estate developer Robert Bartlett who then loaded them on barges on Lake Michigan and floated them across the water to Beverley Shores to entice buyers to his new, exclusive community resort.[1]

'Homes of tomorrow' were sponsored by large electrical, home appliance and communications corporations such as General Electric, Kelvinator and institutes such as MIT (Horrigan 1986). They showcased the engineering and architectural possibilities as part of a drive towards the technologisation of domestic space. Futuristic homes presented Disney-like architectural domestic utopias yet many never moved further than the planning or exhibition stage (Spigel 2001a). For example, Monsanto's 'House of The Future', a prototype house built by Monsanto Company's plastics division in 1957 unveiled its novel plastics technology for the home at Disneyland in California in 1957 as part of Disney's *Tomorrowland*. Over 435,000 visitors were drawn to the Monsanto House in the first six weeks of opening and attracted over 20 million sightseers before it was dismantled in 1967 (Keegan 2017). This prototype house presented novel electrical devices such as a microwave oven and dishwasher, appliances barely heard of by the wider public at that time.

Early corporate films of 'homes of the future'

These early smart homes survive today not so much in material form but as photos and design plans. But among the records are a small number of speculative films, sponsored by the companies that project yesterday's visions of the future within imaginings of 'future homes'.[2] A documentary-style film of Monsanto's 'House of The Future' from 1957 is part of a genre of past and present corporate speculative films and videos that promote technologised home futures. Monsanto's 'House of The Future' imagined a house situated several years in the future, in the year 1986.[3] A new film produced in 2015 as part of Disneyland's Diamond celebration called *Disneyland: 60 Years of Imagineering* [sic] *Monsanto's House of the Future* records sections of the original 1957 film.[4] It reveals the dwelling's interior shot by a camera that follows a white nuclear family around the home. Describing the growing use of plastics in buildings, from floors to insulation, the film's narrator guides us through spacious, open-plan rooms. The living room contains a TV with a giant screen mounted in white plastic surrounded by inlaid seating. Smaller portable versions of TV consoles in space-age styling were displayed all over the home in bedrooms and kitchens – rooms not yet populated by this media technology. As a Disneyland exhibit, this plastic-laden Monsanto House formed a 'stylish promiscuity' (Featherstone 2007). 'House of the Future' foretold a future that 'never was': a technoscientific future home, never inhabited (Tutton 2017). Spawned by a generation of new electrical and communication technologies and framed in a Disneyland cultural backdrop, the Monsanto House formed what we might call a 'simulational culture' (Baudrillard 1983, 1994; and see Chapter 1).

Whilst such visions of the future staged at the New York World's Fair were largely unattainable, these fantasies gained momentum from the late 1960s (Tutton 2017). The space-age imagery that inspired styling of the period chimed with ideas of the New Frontier inspired by President Kennedy's drive to exploit space travel as a definitive symbol of national progress. Space-age motifs coincided with the articulation of a technology-driven 'information age' in which public imaginaries about public and private space were transforming ideas of home. The popular media fascination with ideas of travel from home coincided with the allure of space exploration to underpin an expression of a *modernised* family life. For example, the metaphor of home as 'theatre' competed with imaginings of home as a machine launched into orbit (Baudrillard 1983; Spigel 2001b).

Importantly, corporate promotional films of homes of the future were sponsored by companies such as Ford and General Electric (GE). For instance, a film made in 1967 titled *The Home of the Future: Year 1999 A.D.* [5] was found in 2017 among materials in a collection of 'ephemeral films' in the Prelinger Archives acquired by the US Library of Congress's Motion Picture, Broadcasting and Recorded Sound Division.[6] This 24-minute fictionalised film was funded by appliance and radio manufacturer, Philco-Ford Corporation to celebrate their 75th anniversary (Chambers 2019). It offers a rather unnerving utopian vision of a future home set more than three decades into the future in 1999 – a year which came and went. It prophesies developments in computer science through computer applications in the home of the future. The film's narrative revolves around a young white nuclear family who live in a hermetically sealed environment controlled by a central computer. The home's interior conveys a *Star Trek* aesthetic via spacious and minimalist rooms housing in-built furniture in mid-century Modernist styles with large screen windows, pale walls and multiple appliances.

Year 1999 A.D. is remarkably familiar in accurately in foretelling a technology-oriented home of the future yet is also somewhat unsettling. This film was sponsored by a subsidiary of Ford Motor Company, the Philco-Ford Corporation. It forecasts the Internet with online shopping and weather checks, computer-aided education and wall-sized media screens. But contrasting with today's personal computers and mobile handheld devices, it predicts an ITC-mediated home run by a *central* home computer linked to individual computer screens devoted to each set of tasks. Computerised power controls environmental conditions, an automatic cooking system, office, gym and 'education room'. This visualisation of home is framed by a popularised space-age imaginary. The film's narrator applauds its engineering innovations, describing the central home computer as 'one of the many twenty-first-century devices that are part of the everyday life of the family'. A computer machine is shown with rows of flashing lights followed by a dashboard with switches, buttons and an electronic display of passing hours, minutes and seconds. Yet this machine is domesticated, presented as an entirely family-friendly system.

In some ways, this scenario resonates with today's digitally controlled smart home with its multiple screens, instant access to banking and entertainment online, and a virtual voice-activated assistant that also monitors the human body. We meet father, Michael, an astrophysicist working on a project on the colonisation of the planet Mars within a space-age trope that propels the film's futuristic theme. Son Jamie watches a wall-sized screen in the home's 'education centre'. The space-age theme continues as Jamie is seen learning about the history of astronomy and space travel. And the narrator emphasises this future home's link to space technology: 'Yes life will be richer … as space-age dreams come true'. Meanwhile, mother Karen is introduced as a 'wife, mother, and part time home-maker who dabbles in pottery-making'. Although introduced in a laboratory-style kitchen, she conveys a reassuring traditional femininity by serving 'split-second lunches' of defrosted food selected from a computer menu, retrieved via conveyer belt, and warmed in a microwave oven. Together with the disposable dishes, the narrator explains that this is 'all part of the instant society of tomorrow, a society rich in leisure and taken for granted comforts'. We later see Karen online shopping using a keyboard, referred to as 'fingertip shopping'. Husband Michael is then observed shaking his head in disbelief at his wife's shopping bill while in his home office paying her bill online. His home office boasts an 'electronic correspondence machine' described as a 'home post office' for instant communication 'anywhere in the world'.

These early speculative films promote an 'instant', 'throw-away' society centred on values that privileged immediacy, speed and disposability. Yet despite celebrating ideas about the human–technology interface, these visions of the future home are firmly organised around traditional consumer-oriented white middle-class family roles comprising full-time housewife and professional, salaried husband. As Morley reminds us, today's high-tech discourse is often still framed by a nostalgic vision of 'family values' (Morley 2007). Conventional gender roles function to dispel audiences' anxieties about the potentially disruptive nature of this future home by *domesticating* technoscientific futures. Although the traditional family trope works to domesticate and familiarise these early homes of the future, a masculinised and technology-driven discourse allows the home to become an office. The depiction of a home-working husband foretells the home as a central place of work for men. Although this approach to home as a work environment resonates with the contemporary porous nature of home and paid work, we now know it was much more likely to be women who took up home working, as mentioned in Chapter 3 in relation to the rise of teleworking.

At Home 2001 is a similar speculative film made in 1967 also sponsored by Philco-Ford.[7] Here, a famous American TV anchor-man for CBS *Evening News* of the 1960s predicts the family home of 2001 (Chambers 2019). The space-age metaphor persists. Cronkite informs the audience that 'This home is as self-sufficient as a space capsule', by extracting electricity from its own fuel cells. Working from home is further promoted in this mock-up 'home of the future' by the separation of rooms into work and leisure zones. Built-in and inflatable plastic furniture are accompanied by walls of luminescent glass panels and a wall-sized 3D colour TV screen. A bulky computer console occupies one end of the living room to 'inform, instruct and entertain the family of the future'. As mentioned in Chapter 3, Philco-Ford was styling and manufacturing not only radios, phonographs, television sets and cars but also missiles. This span of products underscores an interweaving of domesticity, science fiction and space-age technology as fundamental cultural forces that shaped the nature of 'home' in the US (see for example, Barad 2003; Opitz et al. 2016). The space-age theme running through

1999 AD and *At Home 2001* validates the entrance of computers into homes, reflecting the aerospace and defence interests of Ford Motor Co., Ford Aerospace (1956–1990). Bought by Ford in 1961, the Philco Corporation was merged with Ford into Philco Aeronutronic in 1963.[8] In the 1960s, the corporation was NASA's main provider of communications equipment and designed the consoles in Houston's *Manned Spacecraft Center*. As such, these Hollywood-styled speculative films of imagined future homes reflected these space-age ambitions (see Kirby 2010: 46).

Smart homes

In the 1980s and 1990s, smart home developments reflected computer advancements and imaginaries. Presented as information networks, newly designed homes were now conveyed as technologically resourceful spaces for work and leisure: as both a haven from work and a domestic work haven. During this period, specialists in building, electronics, architecture, energy conservation and telecommunications came together to develop home automation systems. Smart homes were designed and built in America, Japan and Europe. For instance, The National Association of Home Builders (NAHB) introduced in the United States in 1984 comprised a home special interest group to integrate smart home technology in home-building methods. Examples include the Honeywell House designed with automation and control systems, built by the multinational company Honeywell; a mobile demonstration house built from 1986 by the US NAHB; and experimental Xanadu House of the early 1980s designed by a US team with Roy Mason (Berg 1994). The Honeywell House which included light and heat regulation, alarm and security control, endorsed the company's thermostats, air cleaners, burglar alarms and fire alarms which were integrated through programmable communication networks within the building. However, the house contained no technologies designed to ease housework.

Despite the promises made about better communication networks, energy-saving systems and entertainment, housework-saving systems were almost entirely overlooked in the promotional literature on these late twentieth-century smart homes (Chambers 2016). Neither Honeywell, NAHB or Xanadu mentioned the alleviation of housework tasks, even though the title page of Xanadu's promotional literature displayed a picture of a robot serving breakfast and claimed to 'reduce drudgery'. When she interviewed the designers of these smart homes, Anne-Jorunn Berg (1994) found them pre-occupied by the technology rather than the house-holders' needs. Ignoring women, designers addressed men who were the social group most likely to be captivated by smart technologies – a problem that has endured to this day, as discussed below. These visionary smart homes drew on extravagant designs and materials yet used rudimentary on–off controller switching systems such as remote control. Moreover, manufacturers failed to convince women of the advantages of smart homes since they neglected the needs of these householders who continue to undertake the bulk of housework (Meyer and

Schulze 1996; Aldrich 2003). Despite their practical ineffectiveness, automated smart homes continued to be popularised in the media as the height of sophistication through their repeated association with the rich and famous.

Visions of digitally automated homes

The acceleration in digitally connected technologies in the twenty-first century marks the next stage in the smart home trajectory, also known as the 'connected home'. Today's smart home boasts automation systems that allow appliances, lighting, heating, air conditioning, TVs, computers, entertainment audio and video systems, security and camera systems to communicate with one another. In 2003, The UK Department of Trade and Industry defined the smart home as 'A dwelling incorporating a communications network that connects the key electrical appliances and services, and allows them to be remotely controlled, monitored or accessed' (Housing, Learning and Improvement Network 2003).[9] By now, giant tech companies were driving a government-backed smart home agenda. But take-up has been patchy. For gadget fanatics, the smart home summons visions of Internet-connected and sensing devices that predict domestic needs and shoulder the burden of monotonous daily tasks for ease and comfort. Smart meters and thermostats can monitor and reduce energy use while the refrigerator can re-order food that needs replacing, and the front door of the house can be opened remotely by smartphone for deliveries. Yet after several decades, the smart home project remains limited in scope and levels of success despite claims and popular symbolisms of 'future living' (Bitterman and Shach-Pinsly 2015).

Nonetheless, speculative corporate videos situated in a fantasised near-future are now commonplace as part of the promotion of the digitally controlled smart home. For instance, *A Day Made of Glass* (2011) is a visualisation of a networked home set in the year 2020.[10] Created for American multinational technology company Corning Inc., *A Day Made of Glass* was produced as a promotional video for Corning's Investor Day in New York City in February 2011. The company produces glass for organic light-emitting diode (OLED) and liquid crystal display (LCD). The daily home routines of a white nuclear family are followed to showcase potential uses of OLEDs as digital displays in domestic media and communication devices (Chambers 2019). The family occupying the 2020 digital dream home interact with glass-based technologies such as wall-mounted television, video screens, wall displays, desktops, countertop screens, handheld electronics, and mirror screens. In less than a month, the video was rated number one on 'Unruly Media's "Viral Videos Chart"'. Even though the video has no dialogue and lasts only five and a half minutes, it drew almost 8 million views on YouTube (Baar 2011).

A Day Made of Glass contains intriguing echoes of *Year 1999 A.D.* made in the analogue age more than four decades earlier. Today's technology, involving IoTs and speciality glass, is showcased in the video which begins with the caption: '7:00am in the near Future', staged in a bedroom with floor-to-ceiling windows. Here, a wide screen wall-mounted TV made of thin LCD television glass comes into view as a touch-activated wake alarm operated by the father to display the morning TV news programme. Then, in the bathroom, a mirror of architectural display glass converts into a computer screen by a touch to enable the mother to update her electronic diary while brushing her teeth. Multitasking, she administers her emails via a flat keyboard projected on the architectural display glass. In the kitchen, father watches a morning news programme screened on to the glass countertop while he makes breakfast. Children play with digitally animated family photo-videos projected on to a fridge door by switching them round, enlarging them and drawing on the photographed faces. The father then holds a Skype chat with grandmother via 'handheld display glass'.

We then see mother driving a car, first to work and then to buy clothes in shops filled with gadgets and glass screens to augment the shopping experience. Here, again, femininity is linked to consumerism. In the evening, the family congregate in the living room in front of a vast 3D TV display glass screen that takes up the whole wall. The image evokes the 1950s TV family circle (Spigel 1992) and echoes the ambiance of the family TV screen in the 1967 film *At Home 2001*. However, what is different is the presence of a hologram image of planets that springs forward to hover over the coffee table in front of the family. The space-age trope extends to bedtime when the father is observed lying in bed reading H.G. Wells' *Time Machine* on portable display glass. This technologised future home creates a narrative of family control and empowerment. The video was brought up to date in 2016 and called *Future Homes Technology* [11] but follows the same narrative and principles.

Future-makers

This kind of futuristic marketing coincides with the showcasing of present and future smart homes and smart gadgetry at international trade fairs such as the annual Consumer Electronics Show (CES) in Las Vegas. With just under 4,000 companies exhibiting their products, these trade fairs involve manufacturers, developers and suppliers of consumer technology hardware, content, technology delivery systems. Press conferences are held at the show by companies such as Samsung, LG, Sony, Fitbit and Netflix to announce their products and services for the following year. Forming part of giant tech companies' marketing strategies, superstar status CEOs such as Apples' Tim Cook and Google's Sundar Pichai perform as cultural pioneers by launching dazzling new products at these theatrical events to the applause of admiring audiences. These performers are today's future-makers: the cultural agents of the future smart home (Chambers 2019).

Accompanied by a host of promotional activities including corporate videos, these conference spectacles are also buoyed by consumer reviews in online magazines and blog reports on items ranging from virtual reality (VR) to smart phones, tablets, cameras, smart TVs and the range of gadgetry that now supports today's digitalised home. Multi-author blogs and online news sites on design and technology include Apples' *Macworld, All Home Robotics, TechAdvisor, Techradar* (sponsored by international media group, Futureplc), *Gizmodo, Engadget, Slashgear. com* and *LiveSmart*, to name a few. Adopting a 'matey' tone, the humour and informality of the reviews are moulded to fit their largely male readership. These websites create a buzz around the smart home industry and its innovations. Performing as future-makers, journalists and commentators offer informative, entertaining, zany and geeky reviews. Their performances are complemented by multiple related blogs and online news sites such as *Wall Street Daily* that provides coverage of market-related issues.[12]

Through these representations and practices, the future home is proclaimed and authorised within a complex range of social, legal, technological, commercial and everyday practices (Adam 2011; Berkhout 2006). This group of commercially led cultural intermediaries normalise and stabilise the meanings of the smart home as a vital stage on which smart home domestication is performed. These future-makers impart visions and shared values about smart home technologies and help construct commercial priorities planned within corporate schemes. Giant tech companies have extensive powers to project a distinctive future home lifestyle dependent on smart technologies. Male experts work on their behalf to produce a social consensus within this smart home culture, evoking a masculinised home futurism.

Despite the hype, smart homes remain problematic even in affluent parts of the world. Smart homes promise to deliver domestic comfort, convenience, security and leisure while at the same time lowering energy use through improved home energy management. Yet fundamental difficulties surrounding smart home expectations combine with unclear definitions and users' roles in smart systems (Darby 2018). A further barrier to smart home adoption is the fear of privacy breaches. A gap therefore remains between the state of the art of technology-based solutions and what is actually adopted in the average home. As well as side-stepping the needs of women, designers of smart technologies for home automation often fail to approach home as a dynamic place involving continuous change in householders' needs and lifestyles (Pillan and Colombo 2017).

In a study of the domestication of smart home technologies in ten households, Tom Hargreaves, Charlie Wilson and Richard Hauxwell-Baldwin (2018) found four key themes: first, smart home technologies can be technically and socially disruptive; second, smart homes demand modes of adaptation and familiarisation from householders that may limit their use; third, learning how to use smart home technologies is a challenging and time-consuming undertaking for which as yet, there is little back-up support available. Finally, there is scant evidence that smart home technologies will generate substantial energy savings. In fact, the authors argue that there is a risk that smart home technology may lead to forms of energy intensification. And while research on smart homes and smart home users is gradually expanding, there is no clear understanding of who users are and how they actually use smart home technologies. Driven predominantly by male expert technology developers, the major concerns of privacy, control and levels of user expertise have so far been interpreted narrowly.

Digital homes as threatened spaces

Defensible space

Today's digital smart home imagery relies heavily on householders' security concerns, forming contrived home precarities. Spatial security is a dominant theme in smart home technology discourse propelled by approaching home as a place of risk and vulnerability – from locks to electronic alarms and preventative practices to protect particular spaces (Caluya 2007). Alarm systems are upgraded to smart system intruder alarms, smart phone warning devices, access control and closed-circuit television. This sense of spatialised insecurity cultivates notions of 'defensible space' as latent territoriality (Newman 1973). Drawing on Newman's notion of defensible space, Gilbert Caluya argues that a sequence of defensive performances and preventative strategies are produced and distributed around the home to regulate security risks and create a form of amplifying surveillance (Caluya 2007). Homes have always been constituted by their relations with the public sphere, whether breached by media, work or intruders. But the question here is: why is the futuristic smart home mobilised as a sealed personal space invoked by a fear of security breaches?

For the last two decades, architectural and technological defensiveness of both individual homes and neighbourhoods have escalated. The smart home-generated sense of defensible space conceives of homes as private possessions separated from their community environments (Caluya 2007). This smart home imaginary is an outcome of key structural conditions involving neoliberal state policies (Blandy 2018). Referring to home safety publications aimed at the 'average householder' by organisations such as the UK Design Council and the Department of Housing and Construction in Australia, Caluya (2007: 21) argues that they incite their readers to take action within an urban war that turns the homeowner into a citizen-soldier. Neoliberal policies and a lack of government strategies to prevent trends such as the further growth of gated communities enable developers, security and insurance industries to profit from the contrived home precarities that invoke security anxieties as part of a wider discourse of domestic precarity. A fear of crime fuelled by the news media combines with a loss of place-based community (Blandy 2018).

Such smart home manifestations of security involve contrived precarities that invoke an urban jungle by drawing on 'the principles of warfare' (Caluya 2007). They point to a dramatic shift in discourses of 'home' from a sublime space of belonging and attachment to a precarious, threatening and risky space: a space under siege from multiple sources of danger and therefore in need of fortification. Whether these dangers range from safety and security associated with intruders, crime and vandalism or natural disasters such as floods, fires and climate change, our understanding of home is now shaped by emotional imageries fed by an 'exclusionary and contested distinction between the "domestic" and the "foreign"' (Blunt and Dowling 2006: 168).

The Internet of Things and home surveillance

Related to the discourse of home insecurity is the problem of privacy and surveillance, prompted by the growing number of devices connected to the Internet. Since 2014, the Internet of Things opened up a new era of converged technologies including the Internet, embedded systems and micro-electromechanical systems. This digital innovation entails the extension of network connectivity to everyday objects by designing them to send and receive data. Whilst new forms of personal and household control over the home's appliances are enabled, new concerns are raised about the invasion of our privacy by security and tech companies that can monitor household activities and collect data for marketing purposes. A whole range of domestic objects can now be converted into smart entities by equipping them with sensors, actors and connectivity technologies including embedded and wearable computing. Recognised as the next stage of the information revolution, governments and commercial organisations are investing significant funds in this technology, leading to what we might call the 'datafication of home'. For example, the UK government allotted millions of pounds to support research on the Internet of Things in 2017 to augment the interconnectivity of systems for medical devices, urban transport and domestic devices.[13]

The Internet of Things (IoT) gained traction with the unveiling of virtual voice-activated assistants as Amazon Alexa and Google Home which were made available on the market from 2014 and 2016, respectively. With far field microphones that support voice recognition, these devices provide hand-free operation for purposes ranging from playing music, information retrieval and environmental control. Voice-activated assistants are now embedded in home life, demonstrated by the 2019 inclusion of Amazon's Alexa in the average 'shopping basket' that regularly measures inflation in the UK (Office for National Statistics 2019).[14] Google Home is operated by an artificial intelligence (AI) assistant called Google Assistant that has uninterrupted access to Google and other Google related services such as Gmail, Google Calendar, YouTube and Google Keep. These devices are materially unobtrusive: Google Home is the size of a large mug, is easy to set up and able to automatically detect the wireless Internet signal and connection to the user's smartphone. If used effectively, IoT are expected to have widespread and beneficial effects according to the Pew Research Internet Project (Anderson and Rainie 2014). For retrieval of information, Google Home can search the meaning of words; perform as a calculator, check facts, including cooking recipes, nutritional information, the news, traffic information and weather; and act as a diary, an appointment reminder, a translator and can set schedule reminders for the user.

For the elderly and the disabled, Amazon's Alexa and Google Home have the potential to enhance well-being. Voice-activated smart speakers used as environmental control units (ECU) can enhance a person's independence and general well-being (Noda 2018). They can support users with disabilities as simple Environmental Control Units (ECU), wirelessly connected to appliances (Noda 2018). Voice-activated devices can remind householders of medication regimes and appointments and even make phone calls, for example to emergency services or for ordering taxis. In terms of navigating multimedia, Google Home can switch on and off the TV set through a voice command via a HDMI wireless device, and can operate streaming services, post on Facebook and comment on Twitter. The device can also control lighting around the home by connecting with Philips Hugh light bulbs; lock and unlock doors via Samsung's SmartThing kit; regulate air-conditioning settings; operate window blinds and robotic vacuum cleaners; water plants and activate or deactivate alarm systems. The domestication of these virtual voice-activated assistants therefore summons dramatic changes in home life. With the capacity to adapt to individual needs in health care as well as entertainment, the field of home automation is predicted to grow as it becomes progressively user-friendly. However, for the elderly and disabled, finding the money to pay and install these devices, and learning how to use and maintain them, is a serious dilemma yet a matter of vital concern in a society with a shrinking welfare state and unstable social care services.

Notwithstanding their potential health care benefits, voice-activated assistants and other IoT devices raise critical questions about privacy. This Internet-embed-ded domestic environment enables the continuous collection of vast amounts of personal data about our eating, leisure, sleeping and working habits. This generates anxieties about breaches of privacy and cyberattacks on hardware, software and data. Designed to be 'always on' in the background but not necessarily recording, these devices are not infallible. Some smart systems are susceptible to personal data hacking for criminal purposes or the switching off of security or power. In addi-tion, there have been many cases of security vulnerability where individuals have found that their conversations have been recorded and that the recording has been sent to somebody in their phone book. Ironically, then, IoT enabled items are designed to generate a sense of security and control over the home yet these same devices generate palpable home precarities by causing breaches of privacy. Control over personal and household data is removed from the user and placed in the hands of the companies supplying these devices. Smart home companies may misuse data for marketing goals and/or pass on details to insurance companies to establish profiles on the levels of lifestyle risks of household residents. However, many households that adopt smart equipment are unaware of the extent of personal data accessed by smart home companies, and how companies use the data.

These home precarities are demonstrated by certain well-publicised incidents concerning smart home devices which have confirmed the need for caution. In 2017, a security researcher in the UK, Mark Barnes, revealed how to hack an Amazon Echo smart speaker to eavesdrop on activities in a person's home by installing malware with his proof-of-concept code to stream audio from the gadget to his personal server, undetected. In the same year, the tech giant Apple was required to resolve a security breach in its HomeKit smart home system. Hackers were given access to users' smart locks or other devices via a bug in iOS 11.2 that granted unlicensed remote control of a range of HomeKit-assisted devices includ-ing not only smart lights and plugs but also locks and garage door openers. And the humble TV set has come under criticism. One of the largest smart television developers, Vizio was imposed a fine of US$2.2 million in 2017 when the US Federal Communications Commission found it was tracking householders via its smart TVs. Soon after this incident, the whistleblowing platform 'Wikileaks' released several documents claiming that the CIA had developed tools to transform smart TVs into bugging devices (Cousins 2018: 14).

While users are aware of the need for password secrecy for personal computers, the scale of the attack surface in smart homes extends to include a range of ordinary items including thermostats, vacuum cleaners and even light bulbs connected to the Internet. Another example concerns home smart meters that operate on distinct wireless networks connected to outside networks. A security flaw in the system was spotted during the 2016 unveiling of smart meters in the UK. This involved the UK intelligence agency GCHQ, who stepped in to enforce improved encryption. With many manufacturers failing to prioritise data security, certain providers have been forced to improve systems to tighten protection. For instance, Nest has inserted elective verification on apps to stop unauthorised agents from accessing users' accounts while a Code of Practice for smart building installations is being developed by the Electrical Contractors' Association (ECA) to protect consumers and contractors' businesses.

It is ironic that the smart home's technology has generated palpable home precarities of this nature, undermining the notion of 'home' as a sanctuary from the outside world. The privacy implications stretch from targeted marketing guided by data from Internet connections, microphones and cameras to statistics on household habits gathered by insurance firms to calculate health risks and increase insurance cover. These privacy implications were revealed when iRobot, the manufacturer of the automated vacuum cleaner Roomba, admitted to Reuters news agency in July 2017 that the mapping technology used by the device to learn floor plans of customers' houses could be shared with companies such as Apple, Amazon and Google. Unsurprisingly, then, the sale of smart home systems and devices are held back by privacy and security unease. The results of studies on levels of consumer acceptance of IoT reveal that trust and security risk play a significant role in smart home acceptance (Mobark et al. 2018). By the end of 2017, the world market for smart home devices was optimistically expected to amount to US$9.4 billion and increase to US$9.4 billion in 2021 (IHS Markit, cited in Cousins 2018: 13). Yet householders are distrustful of private companies' capacities to hack or misuse personal data on the IoT network. Nearly 40% of consumers in a 2017 report by Deloitte expressed their concern about the tracking potential of smart devices in the home. Most potential consumers concurred that the companies making these devices were failing to draw attention to the security risks. And less than 20% of respondents claimed to be knowledgeable about these risks involved (Cousins 2018).

Digital housekeeping

The automated vacuum cleaner Roomba – with the s9 and s9+ series introduced by iRobot in 2019 – draws attention to issues of gender and power in the context of what we might call 'digital housework'. This is reminiscent of the predictions, at 1930s Ideal Home Exhibitions, of the 'Nursery of 1960' that staged helmeted mothers using robotic devices to replace nurses and ensure a hygienic distance between mothers and the nurturing of their children in crèche and nursery settings (Ryan 1997). In the 1960s, a time when robotic nurseries had clearly not been warmed to, an American animated science fiction sitcom called the Jetsons (1962–1963) was watched by millions on TV. Described as a space-age counterpart to the Flintstones, the Jetsons depicted an idyllic technology-driven future. This utopian future featured flying cars and a family home crammed with high-tech devices including video-chat flat screens, push-button food and a robot housekeeper dressed in an apron called Rosie.

While the robot housekeeper remains elusive, the Jetsons predicted a startling host of automated devices now regarded as commonplace. But rather than serving to reduce housework tasks, new technologies often generate considerable work involving the setting up and maintaining of home networks (Tolmie et al. 2007: 332). Today's smart home trend raises questions about whether smart technology relieves housework and the level of digital expertise required to sustain a smart home. Jenny Kennedy, Bjorn Nansen, Michael Arnold, Rowan Wilken, Martin Gibbs (2015) consider the digital labour needed for the upkeep of smart homes and what 'digital housekeeping' means today (Kennedy et al. 2015). They studied 22 households in Victoria, Australia, connected to high-speed broadband with varying complexities of smart devices ranging from the simple to the highly complex 'bleeding edge', pushing the limits of the capabilities of technologies within their household. Their research uncovers the ways in which digital housekeeping tacitly generates technology work within the home in the role of the digital 'housekeeper', a practice complicated by gendered sensitivities.

Earlier feminist studies on the adoption of labour-saving technologies in the home drew attention to gendered household labour, highlighting the changes in women's housework practices brought about by washing machines and vacuum cleaners (see, for example, Hochschild and Machung, 1989; Malos, 1975; Vogel, 1995). The introduction of appliances allowed men and children to undertake less housework while the time women take to perform housework was not reduced significantly (Cowan, 1983). Likewise, digital housekeeping is influenced by gendered considerations concerning both the traditional distribution of domestic labour and the gendering processes of technology (Berg 1994). Not only is digital expertise attained unequally between men and women, but so is the value attributed to it, with male skills esteemed. Census surveys that document the distribution of these digital tasks in the home repeatedly identify gender inequalities in terms of the number of the hours dedicated to performing these tasks (Australian Bureau of Statistics 2009; Office of National Statistics, 2016).

In the smart home, we find that locating, accessing, storing and organising digital content is time-consuming (Tolmie et al., 2007). In households with slow broadband connections, downloading content takes up time while for fast broadband connections, the process of storing digital content involves fastidious planning and concentration – such as the reorganisation of content – so that other household members can identify stored items. These tasks involve interoperability between new and current devices, as Kennedy et al. explain:

> The labour required to get the devices to 'talk' to one another, and to re-establish rhythms of family media use, is significant. Digital housekeeping is especially laborious and frustrating when the interoperability of devices in the networked ecology is opaque, and expertise falls short. (Kennedy et al. 2015)

These complex tasks not only point to the difficulties involved in adopting new devices in the smart home but also to the need for expertise and ongoing digital maintenance.

Kennedy et al. (2015) found three key measures used by householders to distinguish expertise: (1) comprehending systems, (2) the ability to transfer knowledge, and (3) automation of practice. Each of these measures require various forms of digital housekeeping such as 'accessing content, managing content, managing the aesthetics of devices, constructing functional networks of devices, deploying these networks, transferring knowledge about these devices and networks, automating the use of the devices and calling upon external expertise when required' (Kennedy et al. 2015: 414). Kennedy et al. found that many participants regarded male household members as the experts that managed these new housekeeping regimes. Most women participants claimed to be digitally competent yet were 'disinterested' or surrendered expertise to the male householder allowing him to be the digital technology-oriented decision-maker. 'Often it seems, expertise is a proxy for identity' (Kennedy et al. (2015: 415). Women participants tended to default to 'the household expert' in deliberations about technology operability and adoption and asked these other members for help.

> The most pronounced example of this occurred during the interview with Jeremy's household, when researchers repeatedly attempted to engage his wife Amy in the discussions. Amy enthusiastically engaged with the researchers only on her own technology use, and the biography of herself and Jeremy as a couple in terms of how long they had lived in their home, leaving all other conversation topics to Jeremy to answer. Amy also remained in the family area rather than join us in the technology tour of the household, delegating the responsibility of demonstrating and describing the household's media ecology to Jeremy. (Kennedy et al. (2015: 416)

As Kennedy et al. (2015) emphasise, participants use a discourse of 'choice' when describing digital housekeeping which replicates claims that women's domestic labour is somehow actively desired by women. If housework is expressed as a choice, then the tasks are construed as voluntary. Yet when it comes to digital labour, a fair amount of the work of the digital expert in the home is interest-based, rather than based on necessity. Many of these interests generate a need for more household work since the work involved has the power to disrupt normal routines. For example, the Internet or TV recording may be down while the male householder organises and regularly readjusts the system. The practice of tinkering with the technology in the home advocates innovation by adopting technologies that are not necessarily efficient or do not necessarily ease home-based entertainment. Moreover, those with expertise have the most agency and control by making decisions that may not be beneficial to the whole household. This predicament resonates with earlier studies of media labour that found that men tend to take over the remote-control device to 'channel hop' and decide on which TV programmes to watch (Gauntlett and Hill 1999, see Chapter 4). As Kennedy and colleagues point out, such a predicament forms part of a range of media-related activities which confirm that gendered power relations are involved in experts' manipulation of the technology (Gray 1992; Morley 1986; Walker and Bellamy 1993).

In the case of digital housekeeping, the ongoing process is conducted in relation to other competing pressures. As women tend to take on the conventional housework tasks, they have less time to digitally tinker, and do not benefit from repeated performance. This means it takes them longer to complete a digital task, each time. The tendency, then, is to defer to the male member of the household as the expert. 'However, the material flows of technoculture mean that expertise is hard won and fleetingly held. Expertise is a constant, dynamic process' (Kennedy et al. 2015: 418). There is a sense in which the technology is changing too rapidly to grasp it and then use that knowledge gain, later. By deferring to the expert, women become less motivated to learn for themselves. As a result of the extra effort involved each time, women tend to ask husbands or partners to download movies and TV programmes out of convenience, to save time. Whilst this seems logical, if men are repeatedly the agents involved in setting up the network systems in the homes, women are relinquishing control over their environment.

Kennedy and colleagues conclude that digital practices in the home reinforce the gendered social relations found in earlier research in both domestic work and media work, in the home. The smart home becomes an unfamiliar and challenging space for women, indicating the palpable home precarities involved in digitalising the homes. Such research casts light on the new kinds of relationships we are developing with our homes in the age of smart dwellings. Similar issues are highlighted by Melissa Gregg who, in an interview with Nellie Bowles (2018), draws attention to a significant reluctance among women to implement smart home devices. She argues that not only should women be the very householders most helped by smart technologies. Women also need to be centrally involved in the actual designing of technologies whether for the home or beyond. Gregg warns that 'if men are setting up the devices, and the rest of the family aren't informed about how those decisions are made, what happens if that protector becomes a threat?' (in Bowles 2018; and see Strengers et al. 2018)

Conclusion

This chapter has traced the shifting imaginaries of home from a place of belonging and intimacy to a digitally mediated environment. Technologies that track and monitor the behaviour of household members have generated a new kind of datafied home, one that has the potential to be an efficient networked space. Yet, at the same time, this raises serious questions about security vulnerabilities within a surveillance culture (Lyon 2018). Today's smart space forms part of a history narrowly framed by corporate ventures. Shaped by preoccupations with technologised solutions to domestic living, early future homes invoked utopian visions of a technology-driven domestic space, drawing on Modernist aesthetics and space-age fantasies. Past and present speculative films and videos of 'homes of the future' underline the role of corporate films and videos in the imaginings of technology-oriented home futures. Today's tech companies' trade shows and news reviews combine with speculative films of smart homes to form 'future-makers' as key agents that have the power to turn utopian smart home futures into palpable home precarities. Comprising discourses of home futurism, future makers promote the visual rhetoric of not-yet-experienced, about-to-be launched technologies for living. Their corporate visions of technology-driven futures embody masculine values, fuelling present-day aspirations with the power to sway impending policy on home constructions.

More recent smart home systems involve contrived home precarities by approaching home as a site of risk and danger that invoke householders' fears of intruders and vandals. The desire to manage security risks summons householders, as defenders of home space, to engage in an elaborate set of precautionary practices. In this smart home imaginary, ontological security can only be attained through smart systems. Yet the precarious nature of home is doubly accented, first by the sense of danger and vulnerability associated with home, and second by the sense of being watched by those same security systems. Ironically, these very same smart systems are now found to be intruding upon householders' privacy as devices of surveillance. Not only are hardware and software susceptible to the hacking of personal data but homes are now vulnerable to the misuse of data by smart home companies for marketing purposes. With commercial companies now capable of eavesdropping in apparently private, intimate spaces without our knowledge – or even with our knowledge – we must ask how the home is being reconceptualised in today's smart home imaginaries. It seems that 'future home' imaginaries have shifted from utopian visions of technology-led solutions to dystopian nightmares of technology surveillance and home datafication.

With households increasingly wrapped into the cross-digital ecosystems of smart homes, the datafied home forms part of a surveillance culture in an era of digital modernity. It raises questions not only about new digital household encounters with this new datafied domesticity but also about emerging possibilities and challenges associated with a new kind of digital citizenship (Lyon 2017). The wider cultural and political consequences of this datafied home stretch beyond issues of privacy to include transformations in the conditions under which citizenship is performed. First, the intelligence accumulated by smart companies that track and monitor behaviour can set limits on the ways in which home futures are determined in terms of health and access to information. This has consequences regarding rights to privacy,digital connection and participation in wider society beyond the home. Second, the datafication of the home sets limits on the ways in which future homes can be imagined and redesigned to cope with climate change (see Chapter 10).

The smart home agenda also foregrounds issues of gender and power with several examples highlighted in this chapter. First, by prioritising masculine discourses of technologised homes, smart homes have failed to address housework needs while celebrating the home as an efficient workspace. Second, in terms of adopting and maintaining smart home systems, the 'digital housekeeping' involved in setting up and maintaining the technology is largely undertaken by men. Male householders tend to establish themselves as the experts who manage these new digital regimes. Women are finding that they lose control over smart home systems since they are busy with homemaking tasks and eventually concede to the male expert in the home. Smart homes cast light, then, on the unequal ways in which men and women are grappling with digitally networked domestic space as part of a new kind of digital domestication. Despite attempts to 'modernise' the housewife during the late nineteenth and twentieth centuries by transforming her into an efficient homeworker, smart home agendas address men as a group more likely to be enchanted by smart imaginaries. Meanwhile women's lack of agency in this space becomes apparent. Women find this home space less homely, more alien and uncontrollable while they struggle with home working, both paid and unpaid.

Notes

1 See, for example, a video of the futuristic homes at the1933 Chicago World's Fair, available at https://www.youtube.com/watch?v=7ixX45Fqc4M (accessed 2 July 2019).
2 For example, Prelinger Archives in the US preserves corporate speculative films among its collection of 'ephemeral films', available at https://publicdomainreview.org/prelin ger-archives/ (accessed 22 June 2018).
3 'The Monsanto House of the Future' by Monsanto Company's Plastic's Division at Disneyland, Bay State Film Productions, Inc. available at https://www.youtube.com/wa tch?v=DoCCO3GKqWY (accessed 28 May 2018).
4 *Disneyland: 60 Years of Imagineering Monsantos' House of the Future* by Rick Conant, available at https://www.youtube.com/watch?v=2UTueKrIuvw (accessed 28 May 2018).
5 Tom Thomas Organization, presented by Philco-Ford Corporation, available at https://www.youtube.com/watch?v=TAELQX7EvPo (accessed 24 May2018).
6 Prelinger Archives, available at https://publicdomainreview.org/prelinger-archives/ (accessed 22 June 2018).
7 *At Home 2001*, Homes of the Future – Cronkite 1967, available at https://www.you tube.com/watch?v=vEtlfoS-toU (accessed 17 June 2018).
8 Carlos A. Altgelt, 'A Brief History of Philco', available at www.oldradio.com/archives/ hardware/philco.htm (accessed 17 June 2018).

9 Housing Learning & Improvement Network (2003) DTI Smart Homes Project Department of Trade and Industry, available at https://www.housinglin.org.uk/_assets/Resour ces/Housing/Housing_advice/Smart_Home_-_A_definition_September_2003.pdf (accessed 8 December 2019).
10 *A Day Made of Glass* is available at https://www.youtube.com/watch?v=OptqxagZDfM (accessed 24 June 2016).
11 *Watch Your Day in 2020*, available at https://www.youtube.com/watch?v=Optqxa gZDfM, (accessed 17 June 2018).
12 *Wall Street Daily* is available at www.wallstreetdaily.com/2016/06/22/invest-smart-hom e-technology/ (accessed 24 July 2016).
13 See, for example, https://www.opengovasia.com/articles/6582-uk-government-launche s-iot-programme-as-part-of-40m-investment; and the government review, Made Smarter: Review 2017, available at https://assets.publishing.service.gov.uk/government/up loads/system/uploads/attachment_data/file/655570/20 171027_MadeSmarter_FINAL_ DIGITAL.pdf (accessed 17 June 2018).
14 See Office of National Statistics news release, Consumer price inflation basket of goods and services: 2019, available at https://www.ons.gov.uk/economy/inflationandpriceindices/arti cles/ukconsumerpriceinflationbasketofgoodsandservices/2019 (accessed 8 December 2019).

References

A Century of Progress International Exposition. (1933 to 1934) *Official Guide Book of the Fair: Chicago World's Fair*. Chicago: Administration Building. https://archive.org/details/ officialguideboo00centrich (accessed 26 March 2019).

Adam, B. (2011) 'Wendell Bell and the sociology of the future: Challenges past, present and future', *Futures*, 43, 590–595.

Aldossari, M.Q. and Sidorova, A. (2018) 'Consumer acceptance of Internet of Things (IoT): Smart home context', *Journal of Computer Information Systems*. doi:10.1080/ 08874417.2018.1543000.

Aldrich, F.K. (2013) 'Smart homes: Past, present and future', in R. Harper (ed.), *Inside the Smart Home*. London: Springer, pp. 17–40.

Anderson, J. and Rainie, L. (2014) 'The Internet of Things will thrive by 2025', Pew Research Centre. www.elon.edu/docs/e-web/imagining/surveys/2014_survey/Elon% 20Pew%20Future%20of%20the%20Internet%20of%20Things%20Report%205-14-14.pdf (accessed 26 March 2019).

Australian Bureau of Statistics. (2009) 'Trends in household work'. Australia, cat. no 4102.0. Canberra: ABS.

Baar, A. (2011) 'Corning glass video goes through the roof', *Marketing Daily*. www.mediap ost.com/publications/article/146462/ (accessed 26 March 2019).

Barad, K. (2003) *Posthumanist Performativity: Towards an Understanding of How Matter Comes to Matter*. Chicago: University of Chicago Press.

Baudrillard, J. (1983) *Simulations*. New York: Semiotexte.

Baudrillard, J. (1994) *Simulacra and Simulation*. Michigan: University of Michigan Press.

Berg, A.-J. (1994) 'A gendered socio-technical construction: The smart house', in C. Cockburn and R. First-Dilic (eds), *Bringing Technology Home: Gender and Technology in a Changing Europe*. Maidenhead: Open University Press, pp. 165–180.

Berkhout, F. (2006) 'Normative expectations in systems innovation', *Technology Analysis and Strategic Management*, 18, 299–311.

Bitterman, N.and Shach-Pinsly, D. (2015) 'Smart home – a challenge for architects and designers', *Architectural Science Review*, 58(3), 266–274.

Blandy, S. (2018) 'Gated communities revisited: Defended homes nested in security enclaves', *People, Place and Policy*, 11(3), 136–142.

Blunt, A. and Dowling, R. (2006) *Home*. London: Routledge.

Bowles, N. (2018) 'Thermostats, locks and lights: Digital tools of domestic abuse', in conversation with Melissa Gregg, *New York Times*, 23 June 2018. www.nytimes.com/2018/06/23/technology/smart-home-devices-domestic-abuse.html (accessed 2 July 2019).

Caluya, G. (2007) 'The architectural nervous system: Home, fear insecurity', *M/C Journal*, 10(4). http://journal.media-culture.org.au/0708/05-caluya.php (accessed 26 March 2019).

Chambers, D. (2016) *Changing Media, Homes and Households*. London: Routledge.

Chambers, D. (2019) 'Media futurism: The role of speculative films and corporate videos in creating the time warps of future media homes', in M. Hartmann, E. Prommer, K. Deckner, and S.O. Görland (eds), *Mediated Time: Perspectives on Time in a Digital Age*. London: Palgrave.

Colomina, B. (1996) *Privacy and Publicity: Modern Architecture as Mass Media*. Cambridge, MA: The MIT Press.

Colomina, B. (2001) *Domesticity at War*. Barcelona: ActarD Inc.

Cousins, S. (2018) 'The dark side of smart homes: What can they do with our data?' *Construction Research and Innovation*, 9(1), 13–16.

Cowan, R.S. (1983) *More Work for Mother: The Ironies of Household Technology from the Open Hearth to the Microwave*. New York: Basic Books.

Darby, S.J. (2018) 'Smart technology in the home: Time for more clarity', *Building Research & Information*, 46(1), 140–147.

Featherstone, M. (2007) *Consumer Culture and Postmodernism*. London: Sage.

Ganz, C.R. (2012) *The 1933 Chicago World's Fair: A Century of Progress*. Chicago: University of Illinois Press.

Gauntlett, D. and Hill, A. (1999) *TV Living: Television Culture and Everyday Life*. London: Routledge.

Gray, A. (1992) *Video Playtime: The Gendering of a Leisure Technology*. London: Routledge.

Hargreaves, T., Wilson, C. and Hauxwell-Baldwin, R. (2018) 'Learning to live in a smart home', *Building Research & Information*, 46(1), 127–139.

Hirshberg, A. and Schoen, R. (1974) 'Barriers to the widespread utilisation of residential solar energy: The prospects for solar energy in the U.S. housing industry', *Policy Sciences*, 5, 453–468.

Hochschild, A. and Machung, A. (1989) *The Second Shift: Working Parents and the Revolution at Home*. New York: Viking.

Jameson, F. (1982) 'Progress versus utopia: Or, can we imagine the future?', *Science Fiction Studies*, 9, 147–158.

Jencks, C. (1973) *Modern Movements in Architecture*. Garden City: Anchor Books.

Keegan, N. (2017) 'Fascinating photos show the plastic 1960s house of the future'. www.news.com.au/finance/economy/world-economy/fascinating-photos-show-the-plastic-house-of-the-future-that-20-million-disneyland-visitors-flocked-to-in-the-1960s/news story/1f.bff5f.11caeabc8f.681cd9d9cf42e41 (accessed 19 March 2018).

Kennedy, J., Nansen, B., Arnold, M., Wilken, R. and Gibbs, M. (2015) 'Digital housekeepers and domestic expertise in the networked home', *Convergence*, 21(4), 408–422.

Kirby, D. (2010) 'The future is now: Diegetic prototypes and the role of popular films in generating real-world technological development', *Social Studies of Science*, 40(1), 41–70.

Lyon, D. (2017) 'Surveillance culture: Engagement, exposure, and ethics in digital modernity', *International Journal of Communication*, 11, 824–842.

Lyon, D. (2018) *The Culture of Surveillance: Watching as a Way of Life*. Cambridge: Polity Press.

Malos, E. (ed.) (1975) *The Politics of Housework*. New York: The New Clarion Press.

Meyer, S. and Schulze, E. (1996) 'The smart home in the 1990s: Acceptance and future usage in private households in Europe', in *The Smart Home: Research Perspectives, the European Media Technology and Everyday Life Network (EMTEL)*, Working Paper No. 1. Brighton: University of Sussex.

Morley, D. (1986) *Family Television: Cultural Power and Domestic Leisure*. London: Comedia.

Morley, D. (2007) *Media, Modernity, and Technology: The Geography of the New*. London: Routledge.

Newman, O. (1973) *Defensible Space: Crime Prevention through Urban Design*. New York: Collier.

Noda, K. (2018) 'Google home: Smart speaker as environmental control unit', *Disability and Rehabilitation: Assistive Technology*, 13(7), 674–675.

Office of National Statistics. (2016) 'Women shoulder the responsibility of unpaid work'. www.ons.gov.uk/employmentandlabourmarket/peopleinwork/earningsandworkinghours /articles/womenshouldertheresponsibilityofunpaidwork/2016-11-10 (accessed 26 March 2019).

Opitz, D.L., Bergwik, S. and Van Tiggelen, B. (eds) (2016) *Domesticity in the Making of Modern Science*. London: Palgrave.

Pillan, M. and Colombo, S. (2017) 'Will smart homes improve our lives? A design perspective towards effective wellbeing at home', *The Design Journal*, 20(sup1), S2580–S2591.

Ryan, D. (1997) *The Ideal Home through the Twentieth Century*. London: Hazar Publishing.

Spigel, L. (1992) *Make Room for TV: Television and the Family Ideal in Postwar America*. Chicago: University of Chicago Press.

Spigel, L. (2001a) 'Media homes, then and now', *International Journal of Cultural Studies*, 4(4), 385–411.

Spigel, L. (2001b) *Welcome to the Dreamhouse: Popular Media and Postwar Suburbia*. Durham, NC: Duke University Press.

Spigel, L. (2005) 'Designing the smart house: Posthuman domesticity and conspicuous production', *European Journal of Cultural Studies*, 8(4), 403–426.

Spigel, L. (2010) 'Designing the smart house: Posthuman domesticity and conspicuious production', in C. Berry, S. Kim and L. Spigel (eds), *Electronic Elsewheres: Media Technology and the Experience of Social Space*. Minneapolis: University of Minnesota Press, pp. 55–95.

Strengers, Y., Kennedy, J., Nicholls, L. and Arcari, P. (2018) 'The 3Ps: Protection, productivity and pleasure for Australian smart home early adopters'. Research report, Centre for Urban Research and Digital Ethnography Research Centre, RMIT University, Melbourne. https:// cur.org.au/cms/wp-content/uploads/2018/09/smart-home-report.pdf (accessed 8 December 2019).

Tolmie, P., Crabtree, A., Rodden, T.*et al.* (2007) 'Making the home network at home: Digital housekeeping', in L. Bannon, I. Wagner, C. Gutwin, R. Harper and K. Schmidt (eds), *ECSCW 2007: Proceedings of the 10th European Conference on Computer-Supported Cooperative Work Limerick, Ireland, 24–28 September 2007*. Paris: Springer.

Tutton, R. (2017) 'Wicked futures: Meaning, matter and the sociology of the future', *The Sociological Review*, 65(3), 478–492.

Vogel, L. (1995) *Woman Questions: Essays for a Materialist Feminism*. New York: Routledge.

Walker, J. and Bellamy, R. (eds) (1993) *The Remote Control in the New Age of Television*. Westport: Praeger Publishers.

10

SUSTAINABLE HOMES

Introduction

In the course of this book, a range of debates and analyses have highlighted the complex social, cultural and political strategies involved in *idealisations* of home. These strategies and processes of idealisation uncover the social tensions and power struggles relating to what I have referred to as 'home precarities'. This final chapter addresses the *palpable* home precarities posed by global warming, confirming that responses to climate change prompt an urgent need to transform ways of living to generate environmentally sustainable, energy saving homes. The chapter identifies the household as a critical site contributing to the severity of the ecological crisis and a key setting in which customs, habits and daily routines can be renegotiated to realise sustainability as a moral imperative.

The Intergovernmental Panel on Climate Change (IPCC) special report on the impact of global warming of 1.5^0 C in October 2018 (IPCC 2018) points out that the 1.5^0 C temperature 'guard rail' is likely to be exceeded as soon as 2030. Staying below this temperature will require urgent, wide-scale changes ranging from governments to individuals and requiring massive financial investments each year of around 2.5% of global gross domestic product for two decades. The report identifies the need for rapid and significant changes in four big global systems: energy, land use, cities and industry. It also urges that because this target cannot be met without changes by individuals, people must make significant lifestyle changes. This involves not only sustainable food consumption and changes in travelling habits but also substantial changes to homes including home insulation and low carbon energy consumption.

Lifestyles, customs and social practices have been recognised for some time as having a central role to play in shaping domestic emissions (see for example, Cabinet Office, 2011; Hargreaves 2011; Spence and Pidgeon 2009). Sprawling developments and the rising number of homes to accommodate demands for smaller households and bigger houses have contributed to wildlife extinction, reliance on fossil fuels, damaging mining practices, the harvesting of forests unsustainably, water scarcity and destruction of prime agricultural lands (Peterson et al. 2013: 3–4). Cultural geographers are now approaching the home and household as a critical scale for the study of the customs and practices that link individual activities with climate change and environmental sustainability. Yet, as a unit, the household remains one of the most under-researched aspects of sustainability and climate change. As such, the household itself must now be placed at the forefront of policy initiatives to combat climate change. What kinds of academic considerations and policy initiatives does this demand, and what kinds of housing and household schemes are under way to support the required levels of sustainable living?

This chapter attempts to deal with these questions by addressing some of the key debates, rhetoric, initiatives and proposed solutions to the universal crisis facing home life in our time. National policy strategies designed to promote 'ecological modernisation' tend to underestimate the diversity and potential productivity of households and the degree of change required at the household scale. On the one hand, it is often believed that an emphasis on the scale of the household is misdirected until economic activity can be separated from fossil fuel usage. On the other hand, if households are acknowledged to be part of the solution to climate change, it is often assumed that straightforward economic incentives can steer demand and that sustainable solutions can be administered through regulation or market pricing. However, householders' choices and judgements are not only economic, involving complex consumption patterns and exchanges among families and communities. As Gibson et al. (2011) point out, householders' decisions are also essentially cultural, shaped by wider customs and values. Research on household sustainability reveals the remarkable range and variety of homemaking and domestic maintenance practices involving the utilisation of resources.

Household energy use and sustainability

Approaching home as a site for reversing climate change draws attention to palpable home precarities, undermining the idea of home as a haven from the world's hazards. The home is one of the main entry points for the implementation of all environmentally friendly policies. However, any modifications made by individual households are inadequate unless linked to wider scale measures. For example, without major changes in water access through current supply networks, decreases in household consumption of water are unlikely to make substantial long-term improvements (Lawrence and McManus 2008). By approaching the household in terms of 'site and scale', the household is recognised as an interconnection of individual judgements and choices about consumption and waste disposal, concerning communal decisions and activities and concerning bad practice and the wider movement and consumption of energy and material goods (Hawkins 2006: 70). An obstacle facing debates and policy formation on greening the 'home' is that homes are individualistic and not collective. Assessing the delicate routines and house-holders' uses of domestic devices that might lower carbon dioxide emissions is complicated. Moreover, variation in household size, from single person to large family households, multiple occupancies and co-housing pose challenges about home boundaries and the kinds of sustainability arrangements required. In turn, these challenges raise questions about how to conceptualise the agency of a household.

Taking Europe as a complex cross-national regional example, buildings in the European Union are responsible for 40% of the total amount of energy needed. This percentage is expected to rise with an increase in future building construction. Accepting the need for meso-level (household) initiatives, the challenges involved in the transformation of household and domestic practices, as major players in energy transitions, are enormous. European nations have signed the 2015 Paris Agreement to combat climate change and accelerate the actions and investments needed for decarbonisation. The challenges entail policy and planning to initiate efficient technologies in the home or transformative changes such as cooperative modes of renewable energy production. Governing frameworks and policies relat-ing to energy use must take account of housing tenure, location, and building stocks followed by climatic and energy cost considerations. The average of equivalent tonnes of CO_2 emissions per capita in the European Union is 8.7 (Naef et al. 2019; European Environmental Agency 2016).

Although energy efficiency forms part of all European national policies, there are significant national differences in their implementation, with variable levels of effectiveness. Demonstrating fragmented energy approaches across the Union, key differences exist in energy production and management with some countries choosing to phase out nuclear fuel and some expanding their nuclear capacity. In response to the 1970s oil crises, energy policies in Denmark have led to the implementation of district heating based on combined heat and power with high uses of wind power for electricity and biomass (Jensen and Quitzau 2019). How-ever, the involvement of households has been somewhat scattered, with transfor-mations focused mainly on the supply side. Hungarian policy emphasises the need to improve energy efficiency with a focus on the household sector, yet the policy support has been uneven (Vadovics 2019). Likewise, in Finland the rhetoric supporting energy efficiency has not been matched by actions until recently (Heiskanen et al. 2019). Across Europe, the retrofitting of older buildings is wide-spread as a method for improving energy efficiency, but the type of renewables and results are varied, depending on local conditions (Naef et al. 2019).

To lower European Union dependency on energy imports and decarbonise the economy, the European Union Energy Policy is being developed across five domains: (i) security of supply; (ii) sustainability; (iii) greenhouse gas emissions; (iv) the role of renewable energy in energy supply and use; and (v) competitiveness of the EU in the energy sector (Genus and Iskandarova 2018: 11). The normalisation of various forms of energy-greedy consumption such as constant Internet con-nectivity, and the use of washing machines and refrigerators, are part of deliberations concerning sufficiency that prompt more fundamental and societal questions including the kinds of services that should be allowed and in what contexts. A definition of 'sufficiency' by Sahakian et al. (2018) supports absolute reductions in resource use while also contesting social conventions on household energy use and fixing upper and lower limits to consumption, drawing on findings from the H2020 ENERGISE1 project. This is based on the principle that sufficiency should be a first step towards efficiency for energy transitions.

Issues of age, gender and social class are significant factors for understanding the link between a household's economic resource, the type of building they live in and their energy habits in relation to current and potential energy-related practices (Gram-Hanssen and Georg 2017). Economic differences between wealthy and poor households involve contrasting patterns of consumption and therefore contrasting technological acquisition and different habitat conditions (Sahakian 2018). Education level is a form of social capital that can influence environmental awareness concerning energy issues. Many scholars therefore agree that thermal conditions should correspond with the type of occupants and type of building (Kunkel et al. 2015; Nicol and Wilson 2011; Bopp 2007; Boerstra et al. 2015). The tenure of the home also influences householders' options for lowering energy demand. Obvious challenges include the lack of incentives on the part of landlords to pay for energy renovations that would help tenants save energy (Laakso and Heiskanen 2017: 12). The type and age of the home also determines energy use with regard to the costs of increasing levels of energy efficiency. Renovation needs are greater in countries with older building stock such as the UK and Bulgaria. Old buildings, and poorly maintained dwellings have very different energy saving needs compared to new and highly automated buildings. In the UK, the housing stock is amongst the oldest in Europe. Houses built before 1918 represented 16% of the housing stock in 2014. The large proportion dating from the Victorian era have poor insulation, indicating additional energy consumption to maintain a certain level of comfort. And in Bulgaria, only 5% of homes were built after 2000 (Naef et al. 2019: 144). Energy use is also determined by the size and type of the dwelling with larger dwellings consuming more energy but multiple rooms allowing rooms to be closed off to regulate temperature.

Variations in the stages of development of smart systems and technologies between countries in Europe show that certain northern countries are more advanced than others. For example, smart energy systems have been advanced in Finland and Denmark with investment in smart grid and smart energy research. Finland has developed smart products for export such as the Internet of Things, building automation and smart controls. Finland also hosts several cities that are piloting smart technologies. An additional factor that affects household energy usage is whether the energy suppliers are private, or state owned. State regulations of energy distribution commonly aim to safeguard consumers' interests, affecting the energy bill. For instance, systems that offer low renewable energy electricity prices can influence household energy use. Meanwhile, fuel subsidies can lower the cost of energy to support people in need. However, growing interest in smart cities has led to calls for a less technology-oriented and more citizen-centric approach (Joss et al. 2017). Citizen-led approaches are discussed below.

Considered together, the range of household energy schemes in Europe highlight the importance of EU funding and related national funding programmes to support innovative initiatives tor lower energy use. They also indicate the value of working with multiple stakeholders to encourage community engagement, an approach regarded as more effective than nation-led, 'top-down' schemes. As Patrick Naef and colleagues state:

> In this vein, there seems to be increasing interest - in policy discourse if not in action - on the need to move away from the 'passive consumer' to the 'active citizen' when it comes to framing the role of households in energy transitions. (Naef et al. 2019: 150)

Although most energy schemes seem to emphasise individual and technological transformation, some encouraging instances of good practice indicate how wider forms of change could be practised effectively. The need to 'embed energy demand in socio-material systems' by addressing questions related to cultural context such as 'car culture' in the case of Germany is also foregrounded by Naef et al. (2019).

State and free market strategies towards green policies

Within debates about effective national strategies to develop low carbon, sustainable homes, academics and policymakers highlight the tensions between 'Green state theory' and a free market environmentalism framework. Green state theory, situated in the tradition of 'ecologism', argues that a commitment to strong sustainability from the state can be considered compatible with liberal principles, including a degree of state impartiality, pluralism, democracy, and a degree of consumer choice (e.g. Barry 1999, Eckersley 2004, Dobson 2007). Green state theory's ecological modernisation literature stresses that governance can foster market innovation in 'win–win' technologies that are efficient ecologically and economically. Forming part of ecologism, Green state theory emphasises community values and cultural ties. For example, Eckersley and Barry highlight the importance of public participation as a way of reaching sustainability goals (Barry 1999: 119–121; Eckersley 2000). But they represent a perspective that supports a 'pragmatic' approach to address policy choices between state and 'market mechanisms', such as environmental taxes and emissions trading, or other forms of regulation to frame market processes (Eckersley 2000: 244).

By contrast, free market environmentalism regards private property rights to be the most efficient approach to direct environmental resources, together with market competition and exchange (Anderson and Leal 2001, Pennington 2008, 2011). However, Greenwood suggests that there is considerable common conceptual ground between free market environmentalism and Green state theory's ecologism (Greenwood 2008). Each challenges the state-market dichotomy by foregrounding the potential for decentralised, evolutionary processes of institutional change in support of zero carbon homes that could involve various combinations of state, locally defined institutions, and markets. Acceptance of the potential for governance processes to guide markets towards sustainability goals through incentives raises questions about how to combine different kinds of 'expertise' in policymaking while also acting on wider public opinion.

Dan Greenwood (2015) draws attention to the implications of interconnections between the ideological traditions of Green state theory and free market environmentalism by analysing the challenges involved in the UK experience. His case study merits close attention here to illustrate national challenges. The Climate Change Act 2008 committed the UK government to an 80% reduction in greenhouse gas emissions by 2050. In 2006, the Labour government declared that all new homes must be zero carbon by 2016. This was supported by environmental bodies such as WWF (World Wide Fund for Nature) and Friends of the Earth. Although acknowledging the extra costs involved for businesses and house-buyers, the government stressed the possibility of lowering costs through continuing innovation supported by policy regulation. This commitment to a state-led ecological modernisation agenda posed challenges for policy coordination by impacting on planning, energy policy and building regulations on energy efficiency.

In tandem with the 2016 zero carbon target, was the Code for Sustainable Homes (CSH), a national standard introduced by government but carried out by a private sector company. In addition, the existence of many private, voluntary building assessment initiatives raised questions about how to assess non-mandatory schemes and their efficacy for the policy agenda. The CSH defined a zero carbon home (Code Level 6) as one which is 'completely zero carbon (i.e. zero net emissions of carbon dioxide (CO_2) from all energy use in the home)' (DCLG 2006: 11). However, this definition was soon contested. After the creation of the UK Green Building Council (UKGBC) in 2007, and later the Zero Carbon Hub, a new consultation took place to assess the practicalities and challenges of implementing the original definition and decarbonising the housing stock more broadly (see McLeod et al. 2012). And low carbon housing has been purposely reframed as a solution to climate change.

Of course, sustainability targets cannot be solely consumer driven because sustainability criteria tend to be much lower priorities for homebuyers than distance to workplace and conveniences. Convincing homebuyers to make informed decisions such as lowering carbon emissions involves considerable collective action, based on public environmental principles stemming from democratic strategies (Pennington 2008, 2011). The pragmatism of Green state theory therefore indicates that reliance on market-based incentives such as carbon tax need to be combined with regulatory approaches as part of a range of policy strategies in market settings (Eckersley 2004, Barry and Eckersley 2005). Although the need for this regulation is broadly conceded across the sector, the intense debate about zero carbon targets within the construction industry has not been reported in the mainstream media or picked up by the general public (see below for a discussion of media reporting on sustainable and 'green' homes). The lack of public engagement in what is a highly technical and specialised debate demonstrates the challenges facing policy. It also implies a central role to be played by experts within governance. Yet advocates of Green state theory's ecological modernisation model offer little guidance on the role of technical and economic expertise in policymaking (Greenwood 2015). Several stakeholders have criticised the narrow policy emphasis on technological solutions for new homes.

While Green state theory and free market environmentalism stress the risks of over-regulatory policy, they both depend on the efficiency and drive of effective government policy. However, local variation in the quality and ambitions of schemes was exacerbated by the British government's 'localism' agenda, adopted in the Localism Act of 2011, which supported decentralised market processes and a surfeit of voluntary standards across the UK. This generated criticisms against the objectives and targets set by local authorities (the local government administrative bodies) for minimising homes' carbon levels. Local authorities were accused of inefficiency, of thwarting sustainability goals and increasing the difficulties for householders. In response, the coalition government condensed and rationalised the standards to be incorporated into local authority plans, initiating a review of national housing standards. However, the government's 2016 zero carbon new homes target and related regulations acted as a major incentive for innovation across the housing sector. If such events highlight the need for coordinated government-led national housing standard definitions and frameworks across scales, they also raise concerns about how to implement and practice sustainable policy. For example, some stakeholders believed that certain key government decisions were imprudent because housing ministers failed to listen to industry expert guidance (Greenwood 2015: 436).

The Zero Carbon Hub was launched as a public/private body in 2008 to support the 'new homes' industry in its objective of supplying the zero carbon homes' programme. The Hub comprised a network of professionals that represented companies and groups across the construction and energy sectors. The body also administered the introduction of higher energy efficiency standards. But although the Labour government pledged to clarify the meaning of 'allowable solutions' in 2009, it made no announcement before it left office in 2010. With indecisions and deferrals, details were never confirmed. Tragically, the Carbon Zero Hub ceased operations in 2016 following a change in government. The Conservative Government made a controversial decision to stop pursuing zero-homes targets to curb the regulation faced by housebuilders. Whilst the closure of the Hub was no surprise to most in the Green building industry, many expressed disappointment at the closure of a body that was helping to promote green best practices.[1] Commenting on closure, UK Green Building Council policy director Richard Twinn commented:

> It's incredibly disappointing to see the closure of the Zero Carbon Hub, although sadly not a shock given the direction of travel in terms of policy. It

> could have helped to guide the industry in delivering better quality buildings during its current housebuilding push. (Mace 2016)

Summing up the sense of failure, Andrew Orriss, head of business development, SIG360 argued that the closure of Zero Carbon Hub (ZCH) was inevitable given the government's 'very weak carbon agenda'.

In addition to the lack of resourcefulness by certain governments and the lack of continuity resulting from a change in government, both the perspectives of free market environmentalism and Green state theory's ecological modernisation are over-dependent on technological innovation as the solution to ecological sustainability. These discourses undervalue the degree of action needed by states to restructure markets in order to move towards environmentally sustainable outcomes. At the same time, Green state theory's ecological modernisation viewpoint, which favours policymaking, provides some key indicators of ways to address challenges by drawing attention to the importance of an effective relationship between policymaking practices, private sector know-how and innovation. Free market environmentalism and Green state theory confirm that processes of governance can bring about coordinated action to address public concerns at the same time as benefiting from stakeholders' technical and economic expertise (Greenwood 2015). Certain advanced schemes and policies on energy, greenhouse gas targets and transport policy have occurred at city and local council levels. For example, Melbourne in Australia and Vancouver in Canada have gained recognition as liveable eco-cities, moving towards dramatic reductions in emissions by 2020. One way in which this vision is achieved is by bringing together several groups and organisations to imagine and then create sustainable cities as exemplified by Vancouver (Holden and Scerri 2013).

Green homes

Despite the poor track records of many governments in implementing policies to advance sustainable housing and deal with old and inefficient housing stock, green homes are now being built globally, either commercially led or in state-commercial partnerships. Used interchangeably with the term 'eco home', a 'green home' is a type of house designed to be environmentally sustainable or ecologically sensitive through the efficient use of energy, water and building materials including recycled building materials. This involves sustainable energy sources such as solar or geothermal energy, the improvement of indoor air quality and production of less waste through use of the home. Whilst the environmental movement today represents multiple shades of 'green' opinion (Jarvis and Bonnett 2013), we have also seen the emergence of green affordable housing. However, in many countries no government standards yet define a green home apart from non-profit certification. The green building movement that began in the US was prompted by the sharp rise in oil prices in the 1970s. Organisations were then founded in the 1990s to promote green buildings. In 2006, the International Code Council and the National Association of

Home Builders began work towards the creation of a 'voluntary green home building standard' exemplified by the US Green Building Council's Leadership in Energy and Environmental design certification and the National Association of Home Builders' Model Green Home Building Guidelines (Yudelson 2008).

Policies across scales and sectors involved in the provision of new homes are needed in order to guide the building and related industries towards lower carbon emissions. At the same time, scope for flexibility and innovation is needed, so that this goal can be balanced in relation to other economic, environmental and social aims. Across different countries, certain projects stand out as successes in sustainability efforts including the development of 'eco-homes'. Eco-home projects demonstrate the need to actively involve and train householders on how to manage these eco-homes. For example, the Perspective Project, a major Dutch research programme in the 1990s trialled low-energy living to show that extensive change is possible. The Perspective Project was conducted in the Netherlands between 1995 and 1998, financed by the then Ministry of Housing, Spatial Planning and the Environment with the target of 40% reduction in energy use. The two-year scheme focused on individual behaviour change and is viewed as a best-practice example by demonstrating that living well, healthily and sustainably can go hand-in-hand. With the aim of reducing their energy use as far as possible over a period of two years, the first 20 households were tutored and monitored throughout the project towards realising a low-energy lifestyle. Among the households selected for participation, it seems that financial gain was a key motivation to participate in addition to environmental gain (Backhaus 2019). The households were informed about basic principles of reducing indirect energy use and provided with information on energy consumption and monitoring.

Most significantly, householders gained monthly coaching involving advice on monitoring home energy consumption, consideration of saving strategies, the planning of monetary spending, and given further details on the energy intensity of products and services. Householders assembled at an event half-way through the project to motivate participants, swap tips and experiences, and generate commitment to the following phase of lowering consumption levels. An additional motivation was the provision of 20% additional household income to imitate economic growth. Households had to follow rules on spending their increased income to conform to the low-energy living principles. Personal coaches recorded the challenges householders faced, such as wanting to travel abroad for holidays and having to remind them of their commitment to the project. They had to take a low-energy holiday instead. These methods of intervention were effective in leading to a reduction in energy use in every category measured including transport, food, living, hygiene, clothing and leisure. As Backhaus emphasises, the Perspective Project is one of many projects presented as best practice to prove that healthy living and well-being living can be sustained through a smaller footprint. (Backhaus 2019). It shows that, rather than targeting individuals, future sustainable energy policies and schemes need to address infrastructures, social norms and collectives.

More recently, a case study of eco-homes in the West Yorkshire, England documented by Lucy Jones (2014) foregrounds the ways that 'ordinary' families and individuals, with no environmental values or experiences of sustainable practices, cope with living in eco-homes. The 520 houses in the Allerton Bywater Millennium Community development were designed to the Building Research Establishment's EcoHomes standard of 'Excellent'. First inhabited in 2007, the research traced the changes in inhabitants' views as they learned to adapt to new ways of living in their new eco-homes. Jones found that 'living-with' an 'eco-home' is like a conversion, involving a journey from denial and frustration towards exploration and transformation. Jones' study shows that any scripting in the design of the eco-homes is not enough to inspire all inhabitants to think and act in a more sustainable way. Unlike the Perspective Project above, the eco-home developers addressed the dwellers as passive recipients of their homes. For some, the scheme sparked significant changes, while for others it triggered none. However, several householders exceeded expectations in their efforts to follow eco-home principles because some did much more than simply follow the eco-home script offered to them. Each household developed strategies of incorporating sustainability into their own values and meanings as part of their life experiences within the transformative encounter.

The research by Jones uncovered the social dynamics of eco-home living with others. She found that 'good neighbours' can 'educate' their neighbours about recycling, water usage and fuel consumption. At the same time, 'bad neighbours' were reluctant to abide by environmentally friendly principles and it was unclear whether competitive mindsets and judgemental outlooks foster or impede abiding relationships between eco-dwellers in ensuring eco- credentials of the eco-development. It was also found that the development of eco-homes depends on the part played by planners, designers, architects and masterplans as they shift from eco-idealist to mainstream housing practices. In turn, the initiative impacts on the everyday lives of ordinary inhabitants of new speculative housing estates built by volume housebuilders. Volume builders often claim to build 'what consumers want'. Yet, significantly, Jones found that the least eco-knowledgeable interviewed couple were open to overt eco-technologies and ideas (Jones 2014).

In several communities across Sweden, including Stockholm, Göteborg, Västerås and Helsingborg, low-energy residences are being constructed called 'passive houses'. These homes are designed to be heated mainly by the energy already found there, such as the energy from people's body heat, electrical appliances, lighting and sunlight. In 2011, the first Nordic Ecolabel multi-family residence was installed in Stockholm. A building with 36 apartments produces half the carbon dioxide emissions of a regular apartment building. Apparently seven out of ten Swedes want to live in an eco-labelled house and would consider paying more for it, according to a survey conducted by a construction firm, Veidekke. In the city of Malmö, Ekostaden Augustenborg is one of the largest European initiatives in the environmental conversion of an existing residential area. The Augustenborg District of Malmö suffered from repeated seasonal flooding as a result of an inadequate drainage system and a high rate of health problems due to poor drainage and unemployment. An extensive urban renovation programme called Ekostaden (Eco-neighbourhood) began back in 1998. By addressing the area as an integrated whole, the Eco-neighbourhood approach transformed the city district into an ecologically, socially and economically sustainable neighbourhood. By setting the priority of working with local residents as well as public and private stakeholders, Eco-neighbourhood combined modern architecture with environmental sustainability to create an environmentally friendly neighbourhood with public space, community-run cafes and other activities as well as sustainable homes. The construction of green roofs solved flooding problems efficiently and sustainably. Similarly, a large construction project in Stockholm's Hammarby Sjöstad district includes 11,500 apartments as part of an eco-cycle approach to showcase ecological and environmentally sensitive construction and living (see for example, Wang et al. 2017; Gosztoni, Stefanwicz, Bernardo and Blomsterberg 2017).

The UK's first low carbon neighbourhood is the £125m Climate Innovation District at Leeds South Bank, built on the edge of Leeds city centre. In 2019, the first residents moved in. The neighbourhood scheme is led by Citu, a small but ambitious property developing company working to accelerate the move to zero carbon cities in partnership with Leeds Beckett University (Smith 2016). Planning permission was granted to turn former industrial land into much-needed housing. Founder of Citu, Chris Thompson spent time visiting housing schemes in Stockholm and Copenhagen, where off-site construction has been the norm since the early 1990s. Using Scandinavian concepts, the Citu team worked with a Swedish architect, White Arkitekter, alongside Manchester-based Ollier Smurthwaite to design the houses, demonstrating the importance of sharing good practice transnationally. The 'Citu Home' is built in a factory in the Climate Innovation District and made of timber-framed panels which are then transported nearby to build 5,015 zero emission homes on former industrial land. The zero emission home was designed to be produced at scale for mass adoption (see Smith 2016).

These Citu homes have green roofs, triple-glazed windows and air tightness based on German Passivhaus principles. Built using passive house tools, the houses are designed to be cheap to run with high energy efficiency, solar panels, mechanical ventilation and heat recovery systems. The homes' modest heating needs are therefore met with renewable energy alone to ensure heat consumption is ten times lower than in a conventional house. The carbon footprint of the home can expect to be reduced by over two tonnes of $CO2$ per year, which contrasts with the average UK household emissions of 2.3 tonnes to heat the home. Each resident is expected to become a member of a Community Interest Company (CIC), to take over when the development is fully sold. The aim is for the CIC to own the landscape, infrastructure and renewable energy systems within the development.

These examples illustrate the types of sustainable dwelling schemes that can be achieved through joint private and public initiatives. They offer suggestions about how householders manage the challenges involved in this new kind of home environment and point to the feasibility of developing eco-homes at scale to create thriving neighbourhoods and even cities. However, given that public awareness performs a vital role in transitioning towards a low carbon housing sector, the question is how are green homes and household sustainability popularised via the media? How do households find out about the tasks and responsibilities involved in the transformation of homes into sustainable dwellings? Such questions lead to a consideration of the significance of eco-lifestyle TV programmes and neighbourhood schemes.

Popular culture and news discourses

Given that practical proposals for sustainable lifestyles must centrally involve the home as a unit, how wider public discourses are addressing the subject of sustainable homes and the need for changes in household habits and routines becomes a vital matter. Books that popularise environmentally sustainable interior design demonstrate that environmental sustainability can be stylish and simple to apply. Spanning appliances, furniture, fabrics, surface materials, plants and window treatments, *Green Interior Design* by Lori Dennis (2010) approaches the home from a green perspective to reduce waste and pollution. This green lifestyle guide shows readers not only how to use sustainable materials such as bamboo, cork and recycled glass but also how to spot 'vintage hidden treasures' in thrift shops and antique stores. It also offers advice on replacing lawns with indigenous plants and edible gardens and how to keep rooms clean with effective and nontoxic products. Other publications, such as *Sustainability in Interior Design* by Sian Moxon (2012) are reference books that target designers by emphasising the need to adapt to sustainable design involving 'the whole life cycle of a project' yet claiming that it can be 'sophisticated and stylish'. However, what is striking about most efforts to popularise the greening of homes is that they remain marginal to mainstream popular culture. They are still considered quirky, unusual, driven by personal preferences and exclusive to the middle classes. And, for those media outputs that target ordinary householders who are not builders or designer-architects, the emphasis is on sustainable solutions that promote sophistication and stylishness, redolent of traditional property makeover TV shows, discussed in Chapter 5.

However, Green Building Podcasts are now available such as 'Green Building Audi Tours' involving audio stories of the greenest buildings led by the Open Green Building Society, a not-for-profit society in Vancouver dedicated to developing tools for sharing information about green building.[2] 'Off Grid Home Design' addresses the motivations for living in an off-grid home and the relationship of off grid home design to renewable energy. Hosted by Ian Woofenden of *Home Power Magazine*, the Podcast deals with solar, wind and hydro systems, biomass, living green, the sustainable house and passive house plants.[3] Social media are now also important channels for information and advice sharing on environmental sustainability. One well-established, independent community-run website hosting discussion forums on different topics in Australia called 'Whirlpool' is compared with a new industry-led interactive website 'Build4Life' by Aneta Podkalicka and Anthony Wright (2019). Their study highlights the importance of trust and transparency in online communities as vital for supporting people in practical ways so that they can make informed choices about consumer products, expertise and labour when transforming existing homes into sustainable homes.

Yet the wide and intense debate about zero carbon targets within the construction industry has barely been reported in the mainstream media or embraced by the general public. The lack of public engagement in what is a highly technical and specialised debate suggests that the challenges concerning incentives and piecemeal information hamper the prospects of public involvement in these policy areas. A study of media discourses of low carbon housing in the UK by Catherine Cherry, Christina Hopfe, Brian MacGillivray and Nick Pidgeon (2015) identified three distinct storylines in British broadsheets: 'zero carbon housing', 'retrofitting homes' and 'sustainable living'. The dominant media discourse promotes zero carbon new builds, by suggesting that low carbon houses offer high technology solutions to the climate problem. This 'zero carbon housing' discourse has been conveyed as a solution to climate change. Zero carbon housing adopts a convincing narrative of revolutionary homes as the answer to climate change by accepting a belief that these houses, rather than occupants' behaviour, will reduce emissions. Discourses on 'retrofitting homes' emphasises the need to reduce emissions within existing housing to deal with both climate change and rising fuel prices. With foundations in Green state theory's ecological modernisation, the 'retrofitting homes' discourse adopts a common-sense narrative by promoting retrofitting housing as a realisable, practical option for reducing household emissions and fuel bills. 'Sustainable living' is a much more marginal discourse that associates low carbon houses to individual identities and 'off-grid' or greener lifestyles. It accentuates individuality and self-sufficiency by focusing on people living outside dominant social norms. As Cherry et al. state:

> Sustainable living does not promote these lifestyle choices, instead portraying them as deeply individual acts expressing personal identities. A tension runs through this storyline, with significant lifestyle changes typically portrayed as undisruptive to households and framed instead as easily translated into new routines. (Cherry et al. 2015: 307)

Whilst such media discourses do not necessarily cause specific behaviour changes, they matter because they motivate policy formulation and institutional planning as well as influencing public values and norms.

Overall, Cherry and colleagues demonstrate that news media storylines of zero carbon home are vague. Green governmentality (the requirement for international climate change governance) and ecological modernisation (the capacity for financial markets and technology to resolve environmental issues) dominate the debate. As mentioned above, after the UK general election in 2010 and the formation of the coalition government, zero carbon housing was increasingly disputed, with zero carbon (in the Code for Sustainable Homes) becoming a focus of the debate. When the political landscape changed, media validation of the government position declined and the ideological divisions between news publishers became more noticeable. *The Guardian* and *The Independent* are newspapers more closely aligned with strong climate change views and offer more critical discussion about the term 'zero carbon' than *The Telegraph* and *The Times*. Yet, these distinctions are largely rhetorical since they do not to change the essential form of the storyline (Cherry et al. 2015).

The challenges surrounding the viability of modelled emissions reductions are largely absent from all three discourses. Other concepts that tend to be excluded from news discourses include individual behaviour change, cultural expectations and social norms. This is despite the fact that significant reductions in domestic emissions will involve fundamental changes in lifestyle and home living and are likely to cause substantial social upheaval (Davies and Oreszczyn, 2012). The emphasis of news media reports tends to be on technical advancement and economic inducements as the route to sustainability, together with a general disregard of the cultural and social implications of this route. Cherry et al. (2015) comment that:

> The absence of these social aspects is strange as one might expect media norms, such as personalisation, to highlight them. We suggest these omissions stem from the implicit assumptions about and blind spots to behaviour change currently found within the dominant technological paradigm of broader decarbonisation. (Cherry et al. 2015: 308)

The quality and spread of these media portrayals of decarbonising housing have far-reaching implications for the effectiveness of transitioning towards low carbon living. It highlights the significant and positive role that needs to be played by the journalism profession in galvanising household action. At the time of writing, the global environmental movement, Extinction Rebellion and the school strike movement led by Greta Thunberg are demanding immediate government action and now having a major impact on climate change debate in the news media.

Popularising alternative eco-lifestyles

Notwithstanding the poor coverage of low carbon and sustainable living, green practices have become a growing trend among communities and suburban areas transnationally. Led by individuals, community groups and networks in advanced consumer societies, this trend involves the rise of a range of initiatives such as community gardens, 'sustainable streets' and 'voluntary simplicity' in the search for innovative strategies and styles for living more ethically and sustainably. Alternative lifestyles that emerged as part of 1960s and 1970s' counter-culture are now being revived in surprising media settings. Leading research by Tania Lewis (2012) reveals that primetime TV schedules draw on the popular makeover genre to narrate and dramatise alterations in everyday habits and lifestyles of 'ordinary', overconsuming folk in the global North.

Eco-lifestyle shows such as *Guerrilla Gardeners* (2009–2011) and *Living with Ed* (2007–2010), which carries resonances of the 1970s BBC series, *The Good Life* (1975–1978), present romantically modulated and televisually mediated experiments in green suburbia. *Guerrilla Gardeners* signals a form of lifestyle politics and ethic that 'is not easily reducible to a neoliberal governmental rationale nor readily dismissed as purely a "discourse of resistance" to governmental hegemony' (Lewis 2012: 324). Contemporary reality-style genres that examine the lifestyles and consuming behaviour of individuals and households such as *Honey We're Killing the Kids* (2005 to date) are accompanied by popular documentaries that follow individuals and families who escape modern life to take up alternative lifestyles in remote places. For example, the New Zealand show, *Off the Radar* traces the encounters of a comedian, Radar, who tries to live sustainably for 10 months on an isolated piece of land. In the UK *River Cottage* (1999 to date), *It's Not Easy Being Green* (2006–2009) and *New Lives in the Wild* (2013 to date) follow the 'back to nature' theme documenting largely middle-class families who attempt to live sustainably by avoiding the pressures and risks of modern city or suburban living.

Examples of early adopters of green lifestyle formats also include an eco-renovation show called *Code Green Canada* (2006) by the Canadian Broadcasting Company, the Australian Broadcasting Corporation lifestyle-advice/ enviro-science show, *Carbon Cops* (2007) on primetime television and an eco-lifestyle format in New Zealand's *Wasted* (2007/8). An analysis of two Australian eco-lifestyle TV programmes: *Guerrilla Gardeners* (2009–2011) and *Eco House Challenge* (2007–current) by Lewis (2012) demonstrates the diverse and sometimes opposing ways in which green citizenship is enacted in suburbia. Using the recognisable domestic makeover genre, these green lifestyle TV programmes present what Lewis calls an 'ethic of experimentation and play, but within the very real constraints of modern suburban contexts and lives' (Lewis 2012: 319). They portray ideas of green citizenship by relating questions of lifestyle to the global scale of environmental matters – ideas once regarded as quirky but now gaining traction, publicity garnered by the global environmental movement, Extinction Rebellion, and related campaign work of the young environmental activist, Greta Thunberg. On the one hand, *Eco House Challenge* exemplifies the shift of environmental issues and responsibilities on to individual citizens through the emphasis on lifestyle and consumption. On the other hand, *Guerrilla Gardeners* not only frames lifestyle politics as privatised rational choices and modes of self-regulation but also expresses green citizenship as a form of creativity, a way of fostering community and romantic imperatives involving the aesthetics of daily life. These series refer to wider trends in suburban nations like Australia where environmentally conscious lifestyle-based 'activism' is realigning understandings of citizenship, particularly in response to the widespread Australian bushfires of 2019–2020.

Guerrilla Gardeners involves the greening of roadside wasteland, concrete jungles and unused neighbourhood land to promote green citizenship as a suburban lifestyle activism. Aimed at Channel 10s Generation X audiences, and using ideas from the global environmental movement, the series documents hit-and-run tactics conducted at night by what are described as six 'young warriors'. These protagonists carry out 'covert operations that transform the biggest eye-sores into an oasis of greenery and recreation for local communities and families to enjoy' Lewis (2012: 320). While *Eco House Challenge* is aimed at an older audience with a more public educational emphasis, it draws on some of the principles framing *Guerrilla Gardeners*. *Eco House Challenge* employs the didactic approach of reality TV makeover series by taking two families on a transformational journey guided by an eco-coach. The greening of their everyday family lives addresses what is referred to as the four 'environmental hot spots' of waste, energy, water and transport by finding ways to lower their consumption to 'sustainable levels'.

By working together with the locals on the wasteland makeover, *Guerrilla Gardeners'* 'experts' ensure that they do not foist their views on the neighbourhood while combining horticultural know-how with creative and aesthetic skills. Their mischievous approach contests civic authorities and suburban dwellers to reconsider suburban spaces as green and sustainable. Rather than downsizing consumption and changing lifestyle behaviour, the series accents a romantic engagement through aesthetics and sensuality to promote the art of everyday living. By contrast, *Eco House Challenge* follows traditional makeover programmes by imposing experts on the participating families. But instead of preaching and disciplining, the show promotes green citizenship by encouraging families to embrace forms of self-surveillance and scrutiny of environmentally damaging domestic lifestyle habits. This tactic resonates with neoliberal discourses of individual accountability. Yet, Lewis (2012) argues that with an emphasis on the household and neighbourhood as spaces of lifestyle transformation, both of these TV shows attend to the ways 'ordinary people' can perform green citizenship by approaching suburbia as a potential space for sustainable living. As such, the accent shifts from global politics to local, domestic lifestyles as the main agents of change.

Based on observations of several grassroots green initiatives around inner urban and suburban Melbourne, Lewis (2015) develops this insight further by exploring small-scale domestic and lifestyle projects comprising a form of 'lifestyle-based activism'. This is exemplified by Permablitz Melbourne, a voluntary initiative that transforms backyards into food- producing gardens. This type of activism is rarely mentioned in the media yet is one that contests common perceptions of citizen engagement and protest-based modes of political action. Such grassroots initiatives digress from yet complement some of the eco-home strategies mentioned above. The gardens, houses and streets of suburbia become 'sites of experimentation' for sustainable lifestyle practices within an emerging community awareness of environmental issues. These projects involve new practices based on the sustainable and self-sufficient ecosystem of permaculture. Drawing on social practice theory to address issues of transformation in relation to everyday practices, habits and habitus (see Introduction above), Lewis considers the rise in what she calls 'lifestyle politics' which underscores today's green citizenship. She argues that green suburban lifestyle schemes such as 'permablitzes' are transformational. They express, materialise and enact far-reaching changes in householders' lives as they pursue the shift from consumption practices to self-sufficiency practices and 'making do'.

Green activism and citizen engagement occur at community levels by converting suburban gardens and backyards into creative food spaces involving the community sharing of horticultural and recycling skills. Lewis (2015) emphasises the importance of projects that traverse civic engagement and everyday lifestyle practices, often prompted by a scepticism towards state environmental interventions at national and regional levels. Lewis expands and develops the notion of 'lifestyle' to move away from the narrow, commercial notion of consumption which has been the conventional discursive frame of lifestyle TV discussed in Chapter 5. By contrast, the ethic of transformation that drives the Permablitz Melbourne initiative entails an important aesthetic dimension, echoing features of the garden makeovers on reality TV series such as *Backyard Blitz*.

Lewis explores the correspondence between the 'makeover practices' of these TV shows and grassroots community initiatives such as Permablitz Melbourne. In fact, she suggests that 'the 'makeover' practices integral to permablitzes offer a *performative* alternative to normative practices around consumption, newness, fashion and instant change:

> The suburban house and garden here is not about a privatized investment in personal status and property values but instead is reframed in terms of a collective, long-term investment in a new way of living, in particular a shared 'lifestyle' of self-sufficiency and 'making do', based on domestic forms of production, reuse and economies of thrift'. (Lewis 2015: 350)

This permablitz example also highlights issues of scale: the inadequacy of only macro or micro considerations of scale for understanding political activism and interventions in social and environmental reform. Everyday lifestyles and small-scale initiatives are entirely implicated in environmental planning. As such, discourses of lifestyle practices form a central part of the study of household sustainability by addressing the need to rethink traditional household, neighbourhood and community practices. Lewis refers to the grassroots green lifestyle initiative exemplified by 'permablitzes' as 'everyday green practices of transformation' (Lewis 2015: 356). She found that many households involved in domestic hard waste reuse had not only developed elaborate ecologies of sharing including repair, storage and recycling of household items with friends and relatives. Lewis explains that some households also organised more planned and more geographically extended networked communities.

For example, as well as using commercial websites such as eBay to trade items, some neighbourhoods used Freecycle Network (www.freecycle.org/) and the Sharehood (http://earthwiseharmony.com/PEOPLE/EH-The-Sharehood.html) websites that support grassroots and non-profit movements involving the sharing of resources such as equipment, vegetables, tools, cars and books. As an example of local transformational practices, Lewis explains that the Permablitz Melbourne 'community' informs a 'politics of scale' through its website (www.permablitz. net/) and by corresponding with relations of care and responsibility at the level of backyards in Melbourne's suburbs. The householders' garden becomes a source not only for permaculture but also for broader 'community'. It is a site of potential food production and a space in which skills and expertise are transferred to other 'blitzers' through activities such as the workshops and talks. A range of activities are documented and publicised via social media as guidance, to draw prospective blitzers and connect with other national and international permaculture networks.

These emerging habitual everyday practices and knowledges are forms of *habitus* that foreground the shared practical understandings and decisions made at a microsocial level. On the one hand, these low-key changes in domestic lifestyles comprise alternative means of 'consuming and living'. On the other, they are potential agents of change, underpinning new arrangements, strategies, routines and forms of habitus.

Conclusion

This chapter has identified the fundamental role to be played by everyday lifestyles, norms and social practices towards environmental sustainability. Changes in household energy and water usage, and the development of supporting municipal, state, national and international policies are required to counter the overuse of resources to halt climate change. Yet the household continues to be neglected in much research on sustainability and climate change. As mentioned in the Introduction, home is both ubiquitous and set apart from everyday life as an unattainable ideal. The palpable home precarities associated with climate change challenge the deep-seated values and routines associated with 'normal' home life guided by time-honoured home ideals. Social network sites have been identified as vital media sources for sharing knowledge and advice on environmental sustainability. However, a strong sense of denial remains in many mainstream news and popular media accounts of climate change and even among heads of powerful nations, such as US President Donald Trump who, referring to the science of climate change as a hoax, withdrew in 2017 from the 2015 Paris Climate Change Agreement to protect national economic interests. This reminds us that political power and both global and social inequalities are deeply implicated in transnational, national and local attempts to tackle global warming.

For instance, it has been known for some time that the housing desires of Western societies and related planning and building principles and practices are contributing directly to the burden of global climate change. Research on greenhouse gas emissions reveals that, even when reductions in transportation or building energy emissions are included, more affluent residents have significantly larger carbon footprints resulting from their consumption habits (Peterson et al. 2013; Rice et al 2019). Affluence is the clearest predictor of carbon footprint and greenhouse gas emissions at all levels, from macro to micro household scale, according to Gibson et al. (2011) who remark that:

> The best way to reduce your environmental impact is to be poor, as economic activity is strongly coupled to fossil fuel use. The rich pollute more through high levels of travel (vehicle and air); more and bigger houses; more food wastage; more consumption generally. Yet the rich and well-educated may be among the strongest advocates of 'green' practices: recycling, composting, buying organic food, taking reusable bags to the supermarket. They may also be leaders in buying still-expensive technology: hybrid cars, solar electricity panels and green energy. (Gibson et al. 2011: 4)

Issues of home sustainability involve tackling middle-class affluence in the West. Yet, as the previous chapters highlight, our personal identities are deeply entangled with idealised homes that inspire homemaking projects and consumption as a form of self-expression. The challenge is to find new ways of tapping into the power of household agency as a fundamental dimension of sustainable homemaking practices. The themes and issues addressed in this final analysis of home provide examples of some of the constraints and possibilities involved in ways of reimagining home as a sustainable unit.

In the context of social adjustments to economic austerity and global warming, sustainable homes offer alternatives to the rhetoric of technologised homes. But in a neoliberal economic and political climate, the problems facing collective and global attempts to inspire sustainable household behaviour are enormous. A significant acceleration of the current environmental crisis from the mid -twentieth century onwards has been identified as a critical turning point (Steffen et al. 2015; Bonneuil and Gemenne 2015). It is no accident that this phase coincided with the reshaping of our global economy by neoliberal policies which propose that the well-being of societies depends on the financialisation of everyday life (Harvey 2005: 39). Contemporary neoliberal policies are supported by commercial marketing which is 'the very sector that has encouraged the unfettered growth and hyper-consumerism that underpin many environmental challenges' (Hobson 2016: 21). As the preceding chapters suggest, these neoliberal policies have contributed to the idealisation of a particular kind of middle-class home which we now acknowledge to be a key contributor to the acceleration of the current crisis. There are, then, serious consequences for households and society regarding a wholly privatised and marketised 'environmental impact', energy efficiency and flood defence.

New ways of approaching home are envisaged via schemes that impact ultimately on our very notions of citizenship and social change. In response to the challenges posed by global warming, several years ago Michele Micheletti (2003) addressed the spread of political culture into people's everyday lives through ideals such as consumption choices, by pointing to a post-political environment that supports the term 'green citizenship'. Since then, unease about the risks and effects of capitalist modernity has spawned not only television documentations of pollution and climate change but also strategies for generating solutions via popular TV programmes to wide audiences. In studies of how these trends are presented in the context of lifestyle television programming and enacted in city neighbourhoods, work by scholars such as Tania Lewis mobilises this notion of 'green citizenship' (Lewis 2012; 2015). As the chapter has outlined, Lewis approaches 'eco-lifestyle' presentations as sites of imaginative experimentation in green living, citizenship and ways to live 'the good life' in the present day.

An ethic of romanticism is expressed in certain creative forms of green and ethical citizenship such as community food markets and the slow food movement. Whilst these initiatives invoke a new kind of idealism associated with home, Lewis argues that the romanticism and creativity associated with the rise of contemporary lifestyle and consumer culture is vitally relevant to the ways we rethink about and perform a green suburban politics. What, then, does it involve? In reply, she states:

> First, it involves recognizing lifestyle politics as a site of potentially progressive grassroots civic activism and as a space in which legitimate forms of empowering citizenship are played out. Second, it suggests that effective, everyday forms of suburban sustainability need to engage with rather than dismiss issues of 'lifestyle', recognizing that everyday ethical and political practices are seldom purely grounded in the realms of rational calculative choice but rather are articulated in complex ways to people's broader lifestyle sensibilities and habits'. (Lewis 2012: 324)

A green lifestyle politics that entails pleasure and affect is likely to be far more successful than penalising ethics of abstinence and austerity. Lewis points to authors such as Kate Soper (2004) who refers to 'alternative hedonism' as part of a body work that considers lifestyle and consumption in relation to issues of care, community and lifestyle ethics (also see Barnett et al., 2005a; Hargreaves 2011; Lewis and Potter 2010; Miller, 2001).

Importantly, concepts and practices associated with green and sustainable homes undermines recent neoliberal individualised versions of 'home', highlighted in the preceding chapters. Citizen-based initiatives identified as sites of experimental sustainable lifestyle practices – involving the permacultural activities of suburban houses, gardens and streets – indicate a growing awareness of the drawbacks of hierarchical, macro-scale environmental policies and multi-scalar strategies of sustainability. This kind of participatory research agenda could be converted into an environmental planning and policy approach to facilitate the shared agency, creativity and efforts of community-led green practices, as indicated by Lewis (2015). Such studies not only emphasise the importance of galvanising popular, grassroots green political advancement. They also demonstrate that the popular media can thwart yet also facilitate far-reaching bonds of solidarity and positive social change. These activities therefore signal the need to reconsider agency and governance (Gibson et al. 2011). To reiterate Naef et al. (2019: 150) mentioned above, it requires a shift from 'passive consumer' to 'active citizen' in policy discourse to tackle the complex scalar dimensions of domestic lifestyle practices, participation and citizenship.

While sustainable homes are necessarily part of the solution, women in hetero-normative households are likely to be the most affected by these transformations – as householders routinely deemed responsible for caring and homemaking. The evidence outlined in earlier chapters suggests that home sustainability is likely to depend on women's invisible labour. A key concern, then is that household strategies of collective action and collaboration required to enact adaptations towards sustainable communities, neighbourhoods and homes may lead to a feminising of responsibility for climate change. A critical intersectional study is therefore required to understand how the varying responses to climate change are configured by the entangled power dynamics of current household practices that form part of social and political relations and inequalities. This includes the need to gauge how sustainable responses to global warming might contribute to personal and household agency, in order to identify potentially empowering paths towards *home* sustainability. As the precarious effects of climate change will dramatically transform future meanings of home, we might then be in a strong position to generate positive imaginaries for sustainable homes.

Notes

1 See for example, 'Zero Carbon Hub to close', 30 March 2016, available at www.zeroca rbonhub.org/news/zero-carbon-hub-close (accessed 2 November 2019).
2 See 'Green Building Audio Tours', available at https://player.fm/series/green-building-a udio-tours (accessed 2 November 2019).
3 See 'How 2 Build Green: The Sustainability Podcast', available at https://how2build green.libsyn.com/off-grid-home-design (accessed 2 November 2019).

References

Anderson, T.L. and Leal, D. (2001) *Free Market Environmentalism*, rev. edn. New York: Palgrave.
Backhaus, J. (2019) 'Turning off the gas tap: Sustainable energy policies, practices and prospects in the Netherlands', in F. Fahy, G. Goggin and C. Jensen (eds), *Energy Demand Challenges in Europe: Implications for Policy, Planning and Practice*. Basingstoke: Palgrave, pp. 71–82.
Barnett, C., Cloke, P., Clarke, N. and Malpass, A. (2005a) 'Consuming ethics: Articulating the subjects and spaces of ethical consumption', *Antipode*, 37, 23–45.
Barry, J. (1999) *Rethinking Green Politics*. London: Sage.
Barry, J. and Eckersley, R. (2005) 'W(h)ither the green state?', in J. Barry and R. Eckersley (eds), *The State and the Global Ecological Crisis*. Cambridge, MA: MIT Press, pp. 255–272.
Boerstra, A.C., van Hoof, J. and van Weele, A.M. (2015). 'A new hybrid thermal comfort guideline for the Netherlands: Background and development', *Architectural Science Review*, 58(1), 24–34.
Bonneuil, C. and Gemenne, F. (2015) *The Anthropocene and the Global Environmental Crisis: Rethinking Modernity in a New Epoch*. London: Routledge.
Bopp, K.-F. (2007) *Housing, Energy and Thermal Comfort: A Review of 10 Countries within the WHO European Region*. Copenhagen: WHO Regional office for Europe.

Cabinet Office: Behavioural Insights Team. (2011) *Behaviour Change and Energy Use*. London: Crown. www.cabinetoffice.gov.uk/resource-library/behaviour-change-and-energy-use.

Cherry, C., Hopfe, C., MacGillivray, B., and Pidgeon, N. (2015) 'Media discourses of low carbon housing: The marginalisation of social and behavioural dimensions within the British broadsheet press', *Public Understanding of Science*, 24(3), 302–310.

Davies, M. and Oreszczyn, T. (2012) 'The unintended consequences of decarbonising the built environment: A UK case study', *Energy and Buildings*, 46, 80–85.

DCLG. (2006) *Code for Sustainable Homes: A Step-change in Sustainable Home Building Practice*. London: Department for Communities and Local Government. www.communities.gov.uk.

Dennis, L. (2010) *Green Interior Design*. New York: Allworth Press.

Dobson, A. (2007). *Green Political Thought*, 4th edn. London: Routledge.

Eckersley, R. (2000) *Democratic Innovations: Deliberation, Association and Representation*. London: Routledge.

Eckersley, R. (2004) *The Green State: Rethinking Democracy and Sovereignty*. Cambridge, MA: MIT Press.

European Environmental Agency. (2016) 'Climate change, impacts and vulnerability in Europe 2016'. www.eea.europa.eu/publications/climate-change-impacts-and-vulnerability-2016 (accessed 30 August 2018).

Genus, A. andIskandarova, M. (2018) Policy paper 1: State of the art and future of policy integration for EU policy on energy consumption. ENERGISE—European Network for Research, Good Practice and Innovation for Sustainable Energy, Deliverable No. 6.4. http://energise-project.eu/sites/default/files/content/ENERGISE_D6.4_300518_Final. pdf (accessed 8 December 2019).

Gibson, C., Head, L., Gill, N. and Waitt, G. (2011) 'Climate change and household dynamics: Beyond consumption, unbounded sustainability', *Transactions of the Institute of British Geographers*, New Series, 36(1), 3–8.

Gosztoni, S., Stefanwicz, M., Bernardo, R. and Blomsterberg, A. (2017) 'Multi-active façade for Swedish multi-family homes renovation: Evaluating the potentials of passive design measures', *Journal of Façade Design and Engineering*, 5(1), 7–22.

Gram-Hanssen, K. andGeorg, S. (2017) 'Energy performance gaps: Promises, people, practices', *Building Research & Information*, 46, 1–9.

Greenwood, D. (2008) 'Non-market coordination: Towards an ecological response to Austrian economics', *Environmental Values*, 17(4), 521–541. doi:10.3197/096327108X368520.

Greenwood, D. (2015) 'In search of green political economy: Steering markets, innovation, and the zero carbon homes agenda in England', *Environmental Politics*, 24(3), 423–441.

Hargreaves, T. (2011) 'Practice-ing behaviour change: Applying social practice theory to pro-environmental behaviour change', *Journal of Consumer Culture*, 11(1), 79–99.

Harvey, D. (2005) *A Brief History of Neoliberalism*. Oxford: Oxford University Press.

Hawkins, G. (2006) *The Ethics of Waste: How We Relate to Rubbish*. Sydney: University of New South Wales Press.

Heiskanen, E., Laakso, S. and Matschos, K. (2019) 'Finnish energy policy in transition', in F. Fahy, G. Goggin and C. Jensen (eds), *Energy Demand Challenges in Europe: Implications for Policy, Planning and Practice*. Basingstoke: Palgrave, pp. 127–136.

Hobson, K. (2016) 'Why the devil does not have the best tunes: A response to Verissimo & McKinley', *Oryx*, 51(1), 21.

Holden, M. and Scerri, A. (2013) 'More than this: Liveable Melbourne meets liveable Vancouver', *Cities*, 31, 444–453.

Intergovernmental Panel on Climate Change. (2018) *Global Warming of 1.50 C: Summary for Policymakers*. Geneva: PCC. https://report.ipcc.ch/sr15/pdf/sr15_spm_final.pdf (accessed 23 March 2019).

Jarvis, H. and Bonnett, A. (2013) 'Progressive nostalgia in novel living arrangements: A counterpoint to neo-traditional new urbanism?', *Urban Studies*, 50(11), 2349–2370.

Jensen, C. and Quitzau, M.B. (2019) 'The role of households in Danish energy policy: Visions and contradictions Inge Røpke', in F. Fahy, G. Goggin and C. Jensen (eds), *Energy Demand Challenges in Europe: Implications for Policy, Planning and Practice*. Basingstoke: Palgrave, pp. 35–46.

Jones, L. (2014) 'Living-with others, living-with an 'eco-home': From frustration to transformation in an eco-development', *Journal of Environmental Policy & Planning*, 16(2), 221–240.

Joss, S., Cook, M. and Dayot, Y. (2017) 'Smart cities: Towards a new citizenship regime? A discourse analysis of the British smart city standard', *Journal of Urban Technology*, 24(4), 29–49.

Kunkel, S., Kontonasiou, E., Arcipowska, A., Mariottini, F. andBogdan, A. (2015). 'Indoor air quality, thermal comfort and daylight', Buildings Performance Institute Europe (BPIE). http://bpie. eu/publication/indoor-air-quality-thermal-comfort-and-daylight-an-analysisof-residential-building-regulations-in-8-member-states-2015/ (accessed 21 March 2019).

Laakso, S. andHeiskanen, E. (2017) 'Good practice report: Capturing cross-cultural interventions', ENERGISE—European Network for Research, Good Practice and Innovation for Sustainable Energy, Grant Agreement No. 727642, Deliverable No. 3.1. https://helda.hel sinki.fi//bitstream/handle/10138/234454/ENERGISE_D3.1_Good_practice_report_cap turing_cross_cultural_interventions.pdf?sequence=1 (accessed 8 December 2019).

Lane, R. and Gorman-Murray, A. (eds) (2011) 'Introduction', in *Material Geographies of Household Sustainability*. Farnham: Ashgate, pp. 9–34.

Lawrence, K. and McManus, P. (2008) 'Towards household sustainability in Sydney? Impacts of two sustainable lifestyle workshop programs on water consumption in existing homes', *Geographical Research*, 46(3), 314–332.

Lewis, T. (2012) '"There grows the neighbourhood": Green citizenship, creativity and life politics on eco-TV', *International Journal of Cultural Studies*, 15(3), 315–326.

Lewis, T. (2015) '"One city block at a time": Researching and cultivating green transformations', *International Journal of Cultural Studies*, 18(3), 347–363.

Lewis, T. and Potter, E. (2010) *Ethical Consumption: A Critical Introduction*. London: Routledge.

Mace, M. (2016) 'Zero carbon hub closes following green building policy changes', *edie*, Sustainability Leaders Forum. www.edie.net/news/6/Zero-Carbon-Hub-closes-after-poli cy-reforms/ (accessed 31 March 2019).

McLeod, R., Hopfe, C.J. and Rezgui, Y. (2012) 'An investigation into recent proposals for a revised definition of zero carbon homes in the UK'. *Energy Policy*, 46, 25–35.

Micheletti, M. (2003) *Political Virtue and Shopping: Individuals, Consumerism, and Collective Action*. New York: Palgrave Macmillan.

Miller, D. (2001) 'The poverty of morality', *Journal of Consumer Culture*, 1, 225–243.

Moxon, S. (2012) *Sustainability in Interior Design*. London: Laurence King Publishing.

Naef, P., Sahakian, M. and Goggins, G. (2019) 'Conclusion: Comparing household energy use across Europe—Uncovering opportunities for sustainable transformation', in F. Fahy, G. Goggin and C. Jensen (eds), *Energy Demand Challenges in Europe: Implications for Policy, Planning and Practice*. Basingstoke: Palgrave, pp. 137–152.

Nicol, J.F. andWilson, M. (2011) 'A critique of European Standard EN 15251: Strengths, weaknesses and lessons for future standard', *Building Research & Information*, 39, 18–193.

Noda, K. (2018) 'Google home: Smart speaker as environmental control unit', *Disability and Rehabilitation: Assistive Technology*, 13(7), 674–675.

Pennington, M. (2008) 'Classical liberalism and ecological rationality: The case for polycentric environmental law', *Environmental Politics*, 17(3), 431–448.

Pennington, M. (2011) *Robust Political Economy: Classical Liberalism and the Future of Public Policy.* Cheltenham: Edward Elgar.

Peterson, M.N., Peterson, T. and Liu, J. (2013) *The Housing Bomb: Why Our Addiction to Houses Is Destroying the Environment and Threatening our Society.* Baltimore: Johns Hopkins University Press.

Podkalicka, A. and Wright, A. (2019) 'Sharing advice online to foster sustainable homes', in P. Newton, D. Prasad, A. Sproul and S. White (eds), *Decarbonising the Built Environment: Charting the Transition.* Basingstoke: Palgrave Macmillan, pp. 469–488.

Rice, J., Aldana, D. andLong, J. (2019) 'Contradictions of the climate-friendly city: New perspectives on eco-gentrification and housing justice', *Internal Journal of Urban and Regional Research.* https://doi.org/10.1111/1468-2427.12740.

Sahakian, M. (2018) 'Constructing normality through material and social lock-in: The dynamics of energy consumption among Geneva's more affluent households', in H. Allison, D. Rosie and W. Gordon (eds.), *Demanding Energy: Space, Time and Change.* Cham: Springer International Publishing, pp. 51–71.

Smith, D. (2016) 'Enter the disruptors', *Construction Research and Innovation,* 7(4), 12–15.

Soper, K. (2004) 'Rethinking the "good life": The consumer as citizen', *Capitalism, Nature, Socialism,* 15, 111–116.

Spence, A. and Pidgeon, N. (2009) 'Framing and communicating climate change: The effects of distance and outcome frame manipulations', *Global Environmental Change,* 20, 656–667.

Steffen, W., Broadgate, W., Deutsch, L. and Gaffney, O. (2015) 'The trajectory of the anthropocene: The great acceleration', *The Anthropocene Review,* 2(1), 81–98.

UKGBC. (2008) *Zero Carbon Task Group Report: The Definition of Zero Carbon.* London: UKGBC.

Vadovics, E. (2019) 'The energy challenge in Hungary: A need for more complex approaches', in F. Fahy, G. Goggin and C. Jensen (eds), *Energy Demand Challenges in Europe: Implications for Policy, Planning and Practice.* Basingstoke: Palgrave, pp. 83–94.

Wang, Y., Kuckelkorn, J., Zhao, F.Y., Spliethoff, H. and Lang, W. (2017) 'A state of art of review on interactions between energy performance and indoor environment quality in passive house buildings', *Renewable and Sustainable Energy Review,* 72, 1303–1319.

Yudelson, J. (2008) *The Green Building Revolution.* Washington DC: Island Press.

Zero Carbon Hub. (2011) 'Energy Performance of Buildings directive', Zero Carbon Hub, April 2011. www.zerocarbonhub.org/sites/default/files/resources/reports/Energy_Per formance_of_Buildings_Directive-_Introductory_Guide_to_the_Recast_EPDB-2.pdf.

INDEX

For Product Safety Concerns and Information please contact our EU
representative GPSR@taylorandfrancis.com
Taylor & Francis Verlag GmbH, Kaufingerstraße 24, 80331 München, Germany

www.ingramcontent.com/pod-product-compliance
Lightning Source LLC
Chambersburg PA
CBHW050705280326
41926CB00088B/2624